THE PHILOSOPHY OF CORPORATE CONTROL

A Treatise on the Law of Fiduciary Duty

David Cowan Bayne, S.J.

LOYOLA UNIVERSITY PRESS
CHICAGO
1986

Imprimi Potest	Howard J. Gray, S. J. Provincial, Detroit Province of the Society of Jesus October 30, 1985
Nihil Obstat	Reverend Anthony Farrell, Ph.D. *Censor Librorum* October 2, 1985
Imprimatur	Most Reverend Gerald O'Keefe Bishop of Davenport October 2, 1985

Loyola University Press
3441 North Ashland Avenue
Chicago, Illinois 60657

Design by J.L. Boden

Library of Congress Cataloging in Publication Data

Bayne, David Cowan, 1918-
     The philosophy of corporate control.
     Includes index.
     1. Directors of corporations—Legal status,
laws, etc.—United States. 2. Trusts and
trustees—United States. 3. Corporation
law—United States. I. Title. KF1423.B39
1986   346.73'06642   86-2983
ISBN 0-8294-0517-8   347.3066642

To
Jerome Ambrose Petz, S.J.
Lawyer, Priest, Jesuit

Contents

Part One
THE FOUNDATION

Part Two
THE SUPERSTRUCTURE

Foreword

When you have listened to an opera of an evening, its melodies often haunt you the next day. So too it is after reading this book by Father Bayne.

The author is a Jesuit. There is no doubt of that. But this is a definite plus, because the Jesuits are moral theologians, and have an unerring eye for human weaknesses. Hence it is natural that a Jesuit would choose an area of the law which seeks to call the unfaithful fiduciary to account.

Just such a field is the law of strict trust. Bayne sees the contrôleur of the corporation as a trustee for the shareholders. And the contrôleur's most critical hour arrives when he must name his successor. Here, above all, is he a fiduciary and therefore must not seek personal gain by accepting a 'bonus' for the transfer of his office—a transaction which Bayne characterizes as a 'premium-bribe.'

The trust is a creation of Equity. It has a Catholic background, originating in the conscience of the medieval Chancellor. The trust has always impressed Continental jurists as a masterwork of the Common Law. One passage of this great work is the thesis: Whoever sells a block of stock for a price above the market value of the individual shares in order to gain control of the corporation must restore the excess over market (the 'premium-bribe') to the corporation.

Here is one of the significant aspects of American law from which Europeans can learn a valuable lesson. (Other examples in contemporary civil law are products liability and liability for the infliction of mental distress.)

The theological background of the trust as a legal entity not only poses a challenge for one who is professor of Corporation law and also a Jesuit. It also inspires him to make full use of the advantages of his educational background, which is so strongly influenced by both Continental and, more important, theological elements.

The *Continental* juristic background engenders a facility in discerning principles and in building a cohesive system rather than merely proceeding from case to case, as many in the Common Law do. Only by bringing together the case-by-case inductive method with the systematic deductive discovery and isolation of principle can success be assured. Thus is truth found, not only for American law but for the European as well, and all the World.

His *theological* education enables Father Bayne to analyze a handful of truly important cases with the perception of a father confessor, to penetrate deeply the souls of the several parties involved by drawing upon the court records. But it also enables him to analyze the duty of the contrôleur to the corporation with the acumen of a moral theologian. Here are found the strictures of Kant's Categorical Imperative: The moral good is good will alone, completely free from personal advantage, yes free even from any self-centered indulgence. In Schiller's ironic words:

> Gerne dien' ich den Freunden,
> doch tu' ich es leider mit Neigung,
> und so wurmt es mir oft,
> dass ich nicht tugendhaft bin.

Such an analysis, simultaneously inductive and deductive, pursued inexorably to the very end, unfolds in the following pages like a detective novel with two malefactors.

First comes the 'old man,' the incumbent contrôleur. He is the most important, most critical figure in the corporation, yet he has thus far not been accorded formal recognition by corporation statutes or charters. Father Bayne brings him from the legal shadows into the bright light of the law as a true fiduciary with legal duties fully defined.

Cast opposite the incumbent is the other malefactor, his successor in control. He, too, is a strict fiduciary, from the very moment he decides to assume the burden of corporate control.

Whenever the transfer and assumption of control occur without regard to the interests of the corporation, when both malefactors line their own pockets, we have premium-bribery. And this premium-bribery mandates disgorgement of the premium-bribe to the corporation and the dismissal of the would-be successor, unsuitable by reason of his own self-seeking.

The whole story of this book is like a labyrinth, crisscrossed with all sorts of corridors, halls and rooms, and it is always exciting. Here we have a talented writer with the highest enthusiasm and force of expression. Often a scholar may speak well but write badly, and vice versa, but all is one in Father Bayne: He is fascinating in the lecture hall—as he so brilliantly demonstrated here at Cologne—and in this book as well.

Although he is not the first to examine corporate control—he embarks from Berle and cites Jennings—he is the only one who does not merely sketch with a pencil but creates an entire mural. Progressing from one law-review article to another and then synthesizing all in this book, he has founded a new discipline in Corporation law.

Translated from the German
>   *Professor Dr. Gerhard Kegel*
>   *Director*
>   Institut für Internationales und
>   Privatrecht der Universität Köln

Prenote
The Mechanics

One overriding objective governed the approaches to the technical trappings of scholarship in this treatise: Ease in reading. When the formal rigidities of tradition confronted facility and comfort, compromise favored the reader.

Footnotes have been eliminated whenever possible. When absolutely necessary they have been pruned to the basics, and stored in the back of the book. All substantive content has been kept in the body. The reader need never resort to a footnote, unless he wishes fuller documentation, an exact citation or technical corroboration.

The *Format* is a blend of the learned-journal inflexibilities with a pragmatic adaptation toward an uninterrupted flow of thought. Thus (1) the *boxed* quotations in the body carry an immediate, sufficient citation—repeated with each succeeding quotation if necessary—thereby obviating altogether the need for a footnote. (2) Other, *nonboxed* quotations are adequately identified in the body to avoid the reader's reference to the footnote unless he needs the technical citation. (3) General *references* to cases will carry no footnotes at all. Their citations are in the appropriate Table.

When the substantive content of this treatise is augmented by the various *Tables*, perhaps the result would be a lesser brag of the book: For the bread-and-butter, fee-in-the-till practitioner, herein contained are all the requisites for either plaintiff or defendant briefs in any sale-of-control litigation.

The *Tables* have been constructed to relieve the body of the treatise and carry the burden of general, scholarly technicality. (1) In the *Table of Cases Cited*, every case appearing in the text is listed, with full citation. This Table, moreover, includes and identifies all major sale-of-control opinions. Similarly, (2) the most important sale-of-control *Literature* is presented in the next Table. Thus the scholar or practitioner is assured of a complete work of basic reference for the beginnings of his study.

Acknowledgments

The seminal concepts for *The Philosophy of Corporate Control* first appeared in *The University of Pennsylvania Law Review* and *The Georgetown Law Journal*. These thoughts were developed successively in the law journals of Saint Louis, Fordham, Cornell, Stanford, Texas, California, Minnesota and Indiana. Alan G. Johnson of the Missouri Bar shared in the early philosophical development.

Support over the years came notably from longtime secretaries Mary Sue Thirolf and Rita Laaveg and from a superb series of research assistants, members of Bayne Associates. The greatest contribution, however, was from the hands of Stephen Luther Rhodes, Managing Director of Bayne Associates.

Preface

> The phenomenon of "control" is perhaps the most important single fact in the American corporate system. As the corporation increasingly is recognized as an institution of primary significance (even Mr. Justice Brandeis called it "a master instrument of American economy"), the importance of control will grow in law as it has grown in economic and social fact. Corporation law has never surrounded this phenomenon. Rules have been developed with respect to isolated aspects of it; but the rules derive chiefly from a time when corporations were still truly private and relatively small . . . .
>
> —Berle, *"Control" in Corporate Law,* 58 COLUM. L. REV. 1212 (1958).

Mr. Berle was right, the "law has never surrounded this phenomenon." It is also true that most of the seriously challenging questions facing corporation law today span out from the problems posed by corporate control. Where does control lie? How did the contrôleur assume his position? Once ensconced, what are the duties of his office? Is he merely a watered-down fiduciary? Or does he transcend 'the workaday world' and rise to a strict trustee? As incumbent, may the contrôleur sell control? And if he does, what of the premium paid? These questions and their answers form the heart of this new and burgeoning field.

But strictly, control has always been at the center of corporation law. Nowhere else is corporate philosophy more fundamental, more intricate, further reaching in effect and implication. Strip away the routine areas—the mechanics of incorporation, procedure, the share contract, the annual meeting, the proxy, the formalities of dissolution—and one is convinced that the contrôleur is the central

xiii

figure of the corporation and affects most intimately its *bonum commune.*

This conviction prompted an intensive effort to 'surround this phenomenon.' The attempt received its first impetus from Jason L. Honigman, of the Michigan bar, with his invitation to sit in on a bellwether control case, the 1961 *Honigman v. Green Giant.* The triple defeat there, on all three Federal levels, was a conclusive goad. The result: The years of study and eventually the present work.

From the earliest days the objective was a technical philosophical system of corporate control, an exposition and analysis of the essentials of fiduciary duty. The developing case law in the field was by no means ignored, as is obvious, but the emphasis nonetheless was on the construction of a complete and cohesive corpus of principles deduced from intrinsic *recta ratio* and the genius of the modern American corporation. The approach emulated the traditional Scholastic philosophers who spurned eclecticism and consciously began with a tabula rasa and strove for an original and unified body of thought. This at worst could point the way to better solutions and at best produce a truly tenable theory.

The undertaking labored under the disability inherent in the erection of any legal dogma: Everything cannot be said at once. The treatise, therefore, proceeds gradually from the basics to the specifics.

David Cowan Bayne, S.J.
Iowa Law School
Feast of Saint Ignatius Loyola, S.J.,
July 31, 1985

THE PHILOSOPHY OF CORPORATE CONTROL

A Treatise on the Law of Fiduciary Duty

With the general principles enunciated in the majority opinion as to the duties of fiduciaries I am, of course, in thorough accord. But, as Mr. Justice Frankfurter stated in [*SEC v. Chenery Corp.*:] "[T]o say that a man is a fiduciary only begins analysis; it gives direction to further inquiry. To whom is he a fiduciary? What obligations does he owe as a fiduciary? In what respect has he failed to discharge these obligations?" My brothers' opinion does not specify precisely what fiduciary duty Feldmann is held to have violated [in his sale of control] or whether it was a duty imposed upon him as the dominant stockholder or as a director of Newport. Without such specification I think that both the legal profession and the business world will find the decision confusing and will be unable to foretell the extent of its impact upon customary practices in the sale of stock.

> —*Perlman v. Feldmann,* 219 F.2d 173, 178 (2d Cir. 1955) (Swan, J., dissenting).

The greatest professional satisfaction comes from nibbling away at such ancient winners, and finally overturning them. (Justice Holmes called this "the genius of the common law"; he liked to talk like that.) As a quick and important example, the clear old rule for the responsibility of corporate managers to stockholders—the great winning argument of an earlier day—had been to adapt the analogy of the strict accountability of a personal trustee. But corporations are much more complicated than personal trusts, and a series of smart, well-paid lawyers began to chew away at the edges of trustee accountability by frightening judges with the prospect of the detailed review of corporate affairs (as in a trust accounting). Thus the principle arose that courts will not question matters of "business judgment." This principle, which began as a minor exception, is now so dominant a winning argument that the only fun left is trying to prove that the business-judgment rule does not cover absolutely *all* forms of corporate theft. Meanwhile, no one outside of the law reviews even has time to suggest that this game be interrupted long enough to devise some relevant rules for corporate responsibility today.

> —Bazelon, *Clients Against Lawyers,* 235 HARPER'S 104, 112 (Sept. 1967).

Part One

THE FOUNDATION

[Directors] hold a place of trust, and by accepting the trust are obliged to execute it with fidelity, not for their own benefit, but for the common benefit of the stockholders of the corporation.

> —*Koehler v. Black River Falls Iron Co.,* 67 U.S. (2 Black) 715, 720-21 (1862).

No better comparison—whether technical or otherwise — could be employed to express the custodial relationship of the contrôleur to the corporation. No child is more completely in the care of a parent than is the corporation when under the total dominion of the contrôleur.

The parent analogy, moreover, is aptly expressive of the relation of trustee to beneficiary. One need only describe a father's custody of a son to define the stewardship of trustee over trust.

> —Bayne, *A Legitimate Transfer of Control,* 18 STAN. L. REV. 438, 442-43 (1966).

Courts have dealt with the problems of control transfers in the light of common-law doctrines seldom designed to encompass transactions involving the peculiar fact of corporate control. As a result the bases of decision are frequently unclear.

> —Leech, *Transactions in Corporate Control,* 104 U. PA. L. REV. 725, 727-28 (1956).

Chapter 1

The Problem
and the Perspective

"Directors of a business corporation act in a strictly fiduciary capacity. Their office is a trust. . . . They must not, in any degree, allow their official conduct to be swayed by their private interest . . . ."

> —*Perlman v. Feldmann,* 219 F.2d 173, 176 (2d Cir. 1955) (quoting *Schemmel v. Hill*).

[A] controlling stockholder is under no duty . . . to refrain from receiving a premium [for control]. There is no obligation under such circumstances, to 'share and share alike'.

> —*Christophides v. Porco,* 289 F. Supp. 403, 405 (S.D.N.Y. 1968).

The latter decades of the twentieth century are witnessing an incongruous phenomenon, a phenomenon seemingly at odds with all the expectable social and moral developments of the age. On every side, the predictable, and baneful, ravages of a quarter century of affluence and unchecked indulgence are debilitating the central structure of Western society: The Family, the Church, the State. Even the most jaded observers are appalled at the abrupt decay. Yet running completely counter to this rampant trend is the inexplicable, or at least difficult-of-explanation, movement toward an ever increasing moral delicacy and sophistication in the recondite area

5

of the legal regulation of the American corporation. When all about is laissez-faire, and laxity is the rule of the day, the deliberate forces of justice and morality seem to be tightening the screws on corporate law: Fiduciary duty, minority rights, securities regulation.

It would seem almost impossible for this tightening to continue in the face of such odds, yet without it much of the hope for a vigorous and effective capitalism will fade appreciably. A robustly healthy corporation bodes well for the future of the American way. And it is truistic to say that the American way bears the primary burden in the world struggle. Clearly, therefore, the moral integrity of the corporate form ranks high as a worthwhile objective.

The Contrôleur

At the helm of every corporation, without exception, stands one man or group of men holding the ultimate direction of all corporate activity. This is an intrinsic necessity. At every minute of time, someone, anyone, must be in charge of the entity. To identify with certainty the specific person in control may at times be difficult or even impossible. Control may shift often, be tenuous or fragile, but control, by inherent logic, must ineluctably be present in every business corporation.

The contrôleur, then, is the topmost person in the corporate hierarchy. In this all-important contrôleur resides the final corporate destiny. Here, therefore, is the center of corporate morality. Or immorality. If the movement toward a sophisticated corporate mores is to progress apace, it must begin with, and branch out from, an exact delineation of the fiduciary duties of this contrôleur. As the contrôleur carries himself, so will the corporation prosper. If the contrôleur is rotten at the center, the whole corporate barrel will decay.

A Corporate-Control Guidebook

This treatise, then, is an attempt at a legal handbook of the fiduciary duties of corporate control. Here are the principles and rules of corporate conduct at the highest level. The right and wrong in the month-to-month and year-to-year direction of the corporation. A moralist would call it: The Moral Theology of Ultimate Corporate

Control. But this is not a moral-theology compendium. It is purely legal. Nonetheless, a contrôleur certainly will find his moral guidelines in these pages. (For the law, if it is to be just, must be exactly conformable to the moral.) As important as these guidelines are, never have they been proposed in a coherent and dogmatic system. Bits and tag ends here and there, but no philosophical corpus. The hope, therefore, is to define at last both the rights and obligations—but particularly the obligations—of corporate control and the contrôleur, since Berle was right: "Corporation law has never surrounded this phenomenon."

The Sale of Control

When the incumbent contrôleur decides to leave his office and pass on the power of control to a successor, he is faced vividly with a complexus of decisions involving the overall well-being of the corporation. At no other time is the total destiny of the entity so completely at stake. Is the prospective contrôleur suitable? Is the corporate future secure under his direction? If, further, the contrôleur exacts a premium from his would-be successor in order to assure the appointment to the office, an entirely new and more subtle set of guiding principles is triggered into action. Is the premium legitimate? If illegitimate, why? And to whom does it belong? All these questions lead to more questions, and in the end the answers to all these questions form an excellent embarkation point for the broader philosophy of the all-embracing fiduciary duty of corporate control.

Do not be misled, however. The elaboration of the law specifically governing the sale of control is only a part of the total synthesis of the control philosophy. But this sale of control is so pivotal to the whole, so pervasive, and so intertwined with the broader body as to be the ideal center for the entire study.

As a practical matter, the control of corporations is sold daily. The barter of control is an omnipresent fact of present-day corporate life. Incumbent contrôleurs are being premium-bribed out of office with almost universal impunity, and in the process giving rise to a constant need for regulation and for a fuller understanding of the moral and legal implications involved. At no other point in the philosophy of control do the dollars and cents, and hence the practicalities, obtrude themselves with such insistence. Throughout this book, therefore, the sale of control will be the matrix onto which the broader study will be superimposed.

The Prototypal Antagonists

The law has approached the concept of control gingerly. At this early stage two roughly antagonistic positions have been taken by the courts, crystallized in the famous *Perlman v. Feldmann* in the midfifties and in *Green Giant* concluded in early 1963. These prototypes point up the antithesis, provide factual settings for the major policy questions underlying the philosophy of control and further set the problem and the perspective for the book.

I. *Perlman v. Feldmann*

> The courts' refusal to adopt the Berle-Bayne approach that control premiums are per se invalid has left an analytical morass of hybrid theories that may be utilized to recapture a control premium. Each theory may seem justified by the facts of a particular case, but when considered collectively, they fall far short of forming a coherent body of law.
>
> —Hazen, *Transfers of Corporate Control,* 125 U. PA. L. REV. 1023, 1060 (1977).

The Newport Steel Corporation in 1950 was a relatively small fabricator of steel with a geographically limited market in the Ohio-valley area around Cincinnati. Newport produced steel sheets for sale to manufacturers of steel products, and was able to keep a shaky operation alive only because of the bonanza of the Korean War shortage. C. Russell Feldmann was the devil in the piece, and handily controlled Newport with combined personal and family holdings of 37 percent of the common. He was thus contrôleur and, as the Second Circuit by Judge Clark put it, was . . .

> . . . not only the dominant stockholder, but also the chairman of the board of directors and the president of the corporation.
>
> —*Perlman v. Feldmann,* 219 F.2d 173, 174 (2d Cir. 1955).

So tight was the supply during those harried years that Mr. Feldmann was able to circumvent the unwritten law of gray-market abstention by a device appropriately called the 'Feldmann Plan.' By interest-free prepayments for every purchase—to guarantee supply—Newport was able to force the hungry end-users to advance substantial sums toward the financing of necessary expansion and plant improvement, and still avoid some of the stigma of price gouging.

But Newport's customers understandably reacted adversely to this modified extortion, and their reaction took the form of a syndicate called the Wilport Company, incorporated in Delaware for the sole purpose of buying out the Feldmann interests and thereby incidentally gaining control of Newport and a captive supply of steel. Predictably, this sale of control would also see the demise of the Feldmann Plan, since the new end-user contrôleur could scarcely be expected to extort interest-free prepayments from itself.

Wilport's plan was simple: To effect the seriatim resignation of Feldmann's minions on the Newport board and in one deft stroke elect the Wilport nominees. To assure these appointments, however, and thereby to install Wilport as the successor contrôleur, C. Russell Feldmann required some substantial inducement. And the inducement was exactly $8 per share over market. In the final event Feldmann received a total premium of $2.1 million. The sale of control was expeditious, and secure, since the tight grip on the proxy-solicitation mechanism left Wilport in indefinite and unfettered domination of Newport. The widely dispersed and typically sheepish shareholder dutifully acceded to Wilport's every wish. Wilport thus became the unchallenged contrôleur of Newport.

The District Court

This was the fait accompli that faced Jane Perlman when she decided to initiate her derivative action in Connecticut on behalf of herself and all the other minority shareholders of Newport. Her objective: To force C. Russell Feldmann to disgorge the "illegal gains which accrued . . . as a result of the sale . . . of [the] controlling interest in the corporation."[1] The suit conformed to the standard derivative pattern and sought recovery by and for the corporation.

The Perlman argumentation was markedly unusual for the midfifties and was highly redolent of the strict-trust philosophy of the turn of the century:

Plaintiffs contend that the consideration paid for the
stock included compensation for the sale of a corporate
asset, a power held in trust for the corporation by
Feldmann as its fiduciary. This power was the ability to
control the allocation of the corporate product in a time
of short supply, through control of the board of
directors . . . .

> —*Perlman v. Feldmann*, 219 F.2d 173, 175
> (2d Cir. 1955).

But Judge Hincks in the District-level *Feldmann* was not disposed
to revert to the rigidity of another era. To him "the power . . . is
not a corporate asset, . . . and there was no breach of fiduciary duty.
. . ."[2] Rather, Judge Hincks espoused the prevailing doctrine that
control was indeed an item of sale and as such belonged to the logical
owner, the incumbent contrôleur, and certainly not to the corporation. Judge Hincks, therefore, refused to grant to the minority "that
share of [Feldmann's] profit which is attributable to the sale of the
corporate power."[3] Rather the District Court held instead . . .

> . . . that the rights involved in the sale were only those
> normally incident to the possession of a controlling block
> of shares, with which a dominant stockholder, in the ab-
> sence of fraud or foreseeable looting, was entitled to deal
> according to his own best interests.

> —*Perlman v. Feldmann*, 219 F.2d 173, 175
> (2d Cir. 1955).

The Second Circuit

The result of the appeal was a strong reversal by Chief Judge
Clark, but with a dissent by Judge Swan. The further, and more important, result was a sharp marcation between the accepted way of
corporate life of the recent half century and the beginning of an un-
nerving trend toward the Cardozo "'punctilio of an honor the most
sensitive.'"[4] While the District Court felt Feldmann "was entitled to
deal according to his own best interests" with his control block, the
Second Circuit was categorical: For Feldmann the "'first principal

duty arising from his official relation is to act in all things of trust wholly for the benefit of his corporation.'"[5]

The Second Circuit, however, did not produce an unqualifiedly perfect application of traditional strict trust to a consciously acknowledged sale of control. On both counts, full-blown strict trust and clean-cut premium-bribery, inaccuracies detracted from the opinion, and from the opinion's later impact on the law of the fiduciary duty of corporate control. But these flaws were far from serious, and the opinion should be justly characterized as one of the most influential corporate holdings thus far in the century.

Furthermore, the few inconcinnities can be readily smoothed out. Some slight reading between the lines soon reduces *Feldmann* to a modern version of the celebrated English Chancery opinion of 1856, *Sugden v. Crossland:* The fiduciary duty of a strict trustee applied to the sale of corporate office. For this reason the opinion can stand as the antithesis to the Hincks holding below, and to *Green Giant* which so forcefully enunciated a relaxed rule for "businessmen of ordinary prudence."[6]

The Sale of Office

A casual reading might classify *Feldmann* as a 'corporate opportunity' case. The majority does speak as if Feldmann had appropriated Newport opportunities to himself, and then passed them on to Wilport for a fee:

> The corporate opportunities of whose misappropriation the minority stockholders complain need not have been an absolute certainty in order to support this action against Feldmann.
>
> —*Perlman v. Feldmann*, 219 F.2d 173, 176
> (2d Cir. 1955).

Throughout the opinion the emphasis is undeniably on the sale of the "ability to control the allocation of the corporate product in a time of short supply."[7] Thus the Court condemns the "actions of defendants in siphoning off for personal gain corporate advantages to be derived from a favorable market situation."[8] Later Judge Clark spoke as if the malefaction were solely the unjustified allocation of the corporate product to favored clientele:

So in a time of market shortage, where a call on a corporation's product commands an unusually large premium, in
one form or another, we think it sound law that a fiduciary
may not appropriate to himself the value of this premium.

—*Perlman v. Feldmann,* 219 F.2d 173, 178
(2d Cir. 1955).

A little reflection, however, and a close perusal of the opinion convince that the Court fully realized that the control of product allocation was impossible without the control of the board, and that the
"unusually large premium" was in fact and necessarily paid to get
control of the board.

Clearly, product allocation was merely one, albeit a notable one,
of the congeries of powers that comprised the totality of 'corporate
control.' Merely because the Court concentrated on the more prominent manifestation of control—more prominent at least in the
Newport/Wilport context—did not mean that the Court failed to realize that Feldmann was selling an inseparable part, product allocation, of an indivisible whole, corporate control, when he accepted
the $2.1-million premium. Early in its opinion, the majority, quoting
the Plaintiff, made this clear: "This power was the ability to control
the allocation of the corporate product . . . through control of the
board of directors . . . ."[9]

Strict Trust

The Second Circuit blended together the reasoning, language
and cases of the old-time strict-trust tradition with the modern ver-
biage and approaches of the Delaware courts. If one were to prescind
from the result, the disgorgement of the premium, one would be hard
pressed to characterize *Feldmann* as either age-old trust or modern
laissez-faire. The opinion was a disconcerting amalgam of both.

Thus, on the one hand, the majority seemed to place prime reliance on a veritable litany of indisputably strict-trust precedents, particularly the 1934 *Irving Trust Co. v. Deutsch,* which the Court dilated
upon, and the invariably quoted 'workaday world' and oft cited
Meinhard v. Salmon—which as pure partnership is necessarily pure
trust—of then-Judge Cardozo. But throughout the opinion there was
a dilutive admixture of language far less rigid. Thus, in conflict-of-
interest situations, said the Court, the law "emphasizes the close

scrutiny to which Indiana subjects the conduct of fiduciaries."[10] And: "'When a director deals with his corporation, his acts will be closely scrutinized.'"[11] "Scrutiny," even "close scrutiny," is not exactly the No Inquiry Rule of inflexible strict trust, which awards all benefits to beneficiary, all losses against the trustee, without inquiry.

The Holding

But when the majority reached the bottom line, the result was truly trust law. Citing the *Restatement of Restitution,* the Court ordered Feldmann to disgorge the $2.1-million premium-bribe. The Court further indicated implicitly that this $2.1 million belonged to the beneficiary of the trust, the corporation, to whom Feldmann, the trustee, must pay it over. Judge Swan in his dissent missed the point, but that is a matter for later.

(Bedeviled by an illogicality that must await study in another chapter, the Court rather remarkably concluded that premium-briber Wilport was guilty and premium-bribed Feldmann was innocent, or somehow less guilty, and that hence the guilty shareholder Wilport must be denied its share of the corporate recovery, but that the innocent Feldmann could keep his sizable percentage of the $2.1-million premium-bribe as long as he gave up the rest to the minority.)

The Modern Prototype

When all the accidentals are put aside, therefore, the substance of *Feldmann* explains the acclaim the opinion has received. The Court held Feldmann and his insiders to the highest standards of a fiduciary: "'Directors of a business corporation act in a strictly fiduciary capacity. Their office is a trust.'"[12]

> "In a transaction between a director and his corporation, where he acts for himself and his principal at the same time in a matter connected with the relation between them, it is presumed, where he is thus potential on both sides of the contract, that self-interest will overcome his fidelity to his principal, to his own benefit and to his principal's hurt."
>
> —*Perlman v. Feldmann,* 219 F.2d 173, 176 (2d Cir. 1955) (quoting *Schemmel v. Hill*).

Thus did the Court set up the primitive essentials of conflict of interest. The director-as-individual negotiates with himself, the director-as-corporation. No one is present to represent the shareholder owners. Feldmann-as-individual on the one hand joins with Feldmann-as-contrôleur on the other to determine the price to be paid for Newport stock. No one is there to champion the minority shareholder owners. They were to receive no share in the $2.1 million.

Faced with such conflict of interest, the Court stated the rule:

> "Absolute and most scrupulous good faith is the very essence of a director's obligation to his corporation. The first principal duty arising from his official relation is to act in all things of trust wholly for the benefit of his corporation."
>
> —*Perlman v. Feldmann*, 219 F.2d 173, 176 (2d Cir. 1955) (quoting *Schemmel v. Hill*).

The Court then bolstered this trust language with resort to the law of agency, which itself applies identical trust rules to the conduct of an agent toward his principal:

> "Directors of a corporation are its agents, and they are governed by the rules of law applicable to other agents, and, as between themselves and their principal, the rules relating to honesty and fair dealing in the management of the affairs of their principal are applicable. They must not, in any degree, allow their official conduct to be swayed by their private interest, which must yield to official duty."
>
> —*Perlman v. Feldmann*, 219 F.2d 173, 176 (2d Cir. 1955) (quoting *Schemmel v. Hill*).

Next, the Court made the obvious nexus between corporation and shareholder owners:

> Both as director and as dominant stockholder, Feldmann stood in a fiduciary relationship to the corporation and to the minority stockholders as beneficiaries

thereof. Pepper v. Litton, 308 U.S. 295 . . .; Southern Pac.
Co. v. Bogert, 250 U.S. 483 . . . .

> —*Perlman v. Feldmann,* 219 F.2d 173, 175
> (2d Cir. 1955).

The Court was satisfied that Feldmann and Wilport did not exhibit
"the necessary undivided loyalty owed by the fiduciary to his
principal."[13]

Upon this solid foundation the Second Circuit applied the
Benefit-to-Beneficiary Rule of strict-trust law and ordered disgorgement of the premium received by Feldmann. The flaw in the disposition of the $2.1-million premium-bribe—for later—marred only
minimally the strict-trust holding of restitution.

The Swan Dissent

One might think that Judge Swan served the praiseworthy purpose of emphasizing further the sharp contrast between the
majority's embrace of strict trust and the modern position. The contrary is true. Judge Swan merely misunderstood what happened.
Very simply Feldmann took $2.1 million in payment for assuring the
election of new directors. He and his minions were premium-bribed
out of office. Swan did not grasp this, else why speak as he did?

> A director is privileged to resign, but so long as he remains
> a director he must be faithful to his fiduciary duties and
> must not make a personal gain from performing them.
> Consequently, if the price paid for Feldmann's stock in-
> cluded a payment for voting to elect the new directors,
> he must account to the corporation for such payment,
> even though he honestly believed that the men he voted
> to elect were well qualified to serve as directors. He can
> not take pay for performing his fiduciary duty.
>
> —*Perlman v. Feldmann,* 219 F.2d 173, 179
> (2d Cir. 1955) (Swan, J., dissenting).

Judge Swan's problem also lay in his misconception of the nature of
corporate control. He conceived corporate control as belonging not
to all the owners but to the owner of a 'control block':

> The power to control . . . is an inseparable incident
> to the ownership . . . of enough shares . . . to control an
> election.
>
>> —*Perlman v. Feldmann,* 219 F.2d 173,
>> 178-79 (2d Cir. 1955) (Swan, J.,
>> dissenting).

Which, as everyone knows, can be no shares at all.

Had Judge Swan mastered the nature of control, he would have joined the majority in demanding that Feldmann "account to the corporation for such payment" of $2.1 million for getting the sheepish shareholders "to elect the new directors," the nominees of Wilport.

On remand, at the direction of the Second Circuit ("for a determination of the question expressly left open below, namely, the value of defendants' stock without the appurtenant control over the corporation's output of steel"[14]), the District Court awarded judgment of $1.3 million directly to the innocent public 63-percent shareholders, and let Feldmann keep his 37 percent of the premium-bribe. This $0.8 million would have inured to Wilport through its 37-percent ownership of Newport.

Nothing was said, from the beginning to the end of the litigation, about keeping a premium-briber in control of Newport. Wilport was unsuitable enough to be denied its share of the disgorgement, but suitable enough to chart the future destiny of the corporation.

II. *Green Giant*

> "This is an area of corporate law [the sale of control] particularly cursed with many shadowy lines and uncertainty born primarily from the need of judicial accommodation of what appear to be diametrically opposed interests." 6 Cavitch, Business Organizations § 120.03 page 751.
>
>> —*Swinney v. Keebler Co.,* 329 F. Supp. 216, 222 (D.S.C. 1971).

The Green Giant Company was founded in 1903, and by 1960 had grown from a handful of employees and annual sales of some $7,000 to sales of $64 million and a net worth of $23 million. The man behind this verdant growth, and the devil in this piece, was

Edward B. Cosgrove, who with his family had controlled the company for six decades.

At its foundation Green Giant had only one class of stock, but in 1923 the Cosgrove-dominated board effected amendment of the articles to create a more tractable situation: Public-held Class-B nonvoting and 44 shares of a Class-A voting. Mr. Cosgrove, of course, held 26 of the 44. Other than the Cosgroves, no Class-B shareholder—there were 428,998 shares held by 1,250 widely dispersed public shareholders—possessed holdings of two percent. Only one difference distinguished the Class A from the Class B: Voting rights. But the Class-B stock nonetheless represented 99.9 percent of the equity, earnings and dividend rights.

By 1960 the drawbacks of the nonvoting stock became disturbingly manifest. Listing on the New York Stock Exchange was foreclosed. Attractive personnel shied away. Mergers were nigh impossible. Equity financing was difficult.

The Glore, Forgan Report

So Mr. Cosgrove and cohorts sought out an old friend, the then Glore, Forgan & Co. A Glore, Forgan partner, Mr. C. S. Vrtis, had for some time been on the Green Giant board. To Glore, Forgan and Mr. Vrtis fell the task of extricating the Cosgroves from their predicament. As the Court so forthrightly put it:

> There is an absence of any showing that any influence was brought to bear on Mr. Vrtis by Mr. Cosgrove or the Directors . . . in any recapitalization which should be proposed. It is reasonable to find from the evidence that this banking concern and Mr. Vrtis, as well as the Directors, approached their task with commendable objectivity and with a desire to propose a plan that would be fair and equitable . . . .
>
> —*Honigman v. Green Giant Co.*, 208 F. Supp. 754, 756 (D. Minn. 1961).

The temptation to digress into a diverting discussion of the Glore, Forgan Report must be resisted for the present. The bolder features of this straight-faced carte blanche to the Cosgroves will appear apropos.

For now, the essentials of Mr. Vrtis's proposal are sufficient to illustrate how well he served the Cosgroves. The Glore, Forgan Report, some 27 pages, proposed a Plan of Recapitalization which provided for a single new class of voting stock. The heart of the Plan was simple. The Class B exchanged share for share. The Class A, 1,000 to one. Class-A equity increased from 0.01 percent to 9.3 percent. Class-A book value from $2,200 to $2,200,000. As a result, the Cosgroves acquired for their Class-A stock 26,000 of the new common. Combined with what they received for their Class-B holdings, they then held about 33 percent of the recapitalized Green Giant. The shareholders sheepishly approved overwhelmingly. Mr. Vrtis and Glore, Forgan were so thorough that a Cosgrove was at the helm well on into the seventies. Control of the proxy, plus a 33-percent block, were unassailable.

Interestingly, the Court placed considerable emphasis on the importance—questionable in the light of the modern mechanics of proxy solicitation in a widely held corporation—of the near unanimity of approval by the Class-B shareholders (the Class-A shares were all cast in favor of the Plan). "'That fact speaks more persuasively than the arguments of those who attempt to theorize on unrealistic principles of so-called corporate democracy.'"[15]

Jason L. Honigman, Esquire

Enter a powerful advocate. Mr. Honigman's wife, Edith, happened to own $75,000 worth of the old Class B, and as he himself phrased it in an exasperated Reply Brief on the Circuit level:

> Here, it so happens, appellant's husband, a lawyer equipped by training and experience to see through the adroit proxy presentation, and sufficiently thereby outraged, was financially able and willing to do something about it. Here before this Court for review is the saga of an expropriation of $2,000,000 in corporate assets ostensibly in exchange for a technical extension of voting rights to scattered small public stockholders in whose hands such right was in fact meaningless.
>
> —Reply Brief of Plaintiff at 8, *Honigman v. Green Giant Co.*, 309 F.2d 667 (8th Cir. 1962).

In a combined derivative and individual action in the Federal District Court for Minnesota Edith Honigman sought to void the recapitalization plan and set aside the issuance of the $2.2-million-premium shares. The complaint alleged principally that the Cosgroves were taking a $2-million bonus for something they did not own, since corporate control as an item of sale, if salable at all, is a corporate asset. Ultimately, the Cosgroves as fiduciaries could not profit at the expense of the corporation and the minority.

Judge Nordbye denied relief. The crux of his decision lay in his readiness to place a premium value on the single element of control, as isolated from all other values. "In these 44 shares was lodged the entire destiny of the company. It was the power of control which was lodged in these few shares which created their value . . . ."[16] The Court advanced no reasons directly explanatory of this extra value, but summarily stated:

> No Class A shareholder could be expected to forego the power of control of a company of this size without receiving in return a consideration commensurate with the value of the control which he foregoes. It seems evident, therefore, that in light of the evidence in considering the fairness of the plan, we must commence with the premise that the A shareholders in surrendering their exclusive voting rights were entitled to a premium in exchanging their stock for the new voting common stock.
>
> —*Honigman v. Green Giant Co.*, 208 F. Supp. 754, 758 (D. Minn. 1961).

The District Court summarized the pervading spirit of its opinion:

> [S]o far as the charge of immoral and reprehensible conduct directed at the Class A stockholders is concerned, suffice it to say that their position in this proceeding must be judged by that which businessmen of ordinary prudence would have done under similar circumstances.
>
> —*Honigman v. Green Giant Co.*, 208 F. Supp. 754, 762 (D. Minn. 1961).

"Whether these Directors are fiduciaries in the strict sense in the promotion of this recapitalization need not be determined."[17]

The Court of Appeals affirmed unanimously, but did not consider the fundamental issue: Is control a salable asset? The Eighth Circuit relied on the reasoning of the lower court and concluded briefly: "We are satisfied that plaintiff has wholly failed to demonstrate . . . that corporate control is a corporate asset. . . ."[18] The petition for a writ of certiorari was duly denied.

The Impact

When the dust settled, *Green Giant* had securely entrenched the status quo of half a century. The District Court for Minnesota and a unanimous Eighth Circuit had aligned themselves firmly with Judge Hincks, and a long line of cases that held:

> It seems wholly unrealistic to suggest, as plaintiff does, that the Class A shareholders should be relegated to the same number of shares . . . when they forego the exclusive voting control . . . .
>
> —*Honigman v. Green Giant Co.,* 208 F. Supp. 754, 757 (D. Minn. 1961).

In a word, the control of a corporation belongs to whoever has it—whether by majority stock ownership, working control, mere-incumbency control, however—and whoever has it may sell it and whoever buys it may—must?—pay a premium for it. Whoever forgoes "the power of control of a company" can expect to receive "in return a consideration commensurate with the value of the control which he foregoes." "Whether these directors are fiduciaries in the strict sense . . . need not be determined."

In *Feldmann* and *Green Giant* the problem and perspective have been set. These were rudimentary, nontechnical, almost loose, statements of the two antithetical philosophical camps lined up against each other in this battle over the nature of corporate control, over the broad elements of the fiduciary duty of corporate control, over the legal ramifications branching out from the sale of the office of control.

Henceforward the discussion will be exactingly technical, and will proceed from the general to the specific and in logical progression.

Chapter 2

The Custodial Concept of Corporate Control

> [S]ome day when English history is adequately written one of the most interesting and curious tales that it will have to tell will be that which brings trust and corporation into intimate connexion with each other.
>
> —F. MAITLAND, *The Unincorporate Body*, in 3 COLLECTED PAPERS 272 (1911).

If one stands on the topmost pinnacle overlooking the whole of corporate law—once the corporation has been satisfactorily located in modern society—the picture one sees, with each succeeding scrutiny, becomes more and more focussed on the contrôleur. Every unit of human society demands an ultimate governor, a person upon whom devolves the final decisions by and for the entity. The corporate entity is no different. The contrôleur, as the final voice in the hierarchy of corporate affairs, possesses by metaphysical necessity the obligation and hence the right to establish and then implement the broadest corporate policy. It is impossible for a corporation to be without a contrôleur. In him necessarily rests the guidance of the entity.

Fiduciary Duty

And if the contrôleur must govern willy-nilly, he must govern according to a rational plan, else he will be acting irrationally and with consequent disaster. More so, he must govern legally and the surest way to govern legally is to govern morally. Certainly corporate morality is the foundation of corporate legality.

The all-important contrôleur, therefore, must in turn be governed himself by an ethicolegal code that will assure a governance that is both ethical and legal. Over the centuries the Anglo-Saxon system has shown a pronounced preference for the term 'fiduciary duty' in describing the foundation of that ethicolegal code. Under the umbrella of 'fiduciary duty' are assembled the major rules of conduct designed to guide the contrôleur in his month-to-month and year-to-year governance of the corporation. But unfortunately fiduciary duty, both the term and the concept behind it, has suffered grievously at the hands of the law. As David Bazelon put it in *Harper's,* time, in the form of lawyers and judges, "began to chew away at the edges"[19] of fiduciary duty to such an appreciable extent that today an exacting philosopher should invariably proscribe the use of the term, unless a qualifying definition is immediately appended.

Fiduciary duty today encompasses every possible meaning attached to managerial obligation, from the most permissive to the most rigid. Central and most fundamental, therefore, to the elaboration of the philosophy of corporate control is the precise exposition of the fiduciary duty of the contrôleur. Such an exposition, moreover, will reduce the remaining control study to a series of logical consequences derived inexorably from the basic premises implicit in fiduciary duty. Any flaws, therefore, in this elaboration will flaw irremediably the consequent philosophy. If, to the contrary, the evolution of the essentials of fiduciary duty is sound, the resultant corpus of the philosophy will be irrefutable. Everything hinges on this exposition.

The Thesis of the Philosophy

The Philosophy of Corporate Control is founded on one premise: The contrôleur is a strict trustee. Fortunately, that term is the beneficiary of the technical learning of centuries of Anglo-American jurisprudence. In essence, fiduciary duty is properly defined as the duty of age-old strict trust. The juxtaposition of the highly opportune *Lionel* litigation, adjudicated in mid-1964 by the New York courts, over against the century-old—but arrestingly fresh—*Sugden v. Crossland* sets a parallel that might well characterize this thesis, and introduce the expatiation and refinement of the Custodial Concept of Corporate Control.

Sugden v. Crossland

In the year of our Lord 1852, William Sugden of Leeds by his will . . .

> . . . devised and bequeathed his real and personal estate to the use of Joseph Sugden and William Crossland, upon certain trusts for his infant son, with the ordinary power to the . . . trustee . . . to appoint new trustees . . . in the place of any trustee . . . becoming incapable of acting.
>
> —*Sugden v. Crossland,* 65 Eng. Rep. 620 (V.C. 1856).

As the event would have it, however, before his death William Sugden removed his two trustees and substituted two others, one of whom was Jervis Horsfield. For reasons left to conjecture William Crossland took ill indeed his displacement as trustee and shortly after Sugden's death sought out his successor Horsfield in the thought that "he should retire from the trust and cause Crossland to be appointed; in consideration of . . . the sum of £75."[20] To this Horsfield was amenable. The money changed hands, Horsfield withdrew, and Crossland was appointed according to the agreement.

Shortly thereafter the administrators of the estate filed a bill against Horsfield with a double prayer: (1) "[T]hat Crossland might be removed from the trust" and (2) "[T]hat the sum of £75 paid to Horsfield might be treated as a part of the testator's estate, and applied for the benefit of the persons entitled under the will. It appeared from the evidence that £75 was paid by Crossland out of his own pocket."[21]

The Vice-Chancellor, Sir John Stuart, granted the double prayer. Since this was a case of first impression, the sureness of his reasoning and unhesitating approach to his conclusions are all the

more remarkable. "This is a very extraordinary case. . . . I do not remember a case where the office of a trustee has been purchased for
money."[22]

The opinion of the Vice-Chancellor was brief, but extremely relevant to the present consideration. In removing Crossland from the
office of trustee the Vice-Chancellor summarized his holding thus:

> Horsfield abandoned his duty and office as trustee
> for a valuable consideration, and made over the trustee-
> ship to a person who was deliberately excluded from that
> office by the testator. Such a transaction, as well as the
> instrument by which it was sought to be carried into ef-
> fect, was entirely unjustifiable, and the deed, in accord-
> ance with the terms of the prayer, must be delivered up
> to be cancelled.
>
> —*Sugden v. Crossland,* 65 Eng. Rep. 620, 621
> (V.C. 1856).

Crossland was removed, not only because of the premium, but also
because he was unsuitable for the office according to the fiduciary
norms for the selection of a successor trustee.

In his response to the second part of the Plaintiff's prayer, Vice-
Chancellor Stuart ordered Horsfield to pay over the money, not to
the out-of-pocket Crossland, but into the trust fund itself:

> It has been further asked that the sum of £75 may
> be treated as a part of the trust fund, and as such may be
> directed to be paid by Horsfield to the trustee for the ben-
> efit of the *cestui que trusts* under the will. It is a well-settled
> principle that, if a trustee makes a profit of his trusteeship,
> it shall enure to the benefit of his *cestui que trusts.* Though
> there is some peculiarity in the case, there does not seem
> to be any difference in principle whether the trustee de-
> rived the profit by means of the trust property, or from
> the office itself. I shall therefore direct that the £75 be re-
> paid by Horsfield and dealt with as a part of the assets . . . .
>
> —*Sugden v. Crossland,* 65 Eng. Rep. 620, 621
> (V.C. 1856).

The *Lionel* Litigation

Hapless Lionel Corporation (electric trains, electronics) had been moved as a pawn so often in a series of control gambits that minority shareholders (primarily Hyman Caplan and Gabriel Industries) finally decided that the game was up. Although details of the machinations were numerous and complex, the essentials of the plan that goaded Caplan and friends to litigation were as stark and simple as the £75 sale by Horsfield to Crossland.

Defiance Industries, Inc. (the 'three muscateers,' Muscat, Huffines, Krock, whom *Fortune* aptly characterized in "What's in It for Eddie, Bob, and Vic?"[23]) had a deferred-sale agreement with the redoubtable Roy M. Cohn (the McCarthy hearings, the Patterson/Liston fight, the United Dye scandal, the Ford v. Ford embroglio), providing for the transfer of Cohn's 55,000 shares of Lionel—just three percent of the outstanding Lionel stock—for a sum of $281,875 ($5.125 per share at market). This agreement was dated March 8, 1963. The other major term of the agreement was the seriatim resignation of six Cohn board members and their replacement on the Lionel board by six nominees of Defiance.

Onto this scene walked A. N. Sonnabend (Premier Corporation, women's apparel, dolls, *Mad*) who immediately consummated a second deal to take over from Defiance the Cohn control package for a sum of $135,000 over the Defiance deal with Cohn. The same condition attached: Seriatim resignation of the Defiance directors.

> [T]he ultimate sale for $415,000 clearly establish[es] that the premium price was being paid for the accompanying transfer of managerial control that was the all important emolument of the transaction.
>
> —*Matter of Lionel Corp.*, N.Y.L.J., Feb. 4, 1964, at 14 (Sup. Ct., N.Y. County).

Sonnabend threw in an extra $75,000 of Lionel money toward salaries over the coming five-year period for outgoing Defiance men.

Sonnabend incidentally felt that it would be to Lionel's interest to take over several Sonnabend companies in exchange for Lionel stock (which fortuitously and fortunately would increase Sonnabend's holdings from three to 30 percent).

> When the transaction is stripped of its somewhat complicated facade, what was originally offered by Cohn, and in turn subsequently offered for sale by Defiance, was Cohn's power, which later became Defiance's power. . . .
>
> —*Matter of Lionel Corp.,* N.Y.L.J., Feb. 4, 1964, at 14 (Sup. Ct., N.Y. County).

In separate litigations in the Supreme Court, New York County, shareholders Caplan and Gabriel Industries respectively sought the same double relief of *Sugden v. Crossland*: (1) "[T]o set aside the election of the board of directors" as "illegal" and (2) To force Defiance to hand over to the Lionel Corporation the $135,000 control premium received from Sonnabend.

> Defiance Industries, Inc., controlled and dominated the board of directors of Lionel [and] sold such control to A. N. Sonnabend without selling a majority of the stock or a clearly defined controlling block of stock and thus made an illegal profit, which profit should inure to the benefit of Lionel.
>
> —*Gabriel Indus. v. Defiance Indus.,* N.Y.L.J., June 17, 1964, at 13 (Sup. Ct., N.Y. County).

In the first litigation, *Caplan-Lionel,* the Court of Appeals affirmed the Appellate Division without opinion. As the four-man Court in the Appellate Division summarized it: "Special Term found the elections to be illegal and vacated them. With this finding and disposition we are in accord."[24] Special Term had founded its holding on a long line of New York cases:

> As early as McClure v. Law . . . and as late as Essex Universal Corp'n v. Yates . . . it is the law of this state that "it is illegal to sell corporate office or management control by itself . . . ."
>
> —*Matter of Lionel Corp.,* N.Y.L.J., Feb. 4, 1964, at 14 (Sup. Ct., N.Y. County) (quoting *Essex Universal Corp. v. Yates*).

It would be misleading to give the impression that the reasoning of Special Term in *Caplan-Lionel* was unimpeachable. The result may well have been correct, but the reasons adduced were neither perfectly clear nor exactly valid.

As for the premium for the sale of control, Special Term in an obiter laid down the governing principle:

> Nor may controlling stockholders receive a bonus or premium specifically in consideration of their agreement to resign and install the designees of the purchaser of their stock, above and beyond the price premium normally attributable to the control stock being sold . . . . The remedies applied where such transgressions have occurred have been to impose liability upon the resigning directors . . . and to require that any bonus received for such transfer of their office be returned to the corporation . . . .
>
> —*Matter of Lionel Corp.*, N.Y.L.J., Feb. 4, 1964, at 14 (Sup. Ct., N.Y. County).

Special Term had particular reference to *Essex Universal* in support of its decision:

> The rationale of the rule is undisputable: persons enjoying management control hold it on behalf of the corporation's stockholders, and therefore may not regard it as their own personal property to dispose of as they wish.
>
> —*Essex Universal Corp. v. Yates*, 305 F.2d 572, 575 (2d Cir. 1962).

Special Term had further resort to *Essex Universal* in a pertinent statement by Judge Friendly:

> "A mass seriatim resignation directed by a selling stockholder, and the filling of vacancies by his henchmen at the dictation of a purchaser and without any consideration of the character of the latter's nominees, are beyond what the stockholders contemplated or should have been expected to contemplate."
>
> —*Matter of Lionel Corp.*, N.Y.L.J., Feb. 4, 1964, at 14 (Sup. Ct., N.Y. County) (quoting *Essex Universal Corp. v. Yates*).

In the second litigation, *Gabriel-Lionel*, the New York Supreme Court built on the foundation established by *Caplan-Lionel*.

> No question of fact therefore remains with respect to this issue of the legality of the [sale] of seats on the Lionel board. When such sale is made, the illegal profit received must be accounted for to the corporation (McClure v. Law, 161 N.Y. 78).
>
> —*Gabriel Indus. v. Defiance Indus.*, N.Y.L.J., June 17, 1964, at 13 (Sup. Ct., N.Y. County).

With that the Court concluded that "Defiance, who controlled the management of Lionel, when it illegally sold such control must account to Lionel . . . for the illegal profit."[25] As Horsfield to the trust.

The *Sugden/Lionel* parallel fulfills a twofold purpose. It supplies excellent materials and subtle questions for later analysis. But perhaps even more important, it suggests the distinct possibility of a working analogy, even an identity, between trustee and contrôleur extending beyond the limits of the single question of the sale of control. At the least it sets the mind to thinking and serves as an apposite introduction.

The General Thesis

Max Pam, writing early in the century, marks a point in the history of the fiduciary-duty concept which asserts strongly that the *Sugden/Lionel* parallel is by no means a new thought:

> The law-books and the decisions of the highest courts of many of the states and of the United States are replete with text and pronouncements holding that the relationship between a director and the corporation is fiduciary, and that the director for all practical purposes is a trustee, the corporation and its stockholders the *cestuis que trustent,* and the property of the corporation a trust fund.
>
> —Pam, *Interlocking Directorates, The Problem and Its Solution,* 26 HARV. L. REV. 467, 471 (1913).

Some years earlier the Supreme Court of Illinois enunciated this same general thesis:

> It is a principle of general application, and recognized by this court, that the assets of a corporation are, in equity, a trust fund, . . . and that the directors of a corporation are trustees, and have no power or right to use or appropriate the funds of the corporation, their *cestui que trust,* to themselves, nor to waste, destroy, give away, or misapply them . . . . Ordinarily, an express trust is created by a deed or will; but there are many fiduciary relations established by law, and regulated by settled legal rules and principles, where all the elements of an express trust exist, and to which the same legal principles are applicable; and such appears to be the relation established by law between directors and the corporation.
>
> —*Ellis v. Ward,* 25 N.E. 530, 533 (Ill. 1890).

In the late twenties—when he was in his earliest thirties—Adolf A. Berle, Jr., in one of his first works, exhibited his usual prescience. Although Mr. Berle was more guarded in his statement, he is reducible to substantially the same strict-trust stand:

> It is believed that examination will show the holders of such management stock to be subject to greater equitable control than generally supposed—control rendering them analogous to trustees, imposing many of the duties which trustees normally have toward their *cestuis que trustent.*
>
> —A. BERLE, STUDIES IN THE LAW OF CORPORATION FINANCE 46 (1928).

These preparatory thoughts set the stage for a general statement of the thesis of the Custodial Concept of Corporate Control:

> *The relation persisting between the office of the contrôleur and the corporation is in all essentials verified in the relationship between the office of trustee and the corpus of the trust. With only accidental qualifications, therefore, the contrôleur is a strict trustee.*

The Beauty of the Trust Doctrine

Such a statement could conceivably raise some hackles. This is, however regrettable, to be expected and undoubtedly makes one scrutinize more closely the advantages of utilizing the trust philosophy in the control field. Undeniably there is no particularly consuming beauty in the technical terms 'trust,' 'trustee' or 'cestui que trust,' but one compelling consideration—beyond, of course, the cogency of the general thesis that the two relationships are virtually identical—does shift the balance in favor of a wholehearted incorporation of trust philosophy, reasoning and rules into the nascent corpus of the law of corporate control.

It comes to this: To ignore, once proven, the intrinsic identity of the two relations would be grossly wasteful of centuries of thorough thinking on trust principles, now apt for application to corporate control. As Maitland said at the turn of the century:

> If we were asked what is the greatest and most distinctive achievement performed by Englishmen in the field of jurisprudence I cannot think that we should have any better answer to give than this, namely, the development from century to century of the trust idea.
>
> —F. MAITLAND, *The Unincorporate Body*, in 3 COLLECTED PAPERS 272 (1911).

It would be prodigal indeed to reject through prejudice the distillate of decades of refined reasoning, trial and error, elimination and retention.

> The philosophy on which these rules of law and equity [rest] came down through the centuries from the Chancellor of Galilee. The wisdom and necessity of such doctrines become more apparent as the forms, in which property is held, multiply under new conditions, and as earning capital, in the custody and control of agents or trustees, follows new enterprises over the world, where it is not under the watchful eye of the owner. Courts of equity do not set bounds to the principles which control the conduct and fix the accountability of trustees. The elasticity of these rules extends their applicability to all of the devices invented by unfaithful fiduciaries to evade their

obligations or to defeat the imperative demands of business integrity and sound public policy.
—*Nebraska Power Co. v. Koenig,* 139 N.W. 839, 842 (Neb. 1913).

The attempt then will be to demonstrate the essential oneness of the two systems, to trace the parallel of the major elements of each relation, to separate the accidentals from the essentials.

The analysis will begin with the nature of the trust itself, the trust essentials, and proceed from there to justify application to corporate control. The viewpoint will be that of the trust, looking outward toward corporate control.

The Fallibility of Trust Law

A caution is in order. It is true that corporate control and the trust are identical relations. It is also true that the trust rules should, therefore, apply with equal logic to corporate control. But it is not clear that every trust rule, down to the most minute, is altogether tenable. Four or five hundred years old they may well be, but in the more specified areas further refinement may yet be required. This fact is important. Justified criticism might well be leveled against this or that trust rule. Insofar, however, as a trust rule applies to the trust relation, so also does it apply, with the same logic, to the relation of corporate control.

Moreover, there will be no attempt here to apply the corpus of trust law to the minutiae of corporate control. Once the parallel philosophy has been established, the implementation in the ad hoc cases will be the journeyman work for the future. Note well: At each stage of progress reflect that what is being said of the trust applies to control. Constant written adversion to this parallel would pall.

Ultimately, the objective is the maximum insight into the subtle concept of corporate control. Even if one were to disagree throughout, some further light on the fiduciary duty of corporate control would nonetheless be inevitable.

The Approach Emphasized

The English, over painstaking decades, constructed the elaborate concept of the trust, designed and engineered to place other people's money in the honest custody of a trustee. The trust concept has been fully developed. Its nature and essence have been explored. The rights and duties consequent on its nature have been laid out.

The modern phenomenon of corporate control is yet emergent. It too places other people's money in the unhampered custody of a corporate contrôleur. The corporate-control concept has yet to be developed. Its nature and resultant rules must now be excogitated.

The present investigation of the mature philosophy of the trust—nature, essence, duties—should yield correspondingly the Philosophy of Corporate Control.

The thesis set for proof will be approached in four parts: *I. The Trust Essentials. II. Custody and Confidence: The Foundation. III. Benefit to Beneficiary. IV. Conflict of Interest.*

I. The Trust Essentials

I am also of opinion that [the directors] are trustees for the plaintiff and the shareholders [of the London Mutual] on whose behalf he sues.

—*Gaskell v. Chambers,* 122 Rev. Rep. 138, 140 (Ch. 1858).

When a number of stockholders combine to constitute themselves a majority in order to control the corporation as they see fit, they become for all practical purposes the corporation itself, and assume the trust relation occupied by the corporation toward its stockholders.

—*Ervin v. Oregon Ry. & Navigation Co.,* 27 F. 625, 631 (C.C.S.D.N.Y. 1886).

Any penetrating comparison of the trust with corporate control must begin with an exact philosophical definition. Such an intensive analysis will permit segregation of the trust essentials for later specific application to corporate control. As a departure point the *Restatement of Trusts* offers the current legal consensus. The trust is...

> ... a fiduciary relationship with respect to property, subjecting the person by whom the title to the property is held to equitable duties to deal with the property for the benefit of another person, which arises as a result of a manifestation of an intention to create it.
>
> —RESTATEMENT (SECOND) OF TRUSTS §2 (1959).

Such a definition requires some expansion and restatement, even emendation. Present purposes, however, would dictate that explanation or justification of any such changes is for later.

The elaboration will build on the two major concepts latent in the *Restatement* definition: (1) *The Relation of Custody* and (2) *Benefit to Beneficiary*. Around these two concepts all the nonessentials group themselves. From these two all the lesser principles are derived. In these two, therefore, lies the fundamental philosophy of the trust.

(1) *The Relation of Custody*

> [A] fiduciary relationship with respect to property ... held ..., which arises as a result of a manifestation of an intention to create it.
>
> —RESTATEMENT (SECOND) OF TRUSTS §2 (1959).

This excerpt contains five distinct elements which coalesce into one concept. Paraphrased it reads: A (1) fiduciary (2) relationship (3) involving property tenure, (4) coupled with an administrative intent (5) specified pursuant to the principle of final causality.

A Relationship

Although the *Restatement* does not specifically state that the relation persists between "the person by whom the title to the property is held," the trustee, and the "property ... held," the trust corpus, nonetheless this would be the only justifiable inference. In this way does the *Restatement* specify the terminal units, the terms of the relation: Trustee as subject, corpus as object.

The *Restatement* would have been better advised to designate the office rather than the officeholder as the subject of the relation. Thus spoke Vice-Chancellor Stuart in *Sugden v. Crossland:* "I do not remember a case where the office of a trustee has been purchased for money."[26] This is more exact terminology since the office continues in existence irrespective of the resignation or death of the trustee. This terminology does not preclude the loose identification of officeholder with office in everyday parlance. Exact thinking, however, must recognize that the person occupying the office is not the office any more than the president is the presidency. The astute Pierre Lepaulle adopted the same approach in 1928 in his reference to the office as "a legal 'person.'"[27]

Further refinement is in order in another terminological particular, as more minute inspection will reveal. Neither the 'office' nor even the 'officeholder' is sold. Rather, the 'occupancy' of the office is the object of sale.

Attention perhaps should next be called to the obvious. The relation is the trust itself, not the office of the trust. It is in the office that the relation inheres. Nor is the relation the trustee himself. Nor finally is it the asset of value, the trust corpus. The corpus, of course, is the object of the relation.

At this point it could be objected that certain prominent terms which have emerged, especially 'custody,' beg the question. They do. Since, however, their legitimacy is to be established apropos, their admirable suitability and the advantage of uniformity dictated their use at the outset.

A Fiduciary Relationship

The term 'fiduciary'—the adjective—in its original Latin form *fiduciarius* was a technical legal term relating to an actual holding in trust. As such it was synonymous with the present-day usage 'in trust.' The English term, however, has been eroded and has far broader applicability. Over the years the 'tenure' element has disappeared. It means, as Webster defines it, "of, relating to, or involving a confidence or trust." Ultimately it is reducible to *fides,* 'faith' or 'confidence.' Thus broadly defined as 'confidence,' the term is a genus of which a variety of species accounts for the variety of nontrust relations, which in turn account for much of the difficulty over the decades with the term 'fiduciary duty.' One of this number of species, however, is the trust. The word, therefore, was not inappropriately included in the *Restatement* definition. The broader note of 'confidence' will have important relevancy in later analyses. The word 'fiduciary'—as involving 'confidence'—takes on genuine importance, however, only when joined to the other elements under consideration.

The Property Tenure

The term 'property'—independent of the tenure—refers to any *asset of value* at all: Patent, plant, formula, money, stock. This asset is the trust fund, the corpus, the object of the relation. It serves, moreover, to distinguish the trust from other merely confidential relationships. Confidence as a genus is unrelated as such to property, or consequently to tenure.

In the apparently insignificant word 'held' is the heart of the trust relation. It is this *holding* of the trust fund, the tenure of the property, which is the intrinsic cause, technically the essence, of the relation. On this philosophical base of property tenure is built the entire law of trusts.

The Custodial Administration

Mere tenure, however, is not the whole of the matter, albeit the base. To actual property tenure must be joined what the *Restatement* calls the "manifestation of an intention to create" the trust. The trustee must accept the stewardship of the fund, either by the direct expression of intent or indirectly by implication or inference of law. The mere physical holding without the intention of custodial administration would result in many another possible relationship, from escrow to bailment, but would not be a trust.

The conjunction of these last two essentials—(1) actual property tenure and (2) an intention to administer as a custodian—gives rise to the custodial relationship of trust. Here is the ultimate genesis of the Custodial Concept of Corporate Control. The *Restatement* could be misleading in this particular. The trust does not arise "as a result of a manifestation of an intention to create it" without the simultaneous property tenure. Both are essential. Neither naked tenure nor mere intention alone would create a trust.

Pierre Lepaulle uses an entirely felicitous term definitive of this conjunction: "Appropriation." The technical *appropriation of an asset of value*, the acceptance of dominion of property by the office of trustee, effects the ultimate essential of the trust: *Custody.* In 'appropriation' there is not only the denotation of a simple passive tenure but also the dynamic concept of an actual administration of the trust. Here also is the actual passage and holding of title which is traditional to a trust. (Appropriation also denotes the initial act of the settlor in creating the trust, but this action is only a condition not a continuing cause of the relation and hence irrelevant to the instant analysis.)

Implicit further in this trust appropriation is the element of 'totality.' In the case of a trust, a 'partial' appropriation is self-contradictory. One either entrusts the asset or one does not. The tenure of the trustee is by definition total. Were it otherwise the trustee would not have true custody. The necessary dominion over the corpus would be lacking. (One could speak of 'partial' custody in the sense that a custodian may be entrusted with a limited sphere of responsibility, as a teacher may be in charge of the child's education and nothing more. But even here, although the custody is 'partial' in that it encompasses education only, it is nonetheless 'total' in that the teacher's control over that limited sphere is complete.)

Thus the appropriation moves a step beyond the reposal of mere confidence. The result is a confidential holding. In this last step the first major trust concept is completed. Custodial tenure is joined to the fiduciary relation.

The Principle of Finality

But a problem arises. The process is incomplete. The mere appropriation, without more, brings the custody into *existence,* but that is all. True, when the settlor carries through with his intention to entrust the assets into the care of the trustee he has effected the existence of the custodial tenure. But he has not spelled out the terms, specified its *nature*. The fact, the existence. But not the nature. The specification of the nature remains.

By some herculean interpolation, therefore, the *Restatement* must be conceived to have injected a second important constituent into its phrase "a manifestation of an intention to create" the trust. Otherwise, the custody created by the appropriation would be ill-defined and amorphous. Thus, the more onerous and subtle role of the *"intention to create"* is the determination of the nature of the custody, not its mere existence. For example, the settlor may entrust $4 million into the trustee's care. Without specification the trustee will never know the true nature of his stewardship. The trustee will not know how to administer the millions. Does he put half of the $4 million in blue chips and half in highfliers? Or all in gilt-edged bonds? Or does he buy a small business outright? Such particulars are of the essence of the nature of custody, and are necessarily included in the "intention to create" the trust.

And this nature of the custody must be determined in rigid adherence to that elemental philosophical principle: Final causality. This driving principle, so basic to all life's activity, is controlling in the specification of the custodial tenure.

The principle of finality—every being acts with its eye on its final goal, from the Latin *finis,* end, objective—is a basic metaphysical concept. Finality is the all-governing norm of every activity, animate or inanimate. By intrinsic necessity every existent being is impelled toward an innate objective. This is the ultimate law of the universe that makes interstellar space intelligible and manageable, that explains the conduct of subatomic particles, that permits the legal theoretician to construct, for example, a cohesive Custodial Concept of Corporate Control. If every being in the cosmos were not driven inexorably by the law of its nature toward a final goal, objective, end, then right order would be unattainable and chaos would be the rule.

The Timepiece

This leads logically to another truism: The end, objective, goal, of any being determines the nature of that being. If one constructs an object in order to achieve a particular purpose, the constituent parts of that object must operate congenially to produce the desired result. The nature of the object must conform to the demands of the objective.

Thus if one wishes to know the time of day and determines on a watch, he must so assemble the watch that it tells time. To conform to perfect rationality every single part of that watch must conduce to telling time. Any part that is directed to any other end is unnecessary, irrational. The nature must conform completely to the end.

Thus if the sole goal is telling time, even adornment is *contra naturam,* or at least *extra naturam.*

So inexorable is this principle of final causality, that the application of its correlative is equally dependable. From a *known nature* one can reason to an *unknown end.* The ticking watch on the desert isle would eventually tell the incredulous native that he had found a timepiece. Nature and end, therefore, are necessary correlatives. The study of one leads to the knowledge of the other.

The Nature Embodies the Means

One logical next step leads to the ready conclusion that the nature of any entity necessarily encompasses a congeries of means suited to the attainment of the desired end. The nature might even be conceived as a collection of means suitable to a stated end.

When the elemental principle of finality, therefore, is expressed in terms of means to end, the rational imperative is clear: Only that specific means may be employed, may be embodied in a nature, which will accomplish the established end. The final goal necessarily dictates the proper means to that end. This simply stated is a patently deducible corollary of the principle of final causality.

As the end or goal determined the nature, so too does the end determine the means at the disposal of the nature. The principles flow from the same font. The nature or essence of a being must be so formed as to be able to effect the activity which is directed to its end. The end, therefore, not only determines the nature, but also determines the means that are to be responsible for producing the end.

Rights and Duties

The next step is equally ready. When, at last, this principle of finality is applied to the realm of human conduct it is expressed in terms of duties and rights. A duty is an obligatory end. A right is a guaranteed, inalienable means to the fulfillment of the duty/end. No one is held to a duty without the corresponding right which will permit performance. The essence and type of the right are defined exactly by the essence and type of the duty. For a congeries of duties there is an appropriate congeries of rights.

Thus, the application of the principle of finality to the concept of custody leads to a definition of the nature, as distinguished from the mere fact of entrustment. Just as the intrinsic nature of the custody is defined and determined by the goal, objective, end, of the custody, so too are the rights/means necessarily defined by the acknowledged duties/ends. The nature of the office—here the office of trustee—must be capable of using the means to the end. The opposite is also necessarily true. No act or activity may emanate from the nature of any office which is not the perfect reflection of that nature. Whence the adage: 'You know the tree by its fruits.' And the older, Latin: *'Nemo dat quod non habet.'*

Since nature and activity, means and end, rights and duties, are all correlative, it is possible by studying one to know the other. Close inspection of the purposes and objectives of the custody will reveal the true nature of that custody. The custody must have the means to achieve its end, the rights to fulfill its duties, a nature conformed to its activities. The purpose, objective, end, goal, of any custody determines the nature or kind of that custody.

In sum, the application of the principle of finality to the custodial relation determines not only the nature of the custody itself but also consequently the collection of those rights flowing from the custody.

The mere appropriation without specification effects the fact of custody. Mere tenure with an intention of administration of some unspecified nature or kind results in custody, determined as to existence, but not as to nature.

Add the settlor's terms to the appropriation, and the nature of the custody becomes specified, specified pursuant to the principle of finality. The legitimate, established objectives of the custody determine the nature and activities of the custody, the means to the end, the rights with which to perform the duties.

(2) Benefit to Beneficiary

[S]ubjecting [the trustee] . . . to equitable duties to deal with the property for the benefit of [the beneficiary] . . . .

— RESTATEMENT (SECOND) OF TRUSTS §2
(1959).

This entire participial excerpt is nothing more than a logical evolution of the initial act of the intentional appropriation of the trust corpus.

The participle "subjecting" is the causal nexus between the intentional appropriation and the consequent *complexus of duties*. The duties, and their scope and nature, are the direct effect of the custody. The custodial appropriation elicits, induces, causes, *gives rise to,* the duties.

The phrase "to deal with the property" is almost redundant, since the duties could scarcely concern themselves in any other manner. Implicit in these duties is the obvious understanding that they will be directed to the *benefit of the beneficiary.* Also implicit is a corresponding *complexus of rights* and a just *remuneration* for the performance of the duties and the utilization of the rights.

The Philosophical Definition

The complexity of the final product prompts a schematized presentation:

The trust is *a relation—*
—a relation *between the office* of trustee *and the corpus* of the trust.
—a relation *inhering in the office* of trustee.
—a relation effected by *the intentional appropriation of an asset.*
—a relation of *total custody—*
—total custody giving rise to a *complexus of duties.*
—a complexus of duties giving rise to a corresponding *complexus of rights.*
—a complexus of duties whose performance merits *remuneration.*
—a complexus of duties directed to the *benefit of the beneficiary.*
—a complexus of duties determined as to scope by *the scope of the custody.*
—a complexus of duties determined as to nature by *the finality of the custody.*

This definition could be stripped to essentials: A trust is a relation of total custody, effected by the appropriation of an asset, giving rise to duties and rights directed to the benefit of the beneficiary.

This rudimentary skeleton will be fleshed out over the remaining pages.

II. Custody and Confidence: The Foundation

> The directors have the custody and control of the assets of the corporation for the benefit of those to whom they belong . . . .
>
> —*Hoyt v. Hampe,* 214 N.W. 718, 720 (Iowa 1927).

In one major respect the role of custody in the philosophy of the trust is unusual. The concept is not only far and away the most important of the trust essentials, but it is the logical base on which all the other essentials—and hence the philosophy of the trust itself—rest. So truly is custody the keystone that it might be described as an exponible proposition in which is latent without more the whole of the trust. But from whatever aspect, the custodial relation remains both the heart and source of the trust.

Over the centuries the equity courts and the trust commentators have struggled continually to penetrate the trust. This court has conjectured one theory, that commentator another. In the main, however, there has been no consensus as to the ultimate and central element. Least of all has there been a recognition of custody as the core and the font.

> "Most of those writers or judges who have attempted . . . a definition have done little to assist the world to a clear conception of what a trust is."
>
> —Long, *The Definition of a Trust,* 8 VA. L. REV. 426 (1922) (quoting J. STRAHAN & G. KENDRICK, DIGEST OF EQUITY).

This is remarkable considering the importance of the philosophical foundation to the elaboration of a body of dependent rules.

Yet the centuries of trust reasoning have been by no means barren. Through the years court and commentator have in fact yielded up all the basic components of the concept of custody. It only remains, therefore, to assemble these components through logical process into the viable Custodial Concept of Corporate Control. This could be the preeminent contribution of this treatise.

Confidence/Reliance/Dependence

From the earliest times the notion of 'confidence' has intruded itself most consistently into the concept of the trust. Lewin, the chief authority of the early 1800s, in his *The Law of Trusts* quotes Coke who virtually equated the two: The trust, "a confidence *reposed in some other.*"[28] In more recent years, both Scott and Bogert leave little doubt about the relevancy of the "confidential relation" to the essence of the trust, but neither of them defines it exactly or relates it adequately to the trust. So too with the courts:

> [The phrase] "fiduciary relations" . . . [has] reference to any relationship of blood, business, friendship, or association in which the parties repose special trust and confidence in each other and are in a position to have and exercise, or do have and exercise, influence over each other.
> —*Curtis v. Armagast,* 138 N.W. 873, 878 (Iowa 1912).

It is understandable that there would be frequent resort to the term 'confidence' since its meaning is synonymous with 'trust' in the broad sense. The etymological derivation, moreover, is the same as that of 'fiduciary,' from *fides,* 'faith,' 'trust,' 'confidence.' For the present analytical purposes, however, it is more important to realize that the essence of 'confidence' is nothing other than reliance on another.

Finally and most important, both 'confidence' and 'reliance' are reducible to 'dependence.' It is interesting that Webster gives two direct synonyms for 'dependence': "reliance" and "trust." The note of 'dependence' is the element most expressive of the true status of one who reposes confidence in another. A dependent person is subject to, in the power of, another. This dependence is coterminous with the orbit of reliance or confidence. The dependence in the one finds the correlative independence of the other. "It is a relation of inequality . . . ."[29]

Dependence is the irreducible element in this entire study.

Dependence

A momentary investigation into this irreducible element will add considerably to the understanding of this concept of custody.

At the foundation of this investigation is a basic ethical principle: The relation between man and man entails a responsibility of the one towards the other. Each man as a human person is intrinsically possessed of a complexus of rights which must be respected by every other human being. When two people come into contact, the responsibility of respecting these rights is immediately operative, but the extent of the responsibility varies with the degree of dependency involved in the relationship. The natural-law aphorism, 'Give to each his due,' summarizes the essence of responsibility.

The principle that relationship begets responsibility is clarified upon reflection on the various types of human relations. The broadest categories of human relations are natural relations and assumed relations. Some of the natural relations are founded on the social nature of man himself, as in the relation of father to son. These are the relations of the greatest dependence, and hence responsibility is the most grave. There are also accidental relationships which arise almost fortuitously but which are nonetheless natural. Thus, in a tortious contact between persons, fleeting and temporary as it may be, there is the responsibility of 'due care.' Since, however, this type of relationship is of relatively less dependency, the corresponding responsibility is relatively less grave.

Man also freely assumes many relationships. These relationships may be either formally contractual, when the parties set down the terms of the relation in the form, for example, of a constitution and bylaws, or inferentially contractual, when the responsibility arises out of justified reliance by one on another. An appropriate instance of an assumed relation is that of lawyer to client. Quite obviously this relationship may be either formally contractual or based on justified reliance. It should be clear, moreover, that these assumed relationships may be a combination of both formal and inferential elements. The formal contract adds the note of fidelity to one's word to the natural responsibility already present without the contract.

Among those freely assumed contractual relationships is the relation of custody with its consequent dependence. Thus this irreducible element, dependence, lies at the base of custody. No more basic constituent of the trust lies beyond or beneath this dependence.

Custody the Ultimate

The *confidence/reliance/dependence* is the quintessence, the prime ingredient, of all fiduciary relations: Guardian and ward, principal and agent, attorney and client, priest and penitent. This element could be aptly called 'fiducial,' the essential constituent of a confidential relationship.

> The ordinary stockholder gives little or no attention to the details or control of corporate affairs. He trusts all with the managing officers, and naturally relies on them in all matters touching his interest in its business and property.
> . . . [P]ower akin to that of an attorney, priest, agent, or copartner is conferred on the directors and officers by those selecting them to manage corporate affairs.
> —*Dawson v. National Life Ins. Co.,* 157 N.W.
> 929, 933 (Iowa 1916).

Although this fiducial content may become greater and greater in any relationship, it only reaches the maximum in the actual appropriation of that asset which is the object of the confidence. Here is the point of distinction between the trust relation and all others (except, of course, corporate control). In every confidential relation the fiducial element is present, but to a partial degree. Only with formal entrustment does it become total. Although dependence remains the essential element, the tenure makes the dependence absolute.

Appropriation

The term 'appropriation' is singularly suited, in its derivation from the Latin *ad proprium,* to express this distinctive blending of the fiducial with the tenure. In *ad* is the dynamic note of 'towards,' denoting not only the handing over of the asset by the settlor but also the dedication to the continuing administration of the custody. More expressive in the *ad* is the principle of finality: The striving toward the goal and objectives of the trust. *Proprium* means 'that which is proper to someone,' 'that which is his very own,' 'something under his own proper dominion,' 'something in his own personal control.'

When joined, therefore, the *ad* and the *proprium* carry to the technical term 'appropriation' certain nuances beyond the two essentials of: (1) Actual property tenure and (2) An undertaking of custodial administration. Beyond the mere dominion is a personal dedication of the administration to goals and objectives that are as exacting as if they were the trustee's own. The trustee acts as he would with his own property. The devotion to the stewardship of another's goods is as individual and punctilious as if it were *ad proprium*.

Both the property and its tenure are indispensable to the trust. Although the property may be of any kind, from a patent to a factory to a bond, property it must be, since with counsel and advice nothing is transferred into custody. This does not mean that property may not be the object of a nontrust, merely confidential, relation. A noncustodial relation may involve counsel and judgment about either property (the purchase of a home, stock) or nonproperty values such as a course of action (marriage, a career). But custody involves only property. As Scott puts it: "In every trust, however, there is something more than a merely personal relationship . . . ."[30] Confidence without custody is dependence on counsel and advice. Confidence with custody is dependence on tenure and administration. Thus the transferral of the property is essential. Short of such transferral there may be a confidential relation, but it is a noncustodial one. All other fiduciary relations (except corporate control) stop short with mere noncustodial confidence or reliance. Although formal passage of title is often involved, this is not necessary for the trust—and certainly not for custody—because the trustee, says Scott correctly, "need not have the legal title to the subject matter, since an equitable interest may be held in trust."[31]

A mere physical holding, however, without the intention to administer as a steward falls far short of a trust relation. The trust asset must not only be removed from the dominion of both settlor and beneficiary and handed over to the complete control of the trustee, it must also be accepted by the trustee upon terms of dedication to the purposes of the trust. Thus Lepaulle: "[T]he essence of such legal institution can only be found in the *res* and its appropriation to some aim."[32] Such entrustment then becomes formal stewardship.

> Trusts appear to us, then, as a segregation of assets from the *patrimonium* of individuals, and a devotion of such assets to a certain function, a certain end.
>
> —Lepaulle, *An Outsider's Viewpoint of the Nature of Trusts,* 14 CORNELL L.Q. 52, 55 (1928).

The trustee has the same custody over the fund as that of "a good father of a family."[33] This is tenure as if *ad proprium,* a true appropriation.

These fundamentals, which distinguish total custody from all other fiduciary relations, are characterized by discernible earmarks. The independence of the trustee is unfettered, unqualified, without conditions. "The whole responsibility for the management of the property is thrown upon the trustee."[34] The judgment of the trustee is final, his power is untrammeled. Correlatively, the beneficiary is completely dependent—because his entrusted asset is totally dependent—with no opportunity for any independent judgment. He can never assert dominion over the trust fund.

On the other hand, in a noncustodial confidential relation, albeit fiduciary, the dependent party still makes the final judgment and consequent decision. He retains possession and control of the asset of value. He may depend in varying degrees, true, on the advice, counsel or judgment of his counsellor, but his is the final and ultimate responsibility. He may act on advice with some reliance, but he it is who nonetheless acts. His reliance is partial. There is no appropriation, no entrustment. Thus a priest may order restitution in a theft case. The penitent may rely heavily on the priest's stipulation, but the penitent remains sui juris and his is the decision to restore or to retain. In merely confidential relations not even partial custody exists.

(An interesting query: Is the difference between the custodial and noncustodial relations merely one of degree? Since the essential element of both is dependence, is it a question of more or less, or does a difference in kind result at the point of total custody? This question has implications in the definition of the fiduciary duty in noncustodial relations. Should the trust rules be extended to all confidential relations? The answer is for elsewhere, and does not concern the trust, or corporate control, since both are truly custodial. To both, application is a fortiori.)

The Custody of Corporate Control

Custody thus elaborated as the first of the two major trust concepts—the Benefit to Beneficiary is the other—is uniformly applicable to corporate control in both nonessentials and essentials.

The relation of corporate control, in parallel to the trust, persists between the office of the contrôleur and the corporation. The relation itself should be called *the corporate control* in analogy to *the trust*. Here too the relation is not the office, which is a legal person in which the relation inheres and which is the subject of the relation. Nor is it the officeholder, who is a nonlegal human person. Nor further is it the corporation viewed as the asset committed to the custody of the office. The corporation, as the appropriated asset, is the object of the relation.

The essential element, the intrinsic cause, of the relation is the appropriation: (1) The tenure and (2) The intention to accept the custody. Bear in mind throughout that these two, tenure and intent, form a single indivisible moral act. The severance of one from the other is conceptual at best.

Property Tenure

For the proponent of the trust theory, it is somewhat unsettling to hear courts and commentators speak of the absence of the actual passage of title as an insurmountable barrier to a trust/corporate-control parallel, let alone an identity. Austin Wakeman Scott, undeniably a modern authority, seemingly so speaks:

> The officers and directors of a corporation are responsible for the management of the corporate affairs. They are in a fiduciary relation to the corporation. They are sometimes said to be trustees, but they are not trustees in the strict sense. They do not hold the title to the property of the corporation which they manage.
>
> —1 A. SCOTT, THE LAW OF TRUSTS §16A (3d ed. 1967).

Yet from the custodial aspect the formal passage of title means nil. Remarkably, even Scott himself said elsewhere that the trustee . . .

> . . . need not have the legal title to the subject matter, since an equitable interest may be held in trust.
>
> —1 A. Scott, The Law of Trusts §2.6 (3d ed. 1967).

The property tenure of corporate control is fully tantamount to actual possession of title and could scarcely be more complete.

Sveinbjorn Johnson, whose 1929 commentary is excellent, was diverted by this title-passage obstacle. Trust and trustee were traumatic words to Johnson (his mother, enceinte, must have tangled with a trustee), yet Johnson in arguing almost fulsomely against the trust/control thesis is willy-nilly an effective proponent.

> The title to the property is not vested in the directors or the officers, but in the corporation. Power is given the directors to control and set in motion that intangible and utterly helpless creature, the holder of the title to all the property committed by the shareholder to the business venture for the promotion of which the corporation was launched. They (the directors), through the joint operation of statute and the action of the members, are the recipients or donees of a power which is primarily lodged in the shareholders, namely, to control the business in which they have associated themselves under the corporate form. The donors (the shareholders) of this power, through election to the board, have not vested title to the property in the directors; that title is in the legal person, the corporation; but they have clothed them with the power of full *control* over the inanimate legal person in which the legal title is lodged.
>
> —Johnson, *Corporate Directors as Trustees in Illinois,* 23 Ill. L. Rev. 653, 669 (1929).

Once prescind from the title problem and Johnson's analysis is unassailable. Correctly he refers to corporate control as "a confidential relationship, the essence of which lies in the grant of power of management and control of the artificial person which holds the legal title for certain definite objects."[35] Johnson correctly places the corporation itself in the custody of the contrôleur. Johnson has commendable insight.

> The directors are not trustees of an express trust in any other sense than this: They are donees or recipients of powers of control and management, which it is their duty to execute, given them under statutes and through election by the original owners, to be carried out in good faith and lawfully for the accomplishment of the purposes the stockholders intended to realize when they organized the corporation. It is not a power, in the technical sense, for the duties devolving on the directors are imperative; it more resembles a trust power which must be executed.
>
> —Johnson, *Corporate Directors as Trustees in Illinois,* 23 ILL. L. REV. 653, 670 (1929).

Here are all the essentials to the total tenure of actual passage of title. Johnson reasons through every stage short of the formal denomination of the contrôleur as a strict trustee. The property held is the corporation with every conceivable asset of value, both tangible and intangible, aggregated to it as an entity.

An early opinion of the New York Court of Appeals regarded the passage of title as the mere technicality that it is and consequently located corporate control where it properly was.

> While not technically trustees, for the title of the corporate property was in the corporation itself, they were charged with the duties and subject to the liabilities of trustees. Clothed with the power of controlling the property and managing the affairs of the corporation without let or hindrance, as to third persons they were its agents, but as to the corporation itself equity holds them liable as trustees. . . . While courts of law generally treat the directors as agents, courts of equity treat them as trustees, and hold them to a strict account for any breach of the

trust relation. For all practical purposes they are trustees when called upon in equity to account for their official conduct.

—*Bosworth v. Allen,* 61 N.E. 163, 164-65 (N.Y. 1901).

The Intention to Control

When the contrôleur accepts dominion, either implicitly or explicitly or effectively (by inference of law), and undertakes the stewardship of the entity, the relation of custody commences. The continuing act of dominion, the exercise of control over top-level policy of the entity, is technically the intrinsic cause of the control relation. Mere high-office incumbency—chairman, chief executive officer, chairman of the executive committee—without more is not enough. There must also be actual assumption of ultimate authority.

An early Federal case, showing rare insight, defined the essence of the relation as the power of control:

> In this country the courts have accepted the essential principle laid down in the English cases, and hold, with scarcely any variation, to the doctrine that the promoter of a company stands in the relation of a trustee to it and those who become subscribers to its stock, so long as he retains the power of control over it.
>
> —*Yeiser v. United States Board & Paper Co.,* 107 F. 340, 348 (6th Cir. 1901).

The manner of control takeover is various. At incorporation the promoters may assume and maintain control. In other instances the initial parties entrust control immediately to another, either indefinitely or for a limited period. Corporate control may be wrested legitimately—or illegitimately—in a power struggle. It may drift to management imperceptibly over years of slow stock dispersal and remain by mere management incumbency. Where corporate control belongs as a matter of right is an interesting and important question, but for elsewhere. The genesis of corporate control is no present matter. At some point the various parties to the corporate venture find themselves in total dependence, for the ultimate disposition of the corporate entity holding their contributed assets, on the judgment and act of the contrôleur. Entrustment has been joined with acquiescence in dominion. A technical appropriation has been effected.

Excepting only formal title, therefore, the custody of corporate control parallels perfectly the trust. The logical consequences of such custody—both ad hoc rules of law and broad philosophy—cannot be ignored. The philosophical consequences find chief expression in the traditional duty of custodial loyalty: All benefit inures to the beneficiary.

III. Benefit to Beneficiary

> The sole appropriate remedy is a declaration that the consideration paid to the trustees by Lytton Financial Corporation allocable to a transfer of control of the Association is an asset held for its benefit in the hands of the trustees.
>
> —*Beverly Hills Fed. Sav. & Loan Ass'n v. Federal Home Loan Bank Bd.*, 371 F. Supp. 306, 319 (C.D. Cal. 1973).

The first of the two major trust concepts, the custodial tenure, is the cause of the second: All benefit from the administration of the trust must redound to the beneficiary.

Inexplicably, trust theorists have never attempted an intensive breakdown of this principle. They accept it, enunciate it, never question it. Necessarily they vaguely understand its rationale, albeit subliminally. Here and there they even inadvertently express its philosophy.

The full import of the rule, however, as is often the case when the organized philosophy is weak, can only be gleaned from its application to specific cases. Traditional trust law has not constructed a systematic philosophy of the Benefit-to-Beneficiary Rule, but rather intuited a set of rules from a brooding sense of the principle.

Although the present deductive approach seems more rational, support for this second axiom could be gathered inductively, as Mr. Berle does in two separate treatises. In one early article on control he sets up three major corporate areas—"[s]ince a general principle like that stated may have an indefinite field of application"[36]—where the rigid trust theory can be found in practical application. In "Corporate Powers as Powers in Trust,"[37] he uses four such categories. The

proof of a general principle from a multitude of applications, however, is always risky. First, an infinite number of specific instances
can arise. Second, as the specificity increases so does the danger of
error. Third, one false application undermines confidence in the validity of the principle itself. Better to reason to a sound theory and
relegate the application to the day-to-day work of the courts.

The Philosophy of the Rule

The explanation of the dearth of intensive trust commentary
could be simple. The principle is axiomatic and therefore virtually
indemonstrable. Hence it has been taken for granted and no one has
dared to explore it deeply. Yet it is possible to evolve the chief constituents of the rule from the principles thus far deduced as latent in the
custodial relation.

The essence of custody is the confidence/reliance/dependence
carried to the maximum in the formal appropriation of the asset to
the trustee.

Beginning with this dependence, therefore, the reasoning
moves one uncontroverted step forward to the elemental conclusion:
Dependence begets responsibility.

> From the conception of a trust as a confidence re-
> posed in the trustee it is easy to pass to that of a trust as
> an obligation resting upon the trustee, and a trust has
> often been defined from this point of view.
>
> —Long, *The Definition of a Trust,* 8 VA. L. REV.
> 426, 429 (1922).

"[R]esponsibility goes with power."[38] Merrick Dodd writing in the
thirties could have been more forceful in expressing this same
thought: "Power over the lives of others tends to create on the part
of those most worthy to exercise it a sense of responsibility."[39]

The obvious extension of this principle produces the next major
axiom: "The greater the independent authority to be exercised by
the fiduciary, the greater the scope of his fiduciary duty."[40] "The standard required of them varies as the confidential nature of their position varies . . . ."[41] The responsibility is always in direct ratio to the
dependence. "[T]he rigor of . . . application is [governed] by the varying dependence of the beneficiary on the fiduciary's judgment."[42] In
every case the reliance must be justified, either by implicit or explicit

acknowledgment or inference of law. No responsibility could be consequent on anything less than a justified reliance.

The junction of these two—(1) dependence as the chief determinant and (2) the direct ratio to responsibility—supplies the material for further illation.

Because this dependence is total in the complete appropriation of the fund—a total tenure tantamount to title plus acquiescence in the stewardship status—the resultant responsibility is total. "This duty of loyalty extends to every incident of their position and requires of them an unbending adherence."[43] Implicit, of course, in such total responsibility is the absence of all ownership in the trustee. If the trustee owned some of the asset, he would obviously not be responsible to another for it. Any personal ownership is inconsistent with stewardship, which concerns another's property. Acknowledgment by the trustee (1) that ownership of the asset is in another and (2) that the asset is dependent fully on the trustee for complete care, gives rise to the obligation to act in accordance with this acknowledgment.

This total responsibility for the stewardship of another's assets is merely a collective noun describing a complexus of duties in regard to these assets. This complexus is the essence of the Benefit-to-Beneficiary Rule. This in turn is only another way of saying that the custodian has a duty to care for the assets entrusted to him as if they were his own.

This reasoning coalesces into one simple unqualified rule enunciated in the *Restatement:* "The trustee is under a duty to the beneficiary to administer the trust solely in the interest of the beneficiary."[44]

Over the years the Benefit-to-Beneficiary Rule has often been called the Duty of Loyalty. Austin Wakeman Scott entitled one of his articles "The Trustee's Duty of Loyalty"[45] and wrote another on the subject in which he discussed Josiah Royce's *The Philosophy of Loyalty.*[46] Royce defined 'loyalty' as "the willing and practical and thoroughgoing devotion of a person to a cause."[47] "In loyalty, when loyalty is properly defined, is the fulfillment of the whole moral law."[48]

Whatever the designation, trust writers and courts have been uniformly successful in the statement of the rule, at least in its broadest sense. Scott goes to the heart of the custodial obligation in describing the trustee as a steward.[49] One court held the trustee to "the diligence . . . [of] a good father of a family"[50] which is the prototypal norm of custody. In 1810 the Maryland Supreme Court noted the element of acquiescence to the appropriation in its enunciation: "[H]e who accepts a trust takes it for the benefit of the persons for whom he is trusted, and not to benefit himself."[51]

Lewin, in his classic of the early 1800s, likened the care and diligence to that of a person supervising his own property:

> Lord Northington once observed, "No man can require or with reason expect that a trustee should manage his [another's] property with the same care and discretion that he would his own," but the maxim has never failed, when mentioned, to incur strong marks of disapprobation. A trustee is called upon to exert precisely the *same* care and solicitude in behalf of his *cestui que trust* as he would do for himself; but *greater* measure than this a court of equity will *not* exact.
>
> —T. LEWIN, THE LAW OF TRUSTS AND TRUSTEES 299 (London 1837).

Willis, in a work contemporary to Lewin, founded his rule on the custodial relation: "So long as they retain possession of the trust property, the trustees are bound to act respecting it with the care and diligence of provident owners."[52]

The Finality of the Trust

The reasoning thus far has established the existence only of a broad undefined responsibility, with a scope that is all-compassing, true, but without definition of the subtleties and nuances of its nature. Merely to state the general rule and the extent of the duty does not specify the kind of duties, their quality, nature or essence. Recall that the finality of the timepiece determined the nature of its mechanism. So also does the purpose of the trust reveal the nature of the trustee's duties. Whatever the deficiencies of traditional trust philosophy, astute perception and the principle of finality can produce a reliable synthesis of the nature and quality of the complexus of duties. Willis in 1835 stated the approach: "The duties of trustees may, however, be more particularly collected from an investigation of their powers and responsibilities."[53]

These purposes may be discerned in the indenture, the conduct of the parties and the circumstances of the entrustment. Principally, however, the finality is disclosed in the intrinsic nature of the trust itself, e.g., the management of real estate, the supervision of a portfolio, the manufacture of a commodity. Beyond the fact, again Willis, of "the general rule, that every act of the trustee should tend to the benefit of the *cestui que trust,*"[54] it is more to the present point "that trustees must execute their trust faithfully, according to the terms of them, and the intention of the parties by whom the trusts have been created."[55]

Arguably, the finality of a trust is also implicitly reiterated in the *Restatement* phrase "interest of the beneficiary." This is true, but it remains necessary to distinguish the quality and nature of the duty from its mere existence and scope. The latter results from the simple fact of custody. The former, however, determined by the principle of finality, can be discerned only by study of the purposes of the trust. Of all the modern commentators Pierre Lepaulle has shown the greatest insight into this distinction. Moreover, his felicity of expression persists. He begins the discussion of finality by an extremely succinct but complete definition of the trust as "a *res* and an appropriation of that *res* to some aim."[56] He next embarks on an incisive analysis of the nature of the trust obligation:

> The rights and obligations of the trustee will vary according to only one thing, his mission. Such mission always consists in insuring that the *res* be *properly appropriated to the aim* to which it has been devoted, either by the settlor, by the court, or by operation of law.
>
> —Lepaulle, *An Outsider's Viewpoint of the Nature of Trusts,* 14 Cornell L.Q. 52, 55 (1928) (emphasis added).

In the word "properly" is the limitation of the activity of the trustee to what is just, what is right, neither more nor less, neither this quality nor that, but exactly the proper quantity and quality, exactly that activity best suited to the aim of the trust.

Thus far in this analysis the existence of a complexus of rights correlative to the complexus of duties has been somewhat taken for granted. Lepaulle remedies this neglect and correctly groups rights with duties.

The rights that the trustee will have in each particular case depend on his obligations; they are tools given to him for the fulfillment of his duties, and such duties are determined by the appropriation to which the *res* has been devoted. Hence, it is apparent that: trustee, *cestui*, rights and obligations of either of them are only means for reaching an end . . . .

> —Lepaulle, *An Outsider's Viewpoint of the Nature of Trusts,* 14 CORNELL L.Q. 52, 55 (1928).

Since rights correspond to duties, it follows that both "are determined" by the appropriation, although Lepaulle does not so state. Thus the finality of the custody extends its influence through the duties to the rights.

At another point Lepaulle defines the trust again. Here he implicitly enunciates the principle of finality and repeats the correlative nature of rights to duties:

> We are therefore in a position to propose the following definition of the trust: an appropriation of assets realized by means of a legal "person" who is subjected to the obligation of taking all reasonable steps to realize such appropriation, and who has all the rights necessary to fulfill such obligation.

> —Lepaulle, *An Outsider's Viewpoint of the Nature of Trusts,* 14 CORNELL L.Q. 52, 57 (1928).

But probably Lepaulle's best statement of the finality of the trust comes on the concluding page of his provoking commentary:

> The only possible theory is that the *rights of the trustee have their foundation in his obligations:* they are *tools* given to him in order to achieve the work assigned to him. The trustee gets all the tools necessary for such end, but only those, in order to allow him to insert his effort in society and to work either for someone else, or for an idea recognized as worth while in the community in which he lives.

> —Lepaulle, *An Outsider's Viewpoint of the Nature of Trusts,* 14 CORNELL L.Q. 52, 61 (1928).

The application of the principle of finality to the unqualified trust duty specifies its nature and gives the full compass of the Benefit-to-Beneficiary Rule.

The Lesser Loyalty Rules

With both scope and nature of the duty of loyalty thus described, whatever follows is simply exposition, expatiation. The lesser rules as derivatives obviously support the principal rule and clarify as they specify.

The Benefit-to-Beneficiary Rule may be analyzed in three major subrules: (1) Both the office and its assets belong to the beneficiary, (2) Any increment in the assets inures to the beneficiary and (3) The remuneration of the trustee is limited by contract and labor expended.

(1) The Office and Its Assets

Trust law has always realized that every asset originally appropriated belongs completely to the beneficiary. However, some hesitation has persisted in latter years in determining who owns the office. *Sugden v. Crossland* was apparently without precedent. (The equally insightful *Gaskell v. Chambers* followed it by two years in 1858 in England.) Vice-Chancellor Stuart knew he had a question beyond mere ownership of assets. Yet he summarily concluded that the office also belonged to the fund:

> Though there is some peculiarity in the case, there does not seem to be any difference in principle whether the trustee derived the profit by means of the trust property, or from the office itself.
>
> —*Sugden v. Crossland,* 65 Eng. Rep. 620, 621
> (V.C. 1856).

Concededly some meditation is required to conclude that the officeholder does not himself own the office. Why could not Horsfield sell the office to Crossland? The answer lies in the fact that the office remains always integral to the relation. It was the occupancy of the office that Horsfield sold. The original appointment to the trusteeship was the privilege of the settlor. The duty of successive appointments was one of the several duties placed on the trustee.

Neither did the settlor give the first trustee the office itself—rather merely its occupancy—nor did the succeeding trustee receive it as his own. Once incumbent the trustee assumed all the duties, directed to the benefit of the beneficiary, among them the duty to appoint a successor. For the proper performance of these duties he received a compensation but he did not receive the office itself. That belonged to the settlor first and later passed with all the other assets to the beneficiary.

When it is understood that the right to appoint a successor trustee rests in the incumbent trustee and that the actual appointment for a price is the so-called sale of the office, it is a ready step to the realization that two, not one, questions are involved in this sale of the office: (1) May the office ever be sold at all? and (2) If sold, where does the sale price belong? The answers: (1) The legitimacy or propriety of the 'sale' depends on the definite norms of selection determined ultimately by the fiduciary duty of the custodian and obviously directed to the benefit of the beneficiary. (This is the complex subject at the heart of the Philosophy of Corporate Control.) (2) If 'sold,' the price indisputably belongs to the beneficiary. These insights Vice-Chancellor Stuart may not have had. But his was the correct conclusion, whether from intuition or a visceral sense: (1) That the price for the sale belonged to the fund and (2) That the right and obligation to select the trustee was a matter for the prudence and discretion of the officeholder, true, but a duty shaped by the fiduciary relation governing the suitability of the appointment. He directed the £75 into the trust corpus and removed Crossland from the office.

Perhaps no case is more pertinent to the Benefit-to-Beneficiary Rule (or to the broad thesis of this study) or a better junction between the trust case *Sugden* and the corporate-control case *Lionel* than the oft quoted *McClure v. Law*. In the 1899 New York *McClure* the facts were on all fours with *Sugden* and *Lionel*. The Court not only reached the same conclusion but applied *Sugden* by name to the corporate situation and quoted Perry to the following effect:

> "Trustees hold a position of trust and confidence, the legal title to the trust property is in them, and generally its whole management and control is in their hands. * * *

They cannot use the trust property, nor their relation to it, for their own personal advantage. All the power and the influence which the possession of the trust fund gives must be used for the advantage and profit of the beneficial owners, and not for the personal gain and emoluments of the trustees. * * * So, where a trustee retired from the office in consideration that his successor paid him a sum of money, it was held that the money so paid must be treated as a part of the trust estate, and that the trustee must account for it, as he could make no profit, directly or indirectly, from the trust property or from the position or office of trustee."

> —*McClure v. Law*, 55 N.E. 388, 389 (N.Y. 1899) (quoting J. PERRY, A TREATISE ON THE LAW OF TRUSTS).

The nexus with corporate control was further emphasized by the Court of Appeals in resort to Cook:

> "It is a well-established principle of law that a director commits a breach of trust in accepting a secret gift or secret pay from a person who is contracting or has contracted with the corporation, and that the corporation may compel the director to turn over to it all the money or property so received by him."

> —*McClure v. Law*, 55 N.E. 388, 389 (N.Y. 1899) (quoting W. COOK, A TREATISE ON THE LAW OF CORPORATIONS).

Thus understood, both the office and any premium from its 'sale' are directed to the benefit of the beneficiary.

(2) The Increment to the Fund

Trust law has unvaryingly insisted that all trust profits be deposited in the trust fund. The *Restatement* expresses this elementary variant on the duty of loyalty as a corollary:

The trustee is accountable for any profit made by him through or arising out of the administration of the trust . . . .

> —RESTATEMENT (SECOND) OF TRUSTS §203 (1959).

It should be equally clear—although it has not always been— that the time, energy, imagination, judgment and skill of the trustee are all trust assets purchased through the funds of the trust paid as compensation to the trustee. As such these services are also increment from the trust fund and come immediately within the purview of the Benefit-to-Beneficiary Rule.

> While he is employed in his fiduciary capacity, his entire energies must be devoted to the advancement of the beneficiary's legitimate interests.
>
> —Clapp, *A Fiduciary's Duty of Loyalty,* 3 MD. L. REV. 221, 232 (1939).

(3) The Remuneration of the Trustee

The entire answer to the question of the remuneration of the trustee—the last of the duty-of-loyalty discussion—rests in the acknowledgment of one truth: In theory the trustee is being adequately and justly compensated by salary set by contract, express or quantum meruit, by stipend or honorarium, by fee or retainer. If this emolument is proportioned (and if it is not it should be) to the labor and difficulty, the talent and imagination, the time and energy expended in the performance of the trust duties and in the utilization of the trust rights, any occult compensation is patently illicit, whether in the form of assets annexed from the fund or profits pocketed from its administration or premiums received for the sale of the occupancy of the office.

> Although a fiduciary is generally entitled to compensation from the trust estate for his work, he is not permitted to accept additional compensation or commissions from persons with whom he deals in performing his fiduciary duties.
>
> —Clapp, *A Fiduciary's Duty of Loyalty,* 3 MD. L. REV. 221, 229 (1939).

Or for any other work whatsoever for which he has already been paid.

> The rights of the trustee . . . may vary in each case, and
> are simply means allowing him to perform his duties, or
> to be reimbursed, or compensated, for having performed
> them . . . .
>
> —Lepaulle, *An Outsider's Viewpoint of the Na-*
> *ture of Trusts,* 14 CORNELL L.Q. 52, 56
> (1928).

The Loyalty of Corporate Control

The temptation at this point would be to descend to detail in relating the trust philosophy—in particular the benefit-to-beneficiary principle—to corporate control. This is neither necessary nor advisable. Most of the comparison of corporate control to trust has already been achieved in the very exposition of the trust. Wherever the word 'trustee' occurs, simply read 'contrôleur.' The only requisite adversions, therefore, are general appraisals or in questionable areas.

There was a fleeting time—the late 1800s and early 1900s—when some courts conceded the applicability, in varying degrees and jurisdictions, of the trust/corporate-control parallel. As fleeting as it was, it indicates that what once was could again be and that at least the thought did occur to some thoughtful jurists. The Illinois Supreme Court, speaking in the second decade, was reflective of this attitude. Specifically, the Court applied the Benefit-to-Beneficiary Rule to corporate control.

> The directors of a corporation are intrusted with the
> management of its business and property for the benefit
> of all the stockholders, and occupy the position of trus-
> tees for the *collective body* of stockholders in respect to
> such business. They are subject to the general rule, which
> prevails in regard to trusts and trustees, that they cannot
> use the trust property, or their relation to it, for their own
> personal gain.
>
> —*Farwell v. Pyle-Nat'l Elec. Headlight Co.,*
> 124 N.E. 449, 452 (Ill. 1919) (emphasis
> added).

In the Court's reasoning, beyond the succinct enunciation of the duty of loyalty, are contained the essentials for the trust/corporate-control analogy: (1) An entrustment to the contrôleur (2) of the corporate business and property. From this custody and tenure the Court concluded to the Benefit-to-Beneficiary Rule.

This same Court some ten years later retrod the same ground but characterized the rule in rather arresting phrases:

> It requires no very keen moral perception to recognize the obvious justice of this universal rule of law, of justice and of morality.
>
> —*Dixmoor Golf Club v. Evans*, 156 N.E. 785, 787 (Ill. 1927).

Earlier, in 1865, the Pennsylvania Supreme Court had placed directors in a position of confidence and hence denied them the right to "consume that which they are appointed to preserve."[57] As late as 1930 the Indiana Court of Appeals incorporated the strict-trust rule of loyalty into the corporate field:

> Directors of a business corporation act in a strictly fiduciary capacity. Their office is a trust. . . . The first principal duty arising from his official relation is to act in all things of trust wholly for the benefit of his corporation.
>
> —*Schemmel v. Hill*, 169 N.E. 678, 682-83 (Ind. App. 1930).

Interestingly, these very words were quoted as controlling in the Second Circuit *Feldmann* in 1955.

The point is not so much that isolated courts imposed the Benefit-to-Beneficiary Rule on the contrôleur (since such is quite clearly not the case today) but that the intrinsic identity of the two relations should impel court and commentator to reassess the law and return to the turn-of-the-century philosophy. In each of the three subrules of loyalty the parity persists:

(1) The Office and Its Assets

As with the trust, there should be no question of the inviolability of corporate assets. Thus an early Federal court:

His liability rests upon the fundamental principle that one who occupies a position of trust and confidence—such as the president, or a director, of a corporation—shall never be permitted to abuse his official position by dealing with the corporate property for his private gain.

> —*Pepper v. Addicks,* 153 F. 383, 405 (E.D. Pa. 1907).

The ownership of the office, however, has been a tortuous question. The New York courts in *Lionel* adduced no reasons in support of their double decision to remove the contrôleur and hand over the premium to Lionel, but the identity of facts and result with the 1856 *Sugden* should give pause. A full analysis, under the *Lionel* facts, would conceivably suggest that the strict-trust philosophy was the only rational explanation of such a conclusion. Implicit in such a holding is the recognition that the *ownership* of the office of control, as of the trust office, lies in the totality of beneficiaries, here the shareholders comprising the entity. L. C. B. Gower, the capable English writer, places his endorsement on what he conceives to be an American trend:

> [T]he American courts are beginning to come round to the view that directors (or, indeed, other controllers who are not directors) are not entitled to retain the increased price obtained because their shares confer such control. This seems eminently desirable—control is valuable because it enables the company's assets to be dealt with; all members should share rateably in this, not just the lucky few. But this would be a highly novel doctrine in England.
>
> —L. GOWER, THE PRINCIPLES OF MODERN COMPANY LAW 494 (2d ed. 1957).

In this highly technical area of the trust/corporate-control question any expatiation beyond the fundamentals would seem to defeat the purpose in establishing the intrinsic identity of the two relations. The philosophical conclusions and principles resultant on this identity should aid in the solution of specific problems surrounding the ownership of the office and the sale of control.

(2) Increment to the Beneficiary

Max Pam not only equated contrôleur with trustee but applied the trust rule to corporate control:

> It is the unvarying rule that an agent or a trustee dealing with the property of the principal or *cestui que trust* cannot profit thereby. All directors realizing any profits or benefits from such transactions may be held accountable therefor, and required to surrender them to the corporation.
>
> —Pam, *Interlocking Directorates, The Problem and Its Solution,* 26 HARV. L. REV. 467, 477 (1913).

In support of his stand Max Pam quoted Taylor:

> "Corporate officers may not buy from or sell to their corporation and retain any profits from such transactions, unless the profits are known and the transactions acquiesced in by all who could claim any interest in the profits. For all secret profits derived by them from any dealings in regard to the corporate enterprise, they must account to the corporation, even though the transaction may have benefited it."
>
> —Pam, *Interlocking Directorates, The Problem and Its Solution,* 26 HARV. L. REV. 467, 477-78 (1913) (quoting H. TAYLOR, A TREATISE ON THE LAW OF PRIVATE CORPORATIONS).

(3) Remuneration

Here again the parallel with the trustee is so pat as to suggest no further comment. The problem with the compensation of the contrôleur rests not in the simple statement of the rule. All admit that the contrôleur should at least, but only, receive a quid pro quo. The difficulty lies in application. The subtleties which may lead the contrôleur to overcompensation are legion. But these are common to, not distinct from, similar subtleties practiced over the centuries by trustees, and are, therefore, to be dealt with on the same grounds and by the same ground rules.

Sveinbjorn Johnson has deserved so well of this study, in spite of his polemical opposition (at least nominal) to its major thesis, and is so reminiscent of the equally well-deserving Pierre Lepaulle, as to merit the last word. Johnson seems to express all the foundations of the benefit-to-beneficiary rationale and rule, at least implicitly.

> Power is given the directors to control and set in motion that intangible and utterly helpless creature, the holder of the title to all the property committed by the shareholder to the business venture for the promotion of which the corporation was launched. . . . There is an imperative duty resting on the board to set in motion and manage, lawfully, in good faith, and for the ends for which the creature came into being, the corporation . . . . [T]he duty is . . . for certain definite objects, . . . for the accomplishment of the purposes the stockholders intended to realize when they organized the corporation.
>
> —Johnson, *Corporate Directors as Trustees in Illinois*, 23 ILL. L. REV. 653, 669-70 (1929).

This concludes the analysis of the second major trust concept: Benefit to beneficiary. From this principle and the first major concept, the custodial tenure, the remaining corollary concept can be constructed.

IV. Conflict of Interest

> I venture to assert that when the history of the financial era which has just drawn to a close comes to be written, most of its mistakes and its major faults will be ascribed to the failure to observe the fiduciary principle, the precept as old as holy writ, that "a man cannot serve two masters". More than a century ago equity gave a hospitable reception to that principle and the common law was not slow to follow in giving it recognition. No thinking man can believe that an economy built upon a business foundation can permanently endure without some loyalty to that principle.
>
> —Stone, *The Public Influence of the Bar*, 48 HARV. L. REV. 1, 8-9 (1934).

The Conflict-of-Interest Rule—so appealingly expressed by Mr. Justice Stone—has been hedged around with some serious misunderstanding. On first face the rule may appear to have its foundation in causes unrelated to the main body of trust reasoning. The rule has often been presented as purely pragmatic, a blanket, fearful ban rooted in a preoccupation with the innate and inevitable weakness of postlapsarian human nature, a no-exception prohibition founded on the senseless if-you-are-allowed-to-do-it-everyone-will-want-to-do-it fear of opening the dike, an inflexible and unreasoning attempt to avert temptation. None of these present the full truth. Yet so salutary is this rule that its clarification and crystallization could prove to be a major contribution of this study of the trust/corporate-control parallel.

The various applications of the Conflict-of-Interest Rule are legion, the infinity of ways in which one person tries to serve two masters. The application of this philosophy, therefore, is an infinite task.

Loyalty v. Loyalty

A stimulating discourse in *Green Giant* between the District Court and the Honigman expert, Storer, chairman of the investment committee of The Manufacturers National Bank of Detroit, poses an arresting hypothetical instance of the head-on clash between conflicting interests. Here is but one example among the legions.

The relevant dialogue began at the point at which Storer had imposed a strict-trust duty upon the Green Giant contrôleur, Cosgrove, to correct the voting deficiency in the corporate structure, but without the receipt of a premium. (Honigman argued: The contrôleur has a fiduciary duty to correct in 1960 the defect in the capital structure which he consciously created in 1923. The very vote originally withheld must be restored, without the payment of a personal premium of $2 million for such restoration.) The Court interjected: "Now, then, does that fiduciary relationship continue if the stock is sold, if the class A stock is sold?"[58] Storer replied that the duty would accompany control. The Court then set up the conflict of interest:

> Well then, supposing in your bank it so happened
> that someone in connection with the Cosgrove family
> died and left their some 23 shares of class A stock in trust

.... And then supposing a plan of capitalization arose somewhat comparable to this. Would you feel justified in voting the class A stock, the 23 shares that you held on a plan that provided one for one on the part of the class A stockholders?

> —Record on Appeal at 299, *Honigman v. Green Giant Co.*, 309 F.2d 667 (8th Cir. 1962).

Storer's prompt reaction was the correct one: To vote for the benefit of all the shareholders and not in favor of the trust beneficiaries.

> If these, your Honor, were the terms of the proposition which came to me as a question to vote on it, I believe that I would vote favorably on such a proposal.

> —Record on Appeal at 300, *Honigman v. Green Giant Co.*, 309 F.2d 667 (8th Cir. 1962).

To which the Court countered: "Do you think that an ordinary prudent businessman would vote in favor of such a proposal?"[59] Storer hedged for the first time: "I have no clear conviction on that. I am of mixed feelings, sir."[60] The Court pressed its advantage:

> Well, I take it as a trustee you would have to exercise judgment and the care of the ordinary prudent man possessed of business judgment that would generally be attained by a man reasonably experienced in business....
> ....
> You can't put into effect some individual theory of your own if you were trustee, could you?

> —Record on Appeal at 300, *Honigman v. Green Giant Co.*, 309 F.2d 667 (8th Cir. 1962).

At this point, unable to resolve his primary loyalty as contrôleur with his secondary as trustee, Storer began to capitulate.

> No, sir. I would have, in a sense, conflict of fiduciary responsibilities toward the beneficiaries of the trust on

the one hand and toward the stockholders of the corporation on the other.

> —Record on Appeal at 300, *Honigman v.*
> *Green Giant Co.*, 309 F.2d 667 (8th Cir.
> 1962).

The Court sensed the hesitancy.

> But insofar as the beneficiaries are concerned I take
> it that you would recognize that you would have to obtain
> the best business deal for them that was possible in any
> reorganization regardless of any fiduciary relationship
> that may have accompanied the Cosgroves in their hold-
> ing of this stock?

> —Record on Appeal at 300, *Honigman v.*
> *Green Giant Co.*, 309 F.2d 667 (8th Cir.
> 1962).

Storer abandoned the field completely: "As you outline the situation,
sir, my responsibility to my beneficiaries, sir, would be primary."[61]
With this the Court administered the coup de grace:

> And I take it under those circumstances you would
> feel justified in voting for the most favorable considera-
> tion that could be obtained by the beneficiaries even
> though it diluted the B stockholders' equity in the corpo-
> ration?

> —Record on Appeal at 300, *Honigman v.*
> *Green Giant Co.*, 309 F.2d 667 (8th Cir.
> 1962).

Storer closed the discourse with a feeble "Yes, your Honor."[62]

In the Court's hypothesis one salient fact which would have fa-
cilitated the solution escaped the expert Storer's attention. The mere
interposition of a trustee between a beneficiary and a controlling
block of stock does not thereby insulate the beneficiary from the fiduciary duties of the office of control. The trustee is the beneficiary's
representative. The shareholder contrôleur unrepresented by a trustee would have the fiduciary duty of control. Represented, he continues to have the same duty through his trustee. The beneficiary's duties
now become the trustee's duties. The trustee is the alter ego of the

beneficiary, and must act exactly as the beneficial owner would act were he without the trust. To guide his own judgment, therefore, Storer could forget he was a trustee and conduct himself as the contrôleur, with all of the contrôleur's duties.

As the representative of the contrôleur, the trustee owed his primary obligation to the common good of the entity, his secondary to each of the parts, one of which was the shareholding of the beneficiary. His custody as contrôleur was far broader than his custody of the individual shareholdings. As contrôleur, a trustee must inaugurate a corporate structure beneficial to the entire entity. He could neither accept a premium for doing his duty nor favor the beneficial holder of the control block at the expense of the corporation.

In the Court's hypothetical, therefore, the new contrôleur—the beneficiaries as represented by Storer—would be bound as thoroughly as the predecessor contrôleur to correct the structural defects, without exacting a premium for performing his fiduciary duty.

This *Green Giant* instance is merely one of the legions. The possibilities for conflict of interest are limited only by the ingenuity of the human mind. The fallible, susceptible human being who holds the office of control usually occupies another corporate office. The result is invariably a conflict of interest. If the contrôleur is also the chief executive officer, the temptation is a salary in excess of true worth. If a shareholder, a selfish and reckless dividend policy. If a consumer, favored sales allocation at favored prices. And so it goes through every facet of corporate assets, prerogatives and remuneration.

Idealistically the answer would be the elimination of all conflicts. But this is impossible in our present corporate structure. In the end, therefore, the realistic solution is that needless conflicts must be avoided. But since conflicts are always to be present, the study of the Conflict-of-Interest Rule is all the more imperative.

The Business Judgment Rule

A further preparatory adversion is necessary. The strict-trust Conflict-of-Interest Rule obviously has no applicability to the arm's-length dealings of a trustee with a third party. A trustee is always bound to the stringencies of complete loyalty. He must represent the trust with full dedication and devotion. He must exercise due care. But he is protected by the Business Judgment Rule. *Absent a conflict of interest* he is subjected only to those strictures binding any agent representing a principal in third-party transactions.

Any study of the Conflict-of-Interest Rule can best be undertaken in three parts: *(1) The Rule Itself. (2) The Sanctions of the Rule. (3) The Rationale of the No Inquiry Rule.* Over the years the confusion of the rule with the sanctions resultant on the breach of the rule has made a difficult subject more difficult. The philosophy underlying the rule has rarely been discussed.

(1) The Rule Itself

> To hold otherwise, would be to overturn principles of equity which have been regarded as well settled since the days of Lord Keeper Bridgman, in the 22d of Charles second [1681], to the present time— principles enunciated and enforced by Hardwicke, Thurlow, Loughborough, Eldon, Cranworth, Story and Kent, and which the highest courts in our country have declared to be founded on immutable truth and justice, and to stand upon our great moral obligation to refrain from placing ourselves in relations which excite a conflict between self interest and integrity.
>
> —*Cumberland Coal & Iron Co. v. Sherman,* 30 Barb. 553, 578-79 (N.Y. Sup. Ct. 1859).

The basic rule is uncompromising and unadorned with qualifications. In 1837, Lewin stated the historical formulation: "[F]or he who undertakes to act for another in any matter cannot in the same matter act for himself."[63] Bogert uses the California Code, among others, to give the modern statement: "'If a trustee acquires any interest, or becomes charged with any duty, adverse to the interest of his beneficiary in the subject of the trust, he must immediately inform the latter thereof, and may be at once removed.'"[64] In 1880, the Supreme Court of the United States applied the rule to the corporation:

> Directors of corporations, and all persons who stand in a fiduciary relation to other parties, and are clothed with power to act for them, are subject to this rule; they are not permitted to occupy a position which will conflict

with the interest of parties they represent and are bound
to protect.

—*Wardell v. Railroad Co.,* 103 U.S. 651, 658
(1880).

The questions clouding the rule, however, are not to be answered by ascribing its rationale to an arbitrary or pragmatic genesis.
The answer lies in two controlling truths: The Conflict-of-Interest
Rule (1) is ultimately dictated by custodial tenure and (2) is a subrule
derived directly from the basic loyalty of the benefit-to-beneficiary
principle. It is essentially and inevitably related to these first two
major trust concepts.

The misconception surrounding the rule and the standard analyses of its nature may be conveniently grouped at three embarkation
points: (1) Basic Loyalty. (2) Quid pro Quo. (3) Prevention of
Temptation.

Basic Loyalty

One source alone without more could account completely for
the efficacy of the Conflict-of-Interest Rule, could supply the innermost rationale which justifies and explains its inveterate and universal application. This source? The dictates of the basic loyalty of man
to man, of man to a cause. The mandates of the rule are nothing more
than the codification of the elementary commands of human loyalty.

Moreover, the basic allegiance of the trustee and the contrôleur
is a fortiori. It is founded on more than mere fidelity, the adherence
to one's commitment. Whence comes this a fortiori, special allegiance? The basic loyalty of trustee and contrôleur is caused directly
by the commitment of custody. This is not a bare commitment. It
is a commitment expressed and fortified in the formal assumption
of the stewardship of a cause, a person, a corporation. This custodial
commitment is an agreement implicit at the least, solemn possibly,
but morally binding in any case, to keep safe, to guard with vigilance,
to protect always, to hold as one's own, the cause, the person, the
corporation. This commitment has inspired confidence, engendered reliance, created dependence. It has bound the two together,
steward to stewardship, custodian to custody, contrôleur to corporation. This commitment is a complexus of duties, an acknowledgment
of obligation, a recognition of responsibility. Mr. Justice Field reduced his statement of the rule to this obligation:

It is among the rudiments of the law that the same
person cannot act for himself and at the same time, with
respect to the same matter, as the agent of another whose
interests are conflicting. . . . The two positions impose
different obligations, and their union would at once raise
a conflict . . . .

—*Wardell v. Railroad Co.,* 103 U.S. 651, 658
(1880).

This line of reasoning leads only to one thought: The basic loyalty
and unswerving allegiance of custody. (Needless to say, even
noncustodial commitment binds to the most stringent loyalty. The
actual assumption of dominion adds the graver responsibility of custodial loyalty.)

Quite logically, therefore, this dedication of a steward may be
expressed in the first rule of loyalty: Every thought, word and deed
must be directed to the best interests of the cause. Here is the epitome
of loyalty. This is what Royce meant when he said that loyalty properly defined is the fulfillment of the moral law.[65]

It follows, then, that the chiefest breach of loyalty would be the
faithlessness of the steward. "And the Lord commended the unjust
steward, because he had done wisely: For the children of this world
are in their generation wiser than the children of light."[66] Wherein
lay this devil's 'wisdom'? In the rejection of the commitment, in the
delicate embrace of interests antagonistic to the master's. A fundamental repugnance exists in serving two masters. Hence: "He who
is not with me is against me." A man cannot serve "two masters at
once." It is not a question of breach of contract, of illicit gain, but
of simply being "against me." Sworn allegiance has been broken by
the very act of serving the second master. Basic loyalty is an elemental
virtue and goes to the heart of human nature. Without more, just
being on the other side is inconsistent with true honor and devotion.
In the leading corporate case (long since overruled), *Metropolitan
Railway,* a contract between the two concerns was voided because
of "the divided allegiance"[67] of an interlocking directorate.

Basic loyalty becomes vividly realistic when reduced to two simple human participants, father and son, priest and penitent, attorney
and client, husband and wife. The anguish and shock of a son, a penitent, a client, a wife, at the slightest intimation of infidelity are most
forceful expressions of the innermost essence of the virtue of loyalty.

Merely, moreover, because the innocent and trusting party happens to be the one million shareholders of General Motors does not diminish an iota the natural-law demands of the utmost in loyalty. Here the requirement is "[n]ot honesty alone, but the punctilio of an honor the most sensitive."[68]

Later reflection will convince that unqualified custodial loyalty alone accounts for the rule itself and all the stringencies which have been set up around it. Other considerations, however, independently demand and justify the invocation of the rule, and hence thereby add further support to this principal foundation.

Quid pro Quo

Were the trustee, as was the case in the early Anglo-Saxon trust, to serve without emolument, his obligation of unswerving dedication would stem solely from the loyalty consequent on his undertaking of stewardship. The modern custodian, however, whether trustee or contrôleur, is remunerated in one or more of the manifold forms of present-day compensation. This remuneration gives rise to a second, conceptually distinct basis for the rule: Commutative justice. This basis is unrelated to the commitment of fidelity or even to the virtue of loyalty in the strict sense (i.e., custodial). Messner comments that "[c]ommutative justice directs the individual and corporate person to render to each in full measure what he is entitled to claim as his own."[69] He rightly adds: "Since rights and claims of commutative justice come into existence mainly through contracts, it is also called contractual justice."[70] And the essence of the justice of the contract is the equality of the consideration. Commutative justice requires an exact return for what has been received, a just quid pro quo.

Trustee and contrôleur both receive under contract a salary or fee commensurate with the onerousness of the office. The source of the payment is the trust fund or the corporate assets. In return, a trustee and a contrôleur, within the scope of their employment, must devote themselves exclusively to the best of their ability to the prosecution of their undertaking.

(Ultimately, but in a different sense, even the quid-pro-quo basis for the Conflict-of-Interest Rule can be referred to the benefit-to-beneficiary principle and finally to the custodial relation. Since the compensation paid to the trustee or to the contrôleur came from the fund of assets originally appropriated into their custody, the totality of services supplied by the trustee and the contrôleur could be viewed as merely the proper return of assets into the fund. Any activity therefore envisaged as within the scope of the stewardship is properly the property of the fund.)

One of the better modern statements of the correct quid-pro-quo rationale came from England and the pen of Justice Denning:

> It matters not that the master has not lost any profit . . . . Nor does it matter that the master could not have done the act himself. It is a case where the servant has unjustly enriched himself by virtue of his service without his master's sanction. It is money which the servant ought not to be allowed to keep, and the law says it shall be taken from him and given to his master, because he got it solely by reason of the position which he occupied as a servant of his master.
>
> —*Reading v. The King*, [1948] 2 K.B. 268, 275.

As with the loyalty foundation, the quid-pro-quo basis for the rule admits of no exceptions whatsoever. Witness Clapp: "While he is employed in his fiduciary capacity, his entire energies must be devoted to the advancement of the beneficiary's legitimate interests."[71] Speaking in general terms Morawetz applied the rule to the corporation:

> It follows, therefore, that the directors, or other agents of a corporation, have no implied authority to bind the company by making a contract with another corporation which they also represent. Each company would be interested in obtaining an advantageous bargain at the expense of the other company, and each would have a claim upon the best endeavors of its agents, unbiased by favor to others.
>
> —1 V. MORAWETZ, A TREATISE ON THE LAW OF PRIVATE CORPORATIONS §528, at 496 (2d ed. 1886).

Some meditation on the various elements constituting the "entire energies" of Clapp and "the best endeavors" of Morawetz will reveal how all-pervasive is the Conflict-of-Interest Rule. Whatever the talents and abilities, knowledge and skill, prudence and judgment, time and energy, imagination and resourcefulness of the trustee and the contrôleur, they all comprise that totality of services offered in return for the compensation of the office, the quid pro quo. As the English Court in 1854 put it in the prominent *Aberdeen Railway* case: "It was Mr. Blaikie's duty to give to his co-directors, and through them to the Company, the full benefit of all the knowledge and skill which he could bring to bear on the subject."[72] Singling out one of these many elements Lewin remarked: "[A]s he acquires that knowledge at the expense of the *cestui que trust,* he is bound to apply it for the *cestui que trust's* benefit."[73] The conclusion therefore is inescapable: However infinitesimal the diversion of energy or endeavor, it is inconsistent with the custodian's contract of hire.

The simple command of a quid pro quo is not founded on the virtues of fidelity or loyalty, but is a natural-law dictate of contractual justice.

Prevention of Temptation

Of all the traditional arguments in support of the Conflict-of-Interest Rule the most frequently adduced is the prophylactic purpose of shielding the trustee from all temptation:

> Remembering the weakness of humanity, its liability to be seduced, by self-interest, from the straight line of duty, the sages of the law inculcate and enjoin, a strict observance of the divine precept: "Lead us not into temptation."
> —*Hoffman Steam Coal Co. v. Cumberland Coal & Iron Co.,* 16 Md. 456, 507 (1860).

The variations have been numerous, but the result the same:

> It does not appear to me that this [conflict-of-interest] rule is, as has been said, founded upon principles of morality. I regard it rather as based on the consideration that, human nature being what it is, there is danger, in such circumstances, of the person holding a fiduciary position being swayed by interest rather than by duty, and thus prejudicing those whom he was bound to protect.
> —*Bray v. Ford,* 1896 A.C. 44, 51 (H.L. 1895).

Thus, also, the New York Court of Appeals held the director of a corporation as "a trustee," to "the same disability which attaches to all trustees"[74] and founded its reasoning on the prevention of temptation:

> It is against public policy to allow persons occupying fiduciary relations to be placed in such positions as that there will be constant danger of a betrayal of trust by the vigorous operation of selfish motives.
>
> —*Barnes v. Brown*, 80 N.Y. 527, 535 (1880).

As salutary as the objective of prevention may be, this reliance on the avert-temptation argument has been a minor source of confusion and a sometime handicap to the proper understanding of the rule. Clearly the objective is praiseworthy. The harm comes in the inaccurate application of the argument. And the imprecise statement of its import.

John L. Counsellor, Sr., Trustee

An analogy should help, both now and in the later elucidation of the sanctions to the rule. John L. Counsellor, Sr., Esquire, for forty years in private practice, is now a full-time trustee for a small trust, whose chief asset is a fledgling research outfit in the competitive electronics field. Tronics, Inc., is routinely beset by patent-infringement claims. This time, counsel for a competitor—who happens through a strange concatenation of events to be the eldest son, John L. Counsellor, Jr.—seeks $200,000 for an 'adaptation' of a patented device that John L. Counsellor, Sr., Trustee, is prudently convinced is worth at most $100,000 in settlement.

In this context, negotiations commence. How apply the prevention-of-temptation argument to the Tronics, Inc., conflict-of-interest predicament? How test the argument's validity in the dual position—as trustee and as father of his son—of John L. Counsellor, Sr., Trustee? What avenues of disloyalty spread out before him? Begin with a capitulation of the several levels of malefaction—*the malefaction the temptation into which John L. Counsellor, Sr., Trustee, must not be led?*—open to both a trustee and a contrôleur in a conflict-of-interest dilemma. Such a capitulation should lead to the fallacy in the loose enunciation of the avert-temptation reasoning.

(1) **Disloyalty Alone**. At the first level, John L. Counsellor, Sr., in his role as trustee, comes immediately into a direct conflict of interest with himself as weak John L. Counsellor, Sr., parent and pliable human being, at the very instant that he places himself as trustee at the table across from himself as father of his son. Without more—without a single word or gesture—this trustee has already been disloyal to his cause and assumed a role antagonistic to his principal, Tronics, Inc., a role of a father who is necessarily and indisputably loyal to his son, willy-nilly. Here is conflict of interest, disloyalty, without more.

This disloyalty is incontrovertibly present even though Counsellor, from beginning to end of the negotiations, maintained an undeniably 'impartial' stance, even though he argued steadfastly against himself at every turn on every point, even though he never once deserted his ambivalence.

At this first level, then, wherein lay the 'temptation' into which the trustee must not be led? Was it *the conflict itself?* Or something yet to come?

(2) **Counsel and Aid**. Once thus positioned on both sides of the table John L. Counsellor, Sr., Trustee, could now yield to further temptation—further temptation? Was this now at last the 'temptation' into which one is not to be led?—and be guilty of a heightened breach of allegiance, actual support and counsel to the opposition, himself in the guise of his son. A passing hint to opposing counsel that his own Tronics case could be stronger. An intimation that Tronics might be tractable in the end. John L. Counsellor, Sr., Trustee, could well stop at that. Here was nothing more than moral support to an adverse interest. But it was nonetheless further disloyalty.

Or John L. Counsellor, Sr., could perhaps take another step and by night release some Tronics blueprints of the patent infraction. Or let slip the outline of the Tronics defenses in the current negotiations. No money changes hands. John L. Counsellor, Sr., Trustee, has merely given his time and aid to the enemy, his son. Was this the 'temptation'?

(3) **Counsel Fees**. An even more active role in preparing his son's case against Tronics could understandably earn John L. Counsellor, Sr., Attorney at Law, a sizable fee for services rendered. Nothing dishonest, one could cynically aver, only a reasonable charge for reasonable labor expended in the preparation of the most reasonable brief against Tronics. The billing would represent the going rate any lawyer

would charge in a similar, arm's-length arrangement. The dollars would be hard-earned and just. The brief would be honest and well reasoned.

(4) **Illicit Gains.** Finally, John L. Counsellor, Sr., Trustee, could insist that John L. Counsellor, Sr., Attorney at Law, receive a sizable kickback, say $50,000, for a negotiated $200,000 settlement for the valid $100,000 claim. This, at least, could be one approach. In fact, the variety of monetary return—false fees, illegal profits, bribes—available to John L. Counsellor, Sr., Trustee, is considerable. All would be illicit, even if at arm's length.

Note well that each of the four levels of disloyalty of John L. Counsellor, Sr., Trustee, was grievously culpable. The only difference lay in the gravity of the sin. Mere presence, without more, on both sides of the table might not be as reprehensible as the dollars under the table, but it would undeniably be wounding to the victim.

The question persists: What is the temptation into which trustee and contrôleur are not to be led? Are they not to be tempted to descend to any of the four levels? Quite clearly the assumption has been—or so the argument has been stated—that trustee or contrôleur has a perfect right to sit on both sides of the table so long as he does not *thereafter* (1) counsel and aid an adversary, (2) labor for him, even though the work was 'honest' and the fee 'just' were the arrangement arm's-length, (3) indulge in outright kickbacks, bribery, extortion.

Seemingly the only temptation to be guarded against would be the last three levels of disloyalty. But the initial act of disloyalty, the very act of conflict of interest itself, is often not regarded as rapine in the holocaust. Recur to the 1880 New York *Barnes v. Brown,* and emphasize the exact meaning of the Court:

> It is against public policy to allow persons occupying fiduciary relations to be placed in such positions as that *there will be constant danger of a betrayal of trust* by the vigorous operation of selfish motives.
>
> —*Barnes v. Brown,* 80 N.Y. 527, 535 (1880) (emphasis added).

When the New York Court will not allow a trustee or contrôleur to assume a position where "there *will be* constant *danger* of a betrayal of trust," the Court obviously does not consider the adversary position itself as such betrayal. Actual aid, fees, kickbacks, bribery, extortion, are the only "danger" to be averted, the only real "betrayal of trust."

The New York Court—and this court is reflective of the frequent avert-temptation approach—was only concerned with a betrayal *after* the trustee had assumed a conflict-of-interest position, not with the disloyalty of the conflict of interest itself. The fear was a future betrayal—"there *will be* constant *danger* of a betrayal of trust"—on the assumption that the conflict-of-interest position itself was not already a betrayal. The fear was a future aid, fees, kickbacks. That was the temptation to be averted. Everything prior to that was not a betrayal.

Implicit, therefore, in the customary avert-temptation argument is the approbation of the disloyalty itself. The one area assumed to be wrong—the temptation that the rule is calculated to avert—is the subsequent malefaction.

In truth, however, no real connection exists between the 'avert-temptation' rationale and the Conflict-of-Interest Rule. The rule says simply: Only one side of the table at a time. The *conflict itself* is what is to be avoided. The rule itself says nil about later infidelities. The rule forbids disloyalty, not because that disloyalty will expectably lead to later depredations, but because the disloyalty itself, the conflict, is the wrong. The later depredations are prohibited, true—and hence ultimately must be redressed—but by a totally different set of rules, rules unrelated to merely sitting on both sides of a dispute at once. The rule is not designed to avert temptation to loot, but to avert the conflict itself. The wrong prohibited by the rule is the conflict, not the later looting.

What harm in the fallacy, then? The harm—beyond its intrinsic illogic—is this: That courts and commentators should see no need for the rule absent any danger of further malefaction beyond the basic disloyalty, the conflict itself. That they should fail to found the rule on its two true supports: (1) Basic custodial loyalty and (2) Contractual justice. The danger is this: If one once removes the threat of the later wrongs, then, so the argument would go, the reason for the rule ceases. Hence remove the rule against the conflict itself. This is the obvious consequence of founding a rule on a false premise. Destroy the premise, the rule falls. Here, this is particularly dangerous since those who would erode the rule are seemingly not cognizant of its two true bases.

The avert-temptation argument, therefore, should be minimized. Query, even, if the rule would be warranted if there were nothing wrong in representing an adversary, if the only purpose were to shield from the grosser and subsequent forms of malefaction. Why bar conflict itself if it is harmless, if the only true concern is later? Under that hypothesis the rule would seem too harsh. Other rules of law adequately handle illicit aid, 'licit' fees, kickbacks, extortion and bribery.

In the end, then, the Conflict-of-Interest Rule should and does in fact bar (1) mere disloyalty itself, and is not designed merely to avert temptation from further, grosser forms of disloyalty: (2) illicit aid, (3) 'arm's-length' fees, (4) extortion, bribes and kickbacks. These grosser forms are later consequences of a conflict of interest, of course, but are not intrinsic to the conflict of interest itself.

(2) The Sanctions of the Rule

> So careful is the law in guarding against the abuse of fiduciary relations, that it will not permit an agent to act for himself and his principal in the same transaction . . . . All such transactions are void, as it respects his principal, unless ratified by him with a full knowledge of all the circumstances. To repudiate them he need not show himself damnified. Whether he has been or not is immaterial. Actual injury is not the principle the law proceeds on in holding such transactions void. Fidelity in the agent is what is aimed at, and as a means of securing it, the law will not permit the agent to place himself in a situation in which he may be tempted by his own private interest to disregard that of his principal.
>
> —People v. Township Bd. of Overyssel, 11 Mich. 222, 225-26 (1863).

The broad proscription of the Conflict-of-Interest Rule is clear: The trustee must never sit on both sides of the table at once. Never as trustee, e.g., of Tronics, may he deal with himself, whether (1) directly for his own personal account, e.g., toward a kickback, or (2) as agent of a 'third party,' e.g., his son.

But what are the consequences of a breach of the rule? What sanctions are visited on the trustee, or the contrôleur, who deals with himself, either personally, or as a 'representative' of his son, as did John L. Counsellor, Sr.? The answer here is somewhat complex, although the rationale of the sanctions may seem simple. A threefold approach is most logical: (1) Damages. (2) Disgorgement. (3) Disqualification and Reconstruction.

Damages

Courts have characteristically been unable to comprehend the fact that mere disloyalty, without the slightest subsequent wrong, without any admixture of dollar loss to the trust or dollar gain to the trustee, is a very real injury to the beneficiary. The mere 'honest,' 'impartial' negotiation against the interests of the beneficiary is disloyalty. Disloyalty itself is culpable. Consider the parallel in the tort of Emotional Distress. There the 'cost' of the pain is difficult to express in dollars, but is nonetheless poignant and distressing. At all four levels of malefaction, John L. Counsellor, Sr., Trustee, was disloyal, and hence liable in damages, *irrespective of superadded derelictions*. At the first level—the mere positioning against the cestuis—the disloyalty needed no segregation inasmuch as no other transgression was involved. The dedication of a custodian to the interests of the beneficiary was violated. (One might even argue further that contractual justice had also been breached, that Counsellor was 'working' for the opposition on trust time and should reimburse the 'quid' to the trust for the 'quo' he did not supply.) Thus, in its purest form disloyalty is a breach of the elemental command of the total allegiance of a steward and cries out for rectification in damages without proof of further wrongs or added injury beyond the simple turning away from the promised dedication to the trust.

The courts have not tasted this truth, but they have intuited it. The notable *Diamond v. Oreamuno* in 1969 by the New York Court of Appeals came so close:

> It is true that the complaint before us does not contain any allegation of damages to the corporation but this has never been considered to be an essential requirement for a cause of action founded on a breach of fiduciary duty. [Citations.] This is because the function of such an action, unlike an ordinary tort or contract case, is not merely to

compensate the plaintiff for wrongs committed by the defendant but, as this court declared many years ago
(Dutton v. Willner, 52 N.Y. 312, 319, *supra*), "to *prevent*
them, by removing from agents and trustees all inducement to attempt dealing for their own benefit in matters
which they have undertaken for others, or to which their
agency or trust relates." (Emphasis supplied.)

> —Diamond v. Oreamuno, 248 N.E.2d 910,
> 912 (N.Y. 1969).

(Here again is the old fallacious 'avert-temptation' argument clouding up the reasoning. As though the purpose were to avert later self-
dealing, rather than preserve single-eyed, unbiased representation
at the outset.) At least the Court saw no need for "any allegation of
damages." But the Court did not mean this exactly. Injury must always be present. More to the point, disloyalty does injure. Damages
from disloyalty may not be visible in blood or dollars but they are
most palpable to the wounded party. This the Court intuited. The
Second Circuit in 1973 in *Schein v. Chasen* undoubtedly meant the
same thing: "[A]n allegation of damages [for fiduciary breaches] is not
a prerequisite to a recovery."[75]

At the three other levels of malefaction John L. Counsellor, Sr.,
Trustee, added further acts of depredation to the pure disloyalty without more. But the added (1) expenditure of unauthorized labor, time,
counsel, (2) exaction of 'just' fees for services to the opposition, (3)
kickbacks for a false settlement, did not remove or diminish the concomitant and basic disloyalty that was present throughout. This
disloyalty—on all levels of malefaction—demands rectification by
the imposition of damages against the trustee.

Disgorgement

The two underpinnings of the Conflict-of-Interest Rule, custodial loyalty and contractual justice, also explain the second category
of conflict-of-interest sanctions: All gains are disgorged into the
trust, all losses are borne by the trustee. On this proposition courts
have shown unanimity. The *Restatement* puts it succinctly:

> If the trustee commits a breach of his duty of loyalty he
> is chargeable with any loss or depreciation in value of the

trust property resulting from the breach of duty, or any profit made by him through the breach of duty, or any profit which would have accrued to the trust estate if there had been no breach of duty.

> —RESTATEMENT (SECOND) OF TRUSTS §206
> comment a, at 463 (1959).

This rule is the simple extension of the Benefit-to-Beneficiary Rule and the insistence of the quid pro quo of contractual justice. As for the losses, since the trust itself was never a proper party and the trustee was on both sides of the deal, the trust could scarcely be expected to suffer the losses.

The disgorgement rule, distinct completely from damages for disloyalty, covers any emolument, whether 'licit' if it had been at arm's length or illicit, flowing to the trustee resultant on his activities as trustee and while dedicated to the beneficiary. This basic law of disgorgement would certainly cover John Counsellor's conduct on the second, third and fourth levels, the labor and aid, the 'just' fees and the illicit kickback. (Thus Counsellor would be forced to 'disgorge,' on the second level, a quid for the quo of time and energy expended on company time on behalf of the adversary.) Nor would the courts hesitate in so holding. One of the most outstanding corporate opinions of the seventies, if not the century, was *Borden v. Sinskey*. In the 1976 *Borden* the Third Circuit spanned forty years and applied the classic *Guth v. Loft* to a prototypal conflict of interest:

> However, even if we were now to order an accounting, we would not permit Sinskey to retain the reasonable value of his services. Although defendants may be able to distinguish the facts of *Guth* from those of the instant case, they cannot distinguish away the rationale of that decision. . . . [A]ll the salaries he received from Pepsi-Cola while serving as Loft's chief executive . . . were stripped away because Guth had gained them . . . in violation of his fiduciary duties. The court refused to allow him to retain any of the profits or benefits derived from his misconduct in order to deter any disloyalty on the part of a corporate fiduciary.
>
> —*Borden v. Sinskey*, 530 F.2d 478, 497-98 (3d
> Cir. 1976).

The Second Circuit gave earlier support in 1973 with the accepted statement of the Benefit-to-Beneficiary Rule:

> "Corporate officers and directors are not permitted to use their position of trust and confidence to further their private interests. . . . The rule that requires an undivided and unselfish loyalty to the corporation demands that there shall be no conflict between duty and self-interest. . . .
>
> "If an officer or director of a corporation, in violation of his duty as such, acquires gain or advantage for himself, the law charges the interest so acquired with a trust for the benefit of the corporation, at its election, while it denies to the betrayer all benefit and profit. . . ."
>
> —*Abbott Redmont Thinlite Corp. v. Redmont,* 475 F.2d 85, 88 n.3 (2d Cir. 1973) (quoting *Guth v. Loft, Inc.*).

This disgorgement rule and its underlying philosophy have been unchallenged over the years.

Disqualification and Reconstruction

Apart from (1) damages for disloyalty and (2) disgorgement of benefits, the conflict-of-interest trustee often triggers into operation a third sanction. Oftentimes the trustee adds a further element to his basic disloyalty. In a separate class of conflict-of-interest cases, the impartial judgment of the trustee is the central requisite of important negotiations. Here not only does the trustee sit on both sides of the table throughout the delicate negotiations but at the culmination of those negotiations the trustee must pass 'impartial' judgment on a deal involving substantial trust dollars. On the first three levels of trustee disloyalty such an impartial trustee judgment was not involved. Now, however, the trust dollars stand or fall on the unbiased evaluation of the trustee. The hypothetical John L. Counsellor, Sr., Trustee, was doing just that, on the fourth level of his malefactions, when he compromised his trust position without the impartial scrutiny of a third party, when his 'impartial judgment' agreed to $200,000 rather than the correct $100,000. In that case, Counsellor was alone at the bargaining table. Counsellor for Tronics and Counsellor for Counsellor. Loyalty to Tronics and the desire for personal gain were in direct conflict, in a contested settlement. But what of a negotiated contract? A stock appraisal? A land deal?

Disqualification

In all such cases, the result is uniform. When the trustee sits on both sides, the primitive Conflict-of-Interest Rule comes into play automatically, disqualifies the trustee and in effect voids the transaction. The unqualified rule is simple:

> The essence of the test is whether or not under all the circumstances the transaction carries the earmarks of an arm's length bargain. If it does not, equity will set it aside.
>
> —*Pepper v. Litton,* 308 U.S. 295, 306-07 (1939).

This unadorned principle recurs constantly and in all jurisdictions:

> "The policy of the law is to put fiduciaries beyond the reach of temptation, by making it unprofitable for them to yield to it. To that end an act by the fiduciary in which personal interest and duty conflict is voidable at the mere option of the beneficiary, regardless of good faith or results."
>
> —*Holden v. Construction Machinery Co.,* 202 N.W.2d 348, 357 (Iowa 1972) (quoting *Hoyt v. Hampe*).

In this class of conflict-of-interest cases the primary question is not only one of damages and disgorgement, but also the reliability, integrity, validity, of the trustee's judgment in an evaluation in which he has a personal interest, either for his own behalf or for another. And the result at law has always been the same: Immediate disqualification of the trustee, immediate repudiation of the trustee's judgment, whether in a contested settlement, a negotiated contract, a stock appraisal, a land deal.

The No Inquiry Rule

This disqualification and repudiation are so inveterately enforced in the law that even the *implementation* of the disqualification and repudiation has itself been canonized in a distinct rule: The trustee is removed without an inquiry. The contract—or settlement, appraisal, sale—is set aside. The New York Court of Appeals expressed the accepted approach:

> He stood in the attitude of selling as owner, and purchasing as trustee. The law permits no one to act in such inconsistent relations. It does not stop to inquire whether the contract or transaction was fair or unfair. It stops the inquiry when the relation is disclosed, and sets aside the transaction, or refuses to enforce it, at the instance of the party whom the fiduciary undertook to represent . . . .
>
> —*Munson v. Syracuse, G. & C. Ry.*, 8 N.E. 355, 358 (N.Y. 1886).

This is the concise statement of the No Inquiry Rule. Courts over the decades have explored its applications and given substance to its operation.

The distinct origins of the No Inquiry Rule are undoubtedly English. By the 1800s the rule was firmly established. The classic *Aberdeen Railway* case in 1854 carries an early enunciation. Alluding to the Conflict-of-Interest Rule, the Court states:

> So strictly is this principle adhered to, that no question is allowed to be raised as to the fairness or unfairness of a contract so entered into.
>
> It obviously is, or may be, impossible to demonstrate how far in any particular case the terms of such a contract have been the best for the interest of the cestui que trust, which it was possible to obtain.
>
> It may sometimes happen that the terms on which a trustee has dealt or attempted to deal with the estate or interests of those for whom he is a trustee, have been as good as could have been obtained from any other person . . . .
>
> But still so inflexible is the rule that no inquiry on that subject is permitted.
>
> —*Aberdeen Ry. v. Blaikie Bros.*, 149 Rev. Rep. 32, 39 (H.L. 1854).

The rule has been variously phrased but is reducibly uniform.

[N]o agent in the course of his agency, in the matter of his agency, can be allowed to make any profit without the knowledge and consent of his principal; . . . that rule is an inflexible rule, and must be applied inexorably by this Court, which is not entitled . . . to receive evidence . . . as to whether the principal did or did not suffer any injury . . . ; for the safety of mankind requires that no agent shall be able to put his principal to the danger of such inquiry as that.

> —*Parker v. McKenna,* 10 L.R.-Ch. 96, 124-25
> (Ch. App. 1874) (James, L.J.).

The two steps are thus automatic: (1) Immediate disqualification. (2) Voidability of the agreement.

The result has been rigid. As long as the trustee has been alone at the bargaining table, no inquiry has been permitted into (1) his motives, (2) his good faith, (3) the reliability and integrity of his judgment, (4) the fairness of his deal, (5) the final product of his 'negotiation.' Without an arm's-length third party, the taint is all-pervasive and the matter is closed, without more. In sum: The disqualification of the trustee, the repudiation of his 'negotiation,' are automatic, without inquiry. That is the No Inquiry Rule.

In a corporate case involving insider use of nonpublic information, the Supreme Court of Kansas took a predictably earthy approach in its formulation:

When loyalty to a beneficiary and desire for personal gain on the part of the trustee may compete for supremacy as guides to conduct, this court does not permit the trustee to take the witness stand and tell how frank and fair he was in purchasing from the beneficiary. If the trust property be land, all too often valuable mineral resources are discovered as soon as the trustee acquires the interest of the beneficiaries, or he sells the land for twice what he paid for it. If the trust property be bonds or stocks, as soon as the trustee acquires the securities the bonds promptly go to a premium, or a melon is cut. Therefore this court applies to a trustee purchasing for himself from a beneficiary substantially the rule applied to an executor, administrator, or guardian, who purchases directly or indirectly for himself at a sale made in his representative capacity.

A trustee's purchase may be avoided by the beneficiary,
or the beneficiary may recover damages for his loss, on
showing the sale and the relationship of the parties to it.

—*Hotchkiss v. Fischer,* 16 P.2d 531, 534-35
(Kan. 1932).

Clearly, the No Inquiry Rule has vigor only in application to executed contracts. If still executory, simple disqualification achieves
the desired objective. If already executed, the courts are faced with
a variety of possibilities.

Reconstruction

After the implementation of the disqualification and the repudiation through application of the No Inquiry Rule, what then? The
trustee is gone. The contract has been voided. Affairs are in a shambles. What is to be done? The court must now attempt to put together
the pieces, to reassemble the agreement, but under only one format,
a truly arm's-length negotiation. To give reliability, integrity, validity,
to any reconstructed contract, the trust and the underlying beneficiaries must be represented by an honestly impartial person.

Faced with this logical prerequisite, the court may appoint a
new trustee, perhaps permit the beneficiaries to name a trustworthy
successor, even assume the supervision of the negotiation itself, or
appoint a special master to reconstruct as equitably as possible the
contract as it should have been. The manner of reconstruction must
be shaped by the peculiar exigencies of the situation. The possible
variants are illimitable. The sole norm, however, must be the restoration of incontestable impartiality. (Certainly the disqualified trustee
will not be allowed "to take the witness stand and tell how frank and
fair he was.") As long as the trust corpus is in an impartial custody,
the Conflict-of-Interest Rule will thereby be duly respected.

Under any one of these or similar approaches, this last and
fourth level of trustee wrong—the tainted evaluation by a trustee on
both sides of the table—has been righted by the No Inquiry Rule.
Impartial judgment has supplanted biased judgment.

This simple statement of the No Inquiry Rule and the complex
sanctions consequent on its breach would undoubtedly be enhanced
by an understanding of the philosophy at the rule's base.

(3) The Rationale of the No Inquiry Rule

> The *cestui que trust* is not bound to prove, nor is the Court bound to judge, that the trustee has made a bargain advantageous to himself. . . . There may be fraud . . . and the party not able to prove it. It is to guard against this uncertainty and *hazard* of abuse, and to remove the trustee from temptation, that the rule does and will permit the *cestui que trust* to come, at his own option, and without showing actual injury, and insist upon having the experiment of another sale. This is a remedy which goes deep, and touches the very root of the evil.
>
> —*Davoue v. Fanning*, 2 Johns. Ch. 252, 260-61 (N.Y. Ch. 1816).

The No Inquiry Rule, as nothing other than the formal implementation of the 'automatic disqualification and repudiation' of the Conflict-of-Interest Rule, necessarily is founded on the same underlying philosophy as the Conflict-of-Interest Rule itself, and then some. The Conflict-of-Interest Rule forbids a trustee from sitting on both sides of a negotiation. The third sanction for breach of the Conflict-of-Interest Rule—the first two are damages and disgorgement—is the immediate disqualification of the trustee and the voidance of the contract. The No Inquiry Rule is merely the formal canonization of this third, automatic sanction of the Conflict-of-Interest Rule. Thus the rationale is identical for all three: (1) The Conflict-of-Interest Rule, (2) the automatic disqualification and repudiation and (3) the No Inquiry Rule itself.

Recur to the four levels of malefaction of the hypothetical John L. Counsellor, Sr., Trustee. The first three, (1) mere disloyalty without more, (2) counsel and aid, (3) fees and profits, all would be reprobated by the Conflict-of-Interest Rule as breaches of loyalty, violations of the Benefit-to-Beneficiary Rule, unworthy of a custodian. In all first three instances the trustee would in effect be 'disqualified.' The broad rationale underlying this 'disqualification' on these three 'non-tainted-evaluation' levels applies necessarily and equally to a conflict-of-interest trustee who falls to the fourth and lowest level and passes a partial judgment on behalf of both sides of a deal, whether in a settlement, a contract, a stock appraisal, a land sale.

But, and here lies a subtlety, when the conflict-of-interest trustee adds a both-sides 'tainted evaluation' to mere disloyalty, added forces reprobate his position. Not only is the trustee subject to disqualification for mere disloyalty but further reasons call for (1) automatic disqualification, (2) repudiation of his biased judgment, nullification of his work product. The philosophy underlying the reprobation of disloyalty per se, without an admixture of other elements, has been laid out already over many pages. But now, what further causes mandate the automatic disqualification and contract voidance in the peculiar context of a tainted valuation? What additional support upholds the No Inquiry Rule beyond the support common to the reprobation of the first three levels, of all varieties of disloyalty? (Cave: The answers will necessarily contain some overlap. The fourth-level malefaction is, after all, disloyalty as well and that disloyalty is invariably present and hence difficult to ignore.)

This question has been answered variously, and with varying cogency, over the decades. Two reasons are fundamental, and tenable, and would account for the No Inquiry Rule without further help: (1) The Inherent Fallibility of Human Nature. (2) The Impossibility Ever to Know.

Fallible Man

One could argue captiously that even the Deity by intrinsic necessity would be incapable of objectivity if called upon to sit on both sides of a question in which He had a personal stake. By definition, 'the total dedication of a custodian' to two conflicting causes is inherently impossible. But even if divine impartiality was possible, human certainly is not. The human psyche, consistently and as a rule, can never be so detached as to favor a competing cause.

Over the decades, the Anglo-Saxon law of trusts has gained some remarkably reliable insights into man's nature and conduct. Paramount among these has been the categorical conviction that a fallible human person on both sides of a bargain with a personal stake in the outcome is essentially incapable of impartiality. The Supreme Court of the United States had this in mind in *Michoud v. Girod* in the 1840s:

> In this conflict of interest, the law wisely interposes. It
> acts not on the possibility, that, in some cases, the sense

of that duty may prevail over the motives of self-interest, but it provides against the probability in many cases, and the danger in all cases, that the dictates of self-interest will exercise a predominant influence, and supersede that of duty.

> —*Michoud v. Girod*, 45 U.S. (4 How.) 502, 554-55 (1846).

Centuries of legal wisdom have agreed with the Supreme Court and have long since placed detached objectivity far beyond the rational powers of *homo rationalis*. This ultimate principle of human conduct is founded simply on the consistent fragility of human nature. Age-old recognition of this basic handicap of acquisitive man led inevitably to the formal enunciation of the No Inquiry Rule.

The Impossibility to Know

At that crucial moment when the conflict-of-interest trustee reached his valuation in the negotiated settlement, or the contract, the appraisal, the sale, only one single person was in the room: John L. Counsellor, Sr., fragile human being. Into his decision and judgment went unknown prejudices, personal and paternal predispositions, unexplored biases. Only God could ever know what motivated that trustee, what influenced his conclusion.

> He stood in the attitude of selling as owner, and purchasing as trustee. The law permits no one to act in such inconsistent relations. It does not stop to inquire whether the contract or transaction was fair or unfair. It stops the inquiry when the relation is disclosed, and sets aside the transaction, or refuses to enforce it, at the instance of the party whom the fiduciary undertook to represent, without undertaking to deal with the question of abstract justice in the particular case. It prevents frauds by making them, as far as may be, impossible, knowing that real motives often elude the most searching inquiry; and it leaves neither to judge nor jury the right to determine, upon a consideration of its advantages or disadvantages, whether a contract made under such circumstances shall stand or fall.
>
> —*Munson v. Syracuse, G. & C. Ry.*, 8 N.E. 355, 358 (N.Y. 1886).

John L. Counsellor, Sr., spoke only with John L. Counsellor, Sr. No impartial third party was ever admitted to the valuations. Here was a completely private matter. Behind closed doors. Counsellor alone. No outside scrutiny, no current corroboration, no possible double check on Counsellor's figure. The old English *Aberdeen Railway* Court knew this:

> So strictly is this principle adhered to, that no question is allowed to be raised as to the fairness or unfairness of a contract so entered into.
>
> It obviously is, or may be, impossible to demonstrate how far in any particular case the terms of such a contract have been the best for the interest of the cestui que trust, which it was possible to obtain.
>
> It may sometimes happen that the terms on which a trustee has dealt or attempted to deal with the estate or interests of those for whom he is a trustee, have been as good as could have been obtained from any other person . . . .
>
> But still so inflexible is the rule that no inquiry on that subject is permitted.
>
> —*Aberdeen Ry. v. Blaikie Bros.,* 149 Rev. Rep. 32, 39 (H.L. 1854).

By some breakdown in the rules for psychological conduct or under the law of averages, a conflict-of-interest trustee might just come up with exactly the right and honest outcome. But that one could never know.

> The law cannot accurately measure the influence of a trustee with his associates, nor will it enter into the inquiry, in an action by the trustee in his private capacity to enforce the contract, in the making of which he participated. The value of the rule of equity to which we have adverted, lies, to a great extent, in its stubbornness and inflexibility. Its rigidity gives it one of its chief uses as a preventive or discouraging influence, because it weakens the temptation to dishonesty or unfair dealing on the part of the trustees, vitiating, without attempt at discrimina-

tion, all transactions in which they assume the dual char-
acters of principal and representative.

> —*Munson v. Syracuse, G. & C. Ry.*, 8 N.E. 355,
> 358 (N.Y. 1886).

Thus, the controlling truth is still there. In any conflict-of-interest
evaluation, for example a land sale, no impartial person, especially
a ready buyer with his own cherished dollars in hand, has been called
in to put an honest price on the property. No public announcement
solicited an objectively competitive market to evaluate the land, not
theoretically but with hard-earned personal cash. (Obviously, such
an evaluation, whether by ready buyer or general market, would
eliminate any conflict of interest.)

Thus, beneath this age-old No Inquiry Rule is (1) the built-in
human disability, the impossibility of impartiality and (2) the absence of any objective third-party scrutiny.

Here is sufficient rationale for the No Inquiry Rule, without further support. But various courts have adduced various reasons, most
of them specious.

The Kansas Supreme Court in 1932 showed noticeable impa-
tience with the niceties:

> This [No Inquiry Rule] is not applied because of any so-
> phistication about the same person acting in two capaci-
> ties in the same transaction, but because experience
> teaches such transactions too often result in gross fraud.
>
> > —*Hotchkiss v. Fischer,* 16 P.2d 531, 535 (Kan.
> > 1932).

Which reducibly is merely empirical support for the premise already
elaborated that fallible man is inherently incapable of objectivity in
a conflict-of-interest dilemma.

Some courts dodge the issue completely by resort to that phan-
tom, 'public policy,' which is even more reprehensible than the con-
temned avert-temptation argument already rebutted.

> It is against public policy to allow persons occupying fidu-
> ciary relations to be placed in such positions as that there

will be constant danger of a betrayal of trust by the vigorous operation of selfish motives.

> —*Barnes v. Brown,* 80 N.Y. 527, 535 (1880).

To which should be recalled, by way of a delightful divertissement, the deftly turned words of the intriguing Burrough, J., in 1824:

> I, for one, protest, as my Lord has done, against arguing too strongly upon public policy;—it is a very unruly horse, and when once you get astride it you never know where it will carry you. It may lead you from the sound law. It is never argued at all but when other points fail.
>
> —*Richardson v. Mellish,* 130 Eng. Rep. 294, 303 (C.P. 1824).

So, in the end, the absolute inflexibility of the No Inquiry Rule is amply justified by the fusion of two separate factors: (1) The private evaluation of a wholly unknown subject with no independent corroboration, (2) by a single person with interests deeply in conflict with those of the absent party. Understandably the result is automatic disqualification and repudiation. This is the rationale of the No Inquiry Rule.

On this foundation of the strict-trust doctrine will be erected the entire corpus of the Philosophy of Corporate Control. Nothing in the ensuing study is more basic. Everything that follows depends upon it. From here forward each new concept will be an increasingly more specific application of the Custodial Concept of Corporate Control.

Chapter 3

The Definition of Corporate Control

> Courts probably are not capable of coping with the complex questions of corporate policy and practice involved in fashioning new rules and doctrines to govern sale of controlling corporate interests.
>
> —O'Neal, *Introduction* to *Symposium: Sale of Control,* 4 J. CORP. L. 239, 240-41 (1979).

Progress in scientific reasoning is impossible without exactitude of definition. Yet an exact technical definition begs the question. Implicit in the accurate statement of any concept is the entire philosophy underlying it. Because of this, and in spite of it, any attempt at a reasoned body of philosophical principles must begin with an inclusive set of painstakingly refined terminology.

Everything cannot be said at once. This is an inherent disability of scholarship. The proofs, therefore, of the underlying principles cannot be for now. (Beyond, of course, the most underlying of all, the strict-trust custodial concept.) Better to present tentatively a precise definition of the object of investigation, and proceed from there to elaboration, development and proof. Without knowing that about which, one can scarcely know why, wherefore or whither. This is eminently true of the synthesis of the Philosophy of Corporate Control.

One might well ask, therefore, why so elementary an undertaking would not have preceded even the elaboration of the Custodial Concept of Corporate Control? The answer is not easy. In so complex a subject, it simply seemed impossible to plunge immediately into the midst of such complexity. Some basic idea of the foundation

97

seemed indispensable. It further seemed that the strict-trust analogy could be pursued successfully without an absolutely technical definition of corporate control. Now at least the nuances of the definition should be more manageable. In one sense the study of the Philosophy of Corporate Control is even now just beginning, with the basic definition. The ancient Scholastics should not be too grieved at this slightly late attempt at definition.

The years after the hesitant emergence of the concept of corporate control in the midthirties—with Berle's classic on the modern corporation—saw no forthright attempt at truly scientific definition. Understandably, an enforced preoccupation with novel rudimentary problems precluded time-consuming rumination. Yet unhurried meditation alone could formulate the terms of art so indispensable to this complex and adolescent science.

Early adoption of a scientific lexicon of major control terminology, and rigid adherence to the supporting philosophical definitions, could mean much to the law of corporate control. The most unfathomable questions are often answered by a simple statement of the principal terms. The loose usages of the past, however, have not been positively harmful or always inappropriate. They simply failed to facilitate. The time to tighten would seem to be at hand, at the inception of the first dogmatic treatment of the subject.

The Various Definitions

The term 'corporate control' has been regularly used in three distinctly different senses. Instances of each are not uncommon.

In a derived and secondary usage, the Second Circuit in 1962 in *Essex Universal* equated the control with the office and referred to the sale of control as "an agreement for the naked transfer of corporate office."[76] The early English *Sugden v. Crossland* referred to the purchase of "the office."[77]

In a transposition of the custodian for the custody, Berle, employing a tertiary and not uncommon meaning, applied the term to the persons themselves, "the group of individuals who for practical purposes may be regarded as 'the control.'"[78] "[T]he modern corporation [must] serve not only the owners or the control but all society."[79]

Finally, Judge Clark in the famous *Feldmann* was most exact, and characterized corporate control as an "official relation"[80]—"a fiduciary relationship to the corporation."[81]

Corporate control, in each of these usages—as the office, the officeholder, the relation—is correctly employed, because corporate control may and must be viewed from each aspect. But one term for three meanings inevitably confuses. More important, only one of the three is 'corporate control' in the strict sense. Primarily and essentially, corporate control is a relation. As such, the technical term 'corporate control' should be used exclusively for the fiduciary relationship existing between the office of the contrôleur and the corporation. The office and the officer are 'corporate control' only in secondary and tertiary senses.

Ultimately, the complete philosophical definition will encompass not only these two derived uses but the many subdefinitions and varied ramifications.

Preparatory to such a detailed analysis, however, a concise statement of the primary and essential definition could form a matrix for the later development:

> *The corporate control is a relation of total custody, effected by the appropriation of the corporate entity, subsisting between the office of the contrôleur and the corporation, giving rise to a complexus of duties and a corresponding complexus of rights directed to the benefit of the shareholders.*

With the stage thus broadly set, the full scientific definition can be approached in four phases: *I. The Relation of Corporate Control. II. The Properties of the Relation. III. The Office of the Contrôleur. IV. The Contrôleur.*

I. The Relation of Corporate Control

> But when a corporation aggregate is formed, and the persons composing it . . . place the management and control of its affairs in the hands of a select few, so that life and animation may be given to the body, then such directors become the agents and trustees of the corporators and a relation is created, not between the stockholders and the body

corporate, but between the stockholders and those directors who, in their character of trustees, become accountable for any willful dereliction of duty or violation of the trust reposed in them.

—*Verplanck v. Mercantile Ins. Co.,* 1 Edw. Ch. 83, 87 (N.Y. Ch. 1831).

In Aristotelian terms a relation is an accident which inheres in a substance, as quantity and quality are accidents which affect a substance. Thus the relation of custody inheres in the substance, the office of the contrôleur. A relation varies in intimacy, for example, from contiguity, companionship and continuity to friendship, fiduciary and fatherhood. But in any context in which it finds itself it is the *effective* junction of two disparate terms in a binding *union*. The essence of the relation is constituted by that efficient force, whatever it may be, which joins subject and object together and keeps them there.

The generic relation is verified fully in specific corporate control in every particular: *(1) The Object. (2) The Subject. (3) The Essence. (4) The Properties. (5) The Foundation.*

(1) The Object

Viewed from the standpoint of intrinsic importance, the chief concern of the corporate venture is the corporation itself. As part of the relation of corporate control, therefore, the corporation is the first of the two outer terms and is the sole object of the custody and dominion. The corporation, nonetheless, remains passive and is the recipient of the activity of the relation. Considered more realistically the objective term of the relation is (1) the corporation directly and (2) the totality of corporate assets behind the corporate veil, indirectly. Even this must be understood correctly, since the ultimate and primary goal of the enterprise is the welfare of the shareholders, the beneficiaries. The entity is only the conduit of the benefits to its constituents. The contrôleur is held rigorously to the Benefit-to-Beneficiary Rule.

(2) The Subject

From the standpoint of the relation itself the principal and active term is the office of the contrôleur. The entire relation has its base in this subjective term and spans out, as it were, to the objective term, the corporate entity. The relation inheres in the subject. In the office resides the custody.

The officeholder, the contrôleur, can be conceived as integral to the relation in the sense that the contrôleur qua contrôleur is only conceptually distinct from the office he holds, must always be present, is essential to the existence of the office. The contrôleur is the personification of the office, is the official agent of all corporate-control activity.

(3) The Essence

The very heart of the relation—and consequently the very heart of corporate control itself—consists in the custody. The custody is the connection between office and corporation, between subjective and objective terminals. Custody is a holding and in this holding, the tenure, is the essence of the relation of corporate control. Here is another indispensable term of art. Nothing better expresses the innermost nature of this tenure than the word 'custody.' In the Custodial Concept of Corporate Control lies the absolute foundation of the entire philosophy. The terms 'custody' and 'custodial' should be sacrosanct, reserved solely for that peculiar dominion and care with which the office of the contrôleur holds the corporate entity.

This custodial tenure, the essence of the relation, is effected by the appropriation, voluntary or involuntary, of the corporate entity by the collective shareholders into the dominion of the office of the contrôleur. In 'appropriation' is another technical term. This shareholder appropriation, as the efficient cause of the relation, is, however, both *static* and *dynamic*. Static, because it represents a stable condition of tenure, the simple, continuous holding of the corporate entity. Dynamic, because the shareholders' appropriation also signifies (1) an active handing over (2) towards an active acceptance and administration of the corporate enterprise for the benefit of the shareholders.

(4) *The Properties*

Inextricably attached to the relation of custody, but not of its essence, are two necessary properties. These properties flow from the essence of the custody, but are really distinct from it. The inescapable consequence of the acceptance from the shareholders of corporate custody by the contrôleur's office is a complexus of duties. Acknowledge custody, responsibility follows. This complexus of responsibilities is the fiduciary duty inhering in the office of the contrôleur. The contrôleur's fiduciary duty is not identified with the custody but is nonetheless not severable or separable from it. It is, however, implied with logical necessity.

Just as the fiduciary duty flows necessarily from the custodial dominion, so too is a complexus of rights the ineluctable correlative of the duties. This complexus of rights is the authority of the office of the contrôleur.

The fiduciary duty and the authority of the contrôleur are the two major and essential properties of the custodial relation.

(5) *The Foundation*

The ultimate philosophical foundation of the relation of corporate control is the inherent need for someone, anyone, to assume the custody, to assert the dominion over the corporation. Berle sensed this in the late fifties:

> The function of control is necessary and essential in the corporate system. Directors have to be chosen by someone. Absent a stockholder with absolute control, some mobilizer must be found to secure consensus where stockholders are scattered.
>
> —Berle, *"Control" in Corporate Law,* 58 COLUM. L. REV. 1212, 1215 (1958).

The conclusion is inescapable, therefore, that the custodial relation must exist somewhere, must inevitably inhere in the office of the contrôleur. As the social exigencies of man postulate a supreme authority for the state, so also do the intrinsic demands of the corporate entity require a contrôleur.

Early in their formulation, the parallel fields of trust and agency set a pattern for corporate control by employing technical terminology apposite to the three major elements of the respective relations. Thus three sets of appropriate parallels result: (1) Contrôleur, trustee, agent, (2) The offices of the contrôleur, the trustee, the agent, (3) The relations: The corporate control, the trust, the agency.

When used without qualification, therefore, 'corporate control' signifies the relation of complete custody, effected by the shareholders' appropriation of the corporation, subsisting between the office of the contrôleur and the corporation, resulting in the two essential properties, the fiduciary duty and the authority of corporate control, directed to the benefit of the shareholders.

Corollaries to the Relation

In the strictly relational area of control, arguably the most important distinction lies between custody and ownership. In technical control law these relations are mutually exclusive. Common parlance, however, does not draw such clean-cut lines. In fact, even in control writings the full implications of the separation of ownership from custody have not been defined.

The Relation of Ownership

The essence of the ownership relation is the owner's *right* to the control and dominion of his assets. The term 'ownership' always *denotes* this right to dominion. However, the cause for some reflection—and the source of serious pitfalls in the control philosophy—rests in the added fact that the vulgar usage of the term also *connotes* the owner's actual *exercise* of his acknowledged right of control. The actual exercise of this right to dominion, however, is not of the essence of ownership. It may be divorced, indefinitely, even permanently, saving always the right to reassertion.

In corporate-control philosophy this divorce is effected by the shareholder appropriation, licit or even illicit, of the corporation into the custody of the contrôleur. As Webster defines it, the verb "appropriate" signifies: To "set apart for or assign to a particular purpose or use." Appropriation, therefore, removes the *exercise* of dominion from the *right,* separates control from ownership. Appropriation has several aspects. The effective act of the owner first hands over the corporation "to a particular purpose," the benefit of the beneficiaries, the shareholder owners. Next, as an enduring state, the appropriation is a continuing custody, the result of the effective act. Finally, as dynamic, the appropriation is the administration of the corporate entity by the contrôleur as if *ad proprium,* with the care as if his own.

Once the appropriation has been completed, the ownership has been changed, not of its essence because the *right* to dominion remains, but in a real sense because the *exercise* of dominion has been entrusted to the contrôleur. The result: A new relation and another technical term to describe it. The scientific control term 'ownership after appropriation' always postulates, by hypothesis, the rigid separation of the right from its actual exercise, the invariable absence of dominion by the owner. Its distinctive note lies in the location of control in another. It is universally ownership-without-dominion. Ownership control after appropriation is a logical impossibility and contradiction.

The Relation of Custody

On the other hand, the relation of custody resultant on the appropriation entails none of the definitional pitfalls of the severable elements of ownership. Custody by essential definition has a double indivisible denotation: (1) The exercise of dominion (2) over another's goods. The *right* to control remains in ownership. The *exercise* has been appropriated and is of the essence of custody. One never speaks of custody of one's own goods (except in relation to God. In this sense, all goods are from God and are held only in custody). The popular usage of 'custody,' therefore, lends itself admirably to technical application in the corporate-control field. No need for the careful specification and clarification necessary with 'ownership' and 'ownership after appropriation.'

Total Custody

Immediately consequent on the corporate-control hypothesis is the next corollary: The custody of the office of the contrôleur is absolute. By definition, custody qua custody admits of no reservation. Otherwise it ceases to be custody and vitiates (to the extent that dominion is withheld) the very act of appropriation essential to the relation. Any limitation is intrinsically repugnant to the entrustment.

Thus, *fleeting* control is nonetheless total control. While it persists, albeit temporarily, fleeting control is nevertheless characterized by the same total custody and absolute dominion.

So also with *precarious* control. Control may be teetering on the brink of loss, but until it falls it invariably possesses complete custody.

Influence versus Custody

Conceivably only a difference of degree exists between influence and custody, although in their purest forms they are antipodal extremes. General Motors as a sole consumer undoubtedly will exercise more or less hidden pressures on a parts supplier. These pressures, although highly influential cumulatively, do not constitute custody.

As these pressures, however, approach and pass a certain point, mere influence ceases and custody begins. Differences in degree become a change in kind. General Motors moves from minor suggestions to isolated policy dictation to the final assumption of complete custody—through a voluntary or possibly forced appropriation—expressed in the nomination and dictation of the board of directors.

The Power Bases of the Custody

Subjacent to the actual custodial tenure of the corporation lie various bases or sources of the power necessary and able to hold such dominion. The nature, location and function of these power bases have been left unclear by courts and commentators. Here again, canonized terminology and uniform definition are necessary.

What makes dominion possible? How can such tenure be effected? Whence the capability? The power of custody can be founded on five bases:

(1) Total Ownership

To ascribe the contrôleur's position of dominion to a power base of 100-percent ownership involves an inherent contradiction, at least if the common meaning of the term is employed. Ordinarily an *ownership base* signifies that the incumbent contrôleur qua contrôleur founds his control position on at least a 50-percent block of his own personal stock held by him in his individual noncontrôleur capacity. Obviously, therefore, if the incumbent contrôleur's personal ownership reached 100 percent he would cease by that very fact to be a contrôleur and would become a technical owner. A contrôleur may have custody only over another's asset. Thus a contrôleur who, as a natural person, owned 99 percent of the appropriated corporation would found his custodial tenure (of the remaining unowned one percent) on his 99-percent-ownership power base. Thus, strictly, the closest that a power base can come to *total ownership* is perforce something short of total.

One might loosely and incorrectly ascribe a contrôleur's power base to a total ownership in the totally different situation where a 100-percent owner had actually appropriated (for reasons of old age, ill health, ennui, the press of affairs) his wholly owned corporation into the absolute custody of a nonowning contrôleur. But this use of the phrase 'total-ownership power base' is uncommon and, hence, confusing.

(2) Fifty-plus-Percent Ownership

A substantial majority (although less each year) of all modern corporations are held in tenure founded on a power base of actual personal ownership by the contrôleur of more than half of the voting stock. Thus prior to the appointment in 1964 of Mr. Thomas W. Florsheim to the office of contrôleur of the Weyenberg Shoe Mfg. Company, the then contrôleur, old Mr. Weyenberg himself, founded his custody on the 51-percent ownership by himself and his family.[82]

In early 1965 the Attorney General of the United States operating through the Office of Alien Property entrusted the $400-million General Aniline and Film Corporation (later GAF Corporation) into the custody of a group of prominent public servants (Clark Clifford, John A. Coleman, Oveta Culp Hobby, Maurice Lazarus, Lew Wasserman) who thenceforward became a self-perpetuating custodial oligarchy.[83] In the days before this appropriation, the Federal government had based its power position—and hence its capacity to effect the appropriation—on 93.3-percent ownership of the outstanding common of General Aniline.

(3) Working Base

When share ownership slips below fifty percent, the custody is founded on a power base altogether different from majority or 'complete' ownership. The wide dispersal of shares and the sheepishness of the small shareholder buttressed by a more or less large block of stock constitute the power position. This was true, for example, in *Essex Universal* (Herbert J. Yates, the contrôleur, personally held a stock block of 28.3 percent of Republic Pictures Corporation), in *Insuranshares* (the management group owned 26 percent) and in *Republic* (William Zeckendorf, Sr., transferred a 9.7-percent block to the Muscat interests).

(4) Mere Incumbency

With the removal of the central core of stock, the power base may consist completely in widely held shares plus unorganized shareholders. The classic example, of course, of the most secure mere-incumbency power base was the pre-split-up American Telephone and Telegraph. The court-enforced sale in 1961 of General Motors stock by the du Ponts moved General Motors from a working-base to a mere-incumbency category.[84] The mere-incumbency base may become *tenuous* when relatively large blocks of stock threaten the incumbent contrôleur. Thus the Pure Oil contrôleur before the takeover by Union Oil (later Unocal) traced his power to mere incumbency, but faced formidable strength in two or three sizable blocks of dissidents, susceptible to ready collaboration.[85]

(5) Blackmail, Duress

The dominion of the corporation may be achieved by means totally unrelated either to stock ownership or the modern proxy-solicitation mechanics, "for example, by bribe or duress" as Judge Clark put it in *Essex Universal*.[86] These extracorporate methods, however, may provide a source of power as fully effective as stock ownership or the dispersal of shares.

The Legitimacy of the Power Bases

When consideration is directed toward the liceity or illiceity of the various power sources—ranging from 99-plus-percent ownership to blackmail—the question is twofold: (1) Where is custody as a matter of fact? (2) As a matter of right? The use of these uniform terms properly sets the stage for the approach to the legitimacy question: Who has the right to custody? The legitimacy of the contrôleur's tenure lies beneath and outside the investigation of the duties and rights consequent on that tenure, and hence is a vast study for elsewhere.

The Geneses of the Custody

It would be otiose to distinguish the geneses of the custody from its power bases. The various geneses of corporate control are really only corollaries defined by their corresponding power bases. The base is the important thing. The genesis is the inexorable consequence of the capability founded on the base.

Put another way, the genesis of the custody is the active resultant of the exercise of the capacity to entrust custody. The various types of power bases effect corresponding geneses of custody.

II. The Properties of the Relation

> A corporate body can only act by agents, and it is of course the duty of those agents so to act as best to promote the interests of the corporation whose affairs they are conducting. Such agents have duties to discharge of a fiduciary nature towards their principal.
>
> —*Aberdeen Ry. v. Blaikie Bros.*, 149 Rev. Rep. 32, 39 (H.L. 1854).

English literature has long employed the metaphor and the simile, has used the part for the whole, the quality for the substance. In the language of corporate control such literary license is tolerable only out of abject necessity, a rarity, and with the exact understanding that the part does stand for the whole, or the property for the essence.

The splitting of a conceptual hair is not captious in constructing a scientific lexicon. The relation of corporate control has many parts:

Subject, object, essence, properties. Without each, the whole is incomplete. In corporate-control discourse, therefore, synecdoche only confuses, particularly, as here, when one or other property is used for the whole relation or for its essence. These usages, however, do provide some intriguing insights into the psychology of man.

The properties of the relation are two:

(1) The Fiduciary Duty of Control

The totality of all duties incumbent on the office of the contrôleur is the chief necessary property of the relation. So intimately connected with the custody, so patently consequent on the dominion, is this fiduciary duty that here if anywhere one would expect a definition by part for whole. Yet rarely does this obligatory element—which is a commentary on human nature—become the definition of control. When has one heard corporate control defined as the responsibility of the office of the contrôleur? If one were determined on corporate-control metaphor, the logical beginning would be just such a definition: The obligation to administer for the maximum benefit of the beneficiaries, the shareholders.

But as integral as it is, fiduciary duty alone is not corporate control. Nor is it the custody whence it arises. True, custody is the heart of the relation. But the mere holding, without more, says nothing of the responsibility. The next inexorable step in the reasoning, however, leads immediately to the duties. These consequent obligations, although not intrinsic to the essence, are inseparable from it. Really distinct, but inevitably present. Outside the essence but inside the relation of corporate control.

This parallels the marriage relation. The multitude of duties is not the essence of matrimony. The mutual entrustment, perpetual and exclusive, of spouse to spouse is the essence of the relation. Yet the responsibilities are the unavoidable result of the union, are intrinsic to the relation, extrinsic to its essence.

As a parallel, however, marriage is deficient, since not one but two reciprocal relations are present. The union is one of *inter*dependence. The relation of corporate control on the contrary is exclusively one of dependence of the entity on the office.

(2) *The Authority of Control*

The nature of the custodial properties is more clearly discernible in the authority of corporate control. Human nature's proclivity to freedom, and repugnance for responsibility, show themselves vividly in defining corporate control as exclusively a bundle of rights. From the aspect of corporate counsel advising contrôleur clients, this emphasis on powers and rights is understandable. If ever part should stand for whole, better rights than duties. Thus, the dearth of definitions defining control as a fiduciary duty is paralleled by a plethora emphasizing authority. The most common word is 'power.' The *Feldmann* Court referred to corporate control as "a power held in trust for the corporation by Feldmann . . . . This power was the ability to control the allocation of the corporate product . . . ."[87] So too did Judge Nordbye in *Green Giant:*

> No Class A shareholder could be expected to forego the power of control of a company of this size without receiving in return a consideration commensurate with the value of the control which he foregoes.
>
> —*Honigman v. Green Giant Co.,* 208 F. Supp. 754, 758 (D. Minn. 1961).

And again: "It was the power of control which was lodged in these few shares which created their value . . . ."[88] Berle too speaks metaphorically in using the word 'function':

> Control is a function of the corporate mechanism as it presently exists in American law. It consists of the power to choose directors . . . .
>
> —Berle, *"Control" in Corporate Law,* 58 COLUM. L. REV. 1212, 1224 (1958).

Again, Berle's 'function' is a synonym for rights and authority, is strictly a property of control, not corporate control itself.

Powers, functions, capacities, rights, all are descriptive of the authority of corporate control. This second of the major intrinsic properties of control is the necessary correlative of the first. The complexus of duties consequent on custody immediately engenders a complexus of rights toward fulfillment of the duties. Both rights and duties inhere in, are appurtenant to, the office of the contrôleur.

Do not be misled. The authority of corporate control is very much a part of the whole relation, but still only a part. The total relation is constituted by: (1) The subject, the office of the contrôleur. (2) The object, the corporation and all its assets. (3) The essence, the custody or holding. (4) The properties resultant on custody, the fiduciary duty and the authority of the office of the contrôleur. Again, the parallel with matrimony confirms that rights are not the whole of the matter.

This second corporate-control property, as a distinguishable but necessary concomitant, was impressively isolated from corporate control itself by the Federal court in *Insuranshares:*

> With the control, as that term is here used, went plenary power . . . to sell, exchange or transfer all of the securities in the corporation's portfolio . . . .
>
> —*Insuranshares Corp. v. Northern Fiscal Corp.,* 35 F. Supp. 22, 24 (E.D. Pa. 1940).

III. The Office of the Contrôleur

> Therefore committee-men are most properly agents to those who employ them in this trust, and who empower them to direct and superintend the affairs of the corporation.
>
> —*Charitable Corp. v. Sutton,* 26 Eng. Rep. 642, 644 (Ch. 1742).

Around the office of the contrôleur the major corporate-control considerations revolve. To the office the custody of the corporation has been entrusted. In the office the relation inheres. Upon the office the fiduciary duties rest. To the office all the rights belong. From the office, therefore, all corporate-control activities arise.

The subtler nuances of the office can be discerned in various incidents pertinent to its use: Existence and operation.

(1) Intracorporate Existence

The exact location of the office has been insufficiently explored. As yet it exists at law outside the group of formal offices within the corporation. This is unfortunate, and incorrect. The office of the contrôleur rightfully belongs inside the legal entity. In the present state of the law, moreover, the office of the contrôleur is not even classified with the extracorporate parties, creditors, labor, consumer, government. It has been left by the law in a never-never land, somewhere it is true, but the courts have never specified exactly where. As topmost in the corporate hierarchy and the residuary of complete dominion, it is in fact aligned with, and above, the directorate, the chairmanship, the presidency. All four offices are very much integral to the entity.

(2) *Separate Existence*

Equally important, the office is necessarily distinct not only from the corporation itself but from the directorate, the chair, the presidency. Each has its own relation to the entity, with its duties and rights, its defined sphere of activity. Delegation and subdelegation ranging down from the office of the contrôleur through well-defined grades is essential to orderly administration. The failure to mark the boundaries of each has led to confusion and injustice.

(3) *Stable Existence*

One might mistakenly think that the office of the contrôleur moves about, skipping from place to place in the corporate venture. To the contrary, the office itself never changes, is stable and permanent, an immovable and necessary force in the corporate mechanism. Any apparent instability is explained by the succession of officeholders. The human occupants may change monthly, move in, resign or die out, but the office itself stands unaffected. At Lionel, the Muscat syndicate may succeed Roy Cohn, and A. N. Sonnabend follow Muscat—all within eight months in the early sixties—but the office of the contrôleur never left Lionel. It remained untouched throughout the cataclysm.

(4) *Necessary Existence*

Just as the corporation needs control, so control needs a central residency for its activities, an office as a base of operations. The office has a necessary existence by definition. Without the office the control hypothesis would fall.

(5) *The Operation of the Office*

All control activity flows from the two properties, the fiduciary duty and the authority. Both inhere in the office of the contrôleur. The performance of these fiduciary duties and the exercise of the corresponding rights are the official functions of the relation. The custodial appropriation of the entity by the shareholders is principally dynamic, toward effective administration *ad bonum commune* of the corporation. The office of the contrôleur, as the center of this administration, becomes the focal point of all corporate-control activity.

IV. The Contrôleur

> The authorities are agreed that the officers and directors of a company are trustees . . . in the transaction of the business and care of property of the corporation . . . .
>
> —*Dawson v. National Life Ins. Co.,* 157 N.W. 929, 931 (Iowa 1916).

The greatest need for definition surrounds the contrôleur. In preliminary response to this need is the technical term, 'contrôleur.' Nowhere in the control argot was the lack more disconcerting. The "controlling shareholders"[89] (of Judge Lumbard in the Second Circuit *Essex Universal* in 1962) so commonly used is unrealistically circumscribed. Many another may be the contrôleur. To call the contrôleur 'control' or 'corporate control' is both inexact and confusing. The 'holder of control'[90] is an unnecessary circumlocution, as is Berle's cumbersome "the control-holder."[91] Several Latin terms would be more distinctive, but also more obscure. So too with law French in the 'cestui' manner. 'Contrôleur,' however, is redolent of English parallels, yet surely differentiates 'comptroller' and 'controller.' 'Contrôleur' is submitted, therefore, as most apt.

The Contrôleur: A Natural Person

A basic and eminently helpful fact pervades the entire definition of 'contrôleur.' The contrôleur as officeholder is inevitably and ultimately a natural person. As an office, corporate control must ultimately be occupied by a living human being who can assume responsibility and exercise rights.

When on first blush, therefore, a second corporation seems to be the contrôleur of the object corporation, the search for the contrôleur—that ultimate natural person—is merely extended into the second corporation whose contrôleur necessarily becomes the contrôleur of the first corporation as well. Thus, during the early sixties when the control of the Chrysler Corporation apparently had lodged in the consortium of Prudential Life and Consolidation Coal, Chrysler's contrôleur had to be found in a liaison between contrôleurs of those corporations. When Mr. George Hutchinson Love emerged from Pittsburgh to become Chief Policy Officer of Chrysler (as *Fortune* put it, "Coal Man at Chrysler"[92]) he could have been either the agent of this liaison or the true contrôleur resultant on an appropriation of Chrysler into his custody.

(An interesting obiter: The very corporate title attributed to Mr. Love is aptly expressive of his role. Chief Policy Officer is a highly felicitous choice for the exact description of the occupant of the office of the contrôleur. Apparently Mr. Love held no other office beyond contrôleur and performed no functions other than those peculiarly reserved to the contrôleur. Query if ever a contrôleur has been so appropriately named and, as a practical instance, been so isolated from the position of a controlling shareholder, the chairman, a director, none of which Mr. Love held.)

A further caution is in order. The individual human person is not the contrôleur in any sense of the word *before* he assumes the office, the prospective contrôleur, or *after* he departs it, the former contrôleur. More subtly, and hence more important, the same human person is equally noncontrôleur *during* actual tenure when and if acting in his personal capacity. Toward maintaining this distinction, 'contrôleur' should be adamantly restricted to that natural person only when acting officially, during tenure. Contrariwise 'prospective contrôleur,' 'former contrôleur,' and 'natural person qua natural person' may be employed apropos. Further, 'contrôleur qua contrôleur' should be used advertently to set off purely personal activity. Patently the philosophical implications of the distinction are far reaching.

The chief implication concerns the various roles the natural person qua natural person might play during his contrôleur incumbency. C. Russell Feldmann, whose conduct was responsible for the prominent control case, acted out just such a multirole drama. Mr. Feldmann was not only the contrôleur and "the dominant stockholder, but also the chairman of the board of directors and the president of the corporation."[93] For one individual to assume the responsibilities of four official positions simultaneously, majority shareholder, chairman, president, contrôleur—a not uncommon phenomenon—raises pressing questions of intracorporate conduct. Such questions will not receive adequate answers without adequate preparatory definitions.

The Contrôleur and the Office

With these distinctions crystallized, the contrôleur can be related to his office.

Begin with the realization that the office has no real existence, only conceptual, apart from the contrôleur. Without the contrôleur the office would cease. He is a sine qua non. Consider, for example, the water and the river. Remove the water and the river is no more.

The river analogy can carry the reasoning further. The contrôleur is a part to the whole. But at any given instant the contrôleur is identified with the office. Thus he is the whole of the whole. Therefore, only *successively* can he be said to be a part to the whole, as one contrôleur succeeds another. Comparably, the water flows in an unending series of successive parts and thereby constitutes the river.

But this is misleading, both as to river and to contrôleur. Strictly, the contrôleur qua contrôleur never succeeds himself but as officeholder always is. So too with the water in the river. River water qua river water is always river water, and never succeeds itself. It is only water qua water that succeeds itself. So too only natural person succeeds natural person.

Thus, only a rational distinction exists between the office and the contrôleur qua contrôleur. Both practically and theoretically they are identified. (This explains the understandable inclination to call both office and officeholder 'corporate control.') On the contrary, a very real distinction exists between the succeeding natural persons who pass in and out of the office. These persons are constantly changing, while the office, and the contrôleur qua contrôleur, remain stable and permanent. Thus, the relation of corporate control never changes, but always inheres in the office, is always a relation of custody. The office never changes, is invariably integral to the entity. The contrôleur qua contrôleur never changes, is invariably identified with the office. The conclusion is inescapable: Only the natural persons change, come and go, are appointed and resign.

An immediate corollary: There must always be a contrôleur, even though he may be difficult to locate. Thus, in the early 1960s no one yet knew who succeeded the du Ponts as the contrôleur of General Motors. Indisputably, however, General Motors not only had the office of contrôleur but a contrôleur as well. The contrôleur qua contrôleur is fully as necessary as the office itself.

Strictly, the contrôleur is neither the subject nor the object nor the essence nor a property of the custodial relation of corporate control. Yet as identified with the office, the contrôleur thereby can be said to be intrinsic to the relation itself. Thus, if the contrôleur is effectively removed, the office is barren, the appropriation ceases, and the corporation returns to the dominion of the owner. *Ex hypothesi,* therefore, the contrôleur is an indispensable party to the relation of corporate control. No contrôleur, no corporate control.

Next, and consequently, consider the role of the contrôleur. With only a conceptual existence, the office cannot act. Hence it is the contrôleur, the human instrument, who performs the functions—fulfills the duties, exercises the rights—of the office. The contrôleur is the personification of the office. Yet the contrôleur is not the office, is rationally distinct from the office. Nonetheless the contrôleur is the human source of all control activity.

Types of Contrôleurs

These subsumptions permit further refinement. An analysis of the internal workings of the officeholder reveals three types, two legitimate, one spurious:

(1) Individual Contrôleur

The contrôleur may be constituted by a single natural person. Thus His Eminence of Krakow, the officer qua officer of a corporation sole, was, in the seventies, the single living human being, Karol Cardinal Wojtyla. Again, in *Green Giant,* "it was Edward B. Cosgrove who controlled."[94] So too in the fascinating transfer of control of Weyenberg Shoe, the Weyenberg family selected an individual contrôleur in the person of Thomas W. Florsheim.[95]

(In elaborating a philosophy of corporate control, difficult concepts are more easily perceived if the fact situations, both hypothetical and real, are limited to cases involving a single individual contrôleur. Unfortunately, however, the actualities of corporate life never seem so to oblige.)

(2) Syndicate Contrôleur

Several individuals may gather together to constitute the contrôleur. Thus, the looting in *Insuranshares* was effected by two such successive contrôleurs:

> [T]he management group transferred the control of the corporation to the Boston group, none of whom had ever had any interest of any kind in it.
>
> —*Insuranshares Corp. v. Northern Fiscal Corp.,* 35 F. Supp. 22, 24 (E.D. Pa. 1940).

In *Feldmann* "[t]he buyers, a syndicate organized as Wilport Company, a Delaware Corporation,"[96] succeeded to the office of contrôleur of the Newport Steel Corporation upon the payment of a handsome premium to the former contrôleur, C. Russell Feldmann. So too, it has been with the Muscat group, the Murchisons, the Van Sweringens.

(3) Corporate Contrôleur

This is a misnomer. A corporation—or other entity—may only be the apparent contrôleur. Among the multitude of instances over the years: Tracinda Investment Corporation as contrôleur of MGM. Tengelmann Warenhandelsgesellschaft of A&P. General Tire of RKO

General. But the true contrôleur stood somewhere behind Tracinda, Tengelmann, General Tire. For example, Kirk Kerkorian, Herr Haub, the O'Neils of Akron.

Within the Contrôleur

Within the narrow consideration of the contrôleur in his official capacity, two major areas are eminent: (1) Distinctions *ad extra*. (2) Intracontrôleur Government. The viewpoint here is that of the contrôleur, not the corporation.

Distinctions *ad extra*

Consequent on the contrôleur's personification of the office, the same basic distinctions pertinent to the office apply to the contrôleur.

The pervasive hypothesis in the philosophy of corporate control is the absolute separation of ownership from custody. Yet nowhere in the corporate-control field is there greater confusion than between contrôleur and owner, or more particularly part owner. By rigid definition, the contrôleur qua contrôleur must be and is completely distinct from the owner. To the extent the contrôleur becomes owner, he ceases to be the contrôleur.

Here a new technical term, founded on the owner/contrôleur separation, facilitates discussion. The owner qua owner has both the right and exercise of dominion. Contrôleur qua contrôleur has only the exercise. Owner qua appropriator, however, has only the right, never the exercise. In control philosophy the owner qua owner, once he has appropriated the corporation into the contrôleur's custody, slips into the background. The appropriator is the principal figure.

In the control lexicon, therefore, 'owner' refers solely to an owner in both the denotative and connotative senses. The 'appropriator' is an owner or part owner who has handed over (willingly or unwillingly) his corporation to the contrôleur. The contrôleur and the appropriator are genuine antitheticals, mutually exclusive in every sense, possessing no common qualities. The contrôleur has only exercise, no right. The appropriator has no exercise, only right. The owner, on the other hand, possesses both right and exercise. Henceforward the owner qua owner is virtually outside the discussion. Note well: An owner who has not appropriated his asset has thereby forestalled the genesis of the relation of corporate control.

He obviously then cannot be the direct subject of discussion involving corporate control.

(This does not mean that contrôleur and owner are not mutually exclusive. The dominion of the owner is over his own assets. That of contrôleur, over another's.)

The Appropriator Contrôleur

Consider the implications when the same natural person happens to be both appropriator and contrôleur. As contrôleur qua contrôleur he has complete custody of the company. As a nonlegal or natural person he also has some stock in the company. As a nonlegal person he is also an appropriator.

In such a situation, the contrôleur qua contrôleur is strictly custodian only of that portion of the entity which he does not own. Because of the entity theory, however, and because the *entire* entity has been entrusted into the contrôleur's custody, technically he must be considered the contrôleur of his own share as well. This is not exact, however. One may be custodian, and hence contrôleur, only of another's goods. He has scarcely appropriated his own asset into his own custody. He simply never releases dominion, unless the fiction of the entity is rigidly employed (which it is in technical control terminology). In the strictest sense, therefore, Roy M. Cohn, as owner of three percent of the Lionel Corporation, was contrôleur of only 97 percent belonging to public shareholders. In technical control law and parlance, however, Mr. Cohn is correctly called contrôleur of Lionel. A contrôleur, moreover, who as an individual may also own as much as 99 percent of the corporation must be treated at law as the contrôleur, since he is in fact custodian of one percent and since the entity theory precludes any segregation of his own interests. As contrôleur, the fiduciary duty of his position attaches. Since most contrôleurs have some shareholding in the entrusted corporation, the distinctions and definitions surrounding the hypothesis of ownership/control separation should be kept in mind.

The Other Officers

The situation is relatively simple when the shareholder-appropriator is contrôleur and nothing more. But confusion increases when he puts on other hats.

This confusion between contrôleur and appropriator may appear in several possible situations, depending on the types of appropriators involved. The problem is compounded by the divergent philosophies of ownership. One school holds tenaciously to the old-line thesis that the shareholder is the sole owner, that creditors are lenders, management and labor are employees, consumers are buy/sell contractors. A modern analysis, the societal concept, would locate ownership in the amalgam of all parties constituent of the enterprise, from shareholders to government. For present purposes, however, the assumption must be—and correct it is—that the share remains the traditional evidence of corporate ownership.

As illustrative of the necessary distinctions, consider the common case of the single human individual, a natural person, in the three typical situations in which he may find himself. In all cases, his ownership is evidenced of necessity by some stock ownership. Whatever else he happens to be, he is also a shareholder. Else he would not be an appropriator.

Begin with the most complex instance. The human person as a shareholder has appropriated his assets into the corporate custody of the contrôleur, who happens also to be himself. Thus he is shareholder-appropriator-contrôleur. But, further, this same human may also be (1) a consumer, (2) a creditor, (3) a laborer, (4) the government or (5) most important, the CEO. In such a case one must insistently recall that the contrôleur qua contrôleur must be and is really distinct from himself, whatever else he may be, whether as shareholder-appropriator, consumer-shareholder-appropriator or CEO-shareholder-appropriator.

Clearly, then, the contrôleur qua contrôleur is not merely rationally, but actually, distinct from all other officers, even though the same human person happens simultaneously to be contrôleur, appropriator (as shareholder) and, for example, consumer and CEO as well.

In the second type of situation the problems are less. When the CEO-shareholder-appropriator, the director-shareholder-appropriator, the laborer-shareholder-appropriator, the creditor-shareholder-appropriator, the consumer-shareholder-appropriator, the shareholder-appropriator, are not, *as individuals,* also contrôleur, it is not difficult to distinguish these various officers from the contrôleur, even though all are appropriators.

In the third type, when the shareholder-appropriator is neither contrôleur nor the CEO, president, creditor, laborer, consumer, all confusion evanesces.

Intracontrôleur Government

The office of the contrôleur as a legal person may be occupied by three types of natural persons: Individual, syndicate or 'corporate.' Since the 'corporate' is spurious—and reducible to one of the other two—either an individual or syndicate governs the entity. With this limited variety of possible internal makeup, the process by which the contrôleur determines contrôleur governing policy varies accordingly. The individual contrôleur merely thinks through the matter, may obtain counsel, reaches his conclusions and issues his orders. The matter is relatively simple. With a syndicate the procedure may be more involved. Intracontrôleur government, therefore, may assume one of three forms:

(1) Autocratic

An individual contrôleur is willy-nilly an autocrat. His position as sole custodian permits nothing else. If a syndicate is governed within on an autocratic basis, it ceases thereby to be a true syndicate. The syndicate then would be a mere facade. Little imagination envisions the elder Murchison in his day or Mr. Alan P. Kirby or the patriarch Sulzberger of the *Times* dominating the small family group as a virtual dictator of what might appear to be a syndicate contrôleur. If one hypothesized that Consolidation Coal/Prudential Life was the 'corporate-syndicate' contrôleur of Chrysler in the early sixties, a second hypothesis would be justified that George Hutchinson Love was the single contrôleur behind that 'corporate' syndicate. As for Howard Hughes and Toolco, conjectures were unnecessary. No syndicate there. The fear of such single domination pervaded the corporate-syndicate contrôleur (nine oil companies and two individuals) in the 1957 Delaware *Abercrombie* case.

(2) Oligarchic

One of the better known intracontrôleur oligarchies was the late unlamented troika team of Krock, Huffines and Muscat. In whichever corporation—Defiance Industries, Fifth Avenue Coach, B.S.F.—they operated, the three determined intracontrôleur policy by telephone on a strict oligarchical basis. Even in their looting they acted as an oligarchy:

> [D]efendants Muscat and Huffines [were] allegedly "corporate buccaneers" out to loot [the corporation] . . . .
> —*Keers & Co. v. American Steel & Pump Corp.*
> 234 F. Supp. 201, 203 (S.D.N.Y. 1964).

Except for the individual autocratic contrôleur, oligarchic intracontrôleur government is the most common form.

(3) Democratic

The mind can conceive of a contrôleur constituted by such a large group in the syndicate contrôleur that intracontrôleur government ceases to be strictly oligarchic and becomes democratic. The incorporation of a large partnership, for example Merrill Lynch, could involve so many 'partners' as to render the intracontrôleur government democratic. Actual corporate practice, however, suggests that democratic contrôleur government is rare.

The Government of the Corporation

A major distinction must accompany this triple definition of the internal processes of contrôleur government. The contrôleur may make up his mind in an autocratic, oligarchic or democratic manner. But this has absolutely nothing to do with the type of government with which the contrôleur qua contrôleur governs the entrusted corporation. Internal government of self is not to be confused with external government of another.

By hypothesis the contrôleur has received absolute, unfettered, untrammeled dominion over the corporation. In governing the entity, therefore, the contrôleur is perforce an unlimited monarch with dictatorial powers. It is a contradiction of the hypothesis of ownership/control separation to attribute less than autocracy to the contrôleur.

In formulating intracontrôleur policy the process may be autocratic, oligarchic or democratic, but once formulated that ultimate policy becomes a ukase from the czar and is promulgated to the entity as the top-level command of the ultimate policy-making officer of the corporation.

Another distinction. As dictatorial and absolute as the commands of the contrôleur to the corporation may be, they nonetheless must be formally promulgated through the traditional conduits: The annual meeting, the special meeting, board meetings, memoranda, counsel. These conduits carry contrôleur policy to the board, the officers and the lesser agents for year-to-year, month-to-month, day-to-day implementation.

Do not confuse, therefore, (1) intracontrôleur government with (2) government of the corporation by the contrôleur, or with (3) the formal mechanics of meetings and votes necessary for the promulgation of contrôleur policy.

These technical terms form a working lexicon of corporate control. Uniform adherence both to term and definition should speed the construction of the Philosophy of Corporate Control.

Chapter 4

The Fiduciary Duty
of Corporate Control

> In contrast to Berle's approach, Professor
> David Bayne's moralist paradigm places such a high
> duty on the seller of control as to be inappropriate
> in anything but the closely held concern.
>
> —Hazen, *The Sale of Corporate Control,*
> 4 J. CORP. L. 263, 271 (1979).

The Custodial Concept of Corporate Control lays out the broadest duty of the contrôleur: All benefit to the beneficiary. Once the shareholders have appropriated the entity, and consequently all the entity's assets, to the contrôleur—and the contrôleur has accepted the stewardship—the consequent custody automatically triggers into operation the Benefit-to-Beneficiary Rule. If the human mind were unswervingly logical, this treatise could be closed therewith. Rather, however, this broadest of rules must be specified and specified, until the resultant specifics form an easily intelligible corpus of the law governing the contrôleur. The present task, therefore, is to build on to this base. This task will be undertaken in five steps: *I. The Three Areas of Contrôleur Duty. II. The Hierarchy of Corporate Authority. III. The Sale and the Transfer of Control. IV. The Selection of the Successor Contrôleur. V. The Remuneration of the Contrôleur.*

I. The Three Areas of Contrôleur Duty

> The very selection for service is an expression of confidence and the employment the bestowal of power. The shareholder selects the director to serve him in caring for the corporate property. . . . Is he not thereby expressing his confidence? . . . He trusts all with the managing officers, and naturally relies on them in all matters touching his interest in its business and property.
>
> —*Dawson v. National Life Ins. Co.*, 157 N.W. 929, 933 (Iowa 1916).

The overarching objective of the corporate entity is its own common good, which is generally to make profits. This primary goal is merely the corporate expression of the Benefit-to-Beneficiary Rule: The welfare of the entity and ultimately of all the members, the shareholders. The immediate purpose of the office of control, therefore, is to create and maintain the best corporation possible, and thereby benefit all equally. As the officer upon whom the ultimate responsibility for the achievement of this objective devolves, the contrôleur must formulate and establish the overall program of corporate policy and supervise its implementation at the highest level. The extent to which the contrôleur enters into the detail of policy formulation and supervision varies between the extremes of a well-established, smoothly coordinated control pattern and a troubled corporation in need of rehabilitation and major policy overhaul. The exact nature of corporate control shows itself most impressively in the three major divisions of this policy formation.

Logically, the contrôleur's first responsibility is that of providing *the best possible corporate structure.* Prior to incorporation, the contrôleur must reconcile the total common good with his obligations to the constituent members. As the years pass, the contrôleur must continually review the structure to adjust to changing times.

The contrôleur's next responsibility is to establish *an enlightened managerial policy.* If the corporation is a Saks Fifth Avenue, is it to hew invariably to a luxury line? If on the other hand it is a J. C. Penney, must it remain unswervingly in the low-price market or is there room in corporate policy to move into the 'Fifth Avenue' field? In general, the contrôleur must make top-level policy decisions

including what the corporate image should be and when to econo-
mize, expand or retrench.

The contrôleur's final responsibility is to select *competent personnel* for both present and future, personnel especially adapted to
the particular type of activity of the firm.

This triple contrôleur burden is elemental, but does aid the
mind in its view of the contrôleur's broadest fiduciary duty.

(1) *The Corporate Structure*

As abhorrent as it is to the doctrines of the Philosophy of Corporate Control, the 1961 *Green Giant* serves well to illustrate this first
of the contrôleur's broad obligations.

The principal justification advanced by the Court in *Green Giant*
for giving the Cosgroves $2 million was the bestowal of voting rights.
Without voting stock, listing on a major exchange was blocked, mar-
ketability hampered and expansion opportunities, equity financing
and diversification by merger and acquisition were made more difficult. Top-notch talent, moreover, shied away from such close control.
There was a genuine fear among top management that the death of
E. B. Cosgrove would find the control falling into undesirable hands.
This fear was expressed by the insiders as a desire to "promote management continuity."[97] All these disabilities would be removed by the
reorganization of the corporate structure, whose chief feature was
the transfer of voting rights from contrôleur Cosgrove to the
holders of 99 percent of the corporate equity. For the purposes of
a deeper investigation of the nature and duties of corporate control
it must be assumed, contrary to the facts, that the Cosgroves actually
relinquished control. This, of course, was the assumption on which
the two courts stood.

> The argument that the family, relatives and friends
> of Edward B. Cosgrove will continue in control of the
> company is without any foundation in fact.
> —*Honigman v. Green Giant Co.*, 208 F. Supp.
> 754, 765 (D. Minn. 1961).

The Honigmans argued that control remained where it always was,
merely slipping slightly from the absolute security of absolute control to the practical security of working control. The events had it

that the Cosgroves would continue in control of the company well into the seventies.

The Cosgroves, occupying the office of control, had determined to pay themselves $2 million for an improvement in the structure which good business judgment indicated was necessary or advisable for corporate and shareholder well-being. At this point the Court was faced with a dilemma. Either the Cosgroves as contrôleur were paying the Cosgroves as shareholders-directors $2 million for the performance of an official act of control, or the Cosgroves were receiving $2 million for the sale of control without any consideration beyond the control itself.

The District Court was not prepared to admit that unadorned control was being sold by the Cosgroves for $2 million:

> After due consideration, the Court is satisfied that a fair analysis of all the circumstances justifies a finding that . . . the premium shares . . . [are] commensurate with the benefit received by the corporation . . . .
>
> —*Honigman v. Green Giant Co.*, 208 F. Supp. 754, 762 (D. Minn. 1961).

The opinion makes it clear that the improvement of the corporate structure was this "benefit received by the corporation."

The Court's dilemma is highlighted by the fact that it was the business judgment and official act of the Cosgroves which erected the deficient corporate structure in 1923. Not that this really made any difference in 1960.

There is an interesting sidelight in Mr. Cosgrove's testimony as to the principal reason for his continued failure to correct the corporate structure. He had denied voting rights to the Class B only as a temporary expedient.

> I can tell you that my attitude through the whole thing was to keep control until we were well on our way; we did not want to be raided. . . . I wanted to see good management in charge before I let go. . . . Mr. Felton so emerged and I made him president. Prior to the time Mr. Felton took over as president I had not been prepared to give voting

rights to the Class B stock; I had been thinking of it but I wasn't ready to do it.

> —Record on Appeal at 54-55, *Honigman v. Green Giant Co.*, 309 F.2d 667 (8th Cir. 1962).

Whether the contrôleur Cosgrove created the condition in the beginning or not, the contrôleur nonetheless was duty bound to utilize all the rights of his office to correct any structural inadequacies. More specifically, these rights (and consequent duties) were patent: The study of the defective structure, the utilization of the opinion of the board, the advice of investment counsel, the formulation of the recapitalization plan, the submission of the plan to the shareholders for approval, and final implementation. The right of the contrôleur to use these rights and facilities of his office was essential to the performance of his fiduciary duty. This raises the question of whether the contrôleur should be paid $2 million for doing his duty. The expert witness for Honigman, Robert W. Storer, chairman of the investment committee of The Manufacturers National Bank of Detroit phrased this thought aptly:

> In the first place, the progressive divorce between the equity interest and the voting control has arisen over the years since 1923 out of the consistent policy of causing all new common shares to be class B shares. If, as a result of this policy, the corporation is disadvantaged by the present capital structure this has arisen on the initiative and on the consistent policy of the class A stockholders. These, through their control of the membership of the Board of directors, have worked themselves gradually into a position which, to my mind, is tantamount to voting trustees with fiduciary responsibilities to their fellow stockholders. Under these conditions I believe that any action, any affirmative action which can be taken by the class A stockholders, acting through their board to benefit the corporation, which does not result in out-of-pocket cost to them, is affirmative action which they are due to take and should take vis-a-vis the class B stockholders who are essentially the equity and the corporation here.
>
> —Record on Appeal at 280-81, *Honigman v. Green Giant Co.*, 309 F.2d 667 (8th Cir. 1962).

If corporate control is a personal asset, the Cosgroves could conceivably be justified in placing that valuation on it and pocketing the proceeds. If corporate control is a relation inhering in the office of the contrôleur, however, the proceeds belong to all the beneficiary shareholders ratably rather than solely to the shareholders in control.

The Reynoldses

The shift from absolute to working control cost the public investor $2 million in *Green Giant*. In the 1960 Delaware *Manacher v. Reynolds,* exactly the same gambit, used with a far larger firm, was worth $40 million.

> What is arguably an abdication of its supervisory role in the settlement perhaps flows from the court's prior conclusion that the right to any premium rested on the family's power to demand it . . . .
>
> —Comment, 109 U. PA. L. REV. 887, 891 (1961).

The United States Foil Company had, as Green Giant, two classes of stock, identical in every way except voting rights. The Reynolds family held all the 540,000 *voting* Class A. The general public were blessed with a tidy 8.5-million *nonvoting* Class B. Foil was actually a holding company for 50.09 percent of the stock of Reynolds Metals Company. By using these millions of public-shareholder dollars the Reynolds family was in turn able to control Reynolds Metals, the second largest integrated producer of aluminum in the country.

This was an expensive business for the public shareholders of Foil. There were operating expenses for the holding company, and extra taxation on the double dividend declarations first by Metals to Foil and then by Foil to the shareholder. These factors, plus the absence of the vote, were reflected in the value of Foil stock on the Amex. For many years Foil nonvoting Class B had sold at a full one third less than the value of the equity interest which it represented in Reynolds Metals. This so-called 'discount factor' amounted to approximately $140 million.

Understandably the public shareholders of Foil for years had been agitating for the liquidation of the company. If Foil were liquidated, the extra operating expenses, the extra taxes and the $140-million discount would be eliminated. In spite of these years of pleading, the Reynolds family refused to discontinue the use of the public money. When litigation was finally initiated by public-shareholder Manacher, the Reynolds group came forward with a plan which differed only in details from that of *Green Giant*. The Reynolds family wanted three shares of new stock for each of their voting shares, a $40-million premium. Under the Reynolds settlement the family would own 17.4 percent of the new common, which constituted operating control. Without the premium shares, they would receive 14.2 percent of the new Metals common.

Here again was the *Green Giant* problem. Was the corporate structure of Foil the best for the entity and its members, or did it serve only one party who happened also to be in control? Did the contrôleur exercise the prerogatives and rights of his office in the performance of his fiduciary duty to the entity and to all its members? Did he have the right to use these corporate assets for his own personal benefit?

The Court stated the problem exactly:

> The issue is whether the A may fairly agree with the B to take appropriate action to remove the discount in return for a premium amounting to one-third of the discount. . . . This being so, the A shareholders hold the key with which to unlock the "discount" treasure chest for the B. No other factor being present, they may demand a reasonable premium for the use of their key.
>
> —*Manacher v. Reynolds,* 165 A.2d 741, 750, 754 (Del. Ch. 1960).

The key was the vote of the Reynolds board of Foil toward liquidation of Foil and thus the improvement of the corporate structure. This vote was a corporate means to an obligatory end, a right entrusted to the contrôleur to enable him to perform his duties. The use of this key should have been a routine operation, the performance of a fundamental fiduciary duty of corporate control, and the *Reynolds* Court realized this:

[T]he hard fact of life is that the proposed action by the
A [the alteration of the corporate structure] is an indispen-
sable prerequisite to the realization of any benefit by the
B from the elimination of the discount.

—*Manacher v. Reynolds,* 165 A.2d 741, 750
(Del. Ch. 1960).

Mr. Manacher contended that the contrôleur Reynoldses violated
their fiduciary duty, that the violation "consisted of their exacting the
3 for 1 premium as their price for letting 'their' board act on a
merger . . . ."[98] The Court, however, approved the settlement and
was "hesitant to say that the settlement was so unfair that it should
be rejected."[99]

One conclusion emerges from *Green Giant* and *Reynolds.* The
office of corporate control in each case was faced with the responsibility of providing the best possible corporate structure for the entity
and its constituent members. At the disposal of the contrôleur was
the entire corporate apparatus with which to fulfill this responsibility. The utilization of these assets was no more than the performance
of the fiduciary duty of corporate control.

(2) Managerial Policy

The corporate assets at the contrôleur's disposal for the performance of managerial duties range from the picayune perquisites
of the office—yachts, clubs, secretaries, chauffeurs—to the determination of important policies of purchase and sale, of initiation of litigation and declaration of dividends. Entrusted with a profusion of
rights and prerogatives, the temptation is intense to regard these corporate means to the corporate end as private powers. Although they
clearly belong to the corporation in the beginning, they somehow
along the way become mysteriously transformed into personal privileges and chattels belonging to the transient human occupying the
office of control.

The corporate contrôleur has a daily array of lesser corporate
assets placed at his disposal in the performance of his duties. Some
of these, of course, are included contractually, directly or indirectly,
as acknowledged elements of his just compensation. With the remainder and greater majority, however, the contrôleur faces a double
difficulty. First, they may not even be appurtenances of the office of
control at all, but rather set aside for the use of other offices within

the corporate entity. Secondly, if they are properly at his disposal, the contrôleur must remember that they are nonetheless not a personal possession. He may not appropriate them altogether, divert them to purely personal use or preempt assets unnecessary in quantity or quality.

It is a relatively simple matter for the contrôleur to commandeer the plant maintenance crew and have them build a new sun porch to his home or a sprinkling system in his garden. There are many more subtle areas, such as credit cards, business vacations, town clubs, country clubs, hunting lodges. Unless these privileges are acknowledged forms of compensation, their use should be categorized as a direct appropriation of corporate assets. Or a saddling of the corporate budget with expenses unwarranted by the objectives of the entity. The excess may be either one of quantity or quality. The principle of finality draws a definite line as to both. The means must conform to the end.

The *Feldmann* litigation highlighted a far more serious preemption of corporate assets in the managerial-policy field. The Plaintiff described the premium of $2.1 million over the intrinsic value of Mr. Feldmann's shares as "compensation for the sale of a corporate asset, a power held in trust for the corporation by Feldmann as its fiduciary."[100] The Second Circuit concluded that . . .

> . . . in a time of market shortage, where a call on a corporation's product commands an unusually large premium, in one form or another, we think it sound law that a fiduciary may not appropriate to himself the value of this premium.
>
> —*Perlman v. Feldmann*, 219 F.2d 173, 178 (2d Cir. 1955).

The Court could scarcely have expressed the fundamental philosophy more aptly. Here was a corporate means, the managerial policy of product distribution to customers, to the attainment of the overall corporate end, the prosperity of entity and members.

Viewed from this particular aspect, the parallel with *Green Giant* is noteworthy. The Cosgroves had a duty to provide Green Giant with the best possible corporate structure. Feldmann had a duty to pursue the most enlightened management policy for the benefit of Newport.

Perhaps it would be more accurate to regard *Feldmann* from a different viewpoint. One could concentrate on the benefits, the interest-free prepayments, inuring to the corporation instead of the policy which produced the benefits. Thus, the $2.1 million paid Mr. Feldmann could be viewed as a present accumulation of future interest-free prepayments which would otherwise have later benefited corporation and shareholders. From either aspect, however, both the gain from the policy and the policy itself properly inured to the entity, not to Feldmann personally. Therefore, he could hardly sell them. The Court properly held Feldmann to a fiduciary duty to formulate managerial policy for the sole benefit of the corporation:

> [T]he responsibility of the fiduciary is not limited to a proper regard for the tangible balance sheet assets of the corporation, but includes the dedication of *his uncorrupted business judgment* for the sole benefit of the corporation, in any dealings which may adversely affect it. . . . Although [this] . . . is particularly relevant to Feldmann as a director, the same rule should apply to his fiduciary duties as majority stockholder, for in that capacity he chooses and controls the directors, and thus is held to have assumed their liability.
>
> —*Perlman v. Feldmann,* 219 F.2d 173, 176 (2d Cir. 1955) (emphasis added).

The Glore, Forgan Report (Glore, Forgan & Co. has long since been absorbed into successively larger brokerage houses) which outlined the *Green Giant* Plan of Recapitalization also contained a revealing list of so-called 'Advantages of Control.'[101] The list presents an excellent example of the possibilities for personal appropriation of corporate assets in the field of managerial policy. An introductory paragraph restates the popular misconception that these prerogatives of control belong personally to the individual, not the office.

> In considering the advantages of control to Class A stockholders we are not *primarily* concerned with advantages from the possible illegal actions. However, there are many possible actions which might be adverse to the Class B stockholders but are either legal or *on the borderline.* Specific areas of such action are as follows.
>
> —Glore, Forgan Report, Record on Appeal at 338, *Honigman v. Green Giant Co.,* 309 F.2d 667 (8th Cir. 1962) (emphasis added).

The answer filed by the Defendants in the notable Pennsylvania case, the 1914 *Porter v. Healy,* expresses this attitude:

> "The price fixed for the stock itself was $165 per share, * * * and the additional compensation that we were to receive for parting with our control was an entirely private business matter. * * * In the sale of our stock, and in all that we did in connection therewith, we acted solely as individual owners, * * * and never did any act in connection therewith as directors."
>
> —*Porter v. Healy,* 91 A. 428, 431 (Pa. 1914)
> (quoting Defendants).

The Court, however, held that "all money thus made belongs either to the corporation, or, in a case like the present, in common to its shareholders."[102]

Among the "specific areas of such action," the Report lists one which is peculiarly related to the *Feldmann*-type subversion of managerial policy:

> Entering into contracts with suppliers or agents owned by the Class A stockholders could be advantageous. However, opportunities to do this are probably limited and the advantages small. Contracts not made on an arms-length bargaining basis would certainly be open to attack.
>
> —Glore, Forgan Report, Record on Appeal at
> 339, *Honigman v. Green Giant Co.,* 309 F. 2d
> 667 (8th Cir. 1962).

An analysis of the implications of these "Advantages to Class A Stockholders of Control" is intriguing. Three distinct conclusions stand out:

(1) Any inferences of reprehensible past conduct are certainly a temptation, but must, however, remain only that. L. E. Felton, president of Green Giant, testified on cross-examination that "the Class A stockholders did not enter into any adverse contracts with the company."[103]

(2) One could not conclude, without cynicism, that the Green Giant contrôleur would indulge in the future in these suggested practices.

(3) What Glore, Forgan, and hence the Green Giant contrôleur, did have in mind, however, was that a purchaser might indulge in

these possible practices, might pay for the opportunity to avail itself of these advantages, and that the Green Giant contrôleur therefore deserved $2 million because he held the key to unlock these treasures to such a purchaser.

Reference was made passim by various officers of Green Giant that the Report's opportunities for adverse contracts could occur, for example, in the purchase of tin cans, labels and unprocessed vegetables. Numerous other instances can be cited of advantages which are redolent of the Glore, Forgan Report and the *Feldmann* allocation of sales. In the classic Massachusetts case of *Sher v. Sandler* in 1950, one partner bought out the other and thereby guaranteed to himself the undisclosed advantages of a marked increase in corporate business. The Court ordered restitution. In another possibility, the contrôleur might traffic in customer lists, or, as the *Feldman* Court suggests, in the sale of "corporate good will"[104] or latent productive capacity. Yet these are all patently corporate assets.

L. E. Felton, then president of Green Giant, mentioned the use of the corporate trademarks as "one other advantage of the A stock."[105] This would be equally true of such other rights as patents, copyrights and the like. A prolific source of litigation has been the appropriation by the contrôleur of the benefits to an acquiring corporation of a net-operating-loss deduction which may be carried over as a tax credit against future earnings. In *Keely v. Black,* a 1920 New Jersey case, the contrôleur accepted a substantial gratuity for relinquishing territorial rights of a small local telephone company to the Bell System. In the forties in the well-known cases of *Young v. Higbee Co.* and *Clarke v. Greenberg* pending litigation was compromised. All these are examples of the appropriation by the contrôleur of valuable corporate assets in the field of managerial policy.

Porter v. Healy and the companion 1910 Pennsylvania *Commonwealth Title v. Seltzer* are two noteworthy opinions which impose unreservedly on the contrôleur the duty to formulate and implement an enlightened managerial policy. Both opinions, written by the able Justice Moschzisker, describe the duties of directors of corporations, but their analysis is equally applicable to the contrôleur, whoever he may be.

> The principle is well established that those in con-
> trol of the management of a corporation are under an in-

herent obligation not in any manner to use their positions to advance their individual interests as distinguished from the interests they represent . . . .

> —*Porter v. Healy,* 91 A. 428, 431 (Pa. 1914).

In *Porter* the corporate asset involved was a public-utility franchise. The *Porter* Court concluded its opinion with a trenchant analysis of the duties of the contrôleur:

> Although the stock of one who is a director of a corporation is his individual property, to be dealt with as he pleases, and to be sold for such a price as he may be able to get for it, either in association with others or alone, yet, his official position is not his individual property in any sense, and he has no right, either directly or indirectly, to use it for his own selfish ends; when he does so, and thereby derives a gain that can be reasonably traced to such an abuse, all money thus made belongs either to the corporation, or, in a case like the present, in common to its shareholders . . . .
>
> —*Porter v. Healy,* 91 A. 428, 432 (Pa. 1914).

In *Seltzer* the "effort to get control . . . was solely for the purpose of forcing the sale of its property. . . ."[106] The Court held the contrôleurs to "an inherent obligation not to in any manner use their positions to advance their individual interests as distinguished from the interests of their corporation."[107]

> "The director of a corporation is a trustee for the entire body of stockholders, and by assuming the office he undertakes to give his best judgment in the interests of the corporation in all matters in which he acts for it, untrammeled by any hostile interest in himself or others; and all secret profits derived by him in any dealings in regard to the corporate enterprise must be accounted for to the corporation."
>
> —*Commonwealth Title Ins. & Trust Co. v. Seltzer,* 76 A. 77, 79 (Pa. 1910) (quoting Syllabus: *Bird Coal & Iron Co. v. Humes*).

(3) *The Selection of Competent Personnel*

The sixth and last of the "advantages" of the *Green Giant* Glore, Forgan Report evaluates the third category of corporate prerogatives, and duties:

> From a practical standpoint, it would seem that the chief advantage of control is the right to elect the principal officer of the corporation and thereby to obtain the largest salary that could not be attacked in the courts plus other perquisites of the office including such things as stock options, pensions, insurance coverage, et cetera.
>
> —Glore, Forgan Report, Record on Appeal at 340, *Honigman v. Green Giant Co.*, 309 F. 2d 667 (8th Cir. 1962).

An obiter: Could Messrs. Dingman and Hennessy have read the Glore, Forgan Report?

> *$1 Million to Work, $1 Million to Loaf:*
> A golden parachute wasn't good enough for Michael D. Dingman, president of Signal Cos. . . . when Signal and Allied Corp. drew up their merger agreement . . . .
> For starters, Mr. Dingman is guaranteed to become chief executive of Allied Signal after 1990, when Edward L. Hennessy Jr., Allied's chief executive, retires. But that's not even the best part. Over the next five years, Mr. Dingman will get whatever Mr. Hennessy gets—at least a million a year in salary and benefits—whether Mr. Dingman works or loafs.
>
> —*Shop Talk,* Wall St. J., July 18, 1985, at 23, col. 3.

The right of the contrôleur to appoint major officials is undoubtedly one of the chief means of promoting the ends of the corporation. At the turn of the century the New York Court of Appeals in *McClure v. Law* properly characterized the law:

> The election of directors, and the transfer of the management and property of the corporation, were official acts, and whatever money he received from such official acts

were moneys derived by virtue of his office, for which we
think he should account.

> —*McClure v. Law,* 55 N.E. 388, 389 (N.Y.
> 1899).

So also Judge Swan dissenting in *Feldmann:*

> Consequently, if the price paid for Feldmann's stock in-
> cluded a payment for voting to elect the new directors,
> he must account to the corporation for such payment,
> even though he honestly believed that the men he voted
> to elect were well qualified to serve as directors. He can
> not take pay for performing his fiduciary duty.
>
> > —*Perlman v. Feldmann,* 219 F.2d 173, 179
> > (2d Cir. 1955) (Swan, J., dissenting).

(Other advantages suggested by the Report: Obtaining control
to secure a capital gain by liquidating the company, arranging mergers and consolidations advantageous to the contrôleur's outside interests, cutting or eliminating dividends to avoid personal income
taxes, granting stock options.)

What Judge Swan was speaking about was not an ordinary director, who is important indeed, but a director who constituted the
contrôleur, and such a director is the most important member of the
corporate hierarchy because in his hands is the corporate
destiny.

Thus the most crucial contrôleur function is his last, the appointment of his successor. The day-to-day, month-to-month, year-
to-year appointments are important enough, but they can be readily
corrected. But that last appointment of all has an irrevocability about
it. By the very nature of his office, the contrôleur is beholden to no
one, answers to no one and is of indefinite tenure in his position.
The finality and importance of the selection of a successor warrants
greater study appropos.

Whatever may be the particular prerogative or right encom-
passed in the authority of control—whether it concerns corporate

structure, managerial policy or the selection of personnel, present or future—that power is not a personal possession or privilege but an incident of office which remains with the office.

II. The Hierarchy of Corporate Authority

> Relatively little authority has been found by the parties defining the duty to the community of corporate interests in the context of the sale of the control of the corporation to an outsider.
>
> —*Swinney v. Keebler Co.,* 329 F. Supp. 216, 222 (D.S.C. 1971).

By definition and logical necessity all authority is vested in the contrôleur. As the ultimate residuary of corporate power, the contrôleur faces the patent necessity of apportioning this power in a rational pattern of delegation and subdelegation. In establishing and implementing overall corporate policy *ad bonum commune,* the contrôleur cannot do it all himself, whether in striving for the best possible corporate structure, managerial policy or personnel.

But the clear and exact portrayal of this rational pattern of contrôleur delegation and subdelegation is irritatingly hampered by an unavoidable fact of contrôleur life: The office of control refuses to attach itself always and consistently to the same party in the entity. Rather, the contrôleur may at one time be the majority shareholder, another time the board, another an outside third party. Any systematic study of contrôleur delegation, therefore, must adapt to this variety, and can best be analyzed in two steps: *(1) The Corporate Hierarchy: The Pristine Concept,* and *(2) Variations and Aberrations.*

(1) The Corporate Hierarchy: The Pristine Concept

The genius of the modern corporation is an amalgam of centuries of thought, inspired by the exigencies of man's needs. Inevitably these exigencies have produced three classes of human participants in the prototypal model of the corporate form. The position and role of the contrôleur among these three, moreover, have been unvarying from the outset.

The Shareholders

In the Anglo-American corporation as initially constituted, and as theoretically and formally constructed in the statutes to this day, the shareholders are necessarily the contrôleur. In every corporate code in the nation the ultimate power over all the broad policies of the entity—and most important the right to name the board of directors—is lodged in the owners, the body of shareholders. The office of contrôleur, therefore, belongs as a matter of right to the collective shareholders. The contrôleur and the shareholders are identified.

The Directors

The first major delegation by the shareholder-contrôleur is to the board. In the directors rests the full responsibility under the contrôleur. The office of control, therefore, properly delegates responsibility to the directorate, but the contrôleur nonetheless must continually supervise the board's conduct.

As with the father in the home, the contrôleur may never desert final responsibility. The principle was summarized by the *Feldmann* court:

> [T]he same rule should apply to his fiduciary duties as majority stockholder, for in that capacity he chooses and controls the directors, and thus is held to have assumed their liability.
>
> —*Perlman v. Feldmann*, 219 F.2d 173, 176 (2d Cir. 1955).

Thus the contrôleur is responsible for the activities of the least agent of the corporation insofar as these activities are referable to the contrôleur's policy and supervisory responsibility. This duty of continual surveillance, of course, extends as well to corporate structure and managerial policy.

The board of directors has a double objective: To interpret and communicate the philosophy and policy of the shareholder-contrôleur to the officers, and formulate its own broad, albeit second-level, policy, conformable of course to the contrôleur's norms. Both these objectives are carried out in the three main areas of contrôleur policy formation. Thus the board might initiate necessary amendments to bylaws or articles. By resolution of the board, managerial salary policies can be established or changed, general economy programs effected, major litigation approved. Finally, the selection and promotion of top officers is a principal board responsibility.

The Officers

The board of directors in its turn subdelegates a yet narrower orbit of responsibility to the chief executive officer or, in a large concern, to a small group of principal officers. These officers transmit varying degrees of responsibility to others, but the major concentration of control in the hierarchy of corporate authority is in (1) the shareholder-contrôleur, (2) the board and (3) the officers.

On this third echelon, the major objective of the chief officers is the day-to-day implementation of the policy formulated by the contrôleur and interpreted by the board. Except, perhaps, to make recommendations for needed changes, the officers will not be directly concerned with the corporate structure, but rather with managerial policy, the orderly administration of the business, research and development, manufacturing policy, distribution and sales. The chief executive officer selects second-level officers and major department heads. To these, of course, there will be delegation of responsibility on the lowest levels.

The limits and hierarchy of these three spheres are inviolable. If contrôleur, or director or officer, steps over the line he is either out of order, or is rightly assuming a second official position.

This then is the pattern of delegation and subdelegation: From the shareholder-contrôleur to the board to the officers. But this pristine concept of the control hierarchy is rarely verified to the fullest except in the closely held corporation.

(2) *Variations and Aberrations*

The chief variant from the prototypal model is the modern widely held entity. Here the rule is almost invariable: The shareholders by default have ceded to the board the rights and duties of control. An inherent disability in the modern corporate form finds the shareholders widely dispersed, necessarily poorly informed and far too numerous properly to exercise their franchise. This sheepishness is not culpable. Until a major revamping of the current formula bestows an efficacious vote on the shareholders the office of control will inevitably be with the board. This is a wholly legitimate and expectable— albeit regrettable in the eyes of many—result of the current corporate dispensation.

But note, although the rights and duties of the office of control may pass to the board, nevertheless the shareholders have the inalienable right to reassume the office at any time. Why? Because the office of control belongs ultimately to the owners of the appropriated assets, and the shareholders remain the owners. Mere inability to fulfill the burdens of the office does not eradicate the right to the office.

Note further that the board's legitimate accession to control— not to be confused with an illicit usurpation—carries with it full legitimacy in the exercise of all the functions of the office. But this legitimate accession also carries correspondingly the full burden of the duties and obligations of the contrôleur. The board possesses both rights and duties.

The principal focus of this treatise, therefore, has been on the board-contrôleur. This is dictated by present-day corporate reality. However, application of the control philosophy, once elaborated, to the shareholder-contrôleur of the close corporation is ready and simple.

The aberrations from the pristine corporate concept are many. Here, no uniform pattern persists. A nonshareholder, nondirectorate contrôleur may dominate the board through extortion, blackmail, financial or familial subservience, coercion. Human ingenuity can devise many means to subvert the proper hierarchy of corporate authority.

An intriguing illustration of a not uncommon contrôleur was the ill-starred Louis E. Wolfson, who was neither director nor officer nor majority shareholder of the equally ill-starred Continental Enterprises, Inc. Yet Louie Wolfson was indisputably contrôleur:

> Gerbert was a director of Continental. Wolfson was
> not, nor was he an officer, but there is ample evidence that
> nevertheless as the largest individual shareholder he was

Continental's guiding spirit in that the officers of the corporation were subject to his direction and control and that no corporate policy decisions were made without his knowledge and consent.

—*United States v. Wolfson*, 405 F.2d 779, 781 (2d Cir. 1968).

An analysis of any individual aberration must necessarily be ad hoc, but this is not overly difficult since the basic control principles apply with equal vigor to an illegitimate as to a legitimate contrôleur.

A major caution: Those directors who have yielded the field to an illegitimate contrôleur—as pitied as they may well be—are not thereby freed of the obligations of a strict fiduciary. Primary liability may properly lie with the usurper, but the emasculated board remains nonetheless fully culpable and subject to the stringencies of a strict trustee.

III. The Sale and the Transfer of Control

"The process of balancing opposing propositions reaches its apex of delicacy when the central transaction is a sale by the controlling stockholder of his shares."

—*Swinney v. Keebler Co.*, 329 F. Supp. 216, 222 (D.S.C. 1971) (quoting Z. CAVITCH, BUSINESS ORGANIZATIONS).

The transfer of corporate control can be accomplished in several ways. The sale is merely one of them. The orderly, imperceptible transition of control from decade to decade in the established corporations, e.g., General Motors and IBM, is the customary method. A shift of control may take place quietly and without incident at the annual meeting or may occur in a stormy proxy fight, a friendly tender offer or a fraudulent seizure. Control generally passes in the sale of majority stock ownership.

The sale, however, is the transfer of control to a successor in a particular, distinctive manner, namely, for some monetary or other consideration. None of the traditional types pose quite the subtle problems of a transfer by sale.

Yet the transfer of control by sale is not as recondite an operation as would first meet the eye. Strip away the terminology and the apparent complexities, and the transaction lends itself to a gratifyingly thorough understanding.

Begin with the question: What is the object of sale? The office? Scarcely, since the purchaser neither receives nor does the corporation part with the office. What is sold is the occupancy of the office, the tenure of the contrôleur. This leads to an obvious conclusion: The object of sale is the appointment to the office.

The rationale and philosophy of the sale of control, therefore, are reducible to the principles and norms, ultimate and proximate, governing the selection of the officeholder. Ultimately, the legitimacy of the transfer of control rests with the suitability of the appointed successor.

For purposes of terminology, although the 'sale' is a species of the genus 'transfer,' better to ascribe the term 'transfer' exclusively to legitimate successions, and 'sale' to the illicit passing for a premium-bribe.

IV. The Selection of the Successor Contrôleur

> Whoever sells the majority block of stock of a corporation has the duty to it and the shareholders to fully identify the purchaser in order to discover his background and the use to which the control stock is to be put in its management.
>
> —*Estate of Hooper v. Virgin Islands,* 427 F.2d 45, 47 (3d Cir. 1970).

The way is now cleared for the central problem in the transfer by sale. How does the broad responsibility of the office translate itself into the specific obligations surrounding the transfer of control? As a strict custodian, what norms or standards of suitability govern the contrôleur in the selection of his successor pursuant to the duty of his office?

Antecedent to subjection to the test of successor suitability, the incumbent contrôleur faces the legal scrutiny of the legitimacy of the power basis and genesis—as well as the continued tenure—of his own control. Although an illicit contrôleur may have escaped the sanctions at any prior stage, he is nonetheless incumbent, nonetheless a custodian, and faced with the same obligations of the office as his legitimate counterpart. The illegitimacy of his power base, his genesis or his tenure, does not mean by that very fact that his performance of these obligations will be deficient—although it does mean that he himself was rendered unsuitable by the very act of his illegitimate accession—or that, more to the point, his selection of a successor in the transfer of control will thereby be judged a bad one. Or a good one.

The Fiduciary Duty in the Selection

The custody of the corporation assumed by the contrôleur has engendered a complexus of duties, collectively described as the fiduciary duty of control, which coalesce in one overall obligation: The *bonum commune* of the corporation and benefit to beneficiary, the shareholders. The contrôleur has undertaken to guard, guide, nurture as his own, this asset entrusted to him, or illicitly assumed by him. He must strive to produce the best possible corporation, specified into three main areas.

Integral to the third division of the contrôleur's fiduciary duty is the selection of the most suitable successor. As important as is the chairman, the board, the chief executive officer, the operating head, nevertheless the role of the successor to the contrôleur is transcendent. Those norms of selection of personnel that guided the incumbent contrôleur during tenure, guide him as well in departing that tenure, in the proper and beneficial transfer of control. The choice of a successor is undeniably the crowning act of the contrôleur's career, as well as his last, and hence invites the commensurate scrutiny of the standards of a fiduciary. In fine, this selection is merely another facet, arguably the most important, of the fiduciary duty of the contrôleur.

Writing to the author in the late forties, Nathan Lobell characterized appositely the role of the contrôleur:

> The whole problem of corporate management is a facet of our latter-day split between ownership of wealth and the control thereof. But, if our experience at the S.E.C. has been in any sense typical, the really crucial ethical problems that have arisen in dealing with corporate management have grown out of management's owner-

ship of a stake in the enterprise. While we once stood at the crossroads facing, on the one hand, the path of merging management responsibility with management's stake in the business and on the other, the creation of a class of disinterested fiduciaries, we have—whether we like it or not—taken the second road. It no longer makes any sense to require that either a substantial portion of corporate wealth be owned by the management or that a substantial portion of management's wealth be invested in the corporation. The hope for effective and honest management lies in evolving a class of financially disinterested managers who accept, as part of a working code, the simple rudiments of honest politics.

> —Letter from Nathan D. Lobell, then Executive Advisor to the Securities and Exchange Commission, to the Author (Feb. 7, 1949).

The Proximate Norms of Selection

The contrôleur's fiduciary duty in the selection of a successor may be specified further in two stages: (1) The Proximate Norms of Selection. (2) The Indicia of Breach.

Here is the final resolution of the question posed by the sale of control: Did the incumbent contrôleur's selection conform to the proximate norms integral to his fiduciary duty? The answer is the answer to the legitimacy of the transfer. All other questions have been preliminary.

Prior to any enunciation of the norms of suitability, the proper philosophical thrust should be given concrete expression in a major presumption: *The presumption of propriety:*

> *Until rebutted, a presumption exists at law that the selection of a successor, when made by the incumbent contrôleur pursuant to the duty of appointment, is conformable to the proximate norms of propriety and suitability.*

Such a rebuttable presumption, or at least inference, is the only logical conclusion from either a legitimate or an unchallenged illegitimate custody. A basic working premise should be that he who occupies an office is fulfilling its duties until shown otherwise.

The efficacy of any preliminary attacks on the contrôleur's *right to appoint,* founded on the illegality of his initial accession or tenure, is within the judgment of the court and is to be determined upon traditional law. In short, a vast difference exists between the *right to appoint* and the *suitability of the appointee.* The illicit contrôleur may appoint a superb successor, his licit counterpart an oaf.

(1) The Proximate Norms

Descent to minutiae in delineating the proximate norms is neither advisable nor feasible. The personal qualities required for the corporate contrôleur may be adequately presented in a five-part working pattern for ad hoc application: (1) Moral integrity, (2) Intellectual competence, (3) Managerial and organizational proficiency, (4) Social suitability and (5) Satisfactory age and health. Absent, therefore, a proven legal and substantial deficiency in these qualities, the presumption of propriety prevails.

(2) The Indicia of Breach

The proximate norms (and any concomitant presumptions) are applied according to established tort formulas. The selection may be either intentionally or negligently improper.

Remember that these norms govern the choice of a man for an office. The breach of these norms consists in the choice of an unsuitable person. The indicia of breach are signs pointing to such a person. The transfer by sale may entail many another matter—from a subtle swindle to bald fraud—which is legally reprehensible in its own right. Here, however, the question only concerns the suitability, or lack of it, of the man for the job. Some of the discernible guidelines (Note: These are at best broad, even random, danger signals):

(1) **Predictable Spoliation.** Foreseeable raiding by the successor may constitute either an intentional (including the 'substantial certainty' of the *Restatement*) or a negligent tort. The extent of admissibility of post-factum activity by the successor, e.g., how much and what kind of looting—consider the twin looting cases of the early forties, *Insuranshares* and *Gerdes v. Reynolds*—how many years later, etc., is a question for the discretion of the court.

(2) **Self-Financing.** Closer scrutiny should be given to an appointee in a deal in which he repays the amount borrowed for the

purchase price of the stock with the assets of the controlled corporation. Apparently the plan in *Fenestra.*

(3) **Projected Mergers or Acquisitions.** Motives other than corporate welfare (and hence an indication of the unsuitability of the appointee) could be present in proposals for self-serving purchases (by the controlled corporation) of outside corporations owned or controlled by the new contrôleur-appointee. As with Sonnabend in *Lionel.*

(4) **Questionable Salary Contracts.** Employment agreements accorded the outgoing contrôleur (consultative positions), that may be per se legal but are nonetheless suspect, may constitute substantial overreaching. As in *Lionel* and *Oser v. Wilcox.*

(5) **Fringe Benefits.** "In considering the advantages of control . . . we are not primarily concerned with advantages from the possible illegal actions. However, there are many possible actions which . . . are either legal or on the borderline."[108] This Glore, Forgan summary in *Green Giant* of "the advantages of control" listed several "specific areas of such action" as "contracts with suppliers or agents," the use of corporate trademarks, the opportunity . . .

> . . . to obtain the largest salary that could not be attacked
> in the courts plus other perquisites of the office including
> such things as stock options, pensions, insurance cover-
> age, et cetera.
>
> —Glore, Forgan Report, Record on Appeal at
> 340, *Honigman v. Green Giant Co.*, 309 F.2d
> 667 (8th Cir. 1962).

All of these objectives—especially the spirit that would envisage actions "on the borderline"—would be proper to a man of questionable suitability for the office of ultimate custody of a corporation.

(6) **The Appointee's Character.** Since the entire question of the selection is reducible to the general character of the man, it is perhaps inaccurate to segregate personal qualities as a separate guideline. However, the reputation of a person may be so egregiously malodorous, e.g., emotional instability, alcoholism, notorious immorality, gambling, as to constitute a distinct indicium.

These indicia could not hope to be exhaustive. Or need they be. Deficiencies in intellectual competence, managerial efficiency, age and health, require no particular earmarks for detection.

The Premium-Bribe

But the most important indicium of all is the premium-bribe. What is to be said of the suitability of a contrôleur who bribed himself into office? Would rational shareholder owners appropriate entity and assets into the custody of a premium-briber? Is premium-bribery intrinsically immoral? Or is an otherwise wholesome and pure premium-briber a worthy person, trustworthy and true, into whose hands the destiny of the corporation can safely be entrusted?

These questions will push the Philosophy of Corporate Control to the fullest. Their answers must await far greater specification of principles than has thus far been possible. Remember, however, that the role of the premium-bribe in estimating successor suitability is a preeminent one. If the suitability of the successor contrôleur is the sole criterion of the legitimacy of the transfer of control—which it is—the presence of premium-bribery is correspondingly of overriding consequence in determining such suitability.

The role of the premium-bribe will be a principal constituent of the remainder of this study.

V. The Remuneration of the Contrôleur

> The services performed under such appointments [of trust] are paid for by salary or fees, presumed to be adjusted by law to the precise point of adequate remuneration for them.
>
> —*Eddy v. Capron*, 4 R.I. 394, 397 (1856).

> These cases are all quite clear to the effect that the trustee will not be allowed to make gain to himself, beyond his allowed compensation, by reason of his office and influence as such trustee.
>
> —*Bent v. Priest*, 86 Mo. 475, 486 (1885).

An adequate compensation is the reward for the proper utilization of the rights and the performance of the duties of custody. Remuneration is proportioned to performance. The compensation due the contrôleur is relative to the manner in which he employs the prerogatives of the office. This is the principle of quid pro quo so assiduously protected by commutative justice.

The delicate balance between performance and emolument is not peculiar to the office of control alone. No party to the corporate venture should be compensated for performance of the duties of another office, or for work he should have done but never did. The labor done determines the remuneration.

Four primary tenets must be emphasized: The office possesses the duties. The office possesses the rights. The officeholder receives the emolument. Upon relinquishment of the office, the successor accedes to the duties, rights and emolument.

Two popular fallacies have resulted from failure to apply these tenets: That the contrôleur may somehow continue to receive compensation even after he quits control. That some forms of compensation become permanent possessions of the individual and are not perquisites attached to the office.

The failure to distinguish corporate assets at the disposal of the office from personal possessions of the individual is the first great source of error plaguing the concept of contrôleur remuneration. The second major problem is confusion between compensation for labors actually performed and compensation for work never done, either before, during or after the period of employment.

Monetary Compensation

Theoretically, and also practically, the contrôleur is the most important and most valuable party to the enterprise. The contributions of the top-level control group to a complex modern corporation may appear slight in point of time and physical energy expended, but they are undeniably the prevailing and crucial element in the success or failure of the venture. The compensation of the contrôleur must match these enormous benefits. This fact has produced a marked antithesis in the present extralegal status of the contrôleur. On the one hand, the contrôleur deserves great rewards which should be distributed through appropriate and acknowledged channels. On the other, the contrôleur cannot be permitted to retain unowned assets and unearned recompense. This antithesis burdens the law with a paradoxical challenge: To establish standard and acceptable processes for adequately compensating the contrôleur for his vast abilities, and to outlaw both the individual's personal appropriation of official, corporate assets, and the officeholder's personal retention of unjust compensation either during or after the tenure of office.

Meeting the first challenge would help to eliminate the second. Were the contrôleur properly compensated, the temptation to appropriate would diminish. Ideally, there should be two distinct categories of contrôleur compensation: Direct emolument awarded in the traditional manner, and indirect benefit flowing to the contrôleur as an individual through his customary second position in the enterprise, such as shareholder, bondholder, director or officer. Thus, dividends to the shareholder, interest on the bonds, salary.

The contrôleur should not be forced to secure a just recompense by the temporary occupancy of an acknowledged, traditional position. This does not mean, however, that if the contrôleur is actually performing the duties of two offices, he should not be paid for both. The point is that whatever else the contrôleur does he should also receive the proper rewards for the labors of the office of control.

The facts in *Green Giant* provide an apt illustration of this double deficiency which the law must correct. Mr. Cosgrove was ostensibly being paid one salary for the performance of three offices. There was little harm in this, however, since the total $70,000 per annum (in 1959 dollars) plus collateral benefits seemingly compensated him for all his labors. It would have been healthier, however, to ascribe the sum to its specific sources.

This failure to denominate properly the compensation for each of Mr. Cosgrove's three offices, contrôleur, board chairman, chief executive officer, occasioned him some unnecessary and unjustified embarrassment during the *Green Giant* litigation. For six to eight years Cosgrove continued to receive approximately $70,000 per year even though he had not occupied the presidency during this period. Perhaps he was properly apologetic in that he had not taken any reduction in his remuneration upon relinquishment of the presidency, but he nonetheless performed the valuable services of contrôleur and board chairman, for which he certainly deserved a substantial recompense. Had his various emoluments been listed over the years with the proper designations, e.g., contrôleur: $30,000, board chairman: $10,000, president: $30,000, he would have been spared this uneasiness (had he, of course, taken an appropriate, e.g., $30,000-per-year, cut when he resigned the presidency). He declared:

I attribute my job as Chairman of the Board to years of experience with the company and not my ownership of Class A stock [he undoubtedly meant control]. I don't consider what I am being paid excessive for my years of experience; a fellow who starts with three employees and $7,000 worth of sales and runs it into a company with $64,000,000 worth of sales has obviously had a lot of experience.

> —Record on Appeal at 57, *Honigman v. Green Giant Co.,* 309 F.2d 667 (8th Cir. 1962).

Another facet of the *Green Giant* facts provides an instance of the temptation facing the contrôleur when he quits the office. Although the Glore, Forgan Report had taken "all factors into account," Mr. Cosgrove's annual income of $70,000 was an important element in establishing his share of the $2-million premium. The Report capitalized and reduced to present worth an assumed salary of $75,000 per year over a 20- to 25-year period, which produced a valuation of $1 million, just for the salary. Since Mr. Cosgrove's major allegation was that he was relinquishing the office of control there is no perceptible reason why he should continue to be compensated for the office. This salary rightfully belonged to his successor.

It is revealing to compare this capitalization of the salary with the statement in the Glore, Forgan Report:

> [T]he chief advantage of control is the right to elect the principal officer of the corporation and thereby to obtain the largest salary that could not be attacked in the courts plus other perquisites of the office . . . .

> —Glore, Forgan Report, Record on Appeal at 340, *Honigman v. Green Giant Co.,* 309 F.2d 667 (8th Cir. 1962).

Nonmonetary Remuneration

Prestige in the community is an inestimable factor in total remuneration. Remuneration in the form of spiritual values can be the most powerful incentive offered the contrôleur. Strict altruism manifested in a desire to benefit corporation, community and society is rarely a motivation and hence an emolument to the contrôleur. However, it is possible. But the desire to express organizational ability, to feel deeply the sense of accomplishment in a complex job well done, can constitute satisfying compensation for the contrôleur.

One might hastily conclude that these nonfinancial forms of compensation do actually become the permanent possession of the individual. The contrary is true. As with the salary, they go with the office and to the officeholder. The opportunity to organize, the power, the prestige, all belong to the corporation. They are habiliments of the office during tenure and as such are properly viewed as remuneration to the officeholder, but they are not his to keep or to sell to another. They are to be returned to the corporation at the close of tenure and passed on to the successor in office.

The Contrôleur's Further Motivation

Almost universally, control conjoins to another position in the enterprise. Since this is so, all the great efforts of the contrôleur toward benefiting the entity have the immediate effect of enhancing the value of each constituent part, including his own. This is a principal motivation to the contrôleur's activity and his chief remuneration. Mr. Cosgrove described this emolument in a very earthy way: "Because I control the company where most of my money sits. My estate is essentially Green Giant Company."[109]

If the contrôleur is also a shareholder, as was Mr. Cosgrove, his indirect reward will consist in an appreciation in the value of his stock and increased dividends. If he is a member of management his month-to-month efforts will yield higher salary, greater prestige, power, satisfaction. These emoluments are the principal and substantial—and altogether legal—compensation of the contrôleur.

This concludes the Foundation. Henceforward the Philosophy of Corporate Control will be specified with increasingly narrower particularity by a detailed study of the Custodial Concept of Corporate Control as applied to the limited area of the illegitimate sale of control. This notable breach of the contrôleur's third subduty of the overall fiduciary duty of corporate control offers the most relevant opportunity to see the philosophy in vivid dollars-and-cents application.

Part Two

THE SUPERSTRUCTURE

[W]e think it sound law that a fiduciary may not appropriate to himself the value of this premium.

> —*Perlman v. Feldmann*, 219 F.2d 173, 178 (2d Cir. 1955).

No Class A shareholder could be expected to forego the power of control of a company of this size without receiving in return a consideration commensurate with the value of the control which he foregoes.

> —*Honigman v. Green Giant Co.*, 208 F. Supp. 754, 758 (D. Minn. 1961), *aff'd*, 309 F.2d 667 (8th Cir. 1962).

[I]t is generally recognized that majority stock is more valuable than minority stock. Neither is there merit in the argument that appellees, as dominant shareholders, must refrain from receiving a premium which reflects the control potential of the stock.

> —*McDaniel v. Painter*, 418 F.2d 545, 548 (10th Cir. 1969).

We start from one of the "well-established principles of equity" . . . "that a personal trustee, corporate officer or director, or other person standing in a fiduciary relationship with another, may not sell or transfer such office for personal gain." There are ample authorities to support this proposition . . . .

> —*Rosenfeld v. Black*, 445 F.2d 1337, 1342 (2d Cir. 1971).

While the price paid for Hutchison's shares was indeed a premium price, it was nevertheless a premium paid for the element of control of the corporation. . . . The premium payment is . . . justifiable . . . .

> —*Clagett v. Hutchison*, 583 F.2d 1259, 1262 (4th Cir. 1978).

Chapter 5

The Sale of Control and the Premium-Bribe

> Gulf says [without objection from the Court] that the purchase of shares [at a premium] for control of a corporation is a normal everyday occurrence and has solid support in the law.
>
> —*Fenestra Inc. v. Gulf Am. Land Corp.*, 141 N.W.2d 36, 46 (Mich. 1966).

> [C]ontrol of a corporation, either actual or in effect, representing as it does an added element of value, may justify a higher value for a specific block of stock.
>
> —Rev. Rul. 59-60, 1959-1 C.B. 242.

The broadest compass of the fiduciary duty of the office of control embraces every possible activity of the contrôleur in his top-level governance of the corporate entity. As the chief policy officer of the corporation it falls to the contrôleur to set the year-to-year norms for guidance of the directorate in its month-to-month administration. Guided by these ultimate norms the board in turn supervises the top-echelon officers.

As the unquestioned ultimate in this corporate hierarchy, the contrôleur finds his overall fiduciary duty conveniently specified into the tripartite obligation to prosecute the corporate *bonum commune* by striving for: (1) The best possible *corporate structure,* (2) The most enlightened *managerial policy* and (3) The finest *personnel.*

Were each of these three contrôleur subduties to be thoroughly explored, the resultant volumes would contain many pages of expectable material common also to the routine duties of the corporate

157

directors and officers. Such repetition would be wasteful. The repetition would be particularly so in the first two subareas. Even in the third, the selection of competent personnel, the duties of the contrôleur in choosing his subordinates—the directors, and perhaps the major executives were he to usurp that board function—would not differ from the obligations incumbent, for example, on the directorate in its selection of the lesser corporate hierarchy. Here too the repetition would be vain.

But in the appointment of his successor, the contrôleur's obligation to the corporation is unparalleled. At that crucial instant the entire corporate future depends on his judgment. Here then is the height of contrôleur duty. The consequences and implications of that appointment are peculiar to the office of control, completely sui generis, and demand elaborate rules specific to the contrôleur and conformed to the Custodial Concept of Corporate Control.

The Sale of Control

Recall that the legitimate transfer of control—by orderly appointment, by proxy fight, by contested tender, even by insurgency of the board—is also governed by extant, and reasonably well-excogitated, rules of law. No real need here for a pedestrian restatement.

But when the incumbent contrôleur decides to sell the occupancy of his office to the highest bidder—as he has done over the decades from *Sugden* in 1856 in England to *Statesman* in 1985 in the United States—then comes the need for a highly refined specification of the Custodial Concept.

Even more to the point—and apart from the specific law governing the sale of control—the philosophy surrounding this law, and the torturous ratiocination required to construct and elaborate it, yield yet further insights into the nature of corporate control and enlighten the understanding of the Foundation of this treatise.

Thus, in studying minutely the sale of control and the premium-bribe—and that is the sole burden of this Superstructure—one can fill out those remaining areas of the Philosophy of Corporate Control that are distinctively pertinent to the office of control and not at all common to the lesser offices in the corporate hierarchy. This, then, explains the dedication of this Superstructure to a study of the illegitimate transfer, the sale of control.

The 'Premium-Bribe' over the Years

From the earliest days of the modern corporation, from the earliest advent of the transferable share and the control struggle, contrôleurs have been premium-bribed in and out of office with the regularity and predictability—and impunity in the main—engendered by the ingenuity and corruptibility of the legal corporate mind.

The importance of the premium-bribe itself is incalculable. From a strictly extrinsic standpoint, the premium-bribe has occasioned most modern control litigation. Here, after all, is where the money lies. The tangible and estimable harm to the corporation has surfaced in the form of the premium-bribe and has afforded the requisite opportunity to bring the malefactors to justice. Intrinsically, the premium-bribe analysis is the center of the entire philosophy. It poses, and answers, a myriad of questions, thereby illustrating and substantiating the basic control principles. The premium-bribe, its inner nature, its legitimacy or illegitimacy, role and disposition, support the superstructure of the control edifice. The court's award—whether £75 in *Sugden* in 1856 or $0.3 million in *Le Mars* in 1979—is the practical implementation of the philosophical theory. To indulge in metaphor, the premium-bribe is the centerpiece in the control puzzle. In this sense, perhaps, the premium-bribe is of great intrinsic importance. If the centerpiece of the puzzle does not fit, something is essentially wrong.

Any decade in the twentieth century could be prolific of examples of premium-bribery at work. But the sixties, with their profusion of mergers, tender takeovers, proxy fights, are particularly apt for a view of the prevalence of the premium-bribe. A sampling of the 1960-1969 years could well serve for the century. Perhaps those years were egregious, but not disproportionately so. The examples, moreover, are characteristic.

Thus, Norton Simon, the great conglomerateur—Hunt Foods, Canada Dry, Wheeling Steel—of the conglomerate-ridden decade, in the vanguard of his corporate minions raised the premium question in the Wheeling Steel—later to become independent as Wheeling-Pittsburgh—attempted takeover of Crucible Steel. The Circuit Court of Cook County questioned the premium passing from Simon, Hunt Foods and Wheeling to the outgoing Crucible contrôleur in the late 1967 case of *Rubin v. Norton Simon*.

On the state level, in *Fenestra v. Gulf American Land*, the Supreme Court of Michigan in the spring of 1966 left little doubt that the premium paid for control was of no real concern to the Court:

> Gulf says, first of all, that there was nothing unlawful in the means by which it obtained Fenestra's shares. Gulf concedes the obvious, that is, that it paid a price per share greater than the market value of Fenestra but says that there is no law which prevents a purchaser from paying a premium [for control] in connection with the purchase of shares.
>
> —*Fenestra Inc. v. Gulf Am. Land Corp.*, 141 N.W. 2d 36, 45 (Mich. 1966).

(This was the same Gulf American so strongly chastised over many months by the Florida Land Sales Board, later to become GAC and still later, bankrupt.)

A New York Federal court, in *Laurenzano v. Einbender*, faced a simple variant of the complex problem in the redemption of the outgoing contrôleur's stock at an appreciable premium. This was 1966. From late 1967 to September, 1968 the press reported intriguing proposals and arrangements that smacked of the same. Mr. A. King McCord, Chairman of Westinghouse Air Brake, became publicly indignant at Mr. Thomas Mellon Evans, Chairman of Crane Company, for "'inappropriate' financial inducements, including stock options" toward Crane's assumption of control of WABCO. "'I was shocked' at this offer, he says."[110] In the Shearson, Hammill/E. M. Warburg control takeover of Silvray-Litecraft, top Silvray executives "Messrs. Gilbert and Gordon received $137,000 each to resign their [control] posts."[111]

In a suspiciously similar gambit, the incumbent contrôleur of Schenley, Lewis S. Rosenstiel, was accused by a Schenley minority of accepting a substantial premium and acceding to the sale of control of Schenley to Glen Alden "in his own self interest and to the detriment of other shareholders by negotiating a sale of his own holdings in Schenley to Glen Alden at a price 'substantially above' that offered the other shareholders."[112]

Equally questionable was the $7 premium—some 39 percent over market—that Cyrus Eaton exacted from American Export Industries as he handed over two board positions and eventual control of Detroit Steel.[113] That was early 1968. (Eaton's premium of $3.25 million was never attacked in the courts.)

But the sixties had no monopoly. Over other decades premiums were passed with regularity, and although the amount of the premium may have varied, the issues have been the same. In 1856 the amount involved in *Sugden v. Crossland* was a trivial £75, but it was nonetheless a premium for the sale of control. In the 1899 New York *McClure v. Law,* Louis P. Levy succeeded in purchasing "the absolute control and management of the Life Union Association, in consideration of the sum of $15,000."[114] In the 1914 Pennsylvania case of *Porter v. Healy,* the directors "'sold . . . control as their individual estate'" and received an $86,830 "bonus" for it.[115] In the two Reynolds Metals cases, 20 years apart, the premiums were $1.3 million and $40 million respectively.

And so it has gone through all the years—both before and after the sixties—with *Perlman v. Feldmann* in 1955 ($2.1 million), *Green Giant* in 1961 ($2 million), *Essex Universal* in 1962 ($2 million), the New York *Lionel* litigation of mid-1964 ($135,000) and *Ferraioli v. Cantor* in 1967 ($2.2 million). In the 1971 Second Circuit *Rosenfeld v. Black*—probably the most important sale-of-control case thus far in the century—the amount was $2.7 million. In a California Federal court in 1973, *Beverly Hills Federal,* $1.6 million. In the Southern District of New York in the same year, $60 million in *Gordon.* In a lower New York court $1.26 million in *Brecher v. Gregg* in 1975. The year 1978 gave the world premiums of $2.5 million in the Fourth Circuit *Clagett* and $30 over a $60-per-share market in *Yerke* in Indiana. The following year saw a $300,000 premium in *Le Mars* in Iowa. In 1980 in *A&P* it was $8.3 million. The amount was $6.8 million in *Statesman* in the Federal Court in Iowa in 1985.

Premium after Premium

Among the many sources of confusion—and few areas of corporate law are as confused—has been the inconsistency of the judicial treatment of these recurrent premiums. The Michigan Supreme Court in the 1966 *Fenestra* agreed "that there is no law which prevents a purchaser from paying a premium [for control] in connection with the purchase of shares."[116] One could wonder if this was the same premium that the New York Court had in mind in the 1964 *Gabriel-Lionel* when it held that . . .

Defiance, who controlled the management of Lionel, when it illegally sold such control must account to Lionel in this action for the illegal profit.

> —*Gabriel Indus. v. Defiance Indus.*, N.Y.L.J., June 17, 1964, at 13 (Sup. Ct., N.Y. County).

Was it the same "premium price . . . paid for the . . . transfer of . . . control that was the all important emolument of the transaction" according to the same New York Court in *Caplan-Lionel*?[117] What did the same Court in 1964 in *Matter of Carter* mean by: "[T]here was no premium paid for control"[118]? What was the nature of the premium condoned by the Delaware Court in 1960 in *Manacher v. Reynolds* when it stated: "No other factor being present, they may demand a reasonable premium for the use of their key"[119]? In the 1962 *Essex Universal*, Chief Judge Lumbard said for the Second Circuit: "There is no question of the right of a controlling shareholder under New York law normally to derive a premium from the sale of a controlling block of stock."[120] In his concurring opinion, however, Judge Friendly was not so sure of the legality of the premium:

> This seems to me a wrong to the corporation and the other stockholders [the transfer of control with less than 50-percent stock ownership] which the law ought not countenance, whether the selling stockholder has received a premium or not.
>
> —*Essex Universal Corp. v. Yates*, 305 F.2d 572, 581 (2d Cir. 1962) (Friendly, J., concurring).

Did the three concurring judges have the same premiums in mind as the majority? In 1914 in *Porter v. Healy* the Pennsylvania Court reprobated the premium and called it a "'bonus' . . . paid . . . for this control."[121]

The point seems clear. A precise legal definition is imperative, and long overdue. Further, perhaps surprisingly, it will be equally clear that all these were in fact the same 'premium.' Reflection will reveal that each of these variously treated premiums was in truth a premium-bribe. An intensive analysis is clearly in order.

The precise legal definition must represent a *legal* analysis of a discernible premium-bribe, accepted by a consensus, and the discussion must not degenerate into a *factual* quibble over its presence or absence. Grant the factual presence, what exactly are its constituent elements? Leave the factual vagaries, as collaterally important as they are, for another time. This inhibition may be especially annoying to those who have so long desired to unfold the complications of the more involved instances of questionable premiums (to begin at the end instead of the beginning, as it were). Here, however, patience is essential. The very cause for so much chaos has been the refusal to learn first the ABCs of the true premium-bribe before attempting to explore all the confusing variations.

The Working Definition

Remarkably, these somewhat demanding strictures can be met. Courts and commentators over the years from *Sugden* to *Statesman* have ascribed, more often than first meets the mind, one meaning to the various terms, 'bonus,' 'illegal profit,' 'premium.' This meaning relates to the contrôleur's fiduciary duty and is consequently most fundamental and important.

At the turn of the century, the New York Court of Appeals in *McClure v. Law*, quoting the Appellate Division, penetrated to the core, and presented a starting definition of the technical 'premium-bribe' in the sale of control:

> The question is therefore presented whether [William H. Law] is bound to account for the money received from Levy for the transfer to him and his associates of the management and control of the Life Union . . . . *The learned appellate division has treated this transaction as a bribe paid to the directors of the Life Union by Levy . . . .*
>
> —*McClure v. Law*, 55 N.E. 388, 389 (N.Y. 1899) (emphasis added).

The Appellate Division was correct. The premium in the sale of control is nothing other than a bald bribe, some special consideration calculated to influence the incumbent in his appointment of a new man to the office of corporate control. Broadly, the premium-bribe is an inducement paid to the contrôleur to breach his fiduciary duty in the specific area of the selection of his successor.

A Term of Art

Consistent with this tentative definition (but certainly contingent on later elaboration), therefore, and pursuant to an undeniable need for a technical control lexicon, the term 'premium-bribe' is submitted as referable to the concept of a bribe paid for the sale of control.

(There is something gross about the term 'bribe,' but the English language offers no appropriate euphemistic substitute. Try as one might, no circumlocution can hide the fact that consideration paid for the appointment is a bribe. At first, the term 'premium' was thought to be adequate, but it proved to be both too bland and insufficiently pejorative. Besides it is dilute with many another meaning. 'Premium-bribe' seemed a suitable compromise.)

Therefore, let this usage prevail. Designate all other nonbribe emolument or consideration by other terms—blockage, deferred compensation, gift, convenience cost, whatever—but confine 'premium-bribe' to nothing other than a bribe in the sale of control.

The Simplicity of *McClure*

The fallible human mind can discern a delicate nuance and subtle ethical principle when the true-to-life fact situation embodying them is reduced to the utter simplicity of a primitive drama. To the contrary, if the fragile intellect is forced first to extricate the essentials from a bewildering maze of interlocking boards, syndicate contrôleurs, fluctuating market values, working-control stock blocks, and the like, little energy remains to evaluate the legal issues behind the complexities.

The turn-of-the-century *McClure v. Law* has just such an apposite simplicity. No one can dispute the *McClure* facts. Contrary to the camouflaged sale-of-control premium so often before the courts or commentators, the premium there stands large and clear, and apt for definition. Just what it was that was objectionable in *Perlman v. Feldmann*, *Green Giant* or *Essex Universal* might be difficult at first to discern, but in *McClure* no one should have any doubts.

The Life Union Association was a New York mutual life-insurance company. As with all such cooperative or assessment-plan companies, each member was at once an insurer and an insured. No stockholders, only members. No set premiums were levied. Assessments were later laid to indemnify a member's loss. In the late 1800s during the presidency of William H. Law, "the members of the company had every reason to believe . . . that its affairs were in a flourishing condition." This flourishing state of the Life Union was impressive, and "it seems that one Mr. Louis P. Levy desired for his own purposes to procure the control of it, and for that purpose he made a contract"[122] with Mr. William H. Law and the other board members . . .

> . . . to the effect substantially that he would pay them the sum of $15,000, in consideration . . . . [T]he result was that these trustees transferred to Levy the full control of the corporation whose interests they were bound to protect . . . .
> —*McClure v. Law*, 47 N.Y.S. 84, 85 (App. Div. 1897).

The transfer was achieved by the then-novel seriatim resignation of the board. According to the plan, the Law men . . .

> . . . would resign their offices as directors from time to time, as [Levy] might request, and would substitute in their places other persons, to be nominated by him, so that he and his creatures might have the entire control of the corporation. . . . As might be expected, shortly after this transaction was completed the affairs of the Life Union ceased to flourish, and within a few months it went into the hands of a receiver . . . .
> —*McClure v. Law*, 47 N.Y.S. 84, 85 (App. Div. 1897).

As receiver, David McClure undertook to put together again as much of the Life Union as possible. His first step was an action to recover from William H. Law, the former president and director of the Life Union, $3,000 he had gained "out of his trust relationship with the company," and his share of the money flowing from Levy under the agreement by which Law "undertook to deliver . . . the absolute control and management of the Life Union."[123]

Receiver McClure met with success in the New York Supreme Court, but suffered an inexplicable reversal in the Appellate Division on the collateral, antiquated theory that the corporation could not recover under an ultra vires contract. The Court of Appeals, however, was not to be deceived by a logical conclusion from an illogical premise and not only ordered the $3,000 over to Life Union, but adduced in support sound reasoning:

> The question is . . . whether the defendant is bound to account for the money received from Levy for the transfer to him and his associates of the management and control of the Life Union, together with its property and effects. The learned appellate division has treated this transaction as a bribe paid to the directors of the Life Union by Levy, and reached the conclusion that the money did not belong to the corporation. We think, however, that the law does not permit the defendant to avail himself of his own crime as a defense to this action.
>
> —*McClure v. Law,* 55 N.E. 388, 389 (N.Y. 1899).

The Court of Appeals then proceeded to found its decision on *Sugden v. Crossland* (which was on all fours) and to apply the *Sugden* strict-trust reasoning without qualification:

> As president and director of the Life Union, he was bound to account to that association for all moneys that came into his hands by virtue of his official acts, and he cannot be permitted to shield himself from such liability under the claim that his acts were illegal and unauthorized. As an officer he had the right to resign, but the money was not paid to him for his resignation. It was paid over upon condition that he procure Levy and his friends to be elected directors, and given the control and management, together with the property and effects, of the corporation. The election of directors, and the transfer of the management and property of the corporation, were official acts, and whatever money he received from such official acts were moneys derived by virtue of his office, for which we think he should account.
>
> —*McClure v. Law,* 55 N.E. 388, 389 (N.Y. 1899).

The case could not have been simpler. Unencumbered by share-holders and a concomitant sale of control-bearing shares, *McClure* reduces the transaction to the simplicity of a sale of control of Life Union for a $15,000 premium-bribe. Without the onerous, and sometimes impossible, chore of segregating the true investment value of accompanying shares, the *McClure* premium stands stark, in the words of the Appellate Division, "as a bribe."

Just as the court-ordered stock disbursal by the Du Pont contrôleur shifted control of GM to the directorate[124]—which effected a mere-incumbency control—and thereby highlighted a legitimate transfer of control, *McClure* will supply the background for the ensuing definition of the illegitimate premium-bribe.

Clearly, this premium-bribe analysis has a twofold purpose: (1) To define the one central concept, the premium as a bribe, without the double disability of complex legal refinement and cloudy fact situations, and thus (2) To supply a reliable and basic definition of the premium-bribe toward further study of its nature, role and disposition.

The Premium-Bribe in Perspective

A major source of misconception has been the failure to lay bare the mechanics of the sale of control and the place of the premium-bribe. Never have they been seen for what they really are. To get the sale and the premium-bribe in proper focus, recall the two basic premises: (1) Every transfer of control, of whatever kind, is very simply the appointment of a new person to the office of contrôleur. For some reason the incumbent is leaving. He finds a willing successor. Control is transferred. (2) Every transfer of control is not a sale of control, but every sale is a transfer. The 'sale' is a limited species of the genus 'transfer.' The sale is a transfer for a price. The sale, in effect, adds only one new element: The premium paid for the appointment. Never does a nonsale transfer directly posit consideration passing from appointee to contrôleur.

In view of these premises, 'sale of control' should be reserved exclusively for the illegitimate transfer involving a premium-bribe, and 'transfer of control' for all nonbribe appointments. As additions to the control argot, 'transfer' and 'sale' should eliminate some loose terminology and loose concepts underneath.

If one conceives control as "a valuable commodity" with Jennings,[125] or as Judge Lumbard's 'personalty'[126] or Berle's 'corporate asset,'[127] rather than a relation of custody, with rights and duties, questions arise as to the ownership of the commodity, its value, and its salability. The result is a long line of inexact reasoning. So too, if the concept is the 'sale of the office,' rather than the payment of a bribe to induce appointment to the office. To the contrary, the office is never sold, always remains, is essential to the corporation, never leaves or changes, and is always occupied. What is sold is the occupancy, and the price paid for the occupancy is the premium-bribe.

The Kinds of Transfer

Fortunately for the corporate world the overwhelming majority of control changeovers are effected legitimately, and hence never elicit litigation. Thus the release of General Motors by the du Ponts. Far more fascinating, but equally legitimate, was the selection of little-known Albemarle Paper Corporation as contrôleur of the vast GM/Exxon Ethyl Corporation. In the early sixties GM and the then Jersey Standard wanted to divest themselves of the $200-million Ethyl Corporation, and neither wanted to be contrôleur. The solution? The Gottwald brothers who controlled minuscule Albemarle Paper of Richmond, Virginia. A mammoth loan, with Ethyl itself as security, and Albemarle became Ethyl, and another instance of a legitimate, and unbelievable, transfer.[128]

However, the necessary absence of a premium-bribe in a legitimate transfer circumscribes the problem areas and correspondingly limits its value as a vehicle for the study of the fiduciary duty of corporate control. For present purposes the abuse of the power is necessarily more rewarding than its use.

Among illicit transfers the sale is preeminent. Fraud, duress and blackmail are rare. It is also most prolific of problems which require the construction of a code for their solution. Although the culpable appointment of an inept son or an unsuitable associate is an illegitimate transfer—which is not a sale and does pose conflict-of-interest control questions—the resulting problems are not comparable to those created by the outright sale.

Concomitant Stock

The greatest deterrent to the definition of the premium-bribe, the construction of a control code, and the development of a philosophical consensus, has been the intrusion of the fact problems raised by the legitimate sale of a block of stock, controlling or otherwise, concomitant to the sale of control. Undoubtedly, most confusion and consequent dispute would have disappeared if these two distinct and essentially unrelated acts—the sale of stock and the selection of a successor for a price—had been studied and evaluated in completely separate treatises. This is exactly the prerequisite to the present analysis. Whether a premium-bribe was imbedded in the $2 million over market moving from Essex Universal to Yates, in the $2.1 million received by C. Russell Feldmann from the Wilport Syndicate, or in the $6.8 million that passed in *Statesman*, are all complicated *questions of fact.* Let judge or jury so determine the matter. In *Sugden,* no such fact question clouded the legal issue. The £75 stood unadorned and alone, with no stock involved. Similarly, in *McClure,* no estimation of investment value distracted the Court from the sole operative fact: Levy paid Law and friends $15,000 for the control of Life Union. Since no stockholders, there was no stock. Since no stock, no investment-value problem.

Clearly, therefore, the presence or absence of concomitant stock is legally irrelevant to the presence or absence of a premium-bribe. (But *cave,* this is a complex question which deserves and will receive suitable answer later in this treatise.) If a premium-bribe is in fact embedded in the price paid for the stock, the transfer is a sale of control, as apparently in *Feldmann, Essex Universal, Lionel* and *Statesman.* If there is no premium-bribe, the transfer, with accompanying block of stock, is perfectly legitimate, as apparently in GM/Du Pont and Albemarle/Ethyl. Whether the block is controlling, as in Albemarle/Ethyl, or noncontrolling, as in GM/Du Pont, is also irrelevant as long as no premium-bribe prevails.

In summary, four possibilities exist: (1) A transfer of control with neither stock nor premium-bribe, conceivably thus in a transfer of IBM, (2) A transfer of control with concomitant stock, but no premium-bribe, thus Albemarle/Ethyl, (3) A sale of control with both stock and premium-bribe, thus Muscat/Sonnabend in *Lionel,* and *Statesman* and (4) A sale of control, no stock but premium-bribe, as *Sugden* and *McClure.*

The Philosophical Background

To place the premium-bribe in proper philosophical perspective, one must begin with the central philosophical event in the premium-bribe question: The selection of a successor contrôleur. No transfer can be made, no sale of control consummated, no appointment to the office effected, and no premium-bribe paid or accepted, before a specific individual person has been chosen for the privilege and the burden of the office of contrôleur. Every applicant for the appointment, as much an Albemarle as a Levy, inescapably must present himself for approval. Whether the contrôleur seeks to sell or the aspirant buy, briber must meet bribed before a premium-bribe can pass. In this selection all the fiduciary obligations of an outgoing contrôleur coalesce.

The Fiduciary Duty in the Selection

However important his day-to-day and year-to-year decisions, none approach the gravity of the contrôleur's last official act. True, every in-tenure selection of personnel affects the corporate well-being intimately, but the choice of a successor crystallizes completely the contrôleur's contribution to the corporate future. If he fails in the selection of a successor, the contrôleur fails in the end. Consequently, this last act should be subjected scrupulously to the fiduciary norms of the office.

The contrôleur has, by definition, total dominion of the entity. He is the ultimate authority in the policy-making hierarchy, and into his custody the corporation and all the corporate assets have been entrusted. In acquiescing to this appropriation, the contrôleur has accepted an unqualified stewardship, with its attendant obligations. Here is the ultimate manifestation of the Custodial Concept of Corporate Control.

At this point, the third subduty of the total set of obligations—the other two are excellence in corporate structure and managerial policy—is preeminent: To strive for the best possible personnel. Clearly implicit in this third subduty is the fivefold norm of appointee suitability: (1) Moral integrity, (2) Intellectual competence, (3) Managerial proficiency, (4) Social acceptability and (5) Satisfactory age and health. Thus, whatever else transpires in any transfer of control—and no less so in a sale—the central concern is the suitability of the successor. Since contrôleur as incumbent possesses the stewardship, and since successor as appointee has acquiesced in the stewardship, both are bound to the broad duty and the fivefold norm as well.

The Technical Definition

One must bear in mind at the outset that the function of the definition is only to discover the exact nature of the premium-bribe. The definition will not include an analysis of the role of the premium-bribe in the overall philosophy of corporate control, but will serve as a prelude to a later study of that question. The objective now, therefore, is a close scrutiny, element by element, to determine exactly what the premium-bribe is.

Next, do not become impatient with exactitude. Many of the control problems disturbing the courts today are caused by differing points of reference. It would be difficult to be overly exact. How absurd it is, in a later analysis of intrinsic illegitimacy, for example, to be uncertain about the subject of the illegitimacy.

The Five Elements of the Premium-Bribe

Broken down into its five principal parts, the sale-of-control premium-bribe can thus be technically defined as:

> (1) *Some form of consideration, monetary or otherwise,* (2)
> *Flowing to the incumbent contrôleur,* (3) *From or on behalf
> of the prospective contrôleur,* (4) *To induce the appointment
> to the office of control,* (5) *Paid knowingly, scienter.*

Although the premium-bribe is indisputably a bribe, it is a peculiar type of bribe with its own special features. A bribe after all can be used to achieve many objectives other than merely the appointment to an office, especially the office of control. The premium-bribe has all the features of the common bribe, and one more. By definition, unlike the ordinary bribe, the premium-bribe consideration must be passed by the would-be contrôleur himself. In short, the individual character of the premium-bribe can only be discerned in the context in which it is inextricably involved, the context of corporate control.

I. The Existence of Consideration

> For the avoydinge of corrupc̃on . . . be it therefore enacted by the Kinge . . . that yf any person . . . bargayne or sell any office, . . . everie suche person . . . shall ymediatlye . . . be adjudged a disabled person in the lawe . . . .
>
> And be it also enacted . . . [that] everie suche bargaynes . . . shalbe voide . . . .
>
> —An Acte againste Buyinge and Sellinge of Offices, 1551, 5 & 6 Edw. 6, c. 16.

The first of many problems facing the fact finder in the analysis of the premium-bribe is the ascertainment of the presence of some consideration. Consideration must be present or the discussion is over. If present, the definition can go forward.

The chore for the fact finder is simple when the consideration is cash and the parties make no attempt to hide it. Such was the case in *Sugden*, where the £75 was clearly a bribe, and in *McClure v. Law*, where Mr. Levy blatantly contracted with Mr. Law and the board to pay them the sum of $15,000, in consideration for the full control of the corporation.

But the consideration is not always so easily identified. In the eminent *Lionel* the Court found no difficulty in isolating the $135,000 consideration paid by Sonnabend to the Muscat group, because this represented the exact excess over the market value of the small three-percent block. And, even more to the point, it was also $135,000 more than the Muscat men had paid Roy Cohn for the very same stock only seven months earlier. (But all possible conjectures would be unavailing to condemn Roy Cohn himself for a similar consideration from Muscat, unless founded on some highly successful detection and a piecing together of many disparate parts. On the face of things no such consideration could be found.)

Patently, the consideration need not be cash. The form may vary from job patronage to contract allocation to the use of a yacht or a summer home. Even more subtle for the fact finder would be a set of intangibles which forestall not only evaluation but even identification. For years, the incumbent contrôleur may have coveted the presidency of the Detroit Athletic Club, or admission into the Bronxville Square Mile or the Down Town Association of the City of New York. The kinds of consideration are limited only by the ingenuity of human desire. Consider, for example, a cumulative pattern of Christmas gifts, a long-term low-interest loan, or perennial purchases below market.

The point is simple. Judge and jury must conclude that consideration is present in one form or another or the first element of the definition of the premium-bribe is absent.

II. Movement of Consideration to the Incumbent

> Usually the controlling interest in a corporation is transferable at a premium. . . . May the seller accept this premium? As an abstract proposition, it seems generally agreed by the courts that he may, though there are few actual holdings to this effect.
>
> —Hill, *The Sale of Controlling Shares,*
> 70 HARV. L. REV. 986 (1957).

On occasion, the premium-bribe consideration is not only visibly present but its path to a point of rest in the contrôleur is also unmistakable. More often than not, however, the path is more like a maze. In New York in late 1966 in Federal court *Laurenzano v. Einbender* pointed up this difficulty of tracking the consideration to its terminus. Yet nothing could be more essential to the definition. A premium-bribe can scarcely be ascribed to the incumbent unless the consideration can be traced with certainty into his hands.

In *Laurenzano* the two-man contrôleur of Retail Centers of the Americas, Inc., was the team of Dobin and Horne, who owned over 70 percent of the discount chain's stock. In an apparently innocuous transfer of control, National Industries, Inc., "on October 7, 1964, bought 690,100 shares of Retail Centers stock from Dobin and Horne, giving National voting control of Retail."[129] The deal after all seemed simply "a sale by Dobin and Horne of a *bare* majority of Retail's voting stock to National at *less than market value.*"[130] The only conclusion: Dobin and Horne wanted out, and National Industries struck a good bargain. But note, National Industries bought only 50-plus of the 70 percent owned by Dobin and Horne.

Certainly nowhere did any consideration flow visibly to the incumbent contrôleurs, other than the money for the stock, a just price at worst. However, as minority shareholder Laurenzano saw the picture, a second transaction, designed as part of the camouflage, hid the extra consideration that smacked of a premium-bribe. And, what is more important, tied the premium-bribe directly to Dobin and Horne, the incumbent contrôleurs.

This second phase of the deal was effected by the newly appointed contrôleur, National Industries, after Dobin and Horne had left Retail Centers. The stratagem was not overly devious. At the instance of National Industries, its new contrôleur, Retail Centers of the Americas, Inc., graciously determined to redeem the remaining 20 percent still owned by ex-contrôleurs Dobin and Horne. Mr. Laurenzano summarized the move as:

> [A] redemption of the remaining twenty-odd percent of the Dobin and Horne stock at an excessive cost to Retail through National's exercise of its control over Retail (amounting . . . to National's paying a premium for the Dobin-Horne control stock out of Retail's assets) . . . .
>
> —*Laurenzano v. Einbender,* 264 F. Supp. 356, 359 (E.D.N.Y. 1966).

Subject to proof by Laurenzano, here was a routine attempt to disguise the consideration of a premium-bribe, and its passage to the incumbent.

Laurenzano carries a triple message. First, in spite of circuity and camouflage, extra effort can unearth premium-bribe consideration, even though buried in an apparently unrelated transaction (which was also the case in the 1979 *Le Mars* in Iowa). Second, the consideration need not move during incumbency, but may well occur after resignation when seemingly no connection remains. Postresignation payment in no way alters the fact: Consideration passed to the former contrôleur as contrôleur. Third, the dollars need not even be the premium-briber's own, but may come directly from the victim's corporate treasury, as with Retail Centers. And Le Mars. And Statesman Group.

But the subterfuge in *Laurenzano* was hardly challenging. An imaginative contrôleur has an intriguing array of possibilities. An enlightened program (with an added cynical tax value) of charitable donations to the incumbent's alma mater in his honor, or regular gifts to the appointee's longtime but deeply impoverished friend who fortuitously happens also to be the contrôleur's brother-in-law. Favorable, but not alarmingly so, contracts awarded to the wholly owned subsidiary of the incumbent's wholly owned corporation. Or a sinecure, summer after summer, to the son of the contrôleur. All of these are at least slightly more deceiving than *Laurenzano*.

In the end, as with the consideration itself, the task for the fact finder resolves itself into one question: Did the consideration actually pass to or for the incumbent contrôleur? Of course, if the ruse is sufficiently successful the proof will fail. But the objective remains, nonetheless, to strip away the camouflage. With success here, the second essential of the definition is confirmed and one new element is added: The terminus of the consideration must be the contrôleur.

III. Movement of Consideration from the Appointee

Bribery . . .

Every person who shall . . . give to any officer, agent or trustee . . . any money . . . with intent to influence his . . . judgment . . . shall, on conviction, be imprisoned in the penitentiary not more than ten years, or fined not more than one thousand dollars, or both.

—MISS. CODE ANN. §97-11-11 (1972).

As with the identification of the consideration and its proven reference to the incumbent, the verification of the third element is at worst not a greatly demanding assignment for the fact finder. At best, it is as simple as laying the blame on Levy for the $15,000 admittedly paid to Law, or holding Crossland liable in *Sugden* as the source of the £75 paid to Horsfield to bribe him out of office. But whether simple or difficult, an essential to the premium-bribe is the indisputable nexus with the appointee-successor.

Whether there is a patent payment directly from the appointee himself, or indirectly from some third party, or a complicated series of moves from the controlled corporation, one overriding principle prevails: The consideration must be the primary responsibility of the successor. Regardless of appearances, all three sources must be reducibly the same. He must be proven the payor or the debtor and be legally liable for the amount.

Directly from the Appointee

Not all payments are as unencumbered as *Sugden, McClure* or *Lionel*. As with receipt, so it is with payment. The dollars can flow immediately from the premium-briber successor-to-be, but under varying subtle disguises.

Thus a natural-gas supplier, owned by a would-be contrôleur, might sweetly see fit to 'impose' on the purchasing incumbent contrôleur personally a series of rates and charges sufficiently below market, for example, to aggregate in a ten-year period a stipulated premium-bribe of $100,000. This was certainly a direct route from successor to incumbent.

The use of his private plane, his Palm Springs cottage, or his country-club privileges, could coalesce almost imperceptibly into a formidable outlay by an eager suitor to an equally eager contrôleur. Whether the benefits pass before or after a successful sale of control is again irrelevant. Nor does a prorated payment for tax purposes diminish accountability.

Indirectly from Third Parties

Perhaps the most difficult of detection of all devices is the use of a third-party friend, relative or debtor. With such cooperation, the prospective contrôleur can channel substantial sums to the incumbent. Gifts funneled through appointee relatives or friends could probably be satisfactorily concealed. True, if the debtor understandably wishes an acknowledgment of satisfaction, that could be revealing. However, the only clamorous evidence generally would be muffled in the personal accounts of the parties. With no external evidence of a suspicious payment, how untoward to insist on a fishing expedition for an unexplained debt-cancellation or a receipt from an unlikely payor.

In the case of the premium-bribe-prone suitor, increased attention by the courts to the sale-of-control premium-bribe predictably will result in greater resort to such third-party duplicity, and thus diminish the chances of ferreting out the hidden consideration of a premium-bribe.

Indirectly from the Controlled Corporation

Although this definitely begs a later question, let it be said: Nearly every successful premium-bribe is sooner or later recouped from the corporation. Often, however, the new appointee avoids the circuity of a personal payment and later corporate recoupment by an immediate raid on the corporate till. Just such a gambit was too subtle for the Iowa Supreme Court in *Le Mars* in 1979. The appointee Iowa Mutual agreed to later use Le Mars Mutual dollars—in effect, embezzle them—for a pension-fund premium-bribe payable to the outgoing contrôleur of Le Mars. Direct embezzlement also produced the premium-bribe in *Statesman*.

Perhaps the most common method of corporate payment is the unearned-salary or consultation-fee device. In *Lionel,* appointee Sonnabend was prepared to approve a $75,000 outlay by Lionel over a five-year period to the former contrôleur, the Muscat group. In a Ninth Circuit case of the prolific sixties, continuing payments to the outgoing contrôleur were openly stipulated in the contract:

> Woike would cause the corporation to employ Wilcox as consultant for five years at a total salary of $118,541, upon the understanding that Wilcox was not to be required to spend more than twenty-five percent of his regular business hours in performing his duties, and that in no event were such duties to unreasonably interfere with his other activities . . . .
>
> —*Oser v. Wilcox*, 338 F.2d 886, 888 n.2 (9th Cir. 1964).

Possibly as a presage for the future, this consultation-fee formula has been used increasingly in the 'sale' of nonprofit corporations. In the late sixties in a confidential letter a Detroit attorney wrote of his client's intentions to 'buy' a local hospital for over $1 million. When this deal was discouraged, the contrôleur of the hospital, undaunted, concocted a substitute arrangement:

> We now understand that Mrs. —— ——— proposed to donate the capital stock of the Hospital Corporation to a local church and the corporation in turn is to retain Dr. —— ——— and Mrs. —— ——— under longterm employment and consultation agreements providing for, we understand, compensation at approximately the same levels they are presently receiving.
>
> We further understand, incidentally, that Mrs. —— ——— has no formal education or practical training in hospital management (and that Dr. —— ——— is mentally incompetent).
>
> —Letter to the Author, Mar. 10, 1967.

As with the other facets of the premium-bribe consideration, the only limit to the variety of the corporate disbursement is human resourcefulness. Retention of the former contrôleur as honorary chairman could mean important emolument—executive perquisites, continuing prestige and social position, appreciable financial savings and benefits—completely apart from a crass unearned salary. The premium-bribe can also come indirectly from the corporate treasury by the deft use of the manufacturer's-agent ploy.

In *Laurenzano* the successful suitor, National Industries, caused the controlled corporation, Retail Centers, to redeem . . .

> . . . the remaining twenty-odd percent of the Dobin and Horne stock at an excessive cost to Retail through National's exercise of its control over Retail (amounting . . . to National's paying a premium for the Dobin-Horne control stock out of Retail's assets), and a sale of G*E*S to Retail at an excessive price (recouping most of National's cash outlay for the control stock).
>
> —*Laurenzano v. Einbender,* 264 F. Supp. 356, 359 (E.D.N.Y. 1966).

One wonders if Glen Alden/Schenley/Rosenstiel in late March of 1968 envisaged the same corporate-till approach of National

Industries/Retail Centers/Dobin and Horne. After Glen Alden Corporation's takeover of Schenley Industries, the stockholder's suit against Schenley directors and Glen Alden charged that Glen Alden—the bribing would-be contrôleur—intended to use Schenley funds (1) to retire the six-month notes given outgoing contrôleur Rosenstiel as part of the payment for his 945,126 shares of Schenley stock, (2) to pay the public holders the cash portion of Glen Alden's offer for their shares, and (3) to repay Glen Alden's borrowings to finance the cash portion of Mr. Rosenstiel's premium-bribe dollars.[131]

Whatever the device, the result is the same. The appointee passes a premium-bribe, either directly to the contrôleur or through third parties or from the corporation itself. In the end, the establishment of this third element requires proof of ultimate responsibility in the appointee for the amount involved.

IV. Purpose to Induce the Appointment

> [T]he transaction . . . was clearly a promise of an appointment, made on a valuable consideration, if not a sale. . . . [T]he Defendant's discretion was shackled, and . . . he would be induced by the agreement to appoint the Defendant, though he were, of all persons, the most unfit . . . .
>
> —*Richardson v. Mellish,* 130 Eng. Rep. 294, 297 (C.P. 1824).

A conceptual nicety, but a relevant one, is in order. Obviously the premium-bribe in itself does not entail action. It is not an act. Yet the money or consideration involved can never become the premium-bribe without first becoming the sole and principal object of an act. This act is the act of premium-bribery and, strictly speaking, premium-bribery and not the premium-bribe is the more proper subject of this aspect of analysis and definition.

The innermost essence of premium-bribery, and correspondingly of the premium-bribe, lies in its purpose. Here is the crux of the definition. The finality of a given action colors it completely and imparts its moral content. To pull a trigger is arguably indifferent. To pull a trigger at a skeet shoot is recreation. To pull the same trigger at an innocent man is murder. But to fend off an aggressor is praise-worthy. The intrinsic gravity of the turpitude, as well as its presence or absence, lies in the purpose.

Thus, too, the purpose in the 'premium' imparts the moral tur-pitude. If the goal is not the appointment to the office, the premium-bribe is absent. The mere passing of money from appointee to contrôleur is as indifferent as the pull of a trigger. The consideration could be the payment of a just debt, an overdue salary, a commend-able gift. Or the inducement to the appointment. To induce the in-cumbent to appoint must be, by definition, the sole purpose of the consideration.

To Buy or To Loot

At this point, a distinction too rarely made, yet disarmingly sim-ple and altogether essential, must clear the way for much of the later analysis of the premium-bribe. Distinguish two totally different ob-jectives: (1) To induce the appointment, and (2) To loot, or benefit, the corporation. 'To induce' is integral to the premium-bribe. 'To loot' is outside its essence.

Necessarily the purpose of the premium-bribe is to induce the appointment. And the purpose of the appointment may be to loot the corporation. Or not to loot. Or to benefit. No matter. The premium-bribe itself—toward the appointment—in no way in-volves the use and disposition of the appointment once secured.

This distinction is important for several reasons other than its ontological truth. Thus, if one depended on looting—or some simi-lar malefaction such as self-serving contracts, unjustified nepotism, or exorbitant salaries—for the discernment of the premium-bribe, those rare instances would be overlooked in which the briber had such less reprehensible thoughts in mind as social status, personal power, or even the praiseworthy objectives of a Robin Hood. More-over, without this distinction a Robin Hood might intriguingly argue from a praiseworthy end, the corporate good, to a praiseworthy means, the premium-bribe. Faced vividly with the sole goal of in-ducement, however, one could hardly be beguiled by the jesuitical 'end justifies the means.' In defining the premium-bribe, therefore, one must consider only the inducement to the appointment and rele-gate any other contemplated, and collateral, malefactions to discus-sion apropos.

The greatest importance of this distinction, however, lies in its application to the later study of the intrinsic illegitimacy of the premium-bribe. If the premium-bribe necessarily includes post-appointment intentions, good or bad, the premium-bribe correspondingly will be good or bad dependent on those intentions. But if the inducement is the sole purpose, the illegitimacy, or the legitimacy, will be determined correspondingly by that purpose alone. Further, this segment of the definition is not meant to explain why the premium-bribe is a perversion, why even a Robin Hood may not buy an appointment. The definition only adverts to the junction of the five elements. The perversity, or lack of it, is the consequence of this junction.

Note, however, that the evil designs of the briber are, in fact, helpful in discerning, but strictly extraneously, the presence of a premium-bribe. An illicit end does suggest an illicit means. One who has future evil in mind will not generally cavil at a little evil en route. Equally possible, however, is the legitimate acquisition of control, but with the ultimate objective of looting.

The Presumption of Premium Presence

Closer scrutiny of the simple purpose 'to induce' yields many further insights, seemingly collateral commentary but in fact essential to the full definition.

The progress thus far has seen the fact finder present three essentials to the definition: (1) Some consideration (2) flowing to the contrôleur (3) from the appointee. To this has been added, but without more, the major and controlling element, the purpose to induce the appointment.

This single purpose, already sharply delimited, is faced, however, with another major circumscription. Just as the definition of the premium-bribe neither requires nor permits an *excess* of 'purpose' beyond the inducement to appoint—for example, an added purpose to loot once appointed—so too the definition of the premium-bribe does not admit of any purpose *less* than 'to induce the appointment.' Any intent short of inducement falls short of a premium-bribe. Thus, any lesser purpose—for example, to reward an incumbent for work well done, to reimburse for past outlays, to give a gift—fails to satisfy the essentials of a premium-bribe. Any consideration flowing from appointee to incumbent for any other reason, legitimate or otherwise, than 'to induce the appointment,' does not constitute a premium-bribe.

With little difficulty, excess of purpose by would-be con-trôleur—a purpose over and above merely 'to induce,' for example, to loot—can be discerned and eliminated from analysis. But it is not so easy to detect other possible *non-premium-bribe* purposes, pur-poses alien to premium-bribery, purposes less than—or other than—a purpose 'to induce,' for example, a gift or debt repayment. Such non-premium-bribe purposes require close scrutiny.

Clearly Identified Consideration

At this point the justification for the selection of the various case examples becomes clearer. As with most moral analyses, the ex-tremes are patent. In the transfers of control of General Motors and Ethyl, no consideration at all was visible. With *Sugden, McClure* and *Laurenzano,* it was obtrusively present. No quibbling over facts was possible.

A chief cause for confusion surrounding the premium-bribe, however, has been the unhesitating and feckless plunge into the midst of the most complicated fact situations, especially the tortuous 'true investment value' of a 'control block' of stock. For example, who can give an off-the-cuff label to the $2-million premium in *Essex Universal?* Is $2 per share over market—$8 vis-à-vis $6—a premium-bribe? Or is it true investment value? Does the 23.7-percent block of *Essex* differ from the three percent in *Lionel?* Or from the stock-less control in *McClure?* How the fact finder determines the presence of a premium-bribe, and the problems he faces in doing it, should not interrupt this study of its essence. The knotty investment-value question posed by *Essex* will be faced later, with the help of the instant analysis.

Suffice for the present that the fact finder has categorically un-covered in *Sugden, McClure,* the nonprofit General Hospital in De-troit, clear-cut cases unencumbered by the queries of *Essex.* If the *Essex* fact finder must throw up his hands in defeat, the matter is con-cluded. The application of clear principles to fuzzy facts is vain.

The problem now remains: What was the purpose of this con-sideration? Can (1) such consideration passing (2) to the contrôleur (3) from the appointee have any other purpose than 'to induce the appointment'?

The Avowed Purpose to Induce

Remarkably the day is not over when the parties unabashedly announce their purpose:

> A. King McCord, the Westinghouse Air [Brake] chairman, was particularly critical of Thomas M. Evans, chairman of Crane, whom he accused of attempting to "force a combination, one way or another," of the two concerns.
>
> . . . .
>
> ". . . During two of the meetings, Mr. McCord said, Mr. Evans proposed that Mr. McCord become chairman of the executive committee of the surviving corporation . . . .
>
> "In the last meeting . . . (Mr. Evans) added the suggestion that I would receive an option to purchase Crane stock and benefits after retirement, possibly by a consulting arrangement."
>
> —Wall St. J., Dec. 19, 1967, at 6, col. 1.

In the takeover of Silvray-Litecraft, a New Jersey producer of architectural lighting, by Shearson, Hammill and E. M. Warburg, the forthright press release meant exactly what it said:

> In addition, Messrs. Gilbert and Gordon received $137,000 each to resign their [control] posts. Mr. Roisman will continue as president and a member of the board.
>
> —Wall St. J., Nov. 2, 1967, at 4, col. 4.

This press release is highly redolent of the statement of *Porter v. Healy*:

> "The price fixed for the stock itself was $165 per share, * * * and the additional compensation that we were to receive for parting with our control was an entirely private business matter."
>
> —*Porter v. Healy*, 91 A. 428, 431 (Pa. 1914)
> (quoting Defendants).

But such an open avowal may not always be forthcoming. What is to be done when the facts point only to indefinable consideration from appointee to contrôleur? How should one approach the purpose, unaided by an open admission?

The Presumption

The fact may be that the parties are readily able to prove a purpose totally unrelated to a premium-bribe. The consideration flowing at the time of the transfer may in truth be a genuine quid for a legitimate quo, a long-due debt, deferred salary, or even a gracious gift. But these alien purposes must be flushed out, and the burden lies on the payor and payee to do the flushing.

Toward this objective a presumption seems tenable:

> When some consideration, clearly identified, has passed to the incumbent contrôleur from the prospective appointee under circumstances reasonably related to the control transfer, a rebuttable presumption arises that the purpose of such consideration is to induce the appointment.

This *Presumption of Premium-Bribe Presence* imposes the burden of explanation on the parties to the transfer.

(Note that this terminology involves an inaccuracy. The title should read: The Presumption of the Presence of the Purpose to Induce. But the purpose 'to induce' is so predominantly the essential part of the premium-bribe that such a transposition seems acceptable, even preferable. In future usage simply recall that the whole is used for the part, albeit somewhat loosely.)

Note, further, that the presumption itself is founded on a very basic assumption that on first face would seem to require substantiation. The primary purpose of the presumption is truly negative: To remove from discussion all purposes foreign to a premium-bribe. *But* does the absence of a non-premium-bribe purpose prove the presence of a premium-bribe purpose? At first blush the answer is 'no.' On reflection, 'yes.' In the elaboration of the presumption, assume momentarily—but for early support—that every unexplained but admittedly relevant consideration is always 'to induce the appointment.' Thus the present approach is only to show that consideration attendant on the control transfer demands an explanation.

The Rebuttal of the Presumption

The explanation by the parties of any suspicious emolument should not be difficult, unless, of course, the suspicions are well founded.

Indebtedness. Of all possible alien consideration a bona fide debt should be the most easily verified. If a direct deal has occurred, the debtor-appointee will show the sum on his books. In any event the creditor-contrôleur will certainly carry the amount on his. If the debt is long-standing, the bookkeeping evidence should be cumulative. If recent, the causes, occasions and circumstances, as well as any parties involved, should be fresh and readily substantiated. In either event, the quid for the suspect quo should be patent.

Salary. The presumption of premium-bribe presence might not have been so strong in the case of the salaries of Mrs. —— ———— and Dr. —— ————, specified in the 'gift' to the local church, had not Mrs. —— ———— originally attempted to extract $1.3 million for the sale of 'her' nonprofit hospital, and moreover had she not been inexperienced and he demented. Absent such damning circumstances their salaries would be no more suspect than a similar salary for Alfred P. Sloan, Jr., were he to have been retained as consultant to General Motors. But the point in either case is the need, not the ease, of explanation. In fact the New York Court in *Lionel* saw the need and apparently felt that Sonnabend and Muscat were unsuccessful in their explanation of the $75,000 to the Muscats over five years. In *Oser v. Wilcox* one would be justified in demanding a similar explanation from Wilcox and Woike, since the $118,541 paid to Wilcox "as consultant for five years" was virtually indistinguishable from the Muscat $75,000.

Gifts. Christmas and Hanukkah, birthdays and anniversaries, should constitute no particular fact-finding problem. Only when the beneficence transcends the customs of a locality, social stratum, financial competence or the established pattern between donor and donee, does the presumption of premium-bribe presence come into operation. The books are full of apt analogies, especially in the tax field, involving purchasing agents, suppliers, the 'five percenters' and Sherman Adams's historic vicuna coat. The norm is the reasonable gift set off against an amount efficacious enough to constitute a satisfactory premium-bribe.

Deferred Compensation. One of the more appealing methods of camouflaging a premium-bribe is the subterfuge of accrued compensation. In a related context, old Mr. Cosgrove, after retirement from the presidency of Green Giant, felt that the $2 million for the sale of control could well be the capitalization of his former salary.

This device of the deferred compensation perhaps deserves greater study. In sum, however, the principal questions would seem to be: Why was the compensation not paid when earned? Was the original employment contract silent on the matter? Why wait until the transfer of control? And most of all: Why should a third party pay a corporate salary?

All these examples say the same thing. Any yacht clubs, perquisites, any unusual emolument, gifts or payment, demand an explanation. This is not unreasonable or intrusive. All the contrôleur need do is simply show that the debt, the salary, the gift, are completely unrelated to an inducement to the appointment. When an accused can account for the consideration, the premium-bribe evanesces.

The Rationale of the Presumption

Five cogent reasons converge to justify such a demand on the principal parties to the control transfer.

First, at that charged instant when control passes from contrôleur to appointee, the complete custody of the corporation hangs precariously in the grasp of each, the one relinquishing, the other assuming. At this moment, therefore, both are logically strict trustees. As such, both are bound to forgo any emolument of any kind connected with the trust corpus. The very hypothesis of a trust relationship is the Benefit-to-Beneficiary Rule.

Equally logically, then, an immediate explanation is incumbent on both. Why? (1) Both are trustees. (2) Trustees garner all for the beneficiaries. (3) Whatever is passing to trustee rather than to beneficiaries is suspect. (4) Whatever is suspect requires explanation. (5) Whatever is unexplained can only be presumed to induce the transfer. And all this occurred at the time of, and reasonably related to, that all-important transfer of control. The conjunction of the two—transfer and consideration—is the key. The least obligation engendered by this Benefit-to-Beneficiary Rule would be an accounting of the suspect consideration.

Second, of all the acts of his corporate career the most important is probably the contrôleur's appointment of a successor, an act fraught with deep trust implications, determinative of the long-term future well-being of the corporation. How completely unthinkable and unlikely for men of prudence to pass unrelated consideration at this time. Even schoolboy discretion would caution a contrary course. Thus does the presumption of premium-bribe presence arise. Since only a rare trustee would not heed such elemental warnings to wait, any consideration is damning, and without explanation presumably induces the appointment.

Third, these two alone, incumbent and appointee, possess the knowledge. Only they are privy to this important information. No one else knows the true nature of the dollars passing at the time of the transfer.

Fourth, and of equal importance, the trusting owners of the entity, the helpless beneficiaries of the trust, have a vested right to know all about any dealings concerned with the corpus of the trust.

Finally, the premium-bribe presumption could be justified for a far lesser reason: A readiness to explain. As strict trustees at the most, as men jealous of their reputation at least, and certainly impelled by the delicacy of the moment, both contrôleur and appointee would demand the opportunity to explain.

The Presumption Illustrated

In the spring of 1968 Detroit Steel had been plodding along at about $18 per share on the New York Stock Exchange in relatively active trading and the firm had "been the subject of takeover rumors for months."[132] In fact the contrôleur of Detroit Steel, Cleveland financier Cyrus S. Eaton, and William R. Daley, long associated with Mr. Eaton in widespread business ventures,[133] wanted out. Negotiations with the Isbrandtsen interests, specifically American Export Industries, led to just the deal: American Export paid $25 per share for 525,000 shares, or about 13 percent of the outstanding shares of Detroit Steel Corporation. With the stock sale . . .

> Jakob Isbrandtsen, president of American Export, and Albert E. Rising, Jr., vice president of American Export, replace Mr. Eaton and Mr. Daley as directors on the boards of both Detroit Steel and Cleveland-Cliffs Iron Co., a Cleveland-based lake shipping and iron ore concern, which is about 24% owned by Detroit Steel.
>
> —Wall St. J., Mar. 27, 1968, at 4, col. 2.

Apply the presumption of premium-bribe presence to these facts. A sizable consideration, $3.25 million over market—about 39 percent—is flowing from the would-be board members to the incumbent contrôleur under circumstances reasonably related to the actual appointments and the patent transfer of control. In such a situation would not the fiduciary duty of both parties call for an explanation of the $7 over market? Did not the owners of the other 87 percent of the outstanding shares, still plodding along at $18, deserve some word?

(Interestingly, this Detroit Steel/Cyrus Eaton 39 percent parallels the 39 percent in the 1968 Southern District *Ferraioli v. Cantor,* where the total premium was $2.2 million. The shares were sold at $3.50 over the $9-per-share market.)

The 'Inexplicable' Few

Granted the success of the negative aspect of the premium-bribe-presence presumption, does this really end the matter? Does the elimination of all foreign and unrelated consideration mean ipso facto that what remains unexplained was passed solely to induce the incumbent to make the appointment?

Consider the situation. The contrôleur has willingly acknowledged relevant consideration—admittedly money has passed—or, reducibly the same, he has failed to rebut the premium-bribe presumption. But impelled by several sincere reasons, he stoutly denies any premium-bribe purpose. This rather rare contrôleur concedes that the consideration cannot be explained by the usual human commerce, or by understandable quids for traditional quos. It is neither debt, salary nor gift. It is transfer related, true, but nonetheless not designed to induce. There is consideration, yes. Unexplained, yes. But premium-bribe, no. Faced with such a staunch stand, how certain can one be?

The second thoughts to such questions are generally the same: All such protestations are impossibly contrary to fact. The staunch stand is so unreal as to invite derision. How could an incumbent accept out-of-the-blue consideration and seriously disavow a premium-bribe or call it something else?

The 'Justified Gratuity'

However absurd and unreal, the haunting doubt persists: Is every unexplained consideration really a premium-bribe? Is it invariably passed to induce? Or more subtly, may not the appointment be merely the occasion rather than the cause of the payment?

Ninety-nine out of 100 cases clearly support the blanket statement: If dollars pass—neither debt nor salary nor gift—with the passing of control, those dollars are premium-bribe dollars. Every unexplained 'gratuity' related to the transfer is causally related. But what of the one out of a hundred that is not so clearly a premium-bribe? If this present investigation is to be exhaustive, however contrary to fact that one in a hundred may be, it nevertheless must be dissected scrupulously. If such scrupulous dissection concludes to a premium-bribe in such an ultimate, absurdly contrary-to-fact instance, no problem can remain with the other 99. The blanket statement will then stand: Every unexplained 'gratuity' is a premium-bribe.

Several reasons support such a minute dissection of such a 'justified gratuity.' Beyond the simple search for the truth lies a practical incentive. Any sincere proponent of the justified-gratuity thesis would undoubtedly concede the illegitimacy if, but only if, the dollars were first identified as premium-bribe dollars. The question for him is not illegitimacy but the presence of the purpose to induce. He sees merely a gratuity, surely not premium-bribe dollars.

What type of mind can engender such self-delusion? Who could live in such a contrary-to-fact world? Antipolar to the hardened 'operator' who admits the premium-bribe but blandly denies its turpitude, here is the well-intentioned entrepreneur, perhaps a bit callow but certainly sincere. The complexities of the modern control transaction, the blasé approach to any gratuity, the apparent divorce of the gratuity from the control transfer, have all conspired to lead this one of a limited few into such a self-delusion.

The Robin Hood explanation also has some fascination. Once posit such a one-in-a-hundred entrepreneur with the unimpugnable purpose of building up the company, and the equally incredible fact follows: Such a Robin Hood could fail to see the premium-bribe in his gratuity. This is scarcely remarkable since the end justifies the means in far less subtle situations. Such reasoning could color a premium-bribe to look like a gratuity.

The most credible rationale, however, has been concocted by competent corporate counsel. Why should a modified Robin Hood, untrained in the law but eminently self-made and successful, question his Wall Street attorney when he quotes from *Essex*, the dissent in *Feldmann*, and *Fenestra*? After all, in 1962 Chief Judge Lumbard for the Second Circuit in *Essex* seemed clear: "There is no question of the right of a controlling shareholder under New York law normally to derive a premium from the sale of a controlling block of stock."[134] Judge Swan, dissenting, in the same circuit some seven years earlier in *Feldmann* had been equally clear: "Concededly a controlling block of stock has greater sale value than a small lot."[135] The Michigan Supreme Court clearly saw no problem in a similar deal:

> Gulf concedes the obvious, that is, that it paid a price per share greater than the market value of Fenestra but says that there is no law which prevents a purchaser from paying a premium [for control] in connection with the purchase of shares.
>
> —*Fenestra Inc. v. Gulf Am. Land Corp.*, 141 N.W.2d 36, 45 (Mich. 1966).

No wonder that an unsophisticated entrepreneur might conceivably conclude that his is a 'justified gratuity.' The prestigious Second Circuit nowhere defines the 'premium,' certainly does not call it a premium-bribe, and at times openly condones it. True, these very courts in other contexts have spoken directly to the contrary. But that has not destroyed the conviction that this gratuity does not induce the appointment. Certainly these eminent courts would never permit an outright bribe. Therefore, this gratuity, or premium, or bonus, or whatever, could not conceivably induce the appointment and thereby become a premium-bribe. Even though a subliminal sense says caution, such an entrepreneur does not pause long enough to strip the situation bare.

As captious as it may seem, the answer to the justified-gratuity argument lies in a look at the more subtle delusions possible to incumbent and appointee. Consider, therefore, a formula least like a premium-bribe:

The Mere Gratuity

Assume that at no time have the parties discussed any gratuity, any expected acknowledgment of the gratitude and indebtedness owed the contrôleur by the appointee for the opportunity to guide the corporation. Least of all has any mention ever been made of a premium-bribe. Not even remotely has any deal been made.

The incumbent contrôleur has spent long hours in evaluating all prospective successors. In the appointee he has found all the qualities demanded by the fivefold norm of suitability—intellectual, moral, managerial, social, physical—as established by his third subduty of the overall fiduciary duty of corporate control: To strive for the best possible personnel. He then proceeds to make his formal selection, installs the appointee, retires from the scene, and rests content that his fiduciary duty has been done.

With the matter thus completely consummated the appointee then steps forward, impelled perhaps by the modern and pervasive sense of fair play in such matters, and bestows an appropriate gratuity on the former contrôleur. Or the appointee Robin Hood, so happy at the opportunity to help the corporation, effuses gratitude and wants to thank the contrôleur by way of a gift. Assume, necessarily, that the stipend is substantial.

Faced with such a fact situation the immediate reaction is to say that here the 'consideration' was not paid *in order to induce* the appointment since the appointment had already been irrevocably made. The appointee could scarce be buying what he already had. At this point the exact legal philosopher would tend to retreat, to conclude that possibly here truly is a mere gratuity, a nonbribe premium, or perhaps a new, legitimate species. Seemingly, this benefaction is at most 'in connection with' or 'related to,' but certainly not 'to induce' the appointment.

A Retroactive Quid pro Quo

To the contrary, fuller reflection finds no real difference between an avowed purpose to induce and the allegedly legitimate formula of a postappointment gratuity. Three factors must be carefully considered:

First, the would-be contrôleur actually proffered, consciously and deliberately, a substantial sum of money or its equivalent. At the same time, and related to the same deal, the incumbent actually accepted, consciously and deliberately, such substantial sum.

Second, the appointee owed the incumbent absolutely nothing. The incumbent had nothing 'coming' from the appointee.

Third, and possibly most important, the sum involved was not *de minimis.* If it were, the parties would have already explained it as an acceptable gift. With this background, a guideline can be reasonably erected. Two extremes are clear: (1) The consideration, on the one hand, must meet the requirements of an acknowledged premium-bribe. How much, in the estimate of experts, would 'buy the office' involving such prestige, influence, desirability? (2) On the other hand, what would a man of relative affluence, social status and habits present to his counterpart as an understandable gift?

With a firm grip on this tripartite reality, one line of reasoning is inescapable. This 'mere gratuity' is a belated quid pro quo, a retroactive settlement of an implicit or sensed contract of purchase. Such a gift would either be *de minimis* or clearly discernible by its size as a premium-bribe. Never would an appointee pay such a substantial sum unless he sensed somehow that he must do so. But the only reason for such feelings would be the conviction that somehow he owed such an amount. Yet if appointee owed contrôleur, the debt must be *for something.* And the *something* must be the appointment. Which, of course, is the definition of the premium-bribe.

The motives for such a postappointment payment are manifold and irrelevant. Implicit could be the fallacious reasoning encouraged by present-day premium-bribe attitudes that somehow the appointee 'owed' the contrôleur for the appointment. That although unenforceable in practicality or in law, the contrôleur somehow 'had it coming' and the appointee correspondingly 'had to pay' if he wanted the office. In the end the only explicable attitude would be the subliminal assumption on both sides that such payment was part of the total understanding, was really integral to the deal, and was part of the accepted procedure. That the appointment would not otherwise be made. That the payment was in fact a precondition.

Such reflections pose a dilemma. Either the 'mere gratuity' is reducibly a premium-bribe or the parties are simpletons. Gratitude could take on such proportions only in such a rare instance.

The Presumption Confirmed

These reflections complete the analysis of the presumption of premium-bribe presence. The parties to a transfer of control are faced with two governing principles: (1) Any consideration passing at the time of, and reasonably related to, the transfer must be explained. (2) Any unexplained consideration is presumed to have been passed to induce appointment.

V. Paid Knowingly, Scienter

> There is no rule better established respecting the disposition of every office in which the public are concerned than this, *detur digniori* [let it be given to the more suitable]: on principles of public policy no money-consideration ought to influence the appointment to such offices.
>
> —*Blachford v. Preston*, 4 Rev. Rep. 598, 601 (K.B. 1799).

The inability to say everything at once is a particularly disturbing handicap in the case of scienter. Necessarily, scienter has been implicit in every single element of the definition, and is integral to each of the four other essentials. The Latin *scienter* has misled many into the limited meaning of 'knowledge' or more exactly 'knowingly,' but the legal and philosophical 'scienter' has two components, equally essential. Not only must appointee and incumbent have sufficient intellectual appreciation of the full meaning of the transaction—the 'knowingly' of the Latin—but both must also have a voluntary, a free-will determination to go forward with the appointment. Thus sufficient reflection by the intellect and full consent of the will are sine qua non to any moral act. And the moral act of premium-bribery is patently incomplete without each of the four other elements: (1) Consideration passing (2) To the contrôleur (3) From the appointee (4) To induce the appointment. If scienter is absent in any one of these four, the act may be illegitimate and hence reprehensible, but it is not premium-bribery.

This interaction of intellect and will transforms a lifeless, disconnected series of movements into a rational, voluntary, human, moral act. By the injection of knowledge and voluntareity the mere materiality of the consideration becomes the formality of a premium-bribe.

Through scienter the actors assume the act as their own. Only by knowledge of intellect and consent of will does a *homo rationalis* accept liability. Without both, any act is unrational, not his own, and without responsibility. Turpitude in the air becomes through scienter the personal baseness of the premium-bribing appointee and the premium-bribed contrôleur.

The Erroneous Conscience

Here again the subjective state of the parties is pertinent. Distinguish: (1) The parties, lacking scienter, fail to pass a premium-bribe (and hence are guiltless) and (2) The parties act knowingly and willingly, but erroneously judge the act faultless (and hence are guiltless). The subjective moral evaluation of the rightness or wrongness—of the turpitude—of the act of passing a premium-bribe has nothing to do with its presence or absence. Before an act can be judged immoral, an act must be present. The allied question, therefore, of 'the erroneous conscience' concerns the culpability of the parties and arises by hypothesis only when total scienter is present, when premium-bribery has in fact been committed.

Do not confuse, therefore, the person who would never knowingly and willingly, scienter, commit the act of premium-bribery with one who would premium-bribe daily, but blandly—and erroneously—maintain that premium-bribery is blameless.

Scienter and the Purpose to Induce

Confusion could arise between the fourth requisite of the definition, 'the purpose to induce' and the fifth, 'scienter,' the will to premium-bribe. What is the difference between the fourth element of the premium-bribe, the purpose to induce, and the voluntareity of the fifth, the will to perform each of the four other requisites of the premium-bribe? Since the distinction is valid and important, the conceptual stages in the application of the intellect and the will—scienter—to the other four requisites, but especially the fourth, is warranted.

Begin with the recollection that without scienter the other four elements—notably the fourth, the purpose to induce—remain only potential and are not yet reduced to actuality. With this in mind, the interaction of intellect and will may be conceptualized into three steps, with the identical process in both appointee and incumbent. This is the conceptual breakdown of the fifth element: (1) The first four elements are laid out in complete array. (A sum of $135,000 would not seem exorbitant to the suitor, or insufficient by the incumbent, to induce the incumbent to accede to the appointment.) (2) As thus laid before the intellect these four factors are studied thoroughly. Confident, with a full knowledge and understanding of the entire control transfer, the intellect passes judgment, giving its approval, and hands this conclusion on to the will. (3) The will in turn, impelled by the reasoning of the intellect, freely assents to the transaction. This consent of the will to the advice of the intellect is scienter. Only now have appointee and contrôleur knowingly and willingly embraced a potential series of actions and vitalized them into the actual, rational, voluntary and culpable act of passing a premium-bribe to induce the appointment. Here then the four *potential* acts—(1) dollars payable (2) to incumbent (3) from appointee (4) to induce—become *actual* by the application of scienter, the fifth element.

Finally in more specific application of scienter to the fourth element, both parties must (1) knowingly and willingly, 'scienter,' embrace (2) ' the purpose to induce' the appointment. Until 'the purpose to induce' is embraced by the will it is merely a possibility.

All this explains the relegation of scienter to fifth place. Each other element had first to be defined before it could be known, assented to and reduced to actuality from potentiality.

Two to Tango

The question naturally arises: Must both appointee and contrôleur have scienter? Very simply, technical verification of the definition requires every single element. And mutual scienter is an element. This rigidity intimately affects appointee suitability, the culpability of the parties, the role and the disposition of the premium-bribe. Thus a naive appointee lacking scienter could be guiltless and hence suitable, saving the naiveté, even though he passed an apparent premium-bribe. The culpable contrôleur, of course, would be forced to disgorge the 'premium-bribe' and be liable in damages. Whereas a contrôleur lacking scienter—and hence culpability— would also be forced to disgorge, but would not be liable in damages.

Just as the criminal code has stratified homicide according to knowledge and consent, so also with the premium-bribe. In cases short of total scienter the principles and philosophy of the premium-bribe are applicable mutatis mutandis, since some other unnamed but very real malefaction is indubitably present.

A definition often appears to be a simple thing. But as it unfolds one is awed as many of the complex questions left for later begin to answer themselves. So it is with the definition of the premium-bribe. The principal benefit, of course, should be univocity of meaning. No more should there be premiums and premiums. Or at least the premium-bribe is now known for what it really is.

Chapter 6

The Sale-of-Control Premium: The Intrinsic Illegitimacy

A. King McCord, the Westinghouse Air [Brake] chairman, was particularly critical of Thomas M. Evans, chairman of Crane, whom he accused of attempting to "force a combination, one way or another," of the two concerns.

. . . .

... Mr. Evans proposed that Mr. McCord become chairman of the executive committee . . . .

"In the last meeting . . . (Mr. Evans) added . . . an option to purchase Crane stock and benefits after retirement, possibly by a consulting arrangement."

"On each occasion," Mr. McCord continued, "I told Mr. Evans that such proposals were inappropriate and shouldn't be discussed in connection with the suggestion for combining the companies, which should be considered strictly on its own merits."

—Wall St. J., Dec. 19, 1967, at 6, col. 1.

"I was shocked" at this offer, he says.

Mr. Evans, in reply, tells an inquirer with a chuckle that he sees nothing wrong with the offer— except that, since Mr. McCord rejected it, "I guess it wasn't inappropriate enough, wouldn't you say?"

—Wall St. J., May 16, 1968, at 1, col. 6.

197

What, in the calloused twentieth century, could so shock Mr. McCord? Was *The Wall Street Journal* cynical, tongue-in-cheek or simply reportorial? What could the realistic chairman of WABCO find so "inappropriate" in the conduct of his counterpart at Crane? Are stock options, retirement benefits, "a consulting arrangement," even "chairman of the executive committee" so reprehensible? Judge Nordbye showed no such concern over the propriety of a $2-million control premium in *Green Giant*. Nor patience with the expert Storer who did:

> The Court: . . . I take it you are motivated by certain ethical principles and standards which you think should be applied to a business transaction of this kind?
> The Witness: This is the case, your Honor.
> The Court: Rather than what the ordinary hardheaded businessman would do under similar circumstances?
> The Witness: This is correct, sir.
>
> —Record at 300-01 (testimony of Robert W. Storer), *Honigman v. Green Giant Co.,* 309 F.2d 677 (8th Cir. 1962).

The Delaware court condoned a similar premium in the 1960 *Manacher v. Reynolds:*

> No other factor being present, they may demand a reasonable premium for the use of their key . . . with which to unlock the "discount" treasure chest . . . .
>
> —*Manacher v. Reynolds,* 165 A.2d 741, 754 (Del. Ch. 1960).

When Shearson, Hammill and E. M. Warburg "gained control . . . of Silvray-Litecraft" was it 'inappropriate' that "Messrs. Gilbert and Gordon received $137,000 each to resign their [control] posts"?[136] In the spring of 1968, would the $7 over market, $3.25 million, that Cyrus Eaton exacted in the Detroit Steel board changes be equally reprehensible?

In the entire control spectrum, the legitimacy of the premium-bribe is probably the most basic, the most vexing, and certainly the most recurrent, question. Undeniably the question has remained unanswered. Yet, the legitimacy, or illegitimacy, of the premium-bribe is focal to every later sale-of-control analysis: (1) The suitability of the prospective contrôleur, (2) The culpability of the incumbent, (3) Possible damages, (4) The role and disposition of the premium-bribe itself.

Further, in the overall control study the premium-bribe—its definition, inner nature, general role—is the apex of the philosophical line. Here all the theories and principles push forward for concrete dollars-and-cents application in day-to-day interplay.

But the vastness of even the narrow premium-bribe problem raises real obstacles to an intelligible approach. Where to begin? Certainly not with the complexities and nuances of the famous *Feldmann/Green Giant/Essex Universal* series. Before the *factual* questions, the *legal* principles must be established. First determine the essence of the premium-bribe, its inner nature. A gargantuan step toward this beginning is an intensive analysis of the intrinsic illegitimacy of the premium-bribe. Once armed with an understanding of its essential turpitude, the battle with the phalanx of subsequent fact—and legal—problems should be less fearsome.

The Definition of the Premium-Bribe

The 'premium' after 'premium' that have come from judge and justice has now at last been satisfactorily analyzed and categorized. The usages have been many and varied. But now that the dust has settled, one 'premium' should reflect a consensus. The premium-bribe for the sale of control is best defined as:

> (1) Some form of consideration, monetary or otherwise, (2) Flowing to the incumbent contrôleur, (3) From or on behalf of the prospective contrôleur, (4) To induce the appointment to the office of control, (5) Paid knowingly, scienter.
>
> —Chapter 5: The Sale of Control and the Premium-Bribe, *supra* at 171.

To this premium-bribe the questions are addressed: Wherein lies the intrinsic illegitimacy? What is the nature of the turpitude? Obviously this is a gratuitous assumption of illegitimacy and must be proven. The approach here, however, is more didactic than dialectic. The onus is therefore twofold: (1) To establish the illegitimacy, (2) While penetrating the essence.

The twofold objective will be pursued in three parts: *I. The Principle of Final Causality. II Suitability, the Sole Norm of Legitimacy. III The Essence of the Turpitude.*

I. The Principle of Final Causality

> That the sale of controlling blocks of shares is a daily phenomenon of our economic order is evident from a casual reading of the financial pages.
>
> —Hill, *The Sale of Controlling Shares,* 70 HARV. L. REV. 986, 1018 (1957).

> The increasing willingness of courts to invalidate control premiums reflects a growing affinity to the Berle-Bayne analysis.
>
> —Hazen, *Transfers of Corporate Control,* 125 U. PA. L. REV. 1023, 1061 (1977).

Every human institution, familial, governmental, corporate, has its own peculiar personality, is constituted according to determined norms of excellence, norms prescribed by intrinsic right order, or by contract, constitution or charter. These norms are the ultimate criteria of institutional perfection. Only insofar as these determined norms are respected does family, state or corporation achieve its potential.

Set off against these ultimate criteria of excellence are the roles of each member of the organization. An institution is nothing without the humans who vivify it. The totality of the entity is the totality of the conduct of its members.

To these ultimates of group activity is added another fundamental: The operative force of the principle of final causality. Basic to any inquiry into right and wrong, perfection and imperfection, rectitude and turpitude, legitimacy and illegitimacy, is this all-pervading and all-governing principle of final causality. Teleology is the driving power in all ethicolegal conduct. A man's envisioned goal or end (the Latin *finis,* hence 'final')—a single aim or an amalgam of objectives—is the sole compelling cause for the performance of any act. The influx of these final causes—the impulses toward the end or goal—moves the will to action, impels a man toward a course of conduct. Final causality is the lone motivating spirit. Man does nothing that is not directed to a goal.

The perfection or imperfection, and therefore the legitimacy or illegitimacy, of every single institutional act is measured completely by the extent to which the well-being of the entity is the motivating force of the action, that is, the degree of the causal influx of organizational perfection into the act. The determined norms of institutional excellence must be the final cause of the conduct of the members. The member's goal must be the group goal.

How does 'final cause' relate to 'means to end'? The final cause is the end. The causal influx of the end into the specific act evidences itself in the selection of the specific means that best conduces to the determined end. The determined end in the present context is total institutional excellence. As an end—the sole acceptable final cause—this institutional excellence must minutely regulate all elements of institutional conduct. Whatever means leads to that end is commendable. Whatever deviates, reprehensible. Single-eyed devotion to specific goals is the prescription for perfection. Any means to any end is right and just only insofar as it is adapted to the proper end. In this sense, and only in this sense, does the end justify the means. Any digression from the moral path to the goal is turpitude, and illegitimacy. Which is only another way of saying (in a means/end frame of reference) that the final cause of a member's act must be exclusively the determined norms of institutional excellence.

In sum, the legitimacy of the premium-bribe is determined solely by the purity of the causal influx. The final cause impelling contrôleur and appointee must be the excellence of the corporation. This is what Mr. McCord meant when he said "the suggestion for combining the companies . . . should be considered strictly on its own merits."

II. Suitability, the Sole Norm of Legitimacy

> Any businessman who transfers control of his company regards it as his ethical duty to assure himself that his successors conform to at least minimum standards of character and responsibility.
>
> —Berle, *"Control" in Corporate Law*, 58 COLUM. L. REV. 1212, 1220 (1958).

The genius—and norms of excellence—of the modern American business corporation can be discerned only by a hilltop view of all the formative factors that give it life, purpose and power. The manifold corporate codes, securities legislation, the quasi corporate common law, the customs and developments in the business community, all blend together to produce an acceptable consensus of corporate perfection.

Whatever cavil with this consensus may be justified relative to lesser matters, few would long debate over the principal purpose of the corporation. Once posit the ultimate profit motive as controlling, then recall the earlier conclusion that "the contrôleur finds his overall fiduciary duty conveniently specified into the tripartite obligation to prosecute the corporate *bonum commune* by striving for: (1) The best possible *corporate structure,* (2) The most enlightened *managerial policy* and (3) The finest *personnel.*"[137] This third subduty assumes consuming importance at the moment of the control transfer. Here, if ever, must a competent person be selected. Into his hands passes the entire corporate future. No single consideration surpasses the suitability of the successor contrôleur. This norm of suitability has already been justifiably specified further into "(1) Moral integrity, (2) Intellectual competence, (3) Managerial and organizational proficiency, (4) Social suitability and (5) Satisfactory age and health."[138]

The Custodial Concept of Corporate Control

At that intense instant of appropriation, when the total corporate entity, all the assets, the future of the firm, pass into his hands, the contrôleur becomes a complete custodian. He becomes the ultimate power over the corporate destinies. This complete dominion correspondingly begets total entity dependence, with necessary reliance, and confidence, willy-nilly.

In one indivisible act the contrôleur accepts the absolute stewardship of the entity and thereby acknowledges, and accedes to, the mandatory norms of corporate excellence. At that moment he becomes a strict trustee, with all the demands of unswerving loyalty and devotion to corporation and shareholders. He assents unreservedly to every implication of the Benefit-to-Beneficiary Rule. Beyond his agreed compensation, all belongs to the corporation. More to the present point, the paramount requirements of the fivefold successor suitability become integral to his commitment. How fatuous to imagine a thoughtful contrôleur oblivious of the overriding need to seek the best possible man to carry on his job.

Beyond the rigid corollaries of strict loyalty—the Benefit-to-Beneficiary and the No Inquiry Rules—the contrôleur is equally bound by contractual justice, a quid for every quo, and the noncustodial obligations of fidelity and simple honesty, common to all, always.

Simultaneous Contrôleurs

At that split conceptual second when the premium-bribe is changing hands the fiduciary duty of a strict trustee rests with exactly equal weight on the outgoing contrôleur and the incoming appointee. At this transitional moment corporate custody is being entrusted by the one and accepted by the other. The *bonum commune* of the entity rests in a delicate balance between incumbent and successor. Each consequently faces the identical custodial obligation defining the suitability of the successor contrôleur.

Although each plays a different role, one active, the other passive, both embrace the same indivisible act in acceding to the appointment. Prior to consummation, both incumbent and appointee envisage in a broad review all the essentials to the transfer. The contrôleur, cognizant of his present trust position, of the Benefit-to-Beneficiary Rule and of the suitability of his successor, is nonetheless prepared to go forward with the appointment. The successor on his part is equally prepared to accept the custody of the corporation and, thereby, the onus of a strict trustee and the same standards of suitability. With the handshake that seals the deal both assume responsibility for all the elements of the appointment. With complete knowledge of intellect and full consent of will, the integral appointment—entrustment by one, acceptance by the other—becomes the joint and several liability of each. Each adopts the acts of the other as his own. Each accedes to each step, and each is as responsible as each for each. Both have full scienter of all. Although one held the gun and the other pulled the trigger, both are equally accountable for the suitability of the successor.

Suitability and Benefit to Beneficiary

From the aspect of either contrôleur or successor, therefore, the rule is clear: The benefit to beneficiary and the suitability of appointee are the only legitimate considerations at the time of the appointment. Suitability is the sole final cause that may flow legitimately into the selection of the new contrôleur. The appointment of a new contrôleur at WABCO "should be considered *strictly on its own merits.*"

III. The Essence of the Turpitude

> The core of the concept of a bribe is an inducement improperly influencing the performance of a public function meant to be gratuitously exercised.
>
> —J. NOONAN, BRIBES xi (1984).

> [T]here is a unanimous conviction on the part of those who have taken special interest in small stockholders that it is unethical for a management group to sell control of a company to outside interests on terms not made available to all stockholders.
>
> —Vanderpoel, Chi. Sun-Times, Oct. 10, 1951, Finance Sec. at 47, col. 1.

> But the sale of an office of trust has always been deemed illegal.
>
> — *Richardson v. Mellish*, 130 Eng. Rep. 294, 297 (C.P. 1824).

The totality of the turpitude of the premium-bribe consists of three conceptually distinct elements caused by separate breaches of fiduciary duty, each with its own peculiar contribution and coalescing into a distinctive moral unit. This tripartite illegitimacy could be defined as:

> *(1) The perversion of the judgment of the incumbent contrôleur, engendered by an appointment of a successor induced by a cause other than suitability, (2) That is, for consideration illicit in itself, (3) Resulting in the appointment*

of a candidate unsuitable by reason of his own active role in the inducement.

This technical definition states the major thesis set for proof.

The complexities of the essence of the turpitude of the premium-bribe thus conceptually divided could best be further unraveled in four successive steps: *(1) The Perversion, the Principal Illegitimacy. (2) The Illicit Consideration. (3) The Unsuitability of the Successor. (4) The Coalesced Turpitude.*

(1) The Perversion, the Principal Illegitimacy

> To take a bribe is commonly understood as a prostitution of one's office. To pay a bribe is to play the part of a professional seducer. . . . Human beings do not engage in such acts without affecting their characters, their view of themselves, their integrity.
>
> —J. NOONAN, BRIBES 700 (1984).

> [Sales of control] have in England been treated as contracts of turpitude, and have been invariably held . . . illegal and void.
>
> —*Outon v. Rodes,* 10 Ky. (3 A.K. Marsh.) 432, 433-34 (1821).

The deeper one gets inside the premium-bribe the more ramified are the concepts and subconcepts. The overall question of illegitimacy is undoubtedly the focal concern in the broad premium-bribe problem. Correspondingly, at the core of this illegitimacy lies the perversion of the contrôleur's judgment in the appointment of his successor. Although this perversity is not the whole of the matter, it stands foremost among the three components, and even might mistakenly be conceived to constitute the total turpitude. Principal, yes, but only one of three.

The nuances of this perversion are delicate, but nevertheless may be sharply limned. Several definable features characterize the premium-bribe perversion.

Final Causality

The logical synthesis of the perversion could best begin with the basic causality motivating the appointment. Start with the obvious truth that the sale-of-control consideration, the material cause of the premium-bribe, passing from appointee to contrôleur has an effective causal impact on the contrôleur's judgment in his selection of a successor. The definition of the premium-bribe expressed this final causality by the infinitive 'to induce.' Here patently is the purpose, goal, end, *finis,* of the would-be contrôleur. As such it is a proven ingredient of the premium-bribe. This final causality, the inducement effected by the premium-bribe consideration, is certainly fundamental to any perversion. 'To induce' is a prime element in the notion. The contrôleur is drawn, enticed, led on (the Latin *ducere*), pulled, toward an end, goal, the consideration of the premium-bribe.

More properly, however, the causal influx of the consideration is only one of the two principal coconstituents of the perversion. 'To induce' is only one element, a single straight-line pull to the goal. It is almost indifferent, bland, and certainly does not express the full force of the perversion.

Further, 'to induce' carries no pejorative sense to it. Strictly, one may be induced by legitimate objectives, hopes of corporate profits, dreams of a corporate windfall. True, the connotation may carry a certain tincture of the emotional, irrational or unreasoning, as if the will were not fully free, or that 'induced' carried a certain suggestion of 'seduced.' But the exact denotation of the word involves none of this. It is noncommittal. The contrôleur was simply induced to the appointment through a final cause. Whether legitimate or turpitudinous is left unsaid.

A Turning Away

The innermost guts of the perversion, however, is the second of the two coconstituents. To the straight-line element 'to induce' is added the notion of 'turning away' (the *vertere* in the etymology). With this addition the simple concept of 'to induce' becomes a complex constituent, an inducement turning away another inducement. Here is a conflict of final causes. The intrusive premium-bribe consideration turns away the influence of another would-be or, better, should-be, final cause, successor suitability.

But the participle 'turning away' is slightly inadequate. The element of dynamism is lacking. The intrusion, rather, is positive, forcible, almost violent, far from a static supersession. The final causality of the premium-bribe consideration shoves aside the final causality of the suitability. This forcible turning away is the perversion. Syllogistically:

> (1) *The suitability of the successor is the sole final cause that may flow legitimately into the selection of the new contrôleur.* (2) *The consideration of the premium-bribe is totally irrelevant, foreign, antagonistic, to suitability.* (3) *Yet the premium-bribe consideration does flow as a final cause into the selection of a successor.*

Here is the quintessence of the perversion.

The Moral Element

The term 'perversion,' therefore, correctly carries a pejorative meaning—and although the constant repetition of the word may be tedious, no suitable synonym in English even remotely expresses the concept—because the forcible ousting of successor suitability is illegitimate and hence morally reprehensible. The perversion intrinsic to this ouster is, after all, the chief element of the overall moral turpitude of the premium-bribe.

The act of the contrôleur, adopted completely by the appointee, with full knowledge of intellect and free consent of will, consisted in the deliberate rejection of the sole acceptable norm of corporate excellence, the suitability of the successor, and the acceptance of a reprobate consideration, the premium-bribe, in its place. Here is trustee disloyalty in essence: Not so much being against the shareholder beneficiaries as not being with them. Not unsuitability, but turning away from suitability. Moral turpitude is the deviation from acknowledged norms of conduct. Any digression from the straight path to the goal of a suitable successor is culpable. Yet neither 'deviation,' a straying off the *via*, nor 'digression,' *digressus*, a 'side step,' expresses the active, intrusive force of 'perversion.' True, both carry the moral note of wandering from the straight and narrow, but both lack the peculiar turpitude of pushing aside the legitimate final cause as well.

Permanency

An inclination arises to characterize this conflict of causes as a deflection, a bending aside, a diverting from the acceptable objec-

tive, but both 'deflection' and 'diversion' have a quality of imperma-
nence, as though the intrusion of the premium-bribe were only
temporary, that right order would soon return and the suitability of
the successor would then become the sole concern. Both deviation
and digression also lack this necessary note of permanency which
is expressed in the corruption implicit in perversion. The same disability is present in 'aberration,' although 'aberration' has some intimation of permanence.

Perfect Perversion

The prefix 'per' carries the important concept of completeness
into the meaning of perversion. 'Per' is the intensive, not the preposi-
tional, prefix and correctly expresses the idea of thoroughness, totality, as in '*per*fervid,' '*per*lucid' and more aptly in '*per*fect,' unsullied
by any foreign substance, integral. Which is perfectly true of the
premium-bribe perversion. No part of the illicit cash has any relation
whatsoever to the suitability of the successor. It is totally foreign, unrelated, antagonistic, to suitability. It is totally other. As antagonistic,
totally other, this cause enters into the formation of the contrôleur's
judgment of selection (Else why given and accepted?). As completely
foreign, with no element of suitability as a cause, this illegitimate
cause perforce supplants, to the total extent of its influx, the legitimate one. As totally supersessive, therefore, this causal influx is totally perverse. A perfect perversion.

Note well that this says nothing about the *quantity* of the influx,
infinitesimal or overwhelming, only about its *quality*, totally perverse. Thus the relative influence on the contrôleur's judgment by
the premium-bribe and other final causes may vary. Nepotism, expediency, friendship, or even successor suitability, may each contribute
to some degree. But to whatever extent the cause may flow, infinitesimal or overwhelming, that causal influx of the premium-bribe, as totally foreign and substitutive, is *totally* perverse. Although the cold
cash may have only an infinitesimal causal influx, that infinitesimal
causal influx is nonetheless a perfect perversion. Merely because the
premium-bribe is small does not mean that it is any less a premium-
bribe. And all of it is perverse.

(To accord proper recognition to this line of reasoning, the definition of the premium-bribe arguably should read 'to pervert' rather
than the innocuous 'to induce.' Strictly, however, the notion of per-

version is outside the definition itself. Without it, the definition adequately answers the question: What? Indisputably the perversion is latent in the five elements of the premium-bribe. But only by a synthesis and expatiation of the five does it emerge. The reasoning necessary to arrive at the inner nature of the perversion is over and beyond the mere definition. The definition is an exponible proposition and the resultant exposition is appropriately reserved for just such a present study.)

The Perversion Classified

The question next arises: Is this perversion peculiar to the premium-bribe? When the contrôleur rejects the suitability norm for a reason other than a premium-bribe, what then? Is that a genuine perversion also? Or is the perversion of the premium-bribe sui generis, with a special identity discernible even in isolation from the other two components of the premium-bribe turpitude? Or without the other features of the premium-bribe—the illicit consideration and the premium-bribe-engendered unsuitability—is its perversion the usual garden variety, common to every other type?

The answer lies in a comparison of the various perversions possible in a transfer of control. Faced with imminent retirement, a contrôleur may select his successor for many illegitimate reasons. At age eighty, for example, ennui, lethargy, even senility, could land the appointment in the lap of the first person with enough cash to buy the thirty-percent block at market. Or a Harold Geneen, Norton Simon or Charles Bluhdorn could conceivably be too busy with too many firms to avoid an occasional negligent appointment. Or friendship could be the final cause. Possibly the most prevalent non-premium-bribe perversion, however, is nepotism.

In each case—expediency, friendship, nepotism—a causal influx other than suitability determined the contrôleur's selection. In each instance, therefore, his judgment was perverted. Each is an instance, moreover, of the breach of the contrôleur's fiduciary duty in the appointment of his successor and as such is relevant to the overall study of corporate control. But nonetheless irrelevant as such to the premium-bribe. Consider the selection of the contrôleur's son. Paternal prejudice, as a prototype for nepotism, expediency, friendship, perverts the contrôleur's judgment just as effectively as any premium-bribe. From this limited aspect, therefore, the perversion intrinsic to paternal prejudice is absolutely identical to the premium-bribe perversion. That is, the premium-bribe cannot find its distinctive character in the perversion itself, but must look elsewhere for isolation from paternal prejudice, friendship, expediency.

At most, therefore, the premium-bribe perversion may be characterized as the principal constituent of the turpitude, but certainly not the distinctive one. As clearly common to many another illegitimate appointment, therefore, the perversion of the premium-bribe is just another ordinary species of the genus 'perversion,' along with those of parental prejudice, expediency, friendship, et alia.

The Suitable Son

But another question. Is this perversion of the premium-bribe, as common to many another illegitimate appointment, really distinct, as a special type of turpitude, from the turpitude of (1) the illicit consideration and (2) the successor unsuitability? The answer here lies in a stratagem of isolation. Expand the example of the contrôleur's son. Posit one further condition. Not only did no monetary consideration pass—paternal prejudice was the lone motivating force—but the son, moreover, was not only oblivious of the motivation but was suitable to the nth. Here the perversion is perfect, but without either illicit cash or unsuitability of successor.

The perversion qua perversion now stands stark and alone. True, as common to other perverted appointments, it is not sui generis. But it is a turpitude peculiar to itself, completely distinct from the turpitude of both the other coconstituents. Thus set off, the perversion as such demands deeper analysis, especially toward the day when the question of the culpability of candidate and incumbent arises.

The Grades of Gravity

Recall that the premium-bribe, however infinitesimal, is wholly corrupt. But the quality of the perversion, as perfectly perverse, says nothing of its quantity, which may vary from nil and minuscule to overwhelming and complete. Thus a large premium-bribe is totally reprobate, but so is a small one. The extent of the total perversion in the one, however, varies in infinity to the other. What, then, of the quantity of the perversion? (The quantification of a quality is an old legal trick. Witness slight, ordinary and gross negligence.) The turpitude of the perversion can in fact be calibrated according to inherent gravity. This calibration will form the measure for future application apropos.

One overriding truth prevails in grading the gravity of the turpitude: The core of the perversion is the turning away from the sole legitimate norm governing the appointment, the suitability of the successor. Consequently, the extent of this turning away determines exclusively the grade of gravity of the perversion. Mark exactly, no other factor fixes the degree of the perversion. Insofar as the contrôleur is efficaciously influenced by any final cause other than the qualifications of the candidate, that far has his judgment been corrupted. Strictly, that is the whole of the matter. Nothing more need be said, since the perversion consists of only one thing, the rejection of the lone legitimate norm, suitability.

A Conflict of Causes

But this central and governing principle is buttressed by a correlative. When the contrôleur 'turns away from' suitability he perforce 'turns to' something. To what does he turn? What is the correlative of suitability? When the contrôleur rejects qualities of appointee excellence, what does he embrace? The reply is another question. What are all the contraries of suitability? What influential factors drag the contrôleur away from any thought of the merits of the candidate? The answer to this gives the correlative: Blind nepotism, gross paternal prejudice, unthinking friendship, lazy expediency, and the greed of a premium-bribe. Any one of these alone, or a congeries of all, is pulling at the other end of the tug rope. But since this analysis concerns primarily the premium-bribe, put aside the various other possible perversions. Anent the moment, the sole correlative of suitability is the illicit consideration of the premium-bribe. When the contrôleur, therefore, in the context of the sale of control, 'turns away from' considerations of successor suitability he perforce 'turns to' considerations of dollars.

Here, however, a certain conceptual difficulty arises in using the somewhat nontechnical approach of 'turning away' and 'turning to.' Better would be the philosophically exact concepts of final causality. The totality of causal influx effecting the contrôleur's judgment of successor selection must necessarily reach the level of 100 percent. Since the sole legitimate final cause is successor suitability, and by the agreed limits of the present study the sole illegitimate final cause is the illicit consideration, these two conflicting causes must influence the contrôleur in perfectly complementary degrees. As the influx of the one is greater, the other is necessarily less. An infinity of gradations lies between the antipolar extremes. When the premium-bribe is the sole motivating force and suitability plays no part, the perversion is absolute. To the contrary, as the influence of successor suitability increases, the premium-bribe evanesces, finally to disappear.

With this, the grades of gravity of the premium-bribe perversion may be expressed axiomatically:

> In proportion as the premium-bribe consideration has causal influx into the formation of the judgment of selection, thus far must suitability yield and cease to have a causal influx. To that extent is the contrôleur's judgment perverted.

Applying the inapplicable percentages of the physical sciences, therefore: As the influence of premium-bribe money on the contrôleur's judgment increases from zero through 25 to 50, 75 on to 100 percent, the effect of successor suitability decreases from the optimum 100 on down to nil.

Unsuitability vis-à-vis Suitability

All this is irrefutable. And is most satisfying, until someone asks: But what of *unsuitability*? Where is the relevancy of unsuitability? When the contrôleur turns away from successor suitability must he not necessarily turn to unsuitability? Rejection of the one involves perforce the embrace of the other? All else being equal, would not a premium-bribe-bent contrôleur demand a greater kick-in from a grossly unsuitable blackguard than from a high-minded but slightly inept applicant? Would not, therefore, unsuitability rather than suitability be the gauge of the perversion? The less or greater the unsuitability, the less or greater the premium-bribe? Indisputably, an impartial incumbent who viewed each prospect with the dispassionate green of the dollar would logically exact greater tribute from the blackguard. Consequently, unsuitability must measure the grade of the gravity? As a further consequence would not the absence of unsuitability mean the absence of illegitimacy? Remove the unsuitability and the turpitude disappears? Without unsuitability, legitimacy?

A highly theoretical but ideal hypothetical will answer these questions and illustrate the proper place of successor *unsuitability* in the synthesis of premium-bribe perversion. Consider three prototypal candidates for control. Apply possible varying grades of contrôleur competence to a possible appointment of each. The prime prospect is an Iacocca on his mother's side and altogether suitable. A second possibility lacks little of the first, but is not without criticism. The third candidate unfortunately embodies every quality alien to corporate success.

Prepared to be perverted in direct proportion to the actual and estimable qualifications, or in-estimable, of the three aspirants, the incumbent would immediately weigh the current market in contrôleurs, and conclude to a $100,000 exaction from the pitiable third, totally bereft of suitability. By an accurate adjustment he would demand $10,000 from the second, and honestly appoint the first without more.

This fanciful example only serves to confirm the basic thesis. In each instance perversion was engendered by the rejection of successor suitability and the acceptance of a proportioned premium-bribe. Granted, the dollar amount involved may be transposed into correspondingly quantified percentages of appointee *unsuitability*—zero, ten, 100—and thus serve admirably to measure the extent of the dereliction in readily recognized terms. But the perversion remains a turning away from suitability, a turning to the dollars, certainly not a turning toward unsuitability as a cause.

Reflect on a cogent intrinsic argument in support of this. No incumbent in his right mind would appoint a successor *because he was unsuitable.* Unsuitability is unthinkable as a final cause for the appointment. One can be attracted only toward a good. Unsuitability is an evil, undesirable, and as such essentially unable to attract anyone. The most calloused contrôleur would appoint his successor in spite of his unsuitability, scarcely because of it. The perversion, therefore, does not consist, as some might suspect, in appointing an unsuitable successor. Rather it consists in appointing any successor for a reason other than suitability. In the end, the perversion consists solely in turning away from suitability and turning to the premium-bribe consideration.

An Inverse Indicator

But this tendency to relate the perversion to the presence of unsuitability rather than the absence of suitability is an explicable frailty. Under some conditions, the unsuitability of the successor is a reliable guide to the extent of the perversion, even though a negative one. From a certain backwards viewpoint unsuitability does seem to affect the grade of the gravity. In fact, the simple triple hypothetical was constructed to do just that. Although unsuitability cannot possibly have a causal influx on the contrôleur's judgment and the grade of gravity must depend exclusively on the suitability, the causal influx of appointee suitability is on some occasions directly correlative to his unsuitability, and hence unsuitability thereby may become a somewhat accurate measure of the perversion, albeit only accidentally.

The explanation of this phenomenon begins with a truism. Any given human being, and certainly a prospective contrôleur, is a highly personal mix of talents and drawbacks, energies and lethargies, abilities and disabilities. Unless he is either a perfect prospect without blemish or the totally bereft, he is a more or less amalgam of corporate advantages and disadvantages, of suitabilities and unsuitabilities. Pursuant to the obvious law of the human dispensation, these suitabilities and unsuitabilities vary necessarily in a directly complementary manner. The greater the former, the lesser the latter, and vice versa. Thus the more handicaps—social, managerial, ethical—holding down an aspirant, the less suitable he is. Each added excellence, however, decreases his unsuitability.

Apply this law of human personality, the fluctuating ratio of unsuitabilities to suitabilities, to the ad hoc situation of a departing contrôleur searching for a successor, and a substantial premium-bribe.

This incumbent is perfectly realistic. As with the impartial contrôleur who estimated the contrôleur market objectively at $100,000, $10,000 and nil, no suppressive or repressive thoughts, parental prejudices, expediencies or amicitial biases, cloud his judgment. A gross premium-bribe quid must offset the totality of an estimable-unsuitability quo, or no deal. In fine, the incumbent is determined that the respective causal influences on his selection among several prospects will be exactly reflective of reality. He has no intention of blinding himself to the facts. The degree of actual suitability—and hence the corresponding degree of unsuitability—and the number of dollars of the premium-bribe will each exert their full and proportioned influence. When this is true, the degree of *un*-suitability is a reliable inverse indicator of the grade of gravity of the perversion. Why? First, the suitabilities and unsuitabilities in any given human vary reciprocally one with the other. Secondly, an impartial premium-bribe-bent contrôleur will accord an unbiased weight to the objective suitability of the successor and the amount of the premium-bribe. Thirdly, when the causal effect of each reflects reality, the unsuitability, as a perfect correlative of suitability, thereby becomes as well a perfect correlative of the premium-bribe. As such, unsuitability is a reliable gauge of perversity, but only because it indicates lesser or greater suitability, not because it is a cause itself. In the end, the only reliable indicator is the turning away from suitability, not the presence of unsuitability.

Again the Suitable Son

But this seemingly semantic problem becomes acute only when the actual suitability of the candidate is *not* a causal factor in the appointment. Return to an apposite analogy. Reconsider the contrôleur's son: Absolutely ideal for the job, young, vigorous, talented, a veritable Sarnoff in every respect. Not a penny passed, with father incumbent. Yet in making the appointment only one consideration prevailed: Paternal prejudice. The father saw neither suitability nor unsuitability. His son would ascend the throne without more. Knowing none of this, the son unhesitatingly acceded.

Here is a perversion as perfect as possible. Yet not a tincture of unsuitability could be found in the contrôleur's son. Obviously, therefore, the father could not possibly have been turning to unsuitability. This perfect perversion consisted solely in a total turning away from the only acceptable norm, appointee suitability. Rather remarkably, therefore, the actual suitability of the candidate need not affect the contrôleur's judgment at all if he successfully blinds himself to all but paternal prejudice.

The Naive New Yorker

The suitable-son analogy points up the danger of using successor unsuitability even as a negative measure of the perversion. Just as a prejudiced father, so too a premium-bribe-bent contrôleur may prescind completely from suitability. Posit a fully suitable selectee, a naive New Yorker, for example, who listened credulously (and hence guiltlessly) to his Wall Street counsel who assured him: "There is no question," as Chief Judge Lumbard said in 1962 for the Second Circuit in *Essex Universal,* "of the right of a controlling shareholder under New York law normally to derive a premium from the sale of a controlling block of stock."[139] Here then is a fully suitable successor, saving of course the naiveté. Nonetheless, the thought of the selectee's suitability never enters the contrôleur's mind. The maximum or at least the sufficient premium-bribe is his sole concern. Here, patently, unsuitability is not essential to the perversity. Here, as with the totally suitable son, the prevailing point is the total absence of a causal influx of suitability, not the presence of unsuitability. Thus *causal* suitability is everything, whereas *actual* suitability may be irrelevant. The question is not the actual presence of suitability in the appointee, but the extent to which it flows into the contrôleur's judgment as a cause. Actual suitability is relevant only if given causal effect by the contrôleur.

The extent, from total through partial to nil, to which a prejudiced father or a premium-bribe-bent contrôleur prescinds from objective merits will thus determine the grade of perversion, even though the successor is in fact completely suitable.

Interestingly, therefore, the perversion is equally perfect in two antithetical cases: The prejudiced father ignoring the total suitability of the son, and the premium-bribe-bent contrôleur in the triple hypothetical appointing the totally bereft successor. Both are equal instances of a turning away.

The High-Minded Robin Hood

Trouble begins the moment one forgets that the premium-bribe perversion is deliberate disloyalty, a conscious renunciation of a pledge to consider a successor "strictly on [his] own merits." By pushing aside such basics, the casual mind can move easily to dreams of corporate greatness, bulging coffers and abundant dividends. Insidiously, and deep in the subliminal, the old fallacy begins to do its work. After all, 'the end does justify the means.' A lapse of memory, fortified by the pervasive sense of a justified means, invariably permits condonation, even praise, of a premium-bribing Robin Hood. Such laxness is understandable. Panicky shareholders can overlook much, perhaps easiest of all a premium-bribe, if the corporate promise is rosy enough.

But cold logic leads to only one conclusion. The highly touted Robin Hood, with unexcelled credentials and purportedly the finest ambitions for the firm, has nonetheless deliberately determined to twist the contrôleur from his avowed dedication to suitability, and to force himself into office for $100,000 in cash (else why the proffer and the acceptance?). Both high-minded Robin Hood and premium-bribe-bent contrôleur freely and consciously acquiesced in a $100,000 act of disloyalty. To the extent at least of the $100,000, the appointment was made not because of suitability, but because of the cash.

This Robin Hood reasoning could be particularly apropos in any appointment, for example, of Crane as contrôleur of WABCO, or Shearson, Hammill/Warburg of Silvray-Litecraft, or Isbrandtsen of Detroit Steel.

The various examples, from the triple hypothetical to the suitable son, the naive New Yorker and the high-minded Robin Hood, should adequately isolate the perversion from the other two coconstituents of the premium-bribe turpitude, and reaffirm its essence as a turning away from suitability, not a turning to unsuitability. The perversion is the turning away.

In the subsequent syntheses endeavor to keep the perversion qua perversion in its present isolation.

(2) *The Illicit Consideration*

> "Where the president and director of a corporation was paid money by outside parties upon the condition that he procure their election as directors of the corporation with powers of control and management, such money was received by virtue of his office and from official acts and he must account to the corporation for it."
>
> —*Brecher v. Gregg*, 392 N.Y.S.2d 776, 780 (Sup. Ct., N.Y. County, 1975) (quoting N.Y. JUR. *Corporations*).

The perversion of the contrôleur's judgment may be the core

of the premium-bribe illegitimacy, but what of the cold cash that constituted the consideration? After all, as the New York Court said in *Lionel*, the "price . . . being paid for . . . control . . . [is] the all important emolument of the transaction."[140] Does this all-important emolument add anything to the turpitude? If so, what? And what is its nature? Its gravity?

The answers not only explore further the present problem of intrinsic illegitimacy, but ultimately determine the dollars-and-cents disposition of the premium-bribe itself. May the contrôleur keep the cash? Or must he return it to the would-be successor? Or hand it over to the corporation? Or to the shareholders? What of any profits flowing to Mr. McCord from his "option to purchase Crane stock"? And the "benefits after retirement"? These questions give the final fillip to later premium-bribe analyses.

An interjection is in order. Patently, the consideration used to pervert the contrôleur's judgment need not be 'cold cash' or any other tangible enticement. Remember: For years, perhaps, the incumbent contrôleur has coveted the presidency of the DAC, or admission into the Bronxville Square Mile or the Down Town Association of New York. The kinds of consideration are limited only by the ingenuity of human desires. As for instance, Mr. Evans's offer of the chairmanship of the executive committee. For present hypotheticals, however, the use of tangible consideration is more apposite. Any problems peculiar to the intangible nature of the inducement do not arise in the area of the intrinsic illegitimacy as such and will be faced appropriately in later chapters.

For now, therefore: What, if anything, could Mr. McCord find "inappropriate" in these "benefits" and the "option"?

Perversity versus Illiceity

With thoughts of the premium-bribe perversion so vividly in mind, one wonders: Does the "price . . . paid for . . . control" partake of the perversion? Or does it have a turpitude all its own? Does the all-important emolument become tainted by its part in perverting? Does the perversion—essentially the rejection of suitability—so permeate the premium-bribe that the consideration itself becomes perverse?

Only by metonymy could the consideration conceivably be called perverse. To be exact, it is the contrôleur who is perverse. Even more correctly, his judgment has been perverted. The price paid is only the means to the end, an instrumental cause, simply the stick that hit the head. Both money and stick are indifferent means used for a reprehensible purpose. As such, neither takes on the turpitude of the purpose. The malice lies with the battery, not the stick. The perversion is attributable solely to the contrôleur's disloyalty, not to the money that proved it.

The parallel is pat with the other acts of disloyalty. Nepotism, expediency, friendship, equally pervert the contrôleur's judgment, but are not thereby peculiarly tainted. The paternal regard of a father does not become intrinsically less admirable merely because he appoints his son. Figurative speech can mislead. People incorrectly characterize the paternal affection as 'misguided' when, in and of itself, it is perfectly praiseworthy. What is 'misguided' is the father's judgment in ignoring successor suitability.

These popular designations—paternal affection as misguided, the price paid as perverted—do have a reasonable foundation in reality. Both paternal affection and the price paid do take on a quality theretofore not possessed. In fact, the money paid for control will never be the same again. Perforce, it is now the money that perverted the contrôleur's judgment. As such it differs vastly from the money put in the poor box. But in neither case does the money's new quality permeate its essence. Such an accidental designation does not alter the substance. The medieval Anglo-Saxons who chopped up and burned the branch that struck the traveler would undoubtedly burn the premium-bribe money as well. Yet the perversion of the contrôleur imparted none of itself to the money as such.

Any illegitimacy peculiar to the price paid for control, therefore, must be found in a turpitude other than the perversion of the contrôleur's judgment in his selection of a successor.

The Essential Illegitimacy

Arguably, the total turpitude of the premium-bribe has three separate constituents, the perversion, the illicit consideration and the appointee unsuitability. But at most each is only conceptually distinct from the other. Hence, any attempt at analysis of one constituent in isolation from another faces a substantial obstacle: How to prescind from the perversion when dissecting the illegitimacy of "the all important emolument of the transaction"? Or, will not the unsuitability of the successor intrude on any separate study of the illicit consideration?

The logical device of analogy can again deftly sidestep this obstacle by transforming a merely conceptual distinction into a real one. Consider a perfect parallel: Illicit emolument, but without the mind-distracting constituents of perverted judgment and unsuitable successor. Envisage the hypothetical president and chief executive officer of U.S. Bolt and Screw, Incorporated. At an annual salary of $90,000, the head of Bolt and Screw has overall charge of an aggressive firm. But latterly the aggression has gone awry, at least in the president's office. What began as a series of highly effective public-relations appearances—regional meetings of the American Society of Corporate Secretaries, the New York Society of Security Analysts, occasional conventions and conferences—has degenerated into a highly lucrative, image-damaging, barnstorming program. With nary a nod to the firm, or even the industry, Bolt and Screw's leader has become a latter-day, corporate Billy Sunday, at $1,000 per banquet. The upshot? A personal net of $20,000 a year to the apostle of corporate laissez-faire.

Here, standing isolated, is one element common to the premium-bribe, unearned recompense, without the perversion of the officer's judgment or any question of an unsuitable successor. The malefaction is a clear case of illicit emolument, without more. The chief executive officer of Bolt and Screw accepted $20,000 in compensation for corporate acts, performed pursuant to a corporate program, in fulfillment of a corporate duty, in the course of official business, during the regular workweek, for which he was already amply remunerated.

Over against the $20,000 over-the-table honoraria juxtapose another $20,000, for example, in profits from "an option to purchase . . . stock and benefits after retirement" as "the premium price . . . paid for . . . control." Prescinding from any possible perversion as well as successor unsuitability, cannot the price paid for control be justifiably equated with the celery-circuit stipends?

In the premium-bribe the incumbent contrôleur accepted $20,000 for a corporate act, the most important of his corporate career, performed "in fulfillment of a corporate duty, in the course of official business, during the regular workweek, for which he was already amply remunerated."

The parity between the premium-bribe consideration and the illicit compensation bears up under fuller scrutiny. In both cases the all-important emolument was paid by a third party to a top-level executive as a corporate official because of his official position and was pocketed personally, even though every minute of time and ounce of energy had been dedicated to the exclusive benefit of the beneficiary shareholders.

But query. A flaw appears fatal. Neither the speeches nor the appointment were truly acts performed *for* the corporation but rather were *contra* the corporation. At best, both were seriously harmful to the corporate well-being. The response to this query rests in the distinction between the official nature of the performance and its quality, well done or poorly, legitimate or illegitimate. Whether the speechmaking junkets of Bolt and Screw's president enhanced the corporate image or sullied it, no matter. They were official corporate acts nonetheless, a corporate assignment carried out as part of his obligation to the firm. The incumbent contrôleur as well, in naming his successor, albeit without reference to suitability and hence in the most reprehensible way possible, was nevertheless fulfilling his principal corporate function. To confirm the matter, reflect that neither the illicit emolument nor the price paid for control would be illegitimate if not paid in the course of and for an official act. This is an elementary requisite of the definition of the malefaction. Thus in the necessary and essential sense both acts were on behalf of, were 'for the corporation.' Patently this becomes a controlling factor in the later disposition of the premium-bribe.

For the present purpose of unencumbered scrutiny, the parity with the illicit compensation of Bolt and Screw's president segregates admirably the price paid for control. Whatever turpitude, therefore, is inherent in the junket-earned $20,000 is equally inherent in the $20,000 paid for control, but without the slightest taint of perversion or successor unsuitability. Proceed, therefore, with the intrinsic illegitimacy of the $20,000 in honoraria, and forget for the moment the $20,000 in premium-bribe, or at least keep it divorced from the perversion and the unsuitability.

Divided Loyalty

When Bolt and Screw's president originally assumed control of the company he dedicated himself unreservedly to the overall welfare of the firm. As contrôleur he was absolutely unfettered in his custody of Bolt and Screw. As complete custodian he alone represented its interests. No one else could step forward to say either aye or nay. He was Bolt and Screw.

Then came the question of the barnstorming junkets and the $20,000 that stood for them. Bolt and Screw's president faced a simple and sharp conflict of interest. Confronting each other across a figurative bargaining table were antagonistic interests, each strongly contending for the time, efforts and talent—and the representative $20,000—of Bolt and Screw's chief. On one side of the table sat Bolt and Screw, in the person of its president. Facing him was an alien and opposing interest, who happened also to be himself.

The president of Bolt and Screw resolved the dilemma by devoting his energies, time and service to the second master, himself. As complete custodian of Bolt and Screw, and hence a strict trustee, the president breached his fiduciary duty by failing to give his unreserved devotion, loyalty and labor to his beneficiary, Bolt and Screw and its constituent shareholders. Herein lies the principal turpitude of the illicit compensation. The $20,000 in honoraria represented abilities, time and devotion that rightly belonged solely to the corporation.

All this, moreover, must be said regardless of the Bolt and Screw president's $90,000 in annual salary. The chief illegitimacy of the $20,000 rests in the disloyalty inherent in the repudiation of the contrôleur's unqualified dedication of all his endeavors to the general welfare of the firm.

Quid pro Quo

Far less subtle are the marketplace demands of contractual justice. Little clairvoyance is needed to see that the salary contract of Bolt and Screw's president read $90,000, not $110,000, per annum. The $20,000 differential was, quite baldly, unjust recompense. As such it was illicit and partakes of the same turpitude present in any unearned return. The turpitude of the illicit emolument of Bolt and Screw's president is essentially indistinguishable from the illegitimacy intrinsic in $20,000 gained through robbery, burglary, embezzlement or simple conversion, with the additional iniquity of a breach of contract of employment.

Completely apart from custody and the loyalty strictures of a trustee, no employee from contrôleur to custodian can licitly be paid twice for doing his job. The turpitude consequent on the breach of the simple contractual quid pro quo is generally characterized as dishonesty, or in less refined circles as plain old stealing. This particular aspect of the intrinsic illegitimacy of the premium-bribe, stemming from the violation of commutative justice, is completely nonfiducial and unrelated, at least in its primary sense, to the Custodial Concept of Corporate Control.

To conclude the synthesis of the illegitimacy of the consideration, simply return to the parallel between the $20,000 in illicit stipend and "the premium price . . . paid for . . . control." As long as the parity is justifiable, the specific turpitude attributable to the unjust recompense can be equated with "the all important emolument" in the sale of control.

(3) The Unsuitability of the Successor

> The most important act a controlling person performs is to choose his successor. Since that choice is often bound up in the sale of stock by the controlling person, we are justified in examining the necessity of imposing rules on those sales.
>
> —Schwartz, *Sale of Control,* 15 N.Y.L.F. 674, 677 (1969) (citing Berle and Bayne).

Note well: This third coconstituent is limited by definition to *premium-bribe-induced* unsuitability. Prescind for the moment from all other extraneous unsuitabilities, e.g., ineptitude, alcoholism, laziness.

This third major coconstituent, then, presents the same if not greater problems in both synthesis and isolation. At first blush the question appears simple: Does any special, added fault lie in the actual appointment of an inept man for the job? Does successor unsuitability itself contribute its own peculiar turpitude, a separate third class distinct from and superadded to the other two? With both the perversion and the illegality of the consideration defined so distinctively, the answer would seem to be unhesitatingly affirmative.

But does not mature reflection conclude otherwise? The illicit consideration and the premium-bribe-induced unsuitability are certainly poles apart from each other. But has not any turpitude in appointing an incompetent been completely absorbed into the culpability already incurred in appointing for reasons other than suitability? In the present context, without the malefaction integral to the perverted appointment, an unsuitable appointee would never become contrôleur. Unsuitability would then scarce be present. Remove the perversion, and unsuitability vanishes. If no perversion, the sole legitimate norm has been observed. The prime objective of the contrôleur has been attained, to wit, the right man for the job.

The unsuitability of the successor, therefore, seems completely intrinsic to the malefaction and hence to the turpitude of the perversion. Consequently, how can successor unsuitability inject a new kind of iniquity, distinct from the turpitude already referable to the perversion itself, appointing irrespective of suitability? The separation of the illegitimacy of the consideration is readily achieved. But how can the unsuitability add anything not already present in the turning away from the suitability?

The Third-Party Robin Hoods

A final analogical gambit should settle the issue. Necessarily, the highly susceptible contrôleur is "willin'," for the usual $100,000. This time, however, the candidate for contrôleur is not only superbly suited for the office, but is decidedly less seeking than sought. Ten successful years at the helm of the company's archrival have left him with not a thought of such a move. But a minority-shareholder group of modified Robin Hoods, knowing a justified means when they see one, are perfectly prepared to insult the incumbent, ineptitude in essence, with a very substantial bribe. In the event, the $100,000 is sufficient to satisfy. The sought-for candidate, completely oblivious of the collateral carryings on, accepts the appointment at a satisfactory salary, and the deal is concluded.

Here the perfect perversion of the contrôleur's judgment is ideally isolated from any actual or possible appointee unsuitability. The $100,000 was a naked bribe (albeit not a premium-bribe, which by definition must pass knowingly from the would-be contrôleur). Yet the candidate was superbly suitable. Here, then, embodied in one single appointment is the maximum turpitude possible in the perversion, but without a smidgen of unsuitability in the new contrôleur. The conclusion? The turpitude of successor unsuitability has absolutely nothing to do with the turpitude peculiar to the perversion qua perversion.

But what was the point for proof? That successor *unsuitability*, not suitability, is distinct from the perversion. Yet the Robin Hoods' candidate was altogether suitable, not altogether unsuitable. So how does one prove that the unsuitability is distinct? (1) A perfect perversion was possible without any *un*suitability. The contrôleur exacted the maximum dollars. (2) A perfect perversion cannot become more so. (3) Therefore any unsuitability added cannot augment the already perfect perversion. (4) Therefore unsuitability is distinct from the perversion qua perversion. (Recall, unsuitability is neither the final cause nor the gauge of the perversion. The turning away from suitability, not the turning to unsuitability, sets the grade of perversity. Thus unsuitability is divorced completely from the perversion. Forget this, and the inclination persists to include the unsuitability in the perversion.)

But this Robin Hood analogy is nonetheless deficient. The absence of *un*suitability remains a handicap. What was set for proof? That premium-bribe-induced *un*suitability is intrinsically distinct from the perversion, the turning away from suitability. How would one best prove this essential distinction? By a real-life instance of (1) the appointment of a fully *un*suitable successor (2) without the slightest admixture of a perverted turning away from suitability. Then the *un*suitability—not suitability—would be clearly distinct from the turning away, because there would be *no* 'turning away,' only a turning *to* the unsuitability.

But this real-life example is an intrinsic self-contradiction. Hence a rather large burden, indeed, lies on the Robin Hoods analogy. No better proof is possible. An inevitable obstacle intrudes in any attempt to segregate the unsuitability. Why? An actual, unqualified appointment—in reality and not merely conceptually—of a total incompetent never in fact can occur in a sane world. Bolt and Screw's president involved nothing but illicit emolument, true. But how to imagine that real-life example of an appointment of a wholly unsuitable successor, without an accompanying premium-bribe? It is impossible. As intrinsically undesirable, unsuitability alone can never be a sufficient motivating cause. Unmixed evil can never motivate. Only a good can attract. Ineluctably, unsuitability must be pulled along, the reluctant noncausal concomitant of the real reason, nepotism, for example, or expediency, friendship, premium-bribe. This invariable phenomenon poses a problem. Only a conceptual severance, never a real example, can divorce the unsuitability. The best available, therefore, is the third-party Robin Hoods. At least here the mind can isolate the unsuitability conceptually, even if a contrôleur never would so isolate it by an actual appointment of an unsuitable successor, without more. Only a fool would appoint such a person without another reason—a premium-bribe reason—and thus the isolation necessarily fails, in the real world. Only conceptually can it be isolated.

The Essence of the Turpitude

Thus conceptually segregated, what is the inner nature of this turpitude specific to *premium-bribe-induced* successor unsuitability? (Continue to prescind from all other extraneous unsuitabilities.) Particularly, how does it differ from the perversion involved in appointing a successor for reasons other than suitability? As clearly distinct—the perversion can exist without the unsuitability albeit not the unsuitability without the perversion—wherein lies the distinction?

The heart of the perversion was the disloyalty in placing a personal good, premium-bribe dollars, before the corporate good, a suitable successor. The suitability of the successor is the sole legitimate norm of selection. In a conflict of final causes the contrôleur yielded the corporate to the personal.

The turpitude in appointing an unsuitable successor, however, consists simply in foisting an incompetent on the corporation, an unadorned breach of the subduty to strive for the finest possible personnel. Whereas the perversion was effected without regard to unsuitability, here the turpitude is solely dependent on unsuitability. Without unsuitability, there is no turpitude. The perversion consisted of twisting the judgment away from suitability. Here the turpitude consists in inflicting an unsuitable contrôleur on the firm, with all the consequent harm. With the perversion, the maximum turpitude was possible even with a totally suitable successor (witness the suitable son and the candidate of the minority Robin Hoods). With the unsuitability, the minimum turpitude is impossible without a partially unsuitable successor. The turpitude engendered by successor unsuitability stems from the uncomplicated fact that the corporation is therewith burdened with all the potential damage and present disadvantages of an incompetent in the most important position in the firm.

The Grades of Turpitude

Understandably one might assume that the gradations of unsuitability could be envisaged summarily by lining up a long series of prospective contrôleurs, each increasingly less suitable, culminating in the worst man for the job. But the matter is not that simple. Successor unsuitability remains necessarily but one element of an indivisible moral act and intertwines intimately with both the illicit cash and particularly the perversion. This inextricable involvement adds a distinctive feature to an otherwise normal progression from zero to total unsuitability.

The Premium-Bribe-Induced Unsuitability

Return to the high-minded Robin Hood. Here is a singularly successful entrepreneur, thrashing about for new opportunities to put his limitless talents to work. Money has long since ceased to interest him. Altruism is all. Natronics, Inc., has hit the nadir. The incumbent contrôleur is not only incompetent but tired. But he is also bullheaded and avaricious. Does Natronics continue to coast downhill? For anything less than $100,000 the answer is 'yes.' Rationalized to the hilt, the determined Robin Hood capitulates.

Before the final handshake sealing the deal, several deliberate decisions had to be taken by this would-be contrôleur. First, he must resolve to twist the contrôleur's judgment away from his vowed objective and toward the $100,000 premium-bribe. To pervert and let be perverted. Second, what of the $100,000 to contrôleur employee rather than corporation? He must be ready actively to pass and let passively accept. Third, how explain his corporate loyalty, and a character and personality thus prepared to pervert the incumbent and divert the $100,000 at the very moment of his dedication to the corporate welfare? Knowing vividly that such a betrayal of trust entails custodial unsuitability, he nonetheless is determined to go forward, to inflict his unsuitable self on the firm. In acceding to this triple turpitude, the premium-briber both engenders and manifests his unsuitability. Conversely, one who forswears such conduct is not unsuitable. But one who accedes, *eo ipso* is.

Consequently, this minimum (but not inconsequential) unsuitability of the premium-bribing Robin Hood is necessarily intrinsic and the direct result of the premium-bribe itself. Whatever extraneous unsuitability otherwise, at the very least this premium-bribe-induced unsuitability—the willingness to premium-bribe into office—is integral to every true premium-bribe and the character of the premium-briber.

In listing the gradations of successor unsuitability begin, therefore, with the otherwise suitable Robin Hood who is nonetheless a premium-briber, and hence necessarily unsuitable at least to that extent.

The Superadded Unsuitability

But what of those disabilities and deficiencies already clouding the character of a premium-bribe-bent successor? No high-minded Robin Hood here. Just an inefficient, peculous squanderer, who is also low-minded enough to premium-bribe as well. Prescind now from the premium-bribery weakness itself and ask: What connection do a propensity for laxity, for slipping a hand in the till, for social or managerial blundering, for alcohol, for a little looting, have to the premium-bribe? Is such added successor unfitness unrelated to the premium-bribe? How does it differ from the unsuitability induced by the premium-bribe itself? Clearly, premium-bribe-induced unsuitability is of the essence of the premium-bribe. But is not prior extraneous unsuitability another matter? Granted, the incumbent is certainly responsible for such a successor. Such unsuitability would be included in his legal liability for the appointment. But can such superadded unsuitability join the premium-bribe-induced unsuitability as intrinsic to the turpitude referable to the premium-bribe itself?

The answer must begin—but not end—with other questions. Does the premium-bribe place this superadded unsuitability on the corporate doorstep? But for the premium-bribe such unsuitability would be absent. True, but does that mean that the premium-bribe is the proximate cause? It might rather be but a condition or an occasion.

Did not the premium-bribe itself cause the integral appointment? The contrôleur founded the appointment not on successor suitability but on premium-bribe dollars. The premium-briber sold himself, with all his defects, deficiencies and disabilities. The conclusion is inescapable. Clearly, the premium-bribe is responsible for the entire package.

Two classes of unsuitability thus emerge: (1) The character blemish engendered and manifested by the premium-bribery itself and (2) All other imperfections theretofore unrelated to the premium-bribe. At the instant of appointment both indelibly marked the forehead of the appointee. This marked person the contrôleur deliberately and willingly appoints his successor, solely by reason of the premium-bribe dollars. Without such causal influx this double disability would never burden the corporation. The premium-bribe is the proximate cause of the visitation on the entity of this double corporate handicap.

The next question logically follows: How do these two classes—both inflicted on the corporation by the premium-bribe—differ intrinsically? The distinction lies in their different geneses, but not in the single cause that inflicts them on the corporation. Obviously, the propensity to premium-bribery had been previously latent, but became patent only at the time of the sale of control. The unsuitability of premium-bribery, therefore, had its origin in (assuming a first fall) and was directly caused by the premium-bribe itself. The other deficiencies, however, had long been patent and needed no premium-bribe to surface them. Their genesis antedated the premium-bribe. But the premium-bribe visited the whole man on the corporation with his double disability, and hence is solely responsible for this corporate affliction. The premium-bribe did not cause the appointee's prior unsuitability—the appointee had already done that—but it was the proximate cause of the imposition of this burden on the corporation.

The final word therefore—and the answer to the intrinsic difference of the two classes—is this: Although the premium-bribe is the proximate cause of the *presence* of both disabilities, (1) premium-bribe-induced unsuitability is intrinsic to and of the essence, is indispensable to, the true premium-bribe, (2) whereas the superadded unsuitabilities, if present at all, are only accidentally related and are outside the definition of the premium-bribe. But the presence of both, nonetheless, is referable to the premium-bribe, inasmuch as the premium-bribe caused the appointment and the appointment caused the visitation of both disabilities on the corporation.

In strict practicality, therefore, the crucial distinction for future sale-of-control litigation lies in the built-in nature of the premium-bribe-induced unsuitability. No true premium-bribe under any conditions whatsoever can be passed without engendering the triple blemish of the perversion, the illicit consideration, and the resultant premium-bribe-induced unsuitability. To the extent, therefore, that an appointee is prepared to twist the judgment and divert the corporate dollars, thus far is he already an unsuitable custodian. As thus unsuitable he caps it off by imposing a premium-briber, himself, on the firm. Whatever further deficiencies he may possess are only added adornments to this ever present, built-in disability.

All this, of course, assumes the premium-bribe as the sole causal influx. As that influx decreases, successor suitability increases.

Premium-bribe-induced successor unsuitability as a distinct conceptual element concludes the syntheses of the three coconstituents of the premium-bribe turpitude.

(4) The Coalesced Turpitude

> However, when insiders sell control at a premium, they sharpen, if they do not actually create, a conflict of interest between themselves and the remaining stockholders, so that more than the duty of care or of exercising sound business judgment is involved. The conflict between the insiders' interest in the premium and the risk to which they subject the other stockholders—the risk that the buyer will fail in his conduct of the corporate business or will exploit the enterprise for his personal benefit—activates the fiduciary duty of loyalty as well as the duty of care.
>
> —Brudney, *Fiduciary Ideology in Transactions Affecting Corporate Control,* 65 MICH. L. REV. 259, 296 (1966).

Being so long so close to the trees one forgets that the forest is an integral moral unit, the single act of premium-bribery. Correspondingly, the tripartite turpitude is only conceptually divisible. True, each of its indispensable coconstituents—the perversion, the illicit consideration, the premium-bribe-engendered unsuitability—can be individually isolated in the abstract. Each certainly is a distinct turpitude, with its own individuating notes and amenable to specific definition. In losing its identity in the new entity, moreover, each does not fully disappear but remains theoretically identifiable. But these conceptually distinct elements are in fact a premium-bribe and properly belong together in a substantial union. As such they fuse to form a new element, entirely distinct and definable, the premium-bribe turpitude. Here, thus unified, is the intrinsic illegitimacy of the premium-bribe. As such it is sui generis.

But these many pages of painful dissections have not been merely an ethicolegal tour de force. The distinctions, categorizations, nuances, would all be sale-of-control *Wissenschaft* were not each coconstituent individually crucial to the remaining sale-of-control problems: The culpability of the parties, damages, the disposition of the premium-bribe, the premium-bribe presumption of unsuitability. Hence the labored breakdown.

The Coalesced Breaches

The intellect and will of both contrôleur and successor simultaneously embraced an integral act, the passing of the premium-bribe. In its totality this act was intrinsically inconsistent with the acknowledged stewardship of both parties. As incoming and outgoing contrôleurs, both were equally guilty of a strict trustee's capital offense, disloyalty to the corporation. Moreover, the broad precepts of loyalty explicitly embody the encompassing obligation to strive for the finest possible personnel. At every conceptual turn, incumbent and appointee faced this obligation in the clear-cut dilemma of a conflict of interest. And thrice each yielded and placed his interests before his beneficiary's. Confronted with an avowed objective of successor suitability, each chose an alien consideration, dollars, prestige, personal advantage. The perversion resulted. In giving and taking consideration that belonged to the corporation, each subordinated the corporate benefit to his own. In making and accepting the appointment each foisted a premium-briber on the future of the firm. Yet each had pledged a suitable successor when he assumed the custody. Thus these three breaches coalesced into the single act of disloyalty of a strict trustee.

True, "[a] trustee is held to something stricter than the morals of the market place. Not honesty alone, but the punctilio of an honor the most sensitive, is then the standard of behavior."[141] But the law of the strict trustee is not all. The premium-briber and the premium-bribed are bound by more mundane strictures as well. "Honesty alone" and the "morals of the market place" have equally binding prescriptions: The rigid return of a quid pro quo and the inviolable commands of commutative justice. At each turn, thrice, both incumbent and successor breached the simple terms of their contract of hire. As Mechem's hornbook law puts it:

> When the principal employs an agent, the law presumes that he does so in order to secure to himself the benefits of the agent's skill, experience or discretion, and to reap the fruits of the performance of the undertaking. The law presumes that he expects—and it gives him the right to expect—that the agent so employed will endeavor to further the principal's interests, and will use his powers for the principal's benefit.
>
> —F. MECHEM, OUTLINES OF THE LAW OF
> AGENCY §500, at 345 (4th ed. 1952).

In the end, therefore, each conceptually distinct act involved in premium-bribery is a specific breach of the broad fiduciary duty of a strict trustee and the obligations of commutative justice.

The Coalescence

The intricate evolution of the premium-bribe turpitude is a complex series of actions and interactions. Moreover, as academic as it may appear, this fascinating process of the fusion of the three coconstituents has practical implications in later sale-of-control queries. The interaction of each element prompts a captious legalist to wonder whether the total turpitude might not even be greater than the sum of the separate derelictions. The wonder, however, is probably overdrawn. An intensification of the illegitimacy, perhaps, because of the interplay of the three, but seemingly no greater iniquity.

The Interaction

Initially recall that the superadded unsuitability, those defects and deficiencies antedating the premium-bribe, is not essential to the definition of the premium-bribe and becomes involved only accidentally because the premium-bribe is the proximate cause of loading this burden on the corporation. As such, the superadded unsuitability is properly bypassed in this analysis of the interrelations of the essential three. On the other hand, each of the three, the perversion, the illicit consideration, the premium-bribe-engendered unsuitability, is indispensable to the fusion that produces the total turpitude. Each forms the essence, but each performs a different function. Each is sine qua non to the whole.

The Formal Cause

The blending begins with the principal essential, the perversion. Here is the active factor and hence, arguably, the most important of the three. The perversion is the formal element imparting form to the otherwise undetermined matter, the illicit consideration. The central act of disloyalty is the spurning of the avowed custodial norm, the repudiation of the dedication to successor suitability. The crux is the turning away. The illicit consideration, on the other hand, is passive and supplies the content for the perversion. The consideration remains amorphous until it is 'turned to.' The application of the elements of the perversion transforms an otherwise indifferent and merely potential inducement into the peculiar illegality of the premium-bribe. Although the consideration may stand alone, as with Bolt and Screw's president, without the perversion it can never enter the essence of the premium-bribe.

The Material Cause

The blending proceeds with the reaction of the consideration to the perversion. The consideration, albeit passive, does make the perversion this specific kind of perversion, specifically premium-bribe perversion, rather than some other kind, say paternal-prejudice perversion. To be a perversion at all, the perversion requires something to turn *to* and transform, even though the prime factor is the turning away *from*. The perversion without the illicit consideration could be many another type of perversion from paternal prejudice to expediency to friendship. As active it can never stand alone but must always be conjoined with a passive correlative.

Thus the perversion and the illicit consideration are mutually dependent. Not only are both sine qua non to the premium-bribe, but they are necessary conditions to each other. Each may stand apart from the other, the consideration alone, the perversion with another material cause, but apart neither becomes an essential of the premium-bribe. Conjoined, however, they meld to form the first stage in the total process of fusion. Notably, the conjunction of the perversion and the illicit consideration constitutes without more the essence of the standard bribe, lacking only the third requisite to become the strict premium-bribe. Recall the example of the straight bribe of the minority Robin Hoods who bribed the susceptible contrôleur, unbeknownst to the suitable nominee.

Homo Sapiens

An irresistible analogy might add some insights. The essential union of spirituality and corporeality which produces the *animal rationale* of the human species could be a productive parallel to the fusion of the perversion and the illicit consideration. The rationality of the human intellect and will is undeniably the principal and active force that infuses the animate corpus and thus removes it from the animal kingdom. Recourse to this parity apropos is at least intriguing.

The Active Role of the Appointee

At this stage the fusion has produced an old-line bribe. The introduction of the personal action of the would-be contrôleur, however, revolutionizes the process completely. The regular bribe says nothing in its definition about the role of the briber. Undeniably, some individual must do the bribing, but who or how is irrelevant. The crux is the perversion of the contrôleur. By hypothesis, however, the premium-bribe is incomplete without (1) the positive act of the appointee (2) passing something of value of his own to the incumbent contrôleur. This active intrusion of the appointee immediately engenders the third requisite and converts a two-way interaction into a triple fusion, the completed turpitude.

The personal deliberate act of the appointee both passed the consideration and, in thus passing, perverted the contrôleur. In a three-cornered interplay, therefore, the junction of the perversion and the consideration simultaneously produces the appointee unsuitability. Once produced the unsuitability proceeds to meld with both perversion and consideration to produce in turn the total turpitude. This could be pedantically expressed in the formula:

$$P + C (\rightarrow +) U = TT$$

Thus the active role of the appointee, and the consequent unsuitability, produce the final element, and thereby transform the standard bribe into the sui generis premium-bribe.

Here at last would seem to be the distinctive element. Eliminate the active role of the appointee, and the premium-bribe disappears. Add it, and the premium-bribe is complete. The premium-bribe without this unsuitability would be an unadorned bribe. Thus with the case of the minority Robin Hoods, the susceptible contrôleur and the unknowing and suitable appointee.

The injection of premium-bribe-induced unsuitability complicates considerably the three-way fusion. The illicit consideration of Bolt and Screw's president was able to stand alone. The perversion of the prejudiced father could be isolated at least conceptually. Each was distinct one from another. Neither entered the essence of the other, although each was a condition for the other in the formation of the standard bribe. The premium-bribe-induced unsuitability, on the other hand, is wholly another matter. Although it in no way enters the essence either of the perversion or of the consideration, its own essence is constituted completely by the active/passive interaction of the other two. It depends fully on this junction for its essence and existence. Further, only the negative analogy of the third-party-bribing Robin Hoods can give the premium-bribe-induced unsuitability even a conceptual identity. But it is nonetheless an essential of the total turpitude.

Recur momentarily to the *animal rationale* analogy. Would not the premium-bribe-engendered unsuitability parallel the human property of risibility? Certainly both are consequents on the fusion of the two principal elements of the union. The analogy breaks down, however, when the unsuitability enters the essence, and leaves risibility standing outside as a mere property.

With this the coalescence is complete. All three are completely essential to the premium-bribe. Each performs a completely distinctive function in the total fusion. Each alone is illegitimate. Yet no one alone is a premium-bribe. In any of the many possible combinations a definable malefaction is indubitably present, but without the coalescence of all three the premium-bribe is nonexistent. The totality of the turpitude, therefore, is determined exclusively by the three coconstituents interacting in an essential union, the premium-bribe.

The facts in Crane/WABCO, *Green Giant,* Shearson, Hammill/Silvray-Litecraft, Cyrus Eaton/Detroit Steel may never disclose a single premium-bribe. Transitory questions of fact are always difficult to answer. But the intrinsic illegitimacy of the premium-bribe once disclosed can have perennial applicability.

Chapter 7

The Sale-of-Control Premium: The Disposition

The theory is not that all the shareholders are entitled to share in the bribe but rather that one who sells an asset he does not own must turn over the proceeds to the true owner. The true owner is the corporation. The malefactor, according to *Rosenfeld,* is the selling shareholder. He owes that part of the proceeds which is the premium to the corporation that owned the asset.

> —*Gordon v. Fundamental Investors, Inc.,* 362 F. Supp. 41, 45 (S.D.N.Y. 1973).

Section 8.70. Kickbacks, bribes . . . .
Any Corporate director or officer who commits commercial bribery or commercial bribe receiving . . . shall be liable to the corporation . . . for treble damages . . . .

> —ILL. REV. STAT. ch. 32 (Supp. 1984).

The bribe never belongs to the bribee but in equity and morals to the principal for whom the bribee had a duty to act.

> —J. NOONAN, BRIBES 697 (1984).

When C. Russell Feldmann accepted the $2.1-million premium-bribe to hand over the Newport Steel board to the Wilport Syndicate, he opened a Pandora's box of sale-of-control questions, questions far from answered, in spite of the Second

Circuit's creditable attempt and historic acclaim. True, the "famous case of *Perlman v. Feldmann*"[142] is justly "celebrated,"[143] and deserves its praise as a "Judicial Landmark."[144] The commentators are correct. Nonetheless, the Court never really did get all the questions back in the box. What should become of the $2.1-million premium? Must it be disgorged? Why? If so, to whom does it go? To the corporation? To the innocent shareholders alone? And always, why? These final crucial questions were too elusive for the Court, and in the end it failed, and thoroughly so.

The Court's failure in the end is all the more poignant because of its effective reasoning in the beginning. On the basic control problem the Court shone. Even today *Feldmann* of the midfifties remains one of the best judicial statements of fundamental sale-of-control philosophy:

> "Directors of a business corporation act in a strictly fiduciary capacity. Their office is a trust. . . . They must not, in any degree, allow their official conduct to be swayed by their private interest . . . ."
>
> . . . [T]he same rule should apply to his fiduciary duties as majority stockholder, for in that capacity he chooses and controls the directors, and thus is held to have assumed their liability.
>
> —*Perlman v. Feldmann*, 219 F.2d 173, 176 (2d Cir. 1955) (quoting *Schemmel v. Hill*).

From these premises the Court reasoned to the illegitimacy of the premium-bribe, and concluded:

> [W]e think it sound law that a fiduciary may not appropriate to himself the value of this premium.
>
> —*Perlman v. Feldmann,* 219 F.2d 173, 178 (2d Cir. 1955).

Thus did the *Feldmann* Court enunciate in embryo the Custodial Concept of Corporate Control. For such prescience its credit should never be minimized.

Nor has *Feldmann* outlived its usefulness. Granted, it is old. Its contribution to the elemental control principles has been made. It has been analyzed to shreds. But these analyses have never extended beyond the elementals to the Court's intricate apportionment of the $2.1-million premium-bribe. Yet here remains a stinging goad to present exploration. *Perlman v. Feldmann* has left the subtlest premium-bribe problems unsolved, and offers itself again as the ideal vehicle toward solution.

And among the subtlest is the next premium-bribe question logically set for answer: How handle a $2.1-million premium-bribe passing to an incumbent contrôleur from a would-be-successor Wilport?

This broad question and its many subsidiaries will be approached in four stages: *I. The* Feldmann *Disposition. II. The State of the Law. III. The Philosophical Foundation of the Disposition. IV. The Distribution on Disposition.*

I. The *Feldmann* Disposition

> The right of a controlling shareholder to dispose of his interest in a corporation is subject to few restrictions. *Perlman v. Feldmann* . . . raises the possibility that these restrictions may be greatly extended.
>
> —Comment, *Shareholders' Liability for Sale of Controlling Interest,* 22 U. CHI. L. REV. 895 (1955).

> Sale of control without this further ingredient of potential danger to the corporation does not appear to be wrongful. Having said that, however, one must quickly add, with some emphasis, that it is unlawful to buy or sell directorships.
>
> —Connolly, *Perlman v. Feldmann and the Sale of Control,* 26 BUS. LAW. 1259, 1262 (1971).

The *Feldmann* facts are familiar and few, but a brief review is essential to this analysis. A group of Newport's customers was hard pressed during the Korean War to keep an inventory of steel. Eyeing a possible captive supply, they approached C. Russell Feldmann, the contrôleur of the Cincinnati-area firm, with the thought "of the sale . . . of [the] controlling interest in the corporation."[145] The result: Feldmann, family and friends transferred to the Wilport Syndicate the "control block of stock," at $20 per share "although the over-the-counter market price had not exceeded $12 and the book value per share was $17.03."[146] On remand the District Court set "the value of defendants' stock without the appurtenant control over the corporation's output of steel"[147] at $14.67 per share, aggregating a $2.1-million premium-bribe. The further result:

> [T]he resignation of [Feldmann's] own board and the election of Wilport's nominees immediately upon consummation of the sale.
> —*Perlman v. Feldmann,* 219 F.2d 173, 175
> (2d Cir. 1955).

At trial in Connecticut Judge Hincks held:

> [T]hat the rights involved in the sale were only those normally incident to the possession of a controlling block of shares, with which a dominant stockholder, in the absence of fraud or foreseeable looting, was entitled to deal according to his own best interests.
> —*Perlman v. Feldmann,* 219 F.2d 173, 175
> (2d Cir. 1955).

On appeal the Second Circuit reversed.

From the sale-of-control aspect the *Feldmann* case is two-pronged. Before apportioning the premium-bribe to the Plaintiffs—done with two-paragraph dispatch—the Second Circuit had first to find the foundation for the premium-bribe illegality. On first face the reasons for illegality are arguably obiter to an analysis of the premium-bribe disposition itself. But over the years commentators have raised too many doubts about the Court's controlling reason for this illegality. A resolution of the doubts is not without help to later reasoning about the disposition.

(1) The Rationale of the Illegality

The factual nub of the illegality holding was the so-called Feldmann Plan. During the war Mr. Feldmann had considerably enriched Newport by exacting interest-free prepayments from prospective purchasers. This practice was widely reprobated but

nonetheless legal. Of course, Wilport as contrôleur would expectably deal otherwise with Wilport as consumer. On the rationale for
this illegality the *Feldmann* Court is undoubtedly a bit confused, but
one nonetheless could piece together an understandable and tenable
explanation. Even granting some confusion, the *Feldmann* opinion
remains a superb contribution to the sale-of-control philosophy.

The Court's ambivalence caused the confusion. One moment
the premium-bribe illegality is referable to an unadorned sale of control. The next, the harm lies in misappropriating "corporate advantages."[148] Chief Judge Clark's opening paragraph seems to pull in one
clear direction:

> This is a derivative action brought by minority stock-
> holders of Newport Steel Corporation to compel ac-
> counting for, and restitution of, allegedly illegal gains
> which accrued to defendants as a result of the sale in Au-
> gust, 1950, of their controlling interest in the
> corporation.
> —*Perlman v. Feldmann*, 219 F.2d 173, 174
> (2d Cir. 1955).

True, these are the allegations of the Plaintiffs, but later, and even
here, the unadorned sale of control of Newport seems to be the ultimate gravamen of the action. At another point the Court says: "The
price of $20 per share was found by Judge Hincks to be a fair one
for a control block of stock . . . ."[149] Thus, the heart of the wrong appears to be the transfer of the "control block" at a premium. Further:
"Plaintiffs argue . . . [that] the vendors must account . . . for that share
of their profit which is attributable to the sale of the corporate
power."[150] Thus far the Court seems completely in the *Sugden,
McClure, Lionel*, tradition. The contrôleur handed over control of
Newport by the seriatim resignation of the board for a $2.1-million
premium-bribe. For this breach of fiduciary duty the premium goes
over to the Plaintiffs.

But then begins a slight shift of emphasis. No longer is it solely
and simply the sale of overall control.

> Plaintiffs contend that the consideration paid for the
> stock included compensation for the sale of a corporate
> asset, a power held in trust for the corporation by
> Feldmann as its fiduciary. *This power was the ability to con-
> trol the allocation of the corporate product in a time of short*

supply, through control of the board of directors; and it was effectively transferred in this sale by having Feldmann procure the resignation of his own board and the election of Wilport's nominees immediately upon consummation of the sale.

—*Perlman v. Feldmann,* 219 F.2d 173, 175
(2d Cir. 1955) (emphasis added).

Here is the first intimation of ambivalence. Yet here the Court's argument is reducibly unchanged. Thus the condemned malefaction was "the sale of a corporate asset." This asset was "a power held in trust . . . the ability to control the allocation of the corporate product." But this "ability to control the allocation" came only "through control of the board of directors." And "it"—which could mean either the "ability to control the allocation" or the "control of the board"—was "effectively transferred in this sale." The transfer of the "control of the board," of course, would be the sale of overall control. At this stage, therefore, the Court is only saying that "the ability to control the allocation" is just one of the many parts of the control whole. Necessarily, the sale of the whole includes the sale of the part.

Midway in the opinion, however, after an enunciation of the most stringent trust obligations, comes a seemingly forthright turnabout:

> The actions of defendants in siphoning off for personal gain corporate advantages to be derived from a favorable market situation do not betoken the necessary undivided loyalty owed by the fiduciary to his principal.
>
> —*Perlman v. Feldmann,* 219 F.2d 173, 176
> (2d Cir. 1955).

Through several paragraphs the Court dilates on these "corporate opportunities of whose misappropriation the minority stockholders complain."[151] Notable among them, of course, would be the advantages of the Feldmann Plan. Also, "Newport might have used the period of short supply to build up patronage in the geographical area in which it could compete profitably even when steel was more abundant."[152]

But the Second Circuit's final handling of the $2.1-million premium-bribe resolved the ambivalence. The ultimate foundation was the sale of control of the entity. No attempt was made to break down, segregate and evaluate individually those "corporate advantages to be derived from a favorable market situation." A single lump sum, determined not by the several lost opportunities, but by the value of the control 'sold' ("the value of defendants' stock without the appurtenant control" subtracted from the total price of the sale), was awarded for the central malefaction, the sale of control for a price. The Court noted that these opportunities "need not have been an absolute certainty in order to support this action against Feldmann"[153] and hence they were clearly not reduced to an estimable element of the award. Granted, the Court certainly sensed these "opportunities" in the background, but in the end treated them merely as functions or subpowers of the overall corporate control.

Judge Swan, in his dissent, clearly saw it that way, and equally clearly saw nothing wrong with it:

> The controlling block could not by any possibility be shorn of its appurtenant power to elect directors and through them to control distribution of the corporate product. It is this "appurtenant power" which gives a controlling block its value as such block. What evidence could be adduced to show the value of the block "if shorn" of such appurtenant power, I cannot conceive, for it cannot be shorn of it.
>
> —*Perlman v. Feldmann,* 219 F.2d 173, 180 (2d Cir. 1955) (Swan, J., dissenting).

The proposals for a premium-bribe-disposition rationale advanced in this treatise will accept the thesis that Feldmann was held liable for the bare sale of control of Newport for a $2.1-million premium-bribe, irrespective of conjectured ingredients, or later uses, of that broad control once transferred. Should one hold tenaciously to the theory of the "misappropriation" of "corporate opportunities," reconciliation with the principles urged as governing the disposition nevertheless should be possible.

Whatever the theory of its nature—a sale of sole control or of a congeries of opportunities—the Court, quoting Cardozo's 'workaday world' in *Meinhard v. Salmon,* interdicted the malefaction on only one ground, applicable to either theory:

> "A trustee is held to something stricter than the morals of the market place. Not honesty alone, but the punctilio of an honor the most sensitive, is then the standard of behavior."
>
> —*Perlman v. Feldmann,* 219 F.2d 173, 176 (2d Cir. 1955) (quoting *Meinhard v. Salmon*).

And added:

> "The first principal duty arising from his official relation is to act in all things of trust wholly for the benefit of his corporation."
>
> —*Perlman v. Feldmann,* 219 F.2d 173, 176 (2d Cir. 1955) (quoting *Schemmel v. Hill*).

Here was the incipient Custodial Concept of Corporate Control.

As circuitously as *Feldmann* may have reasoned to its conclusion, the upshot may be classed—in reference only to sale-of-control fundamentals—as the lineal descendant of *Sugden, McClure, Porter v. Healy,* and the progenitor of such as *Lionel:*

> [W]hat occurred here was the mere sale and purchase of naked directorial control . . . in violation of the clear mandate of McClure v. Law . . . .
>
> —*Matter of Lionel Corp.,* N.Y.L.J., Feb. 4, 1964, at 14 (Sup. Ct., N.Y. County).

Where *Feldmann* ranks, beyond the fundamentals, is another matter, the second prong of the case.

(2) *The Actual Allocation*

Although reasons abounded in support of the premium-bribe illegality, the intricate distribution of the $2.1 million was almost perfunctory, without explanation or argument, followed by a summary remand.

The Second Circuit faced squarely the traditional rule, and understood fully that recovery would normally be in the "right of the corporation (as in the usual derivative actions)."[154] Judge Clark earlier had adverted indirectly to this rule (albeit in a muddled manner):

> We do not mean to suggest that a majority stockholder cannot dispose of his controlling block of stock to outsiders without having to account to his corporation for profits or even never do this with impunity when the buyer is an interested customer, actual or potential, for the corporation's product. But when the sale necessarily results in a sacrifice of this element of corporate good will and consequent unusual profit to the fiduciary who has caused the sacrifice, he should account for his gain.
>
> —*Perlman v. Feldmann,* 219 F.2d 173, 178 (2d Cir. 1955).

But the Court determined that a variant on the traditional law should prevail. Without pro or con, Judge Clark flatly concluded:

> Hence to the extent that the price received by Feldmann and his codefendants included such a bonus, he is accountable *to the minority stockholders* who sue here.
>
> —*Perlman v. Feldmann,* 219 F.2d 173, 178 (2d Cir. 1955) (emphasis added).

And why not the usual award to the corporation?

> [P]laintiffs, as they contend, are entitled to a recovery in their own right, instead of in right of the corporation (as in the usual derivative actions), since neither Wilport nor their successors in interest should share in any judgment which may be rendered.
>
> —*Perlman v. Feldmann,* 219 F.2d 173, 178 (2d Cir. 1955).

The only reason, if it be one, for denying recovery to the corporation was that Wilport "should" not share in the $2.1 million. And why? Nothing beyond the mere assertion.

The Court then rationalized a bit—as though perhaps it might be having a slight qualm—by stating the obvious, that the Feldmanns . . .

> . . . cannot well object to this form of recovery, since the only alternative, recovery for the corporation as a whole, would subject them to a greater total liability.
> —*Perlman v. Feldmann,* 219 F.2d 173, 178 (2d Cir. 1955).

This, of course, brushed under the rug another, more pertinent, consideration: Whether the Wilport Syndicate, on its part, might "well object to this form of recovery." Nor seemingly did the Court consider whether the Feldmanns *deserved* to be held "to a greater total liability." Perhaps none of the $2.1-million premium-bribe belonged to them, let alone a third of it. The distribution was concluded tersely:

> The case will therefore be remanded to the district court for a determination of the question expressly left open below, namely, the value of defendants' stock without the appurtenant control over the corporation's output of steel. . . . Judgment should go to these plaintiffs and those whom they represent for any premium value so shown to the extent of their respective stock interests.
> —*Perlman v. Feldmann,* 219 F.2d 173, 178 (2d Cir. 1955).

Judge Swan in his dissent was not so complacent about this allocation of the $2.1 million:

> The final conclusion of my brothers is that the plaintiffs are entitled to recover in their own right instead of in the right of the corporation. This appears to be completely inconsistent with the theory advanced at the outset of the opinion, namely, that the price of the stock "included compensation for the sale of a corporate asset." If a corporate asset was sold, surely the corporation should recover the compensation received for it by the defendants.
> —*Perlman v. Feldmann,* 219 F.2d 173, 180 (2d Cir. 1955) (Swan, J., dissenting).

Of course Swan proved to be as cavalier as Clark, because he also gave no supporting reasons for his disposition. Clark simply said, without more, that Wilport should get no share, and Swan said that Wilport should, without more. Thus is the scene set and the line drawn.

The remand itself conformed to the letter. In a lengthy opinion the Court sedulously worked out "the value of defendants' stock without the appurtenant control over the corporation's output of steel."[155] Broken down, "[t]he value of each share of the capital stock of Newport Steel Corporation was, on August 31, 1950, $14.67."[156] Again, conformably:

> The difference between $14.67 and the $20 per share received by the defendants constituted a premium or bonus paid by Wilport Company for control over Newport's output of steel.
>
> —*Perlman v. Feldmann,* 154 F. Supp. 436, 446 (D. Conn. 1957).

With this, the only remaining chore was the arithmetic to determine Wilport's share—to be kept by the Feldmanns—of the $2.1 million.

> The bonuses or premiums of $5.33 per share . . . total $2,126,280.91. The Wilport Company shares, which are barred by the judgment of the Court of Appeals from recovery in this proceeding, constituted 36.99% of the outstanding shares of Newport. This percentage of the $2,126,280.91 amounts to $786,511.29 which, deducted from the $2,126,280.91, leaves $1,339,769.62 due . . . the present holders . . . other than . . . the Wilport Company . . . in proportion to the number of shares each holds.
>
> —*Perlman v. Feldmann,* 154 F. Supp. 436, 446 (D. Conn. 1957).

In rough figures, the total deal saw $8 million pass from Wilport to Feldmann, of which $2.1 million constituted the premium-bribe. The remaining $5.9 million was paid for Newport common at market.

Thus ended the *Feldmann* distribution of the $2.1-million premium-bribe paid by Wilport to Feldmann for control of Newport.

The public shareholders received $1.3 million. Feldmann retained the rest. Nothing went directly to the corporation. Wilport lost all.

II. The State of the Law

> Despite some academic support for the contrary position, the cases seem to continue to hold that the sale of a control block of shares at a price in excess of current market does not create a liability to minority shareholders or to the corporation, except in unusual cases . . . .
>
> —Kaplan, *Fiduciary Responsibility in the Management of the Corporation,* 31 BUS. LAW. 883, 907 (1976).

> In summary, it is our opinion that a majority stockholder who is paid a premium for his stock because of the control that goes with it is under no duty to the corporation or to the minority stockholders to account for such additional profit . . . .
>
> —*Thompson v. Hambrick,* 508 S.W.2d 949, 954 (Tex. Civ. App. 1974).

Gleanings of premium-bribe-disposition principles can scarce be gathered from the antagonistic line—antagonistic, that is, to any recovery, and hence to any disposition, to anyone—beginning with the 1880 *Barnes v. Brown* in New York, running through the Delaware *Manacher v. Reynolds* in 1960, *Green Giant, Essex Universal, Fenestra.* The hundred years ending with the seventies were summarized by the Southern District in *Christophides v. Porco:*

> These cases hold that a majority or controlling stockholder is under no duty to other stockholders to refrain from receiving a premium upon the sale of his stock which reflects merely the control potential of that stock.
>
> —*Christophides v. Porco,* 289 F. Supp. 403, 405 (S.D.N.Y. 1968).

This same antagonistic line stretched on through the decade ending in 1980. Thus *Zetlin v. Gable Industries* in New York in 1975.

So too in Indiana in 1978 with *Yerke v. Batman*. Probably the archetype for the laissez-faire seventies is the Fourth Circuit's *Clagett v. Hutchison* in 1978 which resurrected and relied on the 1969 Tenth Circuit *McDaniel v. Painter:*

> Neither is there merit in the argument that appellees, as dominant shareholders, must refrain from receiving a premium which reflects the control potential of the stock.
>
> —*McDaniel v. Painter,* 418 F.2d 545, 548 (10th Cir. 1969).

Equally categorical was the Southern District in the 1980 *A&P:*

> It is well-settled that a stockholder is neither obliged to refuse a premium for his shares nor required to advise other stockholders that he is receiving a premium.
>
> —*Stromfeld v. Great Atlantic & Pac. Tea Co.,* 484 F. Supp. 1264, 1271 (S.D.N.Y. 1980).

One could hardly expect a disposition rationale from such contra cases.

But even in those cases where the premium was declared illegal, the judicial contribution to a more refined body of law is sparse indeed. In the majority of cases, the bare holding without more of *Sugden v. Crossland* in 1856 was followed without explanation. Thus it was in 1964 with *Lionel:* "[A]ny bonus received for such transfer of their office [must] be returned to the corporation."[157] In fact, without exception—*McClure, Bosworth, Porter v. Healy,* the *Reynolds* cases, *Rosenfeld, Le Mars*—all awarded the premium-bribe to the corporation, but, unfortunately, all equally without exception adduced no reasons at all for the award. One might conjecture that the reasons were too patent, that the premium-bribe so obviously belonged to the corporation that discussion would be otiose. But some experience of the pain suffered in unraveling the intrinsic illegitimacy of the premium-bribe, and its rightful ownership by the corporation, destroys this conjecture. The judicial silence is perhaps rather referable to the very complexities of this illegitimacy. In any event, resort to the adjudicated cases for a premium-bribe-disposition philosophy yields little beyond the unexplained conclusion that the premium-bribe belongs to the corporation, without elaboration.

Damages Distinguished

Somewhat inexplicably, another factor contributed to the judicial fuzziness, or outright silence, on the rationale of the disposition. Rarely have courts segregated the premium-bribe money from any dollar damages for later looting, collateral chicanery, or the harm from disloyalty and conflict of interest. Here are mutually exclusive concepts, one founded in the law of restitution, trust and contract. The other in tort. A court must approach damages and disposition, therefore, from totally distinct aspects.

Yet, interestingly, only two of the major control cases of the century overtly recognized this distinction. The New York Supreme Court in 1941 in the superb *Gerdes v. Reynolds*—in which (1) palpable looting and (2) a substantial premium-bribe made the distinction clamorous—first ordered over the $1.3-million premium ($1.25 per share over the actual value of $0.75) and then mulcted the Reynolds group $903,000 in damages for injury to Reynolds Investing. In the turn-of-the-century *Bosworth v. Allen* in New York the two-pronged approach was equally orderly.

But in all others the courts addressed one or other question, but never both. In such as *Sugden* and *McClure* the oversight was understandable. After the premium-bribe was disgorged, the tort damages from disloyalty, the breach of fiduciary duty, were most intangible, even if not minimal. With *Lionel,* however, the omission of all mention of damages is somewhat surprising, since the Muscats' disloyalty in selling and Sonnabend's malevolent designs in buying were spread across the opinion. The premium-bribe, of course, was far more obtrusive than the damages.

The prime anomaly, however, was *Insuranshares.* Here the Federal Court in 1940 in Pennsylvania took exactly the opposite tack. The premium-bribe, not inconsequential ("The price is strongly indicative of the true nature of the transaction. The sellers obtained $3.60 a share at a time when the price of the stock in the over-the-counter market was $1 to $1.25, and when the book value was $2.25—a figure substantially higher than could have been realized on actual liquidation"[158]), was totally ignored. Thus $178,422.55 in premium-bribe was overlooked, while damages for the tort harm were fixed at $207,358.87. This holding is all the more remarkable since the premium-bribe had been so obviously isolated by the Court from the share value of the stock.

(This fact question of the isolation of the premium-bribe handled so easily in *Sugden, McClure, Porter v. Healy, Le Mars,* and so well in *Bosworth, Gerdes, Insuranshares, Lionel* and *Rosenfeld,* has bedeviled many courts—*Stanton v. Schenck, Benson v. Braun, Essex Universal* in particular—when it never should have. True, the sale-of-control jurist must never fight the facts. The premium-bribe must be proven in isolation or the matter dropped. Delaware in the fifties expressed the idea with a wry smile:

> One cannot but sympathize with plaintiff's counsel.
> A great deal of work was done, and doubtless in the best
> of faith. Still, with all the intricacies and sophistication
> of modern corporation law, we must remember that it is,
> after all, a virtue of our system, and not a vice, that the
> lack of facts remains a vital deficiency.
>   —*Gottlieb v. Heyden Chemical Corp.,* 105
>   A.2d 461, 462 (Del. 1954).

But even when the premium-bribe has been patent, courts have seemingly missed it.)

This instant analysis of the premium-bribe disposition must substantially relegate this intrusive question of damages to later. Such relegation, however, is not uniformly practicable. As the discussion progresses, the impact of a damages award on one's understanding of the philosophy of the apportionment can be great, even though subconscious. But the analysis primarily must concern the disposition and later allocation of the premium-bribe, duly identified and isolated, and leave damages—for looting or the disloyalty itself—for elsewhere.

Distribution upon Disposition

At this point *Perlman v. Feldmann* manifests its singular value as a vehicle for the subtlest disposition problems.

Never before did a court question who would share how much of the premium-bribe award. Why? In many cases the total amount was gobbled up, and justly so, by the corporate creditors. Thus in *Gerdes v. Reynolds* the trustee in bankruptcy claimed the entire premium-bribe. Or as with *Sugden* and *McClure,* the beneficiaries behind the entity were all deserving innocents. Strictly speaking, *Lionel* should have offered the same queries as *Feldmann,* since the premium-bribe money Muscat paid over to Lionel was immediately shared by Sonnabend who had paid it to Muscat in the beginning. The explanation, though not the excuse, for the Court's oversight was probably the small amount, three percent, of Sonnabend's share in the $135,000 premium-bribe. But, howsoever explained, the *Lionel* Court never even asked itself whether Sonnabend—as Wilport— should share in the illegal premium.

Thus *Feldmann* stands alone in the judicial history of corporate control as the first and only court to apportion the premium-bribe among the competing parties, rather than, as *Lionel,* awarding it in toto, without qualification or quaver, to the corporation.

And *Feldmann* undoubtedly raised every possible issue. First and most fundamental, why assume at all that the premium-bribe belongs to the corporation (*Feldmann* did so assume, even if from a visceral sense)? Why deny Wilport its share? Sonnabend got his. Did Feldmann deserve to keep a third of the $2.1 million? Suppose Feldmann had 'sold' control but retained a sixth of the Newport shares, would the Court deny both Feldmann and Wilport a sixth of the $2.1 million? Without doubt *Perlman v. Feldmann* is a stinging goad toward this elaboration of a full philosophy of premium-bribe disposition.

III. The Philosophical Foundation of the Disposition

> [I]t is hoped that courts in the future will rely upon the custodial concept of corporate control to provide a single unifying philosophy.
>
> —Lewis, *The Legitimate Transfer of Corporate Control,* 13 CREIGHTON L. REV. 463, 486 (1979).

On its path to the final allocation, the *Feldmann* Court began to grope as soon as it progressed beyond the Cardozo trust generalities and the rudiments of the Custodial Concept of Corporate Control. Perhaps this is harsh, because, groping or no, several valid proximate, subsidiary conclusions were in fact reached (in contradistinction to the ultimate conclusion of the general liability of Feldmann). And the Court did move successfully from the general fiduciary duty to the specific liability for the sale of control, even though the intermediate steps were in the dark and the final implementation incorrect. Granted, some rationalization is also required to explain the Court's ambivalence in arguing to the naked sale of control. But groping and ambivalence withal, the upshot was nevertheless indisputably true to the broad philosophy of *Sugden, McClure, Gerdes, Lionel, Rosenfeld* and *Le Mars.*

The Three Proximate Subconclusions

Moreover, the later groping among the more proximate principles was not so blind as to be aimless. The Court reached three clearcut and influential conclusions subsidiary to the overall liability of Feldmann. Since every such subconclusion must perforce be founded on a controlling principle, one can justifiably (albeit somewhat forcibly) construct a tenable *Feldmann* philosophy even on this proximate level. In short, the Court's actions were far louder than its words.

The subconclusions? The *first*, logically, and most evident: The corporation was seriously harmed by the Feldmann/Wilport deal and, moreover, the fruits of the deal belonged in justice to the entity. *Second,* but far and away the foremost and most compelling: Wilport's role was seriously reprehensible. The *third* and last but nonetheless important: The Feldmann culpability was almost as great.

These three proximate subconclusions together must next be joined to a highly indicative *fourth* factor. Note that the Court was not at all concerned with damages, but awarded a lump sum exclusively from the $2.1-million premium-bribe paid by Wilport to induce Feldmann to hand over the board. This was pure restitution, with no damages whatsoever. Judge Hincks on the District level was more forthright in acknowledging this distinction:

> In this connection it must be remembered that the plaintiffs frankly are not seeking the recovery of damages for harm done to the corporation by a breach of trust. Instead, plaintiffs rely upon the principle that "a fiduciary

who has acquired a benefit by a breach of his duty as fiduciary is under a duty of restitution to the beneficiary," quoting from the Restatement, Restitution, Sec. 138(1).

> —*Perlman v. Feldmann*, 129 F. Supp. 162, 188 (D. Conn. 1952).

Not only was the Second Circuit attempting a "restitution to the beneficiary" of such "benefit" but in the process the Court laid down the elementary and obvious formula for the identification and isolation of that "benefit," the premium-bribe paid for control:

> The case will therefore be remanded to the district court for a determination of . . . the value of defendants' stock without the appurtenant control over the corporation's output of steel.
>
> —*Perlman v. Feldmann*, 219 F.2d 173, 178 (2d Cir. 1955).

(Furthermore, the lengthy implementation by the District Court of this directive is a feasible pattern for any fact finder in an attempt to segregate the premium-bribe in a sale of control.)

The Premium-Bribe

The conjunction of these four factors forces the question: What must be the nature of a premium that would lead the Court to such drastic conclusions? Or, better: Wherein lay the malefaction in passing such a premium from Wilport to Feldmann? In its three proximate subconclusions has not the Court unwittingly verified all of the five principal parts for a determination of . . .

> . . . the sale-of-control premium-bribe . . . technically defined as: (1) Some form of consideration . . . (2) Flowing to the incumbent contrôleur, (3) From or on behalf of the prospective contrôleur, (4) To induce the appointment to the office of control, (5) Paid knowingly, scienter.
>
> —Chapter 5: The Sale of Control and the Premium-Bribe, *supra* at 171.

With this hypothesis in mind, consider each of the Court's three proximate subconclusions vis-à-vis the technical definition of the premium-bribe.

First, from the early days of *McClure v. Law* and before, courts have uniformly handed over a premium-bribe to the corporation. Thus *McClure:* "The learned appellate division has treated this transaction as a bribe paid to the directors of the Life Union by Levy . . . . As president and director . . . he was bound to account to that association for all moneys . . . ."[159]

Second, a frank description of the deal as premium-bribery would have so characterized the Wilport/Feldmann malefaction as to fortify two of the Court's other three predispositions, namely (1) that the corporation should receive the *entire* $2.1 million and (2) that Feldmann should disgorge *all* of it, not merely two thirds.

Third, the assumption that the premium-bribed, Feldmann, is as guilty (or almost, according to the Court) as the premium-briber, Wilport, would make good sense out of the order to Feldmann to pay over *at least* the $1.3 million. In short, the Court was torn between the respective culpability of Wilport and Feldmann. Why it decided that the premium-bribed was less guilty than the premium-briber one will never know.

The Illegality of the Premium-Bribe

Even more pervasive was the Court's ready realization that this premium-bribe, once identified and isolated, was somehow bad. This, however, is understandable, since most honest citizens, faced with an acknowledged bribe, will reason to its illegality without benefit of complex ratiocination. So it was with the *Feldmann* Court. How far the Court could have gone in dissecting and defining this illegality is a more difficult question. Had the Court penetrated through to the niceties, Feldmann probably never would have kept the third of the premium-bribe, and the Wilport Syndicate, as a shareholder, might have got it. But in any event, few of the conclusions would have been reached had not the Court sensed that the premium-bribe was somehow illegitimate. How this illegitimacy should have been analyzed is a deeper question.

The philosophical questions yet unanswered and the many nuances remaining will be treated in six distinct steps: *(1) The Norms for Disposition. (2) The Turpitude of the Premium-Bribe. (3) The Illicit*

Consideration. (4) The Law of Restitution. (5) The Shareless Sale. (6) The Culpability of the Parties.

(1) The Norms for Disposition

The immediate queries of the overall disposition are clear: Who gets what? How much? Who loses what? How much? Why? The *Feldmann* facts have supplied the spare essentials: (1) The round sum of $2.1 million must be placed in the right hands. (2) One malefactor, Feldmann, exacted the premium-bribe from one other, Wilport. (3) Only one party was injured, the corporation, unless the veil is later lifted to look at the shareholders behind. (4) The malefaction was primitive: Premium-bribery to induce Wilport's appointment as contrôleur of Newport.

On first blush, many conjectures rush forward. The corporation should get all by default, since the guilty premium-bribed should not get any or should the equally guilty premium-briber. But that only excludes the guilty, with no positive reasons for the corporate boon. Possibly *all*, not just $1.3 million, should go to the innocent public shareholders? But that would be a windfall. Should a punitive award go to the corporation? Certainly the malefactors should be punished. What of escheat to the state? Perhaps return the money to Wilport? Or let Feldmann keep his share, $0.8 million, as the Court ordered?

But this immediate query—how to handle the $2.1 million—is superficial indeed. To answer the immediate, one must first answer the ultimate: What is the fundamental norm governing the premium-bribe disposition? Wherein lies the basic rationale for the award of the $2.1 million?

The wrong holds the key. To determine who gets what from whom, one must first determine who harmed whom, how and to what extent. From the nature of the wrong can be discerned the nature of the remedy. The wrong is the causal nexus between wrongdoers and wronged. As the injury flowed from malefactors to victim, so also must the restoration. The ultimate determinant of the disposition, therefore, is the causal impact of the wrong. Wilport and Feldmann committed an indivisible moral act, the single act of premium-bribery. In the essence of this malefaction lie all the ingredients necessary to supply the controlling principles for righting the wrong, for the proper disposition of the $2.1 million.

The heart of every wrong is the breach of a duty. But merely to say 'breach of a duty' is only the beginning, because the breach in premium-bribery is a complicated breach. Granted, premium-bribery is an indivisible, intentional tort: The breach of the trust obligation of loyalty—the fiduciary duty of the contrôleur to administer the entity to the exclusive benefit of the beneficiaries-shareholders—but that is too generic (even though the constituents of the tort are only rationally separable). Why? Because the rationale for the disposition might well be founded on less than the total tort, *on only one or more of its conceptual parts.* To what extent, how much or how little, can the overall Wilport/Feldmann wrong be directly related to the $2.1 million? Were only some aspects of the undivided breach specifically responsible for the dollars of the premium-bribe? In such close reasoning, cause may not be greater than effect, or lesser. Only a deeper analysis of the Wilport/Feldmann breach, therefore, will yield the formula for the premium-bribe disposition.

(2) *The Turpitude of the Premium-Bribe*

The complexities and involutions of the intrinsic illegitimacy of the tort of premium-bribery are the most challenging and important in the entire control study. The early investigation of the atom might be a parallel. On first approach, from the outside, each seems a partless unit, ultimate in simplicity, defying further breakdown. But dig below the surface and a new world lies beneath, parts within parts, relations and subrelations.

The pattern inside the premium-bribe is tripartite. Both principal parties, contrôleur and successor, were guilty simultaneously of (1) passing *illicit consideration* (2) in the appointment of an *unsuitable successor* (3) thereby *perverting the judgment* of selection. These elements coalesce to constitute the total turpitude of the premium-bribe, technically defined as . . .

> . . . (1) The perversion of the judgment of the incumbent contrôleur, engendered by an appointment of a successor induced by a cause other than suitability, (2) That is, for consideration illicit in itself, (3) Resulting in the appointment of a candidate unsuitable by reason of his own active role in the inducement.
>
> —Chapter 6: The Sale-of-Control Premium:
> The Intrinsic Illegitimacy, *supra* at 204-05.

The three elements derive their illegitimacy from various violations of fiduciary duty. As fully compensated corporate custodians, one an incumbent and one an appointee but both nonetheless committed, each had espoused the corporate welfare, particularly in the choice of a new leader. At that electric instant when incumbent passed control to appointee, only one norm could be consonant with corporate well-being: The suitability of the successor. When each agreed, therefore, to an appointment for a reason other than successor suitability, here cold cash, the result was triple: (1) The illiceity of the consideration, (2) the perversion of the judgment of selection and (3) subtly, the appointment of a successor who became unsuitable by his very act of premium-bribery. Here, in fine, is the threefold essence of premium-bribe illegitimacy.

(3) The Illicit Consideration

The joint and indivisible act of Wilport and Feldmann was solely responsible for the premium-bribe. The resultant $2.1 million must be specifically referable to one, two or all three of the conceptual coconstituents of this malefaction. In such constituents, therefore, will be found, necessarily, the rationale for the disposition of the $2.1 million. But which of the three relate to the dollars? The answer can be reached both negatively by the process of elimination and positively by proof of actual causal impact.

The Perversion Eliminated

Contrôleur Feldmann appointed Wilport for $2.1 million. As a desired objective, end, goal, the receipt and retention of this $2.1 million were "totally irrelevant, foreign, antagonistic, to"[160] the sole legitimate norm, successor suitability. The consequent perversion of judgment undeniably became the principal constituent of the total turpitude of the tort. Should not one immediately conclude, therefore, that this principal turpitude is thereby the principal determinant in the disposition of the $2.1 million? To the contrary, whatever other effect it may have, the perversion as such is unrelated to the $2.1 million. A homely analogy can effectively sever the perversion from the illicit cash.

Conceive a highly possible situation. The corporation was family-founded, and family-controlled ever since, but the ownership has long been dissipated among thousands. The reigning patriarch, now in his eighties, finally sees need of a successor. Three suitors seek the succession, the brilliantly competitive executive vice-president (long conceded the job), the miserably bereft president (fortuitously, also his father's only son) and an unscrupulously aggressive consumer syndicate (interestingly, with an under-the-table $2.1 million for the seriatim resignation of the board). Father is unhesitating. With not a nod to the corporate welfare, his choice has only one basis: Paternal prejudice. Here is a perfect perversion. Thoughts of successor suitability never entered the old man's head. The proffered premium-bribe could not have perverted his judgment any more effectively. Yet more to the present point, the perversion had no causal connection with any monetary consideration. Not a single cent changed hands. Thus a perfect perversion may enjoy its full maleficence without any premium-bribe dollars at all. The perversion consists in turning *away* from suitability. *That to which* the incumbent turns does not affect the essence of the perversion. The *that to which* merely characterizes the *kind* of perversion, e.g., paternal-prejudice perversion, premium-bribe perversion, etc. The formula for disposition, therefore, can scarce be found latent in this first of the three constituents.

The Premium-Bribe-Induced Unsuitability

So also with the second constituent. Imagine an embattled corporation, a Chrysler in the Colbert days or again in the eighties, or a Ford before Breech and Henry II, or after. Add another factor: The incumbent contrôleur is not only grossly inept but he is also a New Yorker who knows some law ("[A] majority or controlling stockholder is under no duty to other stockholders to refrain from receiving a premium upon the sale of his stock which reflects merely the control potential of that stock," as Judge Pollack put it in *Christophides v. Porco* in 1968 in the Southern District[161]). Enter a minority stockholder with a perfect candidate for successor, and minimal compunction about passing a bribe. The suitable successor is the guiding genius of a competitor. He is, furthermore, completely oblivious of the back-room negotiations and will be satisfied with the sizable salary and the opportunity to turn the corporation around. The deal is sealed. The $2.1 million passes from the minority Robin Hood to the outgoing contrôleur. The result? A perfectly suitable successor, unsullied by even the tincture of a bribe.

This little story makes it obvious, therefore, that some rationale other than the premium-bribe-induced unsuitability must determine the disposition of the $2.1 million. That question remains unsolved. Thus a $2.1-million bribe can effectively pass without any relation to premium-bribe-induced unsuitability. The explanation must lie elsewhere.

The Ultimate Rationale

With both perversion and successor unsuitability removed from the rationale, the third coconstituent could carry the day by default. Positive argumentation, however, can establish "the all important emolument of the transaction"[162] as the controlling constituent of the triple turpitude. Without support or influence from either perversion or unsuitability, the illicit consideration alone can answer who gets what and how much.

The conceptual unity of the tort's turpitude, however, again forces resort to an apposite analogy. Bring back to mind the story of the president of a mythical U.S. Bolt and Screw, Inc. In his early days he did a good job, was well worth his $90,000 salary, and even developed a national name for himself as a formidable banquet speaker and informative good-will ambassador for the firm. But soon the speechmaking tail began to wag the working dog, and the barnstorming head of Bolt and Screw was netting nearly $20,000 a year in personal income from the junkets.

> Here, standing isolated, is one element common to the premium-bribe, unearned recompense, without the perversion of the officer's judgment or any question of an unsuitable successor. The malefaction is a clear case of illicit emolument, without more. The chief executive officer of Bolt and Screw accepted $20,000 in compensation for corporate acts, performed pursuant to a corporate program, in fulfillment of a corporate duty, in the course

of official business, during the regular workweek, for
which he was already amply remunerated.

> —Chapter 6: The Sale-of-Control Premium:
> The Intrinsic Illegitimacy, *supra* at 220.

The parallel with the $2.1 million seems unassailable. Thus iso-
lated, both $20,000 and $2.1 million justly belong in the corporate
till, and for exactly the same reasons. In both cases "the all important
emolument" was paid by a third party, to a top corporate executive,
as a corporate official, because of his official position, and pocketed
personally, even though every minute of time and ounce of energy
had been dedicated to the exclusive benefit of the beneficiary corporation. Most important in both cases, the money was paid for the performance of an official corporate act, even though concededly that
act was seriously harmful to the corporate well-being.

Join this positive analysis to the negative elimination of the perversion and successor unsuitability. Now the foundation of the disposition has been narrowed to its simplest elements. In essence the
Wilport/Feldmann fiducial breach—*in specific reference to the $2.1
million alone*—consisted solely in the unlawful passing and, more
to the point, the unlawful retention of that very $2.1 million. Al-
though the total tort has a triple turpitude, only the specific turpitude
of the illicit retention is referable to the $2.1 million. Here is the sole
rationale of the disposition.

(4) The Law of Restitution

In rigid logic, the matter of the $2.1-million disposition could
end with a simple tort recovery for misappropriation of corporate
funds. Such recovery would be an unqualified restoration of the $2.1
million and would prescind completely from the concomitant but
intrinsically distinct cause of action for damages for the triple disloyalty integral to the premium-bribery.

But an inherent disability handicaps this simple tort approach.
It does not express the whole truth. Feldmann and Wilport were not
ordinary tortfeasors—regular employees, selling agents, or low-level
corporate officers—they were also fiduciaries who had placed themselves above the "workaday world" on a fiduciary level "stricter than

the morals of the market place."[163] As *trustee* tortfeasors Feldmann and Wilport must be regarded with a more refined eye. Theirs are all the custodial obligations of corporate control and particularly of the highly pertinent Benefit-to-Beneficiary Rule. Thus, although the simple tort recovery for restoration of misappropriated funds achieves the same end result, it does not frame the disgorgement in the exactingly correct legally philosophical terms.

From another aspect the unqualified tort disgorgement is even more inadequate. Concededly the passing of the premium-bribe is the heart of the malefaction. But the captious legal mind can surely discern a second related element, distinct from the mere passing and receiving of the $2.1 million. Strictly one might argue that the *receipt* of the $2.1 million was the last essential act of premium-bribery, and that the *retention* thereafter constituted a second definable wrong: Unjust enrichment.

The illicit retention of corporate funds ("[C]ompensation for corporate acts, performed pursuant to a corporate program, in fulfillment of a corporate duty, in the course of official business, during the regular workweek, for which he was already amply remunerated"[164]) opens up several traditional avenues to recovery. The *Restatement of Restitution* suggests one:

> In some cases, however, the quasi-contractual action of assumpsit is based wholly upon the unjust enrichment of the defendant. Thus a principal is entitled to a bribe received by his agent from a third person, although the principal's profit from the transaction, aside from the bribe, was the same as it would have been if no bribe had been given (see Restatement of Agency, §403).
> —RESTATEMENT OF RESTITUTION §128
> comment f, at 531 (1937).

But a common-law action of assumpsit is encumbered somewhat by the same disability as the simple tort approach. It too ignores the heightened trust obligation of the parties.

The most sophisticated and exacting rationale for the disgorgement is the deft blending of restitution with trust, and the conjunction in turn of this blend with the basic tort action. The law of restitution has a long and reliable history and complements admirably the Benefit-to-Beneficiary Rule of trusts. Thus the *Restatement:*

> Where a fiduciary in violation of his duty to the beneficiary receives or retains a bonus or commission or other profit, he holds what he receives upon a constructive trust for the beneficiary.
>
> —RESTATEMENT OF RESTITUTION § 197, at 808 (1937).

In a general way Judge Hincks was alluding to this synthesis when he noted:

> [T]he plaintiffs frankly are not seeking the recovery of damages for harm done to the corporation by a breach of trust. Instead, plaintiffs rely upon the principle that "a fiduciary who has acquired a benefit by a breach of his duty as fiduciary is under a duty of restitution to the beneficiary," quoting from the Restatement, Restitution, Sec. 138(1).
>
> —*Perlman v. Feldmann,* 129 F. Supp. 162, 188 (D. Conn. 1952).

In drafting the *Restatement,* the Committee on Restitution would have readily included corporate premium-bribery within the ambit of their thinking:

> Comment:
> a. *Bribes and commissions.* The rule stated in this Section is applicable not only where the fiduciary receives something in the nature of a bribe given him by a third person in order to induce him to violate his duties as fiduciary, but also where something is given to him . . . in connection with the performance of his duties as fiduciary. Thus, if a trustee, or corporate officer, or an agent entrusted with the management of property insures the property in a company of which he is an agent, and he receives from the company a commission for placing the

insurance, he is accountable for the commission so received and holds it upon a constructive trust for his beneficiary (see Restatement of Trusts, § 170, Comment *n*;
Restatement of Agency, § 388, Comment *a*).

> —RESTATEMENT OF RESTITUTION §197 com-
> ment a, at 808-09 (1937).

The philosophy and the reasoning of the Committee are thus
far unimpeachable. Their next step, however, encountered a pitfall
altogether too common.

> *c. Where no harm to beneficiary.* The rule stated in this
> Section is applicable although the profit received by the
> fiduciary is not at the expense of the beneficiary. Thus,
> where an agent to purchase property for his principal acts
> properly in making the purchase but subsequently re-
> ceives a bonus from the seller, he holds the money re-
> ceived upon a constructive trust for his principal. *The rule*
> stated in this Section, like those stated in the other Sec-
> tions in this Chapter, *is not based on harm done to the bene-*
> *ficiary in the particular case, but rests upon a broad*
> *principle of preventing a conflict of opposing interests* in the
> minds of fiduciaries, whose duty it is to act solely for the
> benefit of their beneficiaries.

> —RESTATEMENT OF RESTITUTION §197 com-
> ment c, at 809-10 (1937) (emphasis
> added).

(This is redolent of the summary award, without explanation or support, of *Sugden, McClure, Lionel,* et al.) Here manifest is the historical
confusion surrounding the prevention-of-temptation argument as
an explanation of the conflict-of-interest rule. True, the prophylactic
effects of the rule are healthy, but they are strictly by-products. The
ultimate basis is again the Custodial Concept of Corporate Control.
In short, the Comment is incorrect. The Benefit-to-Beneficiary Rule
"stated in this Section" *to the contrary is* "based on harm done to the
beneficiary in the particular case." And the harm in this particular
case—totally unrelated to the added harm from the disloyalty
itself—"is one element common to the premium-bribe, unearned
recompense . . . for corporate acts . . . for which he was already
amply remunerated." Denial of such emolument to the beneficiary
would be a very real harm indeed.

Thus the belabored dissection of the intrinsic illegitimacy of the premium-bribe, and the isolation of the illicit consideration from the perversion and the successor unsuitability, were both necessary processes in uncovering the philosophical fundamentals for the disposition of the $2.1 million. These philosophical fundamentals command restoration to the corporation in any view of the matter—totally irrespective of the separate cause of action for damages for the disloyalty intrinsic to the premium-bribery—whether the approach is simple tort damages or the more enlightened and correct conjunction of the restitution/trust philosophy with the basic tort that originally gave rise to the $2.1 million. Again the *Restatement of Restitution*:

> A fiduciary who commits a breach of his duty as fiduciary is guilty of tortious conduct and the beneficiary can obtain redress either at law or in equity for the harm done. As an alternative, the beneficiary is entitled to obtain the benefits derived by the fiduciary through the breach of duty. Situations involving specific breaches of duty with the resultant creation of a constructive trust and an equitable lien in the proceeds in favor of the injured beneficiary are dealt with in §§ 190-201.
>
> —RESTATEMENT OF RESTITUTION §138 comment a, at 556 (1937).

Thus the intentional tort of premium-bribery is really only rationally distinct from the violation of the Benefit-to-Beneficiary Rule. The same fundamental wrong—retaining illicit consideration—is common to both. The double approach—as captious, even superfluous, as it may be—to the single wrong, however, reflects reality admirably. And founds the disgorgement on an apposite rationale and characterizes the cause of action in the exactingly correct philosophical form.

(5) *The Shareless Sale*

The human mind can more easily penetrate an apparently impervious problem if the complexities are first reduced to the simplicity of A, B and C. Just such a reduction of the Wilport/Feldmann

intricacies is the 1899 New York *McClure v. Law* (which understandably has kept its vigor throughout the twentieth century). The chief
glory of *McClure* is the simplifying absence of all shares and shareholders. The Life Union Association was a mutual life-insurance
company. Business was in a flourishing condition and it seemed "that
one Mr. Louis P. Levy desired for his own purposes to procure the
control of"[165] the firm. The contrôleur, William H. Law, and the rest
of the board readily agreed to "the sum of $15,000, in consideration
. . ., [and] transferred to Levy the full control of the corporation"[166]
by the seriatim resignation of the board.

Stripped of the delicate distribution questions, *McClure* stands
apt for analysis. With no shareholders, only three parties were involved: William H. Law exacted the premium-bribe from Louis P.
Levy for control of Life Union. Beyond the perversion of his judgment
and the appointment of a premium-briber to the office of control,
the incumbent contrôleur accepted $15,000 for a corporate act, the
most important of his corporate career, performed "in fulfillment of
a corporate duty, in the course of official business, during the regular
workweek, for which he was already amply remunerated."

On these facts a court should readily order over, as the *McClure*
Court did, the entire $15,000 to the corporation. The premium-
briber Levy should lose all. The premium-bribed Law should disgorge everything. In such simple circumstances the basic philosophical principles are fully operative, unobstructed by mind-distracting
collateral questions. *McClure* will be a help betimes.

Note well that the *Feldmann* Court really reached all these conclusions as well. Certainly it would have adjudicated *McClure v. Law*
exactly as did the New York Court of Appeals. With a more gingerly
approach to its subtle allocation problems, the *Feldmann* Court
might well have gone on to a correct conclusion itself. But from this
point forward the *Feldmann* Court is on a distinctly different path.

(6) The Culpability of the Parties

But after some reflection, the mind becomes uneasy at an apparent inequity. True, the *McClure* $15,000 was, quite forthrightly, un-
just recompense earned through a corporate act, and properly
belongs to the company. True, too, neither the premium-bribed
should keep any of the $15,000 nor should the premium-briber get

any of it back. But hold. Both Law and Levy were *equally* guilty. Yet Levy, who paid the premium-bribe, loses his full $15,000 and Law, who accepted the premium-bribe, remains unscathed, financially where he was in the beginning, able to walk away with a 'nothing ventured, nothing gained.' The answer to this quandary can be found in several places.

The inequity will partially disappear with this realization: With the chips down, everybody involved really got exactly what he bargained for. The corporation got the $15,000, earned by its president on corporate time. The president himself was already getting his salary, and knew that any extras in the course of official business belonged in the corporate till. Even Mr. Levy, in a certain black sense, got what he bargained for. He paid for a corporate act and he got it, even though not exactly as planned. Certainly he knew in his heart that a premium-briber could lose his premium-bribe.

Damages Distinguished

But any remaining inequity evanesces when an influential and oft overlooked distinction is emphasized. Trial Judge Hincks in *Feldmann* put his finger on it. The *disgorgement* and *disposition* of the $2.1 million and the various *damages* imposed for the multifaceted malefaction are deeply antithetical. Strictly, the question of damages involves a separate cause of action and is obiter to any discussion of premium-bribe disposition. But the legal mind cannot concentrate uninhibitedly on the disposition when flashes of the damages-award inequity keep disturbing it. Recall that, interestingly, only two sale-of-control courts, *Gerdes* and *Bosworth,* have been able to concentrate on both damages and disposition at the same time. All the others were deflected to one or the other.

Since the premium-bribe damages is not a complex question, only a summary is in order. But such a summary could block damages from intruding into the disposition problem.

To say that damages is obiter to the disposition is perhaps an overstatement. Conceded, when the malefactors are *nonshareholders*, like Levy and Law, personal culpability ceases to be a factor after the *disgorgement* litigation is over, since no question can arise concerning the ownership by nonshareholders of the disgorged dollars now in the corporate treasury. All the members own equally. But when malefactor *shareholders* later present their stock at the corporate window for a slice—either by dividends or redemption—of the original premium-bribe money, personal culpability, and hence damages, cannot be ignored.

The present stratagem, therefore, is to carry forward with Levy and Law toward a complete judicial cleansing of culpability, both criminal and civil, in the thought that the final apportionment then can be faced in tranquil isolation, with damages questions resolved. Assume therefore *ex hypothesi:* (1) That Mr. William H. Law has disgorged the $15,000 to Life Union and (2) That thereafter he and Mr. Louis P. Levy are about to be battered by antagonists in every conceivable suit, and all successful to a shuddering degree. Thus with the *disgorgement* effected, now the *damages.*

Criminal

Pursuant to the New York Penal Law the local district attorney initiates prosecution against Levy and Law for 'commercial bribing' and 'commercial-bribe receiving,'[167] which are both perfectly pat. Since Levy and Law were both guilty, as briber and bribed, of a class-B misdemeanor, the jury returns a verdict and each is fined and sentenced to prison for three months.[168] The prison terms are identical, but with the fines the judge lets the punishment fit the crime: Levy $500,[169] as briber, and Law $30,000, as bribed ("double the amount of the defendant's gain"[170]). Levy had lost the money he paid as a bribe, now Law loses that amount and then some.

Since Mr. Law was also guilty under Penal Law Section 155.05 of larceny by embezzlement, and Mr. Levy of conspiracy to commit the same crime, prosecution goes forward, with the same success: Fines of $500 and three months in prison, consecutively served.

Civil

Had Mr. David McClure, receiver for the Life Union, been able to study the two 'looting' cases of the forties, *Gerdes* and particularly *Insuranshares,* he would undoubtedly have initiated a tort action for, as Judge Hincks put it on the trial level in *Feldmann,* "the recovery of damages for harm done to the corporation by a breach of trust."[171] Here after all is the cardinal sin of a trustee, clear disloyalty—triple disloyalty—in the face of a conflict of interests. William Law, as outgoing, and Louis Levy, as incoming, contrôleur, both assumed an identical obligation to promote the corporate welfare.

Yet, first, in the all-important appointment, both placed premium-bribe dollars before successor suitability. Here is serious malfeasance in office and the principal ingredient of the premium-bribe illegitimacy, the perversion of contrôleur judgment. For this "harm done to the corporation by a breach of trust," substantial damages—even punitive, considering the total helplessness of the corporation and the sensitive fiduciary duty of control—should be mulcted by the court.

But perversion was not the sole breach of trust. Secondly, both Levy and Law, again with equal culpability, foisted a premium-briber on Life Union, when both had pledged the best possible personnel for the future of the firm. This was not merely lack of due care but at the least the 'substantial certainty' of Section 8A (Intent) of the *Restatement (Second) of Torts*. The potential for disaster with a premium-briber in the top spot of Life Union was palpable, and damages—solely for the disloyalty—should be awarded accordingly. (Had such a premium-briber been given a little time and latitude—say two or three years as contrôleur—as in *Bosworth, Gerdes, Insuranshares* and *Le Mars*, this particular facet of the total turpitude, successor unsuitability, might have shown itself in further forms of malefaction, e.g., in the steel contracts Wilport might award Wilport.)

Finally and third, in paying over and retaining $15,000 in illicit emolument, both Levy and Law again breached their fiduciary duty of loyalty, since personal welfare was placed before corporate. Such misappropriation of funds is clearly actionable, not merely for the disgorgement but for the superadded damages for the malfeasance itself and the concomitant disloyalty.

The Court, in a summary review of the triple tort breach of trust—the perversion, illicit compensation, unsuitable successor— would hand down awards for example in the amount of $1,000 on each of the several counts. (Surely a benign court would not be oblivious of the previous loss by Levy of the $15,000 in premium-bribe money. And even Law's loss on the criminal level. As an ameliorative factor these would undoubtedly mitigate damages.)

Ouster

As the final fillip, since Mr. McClure faced the *Lionel* problem, surely he would have sought the permanent removal (as he probably did) of Mr. Louis P. Levy from the office of contrôleur. Thus in *Lionel:*

Therefore, some restrictions of the present board are required, so that the Sonnabend group may not take advantage of the position they hold. They shall be restricted to current management problems and other matters necessary for the proper functioning of the corporation and they shall not be permitted to use their present offices as the means to secure stockholder approval for their designated directorial slate, or dealing in matters involving self interest, such as proposed acquisitions from Premier Corporation of America.

—*Matter of Lionel Corp.*, N.Y.L.J., Feb. 4, 1964, at 14 (Sup. Ct., N.Y. County).

But the broader subject of successor suitability is too far afield from the question of disposition. Suffice to say that some assurance of corporate protection from the appointment of a premium-briber as contrôleur would permit the legal mind to focus unblurredly on the distribution of the premium-bribe money.

Thus, with criminal prosecutions, civil damages, removal from office, gone would be any lingering thought of an apparent inequity. Patently Mr. Law or any other contrôleur cannot exact his premium-bribe and take his chances. His day of reckoning will come at other times in other courts. As would Mr. Levy's.

The Philosophy in Globo

Two fundamentals emerge from these simplifications. First, under the simple three-party *McClure*, involving a completely shareless sale, the $15,000 payment over to the corporation—whether through tort law alone or aided by restitution and trust—is founded *exclusively* on the illiceity of the consideration, with no admixture of either the contrôleur's perversion or successor unsuitability. Second, whatever personal culpability either Levy or Law incurred was completely cleansed away by the multifarious criminal and civil actions, climaxed by the disgorging of the $15,000 itself. Both Levy and Law were as white as the driven lamb when they walked out of the last courtroom.

Thus reduced to the simplicity of A, B and C, and shorn of the confounding complexities of malefactor-owned shares, the basic philosophical principles point to a triple conclusion: The premium-bribery money goes in toto to the corporation. The premium-briber loses all. The premium-bribed retains nothing. Now the disposition can proceed into virgin territory, and directly contra to *Feldmann*. Perhaps, indeed, a Procrustes might have even stretched the *Feldmann* Court this far. But not an inch farther.

Now that a hilltop view is possible, perhaps a little retrospect will aid appreciably in the progress of this disposition study.

What the *Feldmann* Court so fatefully failed to see, and what is so crucial, is the sharp division, the categorical splitting, of the broadest disposition question into two relatively unrelated subjects: (1) The philosophy supporting the unqualified award of the entire $2.1 million directly to the corporation. Thus: *The original disposition to the corporation.* (2) The basic principles governing the next stage, the apportionment by the corporation of that $2.1 million so disposed and received. Thus: *The distribution after disposition.* The shareless sale of *McClure* so aptly set off these distinct divisions.

The conclusions thus far have presumably settled the entire premium-bribe upon the corporation. The reasoning has reached a high point, and must now lead to a proper allocation by the corporation. Once in the corporation, how out of it?

IV. The Distribution on Disposition

> The view seems to be slowly gaining acceptance in some courts, probably inspired in part by the work of scholarly commentators, that . . . when a fiduciary sells a controlling block of stock he is required to take some affirmative action to protect the interests of minority shareholders, . . . even by refusing to sell unless the purchaser offers to buy the shares of minority holders on the same favorable terms.
>
> —O'Neal, *Sale of a Controlling Corporate Interest*, 38 U. PITT. L. REV. 9, 26 (1976).

The philosophical fundamentals, the shareless sale of *McClure,* the thorough cleansing of Levy and Law, have supplied the wherewithal for just such an exact allocation of the $2.1 million.

The apparent crux lies in Wilport's ownership of one third of the Newport stock. But that only begins the problem. At three points the *Feldmann* Court crashed head on with the philosophical fundamentals: (1) The corporation did *not* receive the entire $2.1 million. (2) Feldmann did *not* disgorge all, only two thirds. (3) *Shareholder* Wilport was *denied* its third.

The attempt at a resolution of this confrontation will proceed in two successive steps: *(1) The Eligibility to Share. (2) The Severability of the Contracts.*

(1) The Eligibility to Share

The progress of the argument now finds Levy and Wilport, Law and Feldmann, arm in arm and fully purged, leaving the last of their many litigations. Perhaps the only difference in their respective hypothetical purgations would be caused by the relative enormity of the Wilport/Feldmann $2.1-million malefaction.

Another supposition must be added to this hypothesis. Carry forward arguendo with the assumption so elaborately constructed thus far, that Feldmann, as Law, was ordered to pay over directly to the corporation the total $2.1 million, not just two thirds. Apart completely from intrinsic reasonableness, this assumption has extrinsic support. Strict logic commands adherence to a general principle over a specific exception until such time as the general principle has been proven untenable. Philosophical fundamentals bolstered by the traditional rule in *Sugden, McClure, Lionel, Rosenfeld, Le Mars,* suggest that the entire premium-bribe belongs to the corporate entity until cogent countervailing reasons can be adduced. If none appear, the general principle prevails.

To reduce this hypothetical to its narrowest limits, further assume that the eventual ownership of the crucial one-third stock block (actually in Wilport's hands at the moment) remains undetermined. After later issues are resolved, possibly Feldmann will have the block. One thing only is certain at this point. None other than Feldmann or Wilport should receive this block's share of the $2.1 million. Neither the two-third public innocents by a windfall nor the state by escheat.

(The hypothesis of course has excluded the real business possibility that Newport might determine to use the $2.1 million for debt retirement, plant expansion or any of many internal reasons.

Feldmann or Wilport would nonetheless be the owner. The present scrutiny is limited to the viability of the one-third block in the hands of either Feldmann or Wilport.)

Suitability Excluded

Another necessary oversight must be the possible control role of either Feldmann or Wilport after the stock has settled. Wilport's suitability for the office of control of Newport—or even premium-bribed Feldmann's—does warrant further investigation. The distribution after disposition, however, concerns solely the eligibility to share in the $2.1 million, and not the suitability to control the corporation. Whether a court should block Wilport, or Feldmann for that matter, from the office of control, as *Lionel* did Sonnabend, is a fascinating question that ere long will answer itself.

With the field down to Feldmann and Wilport, how would dispassionate objectivity assess the eligibility of each to participate in the apportionment? Looking toward the day, under these circumscribed conditions, when either Feldmann or Wilport finally possesses the controverted block, one can see only two apparent obstacles to their participation: (1) Such *personal culpability* as to render them unfit as individuals for any of the erstwhile premium-bribe money and (2) Such a *taint on the shares* as to preclude the stock itself, in anyone's hands, from any share of the $2.1 million.

If Feldmann and Wilport can surmount these obstacles, they can enter the lists prepared to do battle over the rightful ownership of the one-third block. With Feldmann and Wilport, therefore, these obstacles will be faced successively.

The Levy/Wilport Dilemma

Both Mr. Levy and the Wilport Syndicate lost their $15,000 and $2.1-million premium-bribes. (In a strict sense both premium-bribes could be said to have been disgorged, or less accurately 're-stored,' to the entity.) Both parties were completely battered with damages, fines, imprisonment. If nonshareholder, premium-briber Levy may now walk away cleansed, with no further obligation either to society in vindication or to the corporation in tort damages or trust 'restitution,' so certainly should a similar *non*shareholder Wilport. And if a *nonshareholder* Wilport, why not also a *shareholder* Wilport?

Even assuming a contrary-to-fact assumption that *premium-briber* Wilport must always and forever be identified with *shareholder* Wilport, would not even a premium-briber *shareholder* Wilport be as fully rehabilitated as a premium-briber *nonshareholder* Levy? Only the ownership of shares distinguishes them.

When shareholder Wilport presents its shares at the Newport window should it now be punished an additional one third, $800,000—it lost forever the $2.1 million—by the denial of its one-third share of the $2.1 million now disgorged into the Newport coffers? This one third is increment, return, from an investment *at market*—the $2.1 million was premium-bribe, the additional $5.9 million was the market price of the stock—in 37 percent of Newport common. If Wilport is to be thus additionally punished, should not Levy be called back and also be punished an extra 'third' of the $15,000, since he was just as guilty as Wilport? Levy had already lost the full $15,000, but only $15,000. Wilport had already lost the full $2.1 million, so why more, an additional one third, now?

A Retort

One immediately hears an objection. If Wilport now receives the one-third $800,000, this $800,000 repayment will reduce the $2.1-million disgorgement and Wilport will not have, in fact, disgorged—and hence lost forever—the full $2.1 million, and with that the artfully contrived dilemma would fall. Thus Levy will have in truth lost his full $15,000—since he has no stock to warrant a one-third repayment—but Wilport only two thirds.

A Rejoinder

But further thought restores the dilemma. The captious retort would have won the day had two contrary-to-fact suppositions been true: (1) That Wilport had never in fact purchased a one-third stock ownership, but had merely passed the bald $2.1-million premium-bribe unaccompanied by the purchase of the Newport common (in a word, that no stock passed, only control to Wilport and the $2.1-million premium-bribe to Feldmann) and (2) That shareless Wilport (as shareless Levy) nonetheless received a one-third $800,000, even though Wilport had no stock holding in Newport to warrant the payment.

But neither of these suppositions was verified. Wilport had invested $5.9 million in honest investment dollars—totally unrelated to the collateral $2.1-million premium-bribe—and the $800,000 would be simply the equally honest share of the $2.1 million the corporation honestly earned through the efforts, albeit dishonest, of its incumbent contrôleur, Feldmann, "during the regular workweek, for which he was already amply remunerated."

So in fact Wilport did lose the full $2.1 million, as Levy the $15,000. The $800,000 was totally unrelated to the premium-bribe dollars, was merely return on investment. So the Levy/Wilport dilemma stands.

The dilemma, therefore, is answerable in only one way. Once grant the justice and sufficiency of the punishment, damages and 'restitution,' and premium-briber Wilport disappears, to be supplanted by a new person, shareholder Wilport, untarnished, who made an investment at market unrelated to the premium-bribe.

This Levy/Wilport dilemma was used only because the disposition problem *seems* to center on the Wilport Syndicate. But everything said of Levy/Wilport is obviously applicable to Messrs. Law and Feldmann. Carrying out the same hypothetical, both, once they had received their premium-bribes, disgorged their entire $15,000 and $2.1 million—recall that in each hypothetical each paid over the full amounts to the corporation—and both were fully cleansed. By the same valid argument, therefore, Mr. Feldmann as a *possible* shareholder could correspondingly share in any corporate disbursement of the $2.1 million. Thus from the single aspect of a *personal culpability*, Levy and Wilport, Law and Feldmann, should all be equally eligible to share.

The 15-10-15 Query

Which leads opportunely to another apposite analogy and the question of *tainted shares*. Change hypothetically the pre-premium-bribe shareholdings of Feldmann and Wilport. As support for his mere-incumbency control of Newport, suppose Mr. Feldmann instead possessed at the outset only a 25-percent block of stock. And instead the Wilport Syndicate already held 15 percent. Again Feldmann and Wilport put their heads together, again agreed on the same $2.1-million premium-bribe, but this time varied the script a bit—no doubt as an earnest of Feldmann's confidence in Wilport—by transferring only a ten-percent block of Feldmann stock, *at market*. In addition, of course, to the $2.1-million premium-bribe paid to Feldmann. When the dust settled Wilport held 25 and Feldmann 15 percent. And, of course, the full $2.1 million was eventually and duly disgorged by Feldmann.

Who now may come to the Newport window for a share of the $2.1 million? Neither of the two 15-percent blocks—Feldmann's and the original Wilport—were involved directly in the so-called sale of control. The 15-percent blocks never moved. Only the ten-percent block changed hands. Both 15-percent blocks would hardly be barred at the distribution merely because their owners had otherwise indulged in a premium-bribe. One can conclude, therefore, that the *ownership itself* or the *mere holding* could never indelibly taint the shares.

Patently any personal culpability of Feldmann or Wilport (even granting a residue after the purgings) can scarce contaminate their stock. At worst the premium-bribe turpitude infected the human malefactors, not their nonhuman stock. This, of course, would be equally true even of the transferred ten-percent block, *at least to the extent that it was merely owned or held*. The taint of owners, without more, can never taint the stock itself, whether the two 15-percent blocks, or even the ten. Or even, of course, the Feldmann/Wilport one third.

All this may be true from the mere-ownership, personal-culpability aspect, but the ten percent was more than merely held. It actually passed in connection with and at the time of the premium-bribe. Could such *involvement in the deal* bring ineradicable taint to the stock itself?

The Shareless Sale

But was it actually involved? Recur to the shareless sale of Levy and Law. Embodied in that single deal was every evil possible to premium-bribery: The triple disloyalty of both Levy and Law in the perversion of judgment, the illicit consideration and the appointment of a premium-briber, and finally the retention of $15,000 in corporate funds. Yet obviously none of this collective evil besmirched the shares that passed *in connection with* or *at the time of* the sale of

control. Scarcely so, since no shares existed to pass, or be be-
smirched. Clearly, then, the full turpitude of premium-bribery expresses itself without consequent effect on the stock. No causal
nexus joins the collateral shares to the malefaction of premium-
bribery. Total taint is possible without any shares at all. Thus, arguably, with shares actually present the taint is nonetheless fully
pervasive, but without pervading the shares.

But this at best is a negative proof. Consider the positive role
of the ten percent in the act of premium-bribery. Was it the efficient
cause? No, Wilport and Feldmann effected the deal. Material cause?
That unhappy—but equally guiltless—role fell to the illicit consideration. Instrumental cause? If any, it was the cold cash itself. The stock
was neither the efficient cause nor the material cause nor the instrumental cause. Nor even the condition. Why? Because the stock—
again witness Levy and Law—was not involved in the act of
premium-bribery at all. It figured solely in a separate sale, collateral
to an illegal act of premium-bribery. With no connection at all,
hardly a causal connection, or even that of a condition.

All this, however, has only said why the shares are untainted,
why the stock is *not undeserving*. Perhaps the correct approach is
positive. The stock has a positive right to share in the $2.1 million,
not because it was not involved in premium-bribery, which it was not,
but because it—and all the blocks, the two 15-percent blocks and
the ten—had beneath them an honest investment of cash. This cash
earned a just return on a sudden but legal increment, also justly
'earned' for the corporation by a 'hardworking' employee in the
course of his employment. The $2.1-million increment should inure
to all untainted shares alike.

Further support, if needed, could be garnered from any stock
owned by Bolt and Screw's president. Such presidential shares would
hardly be so tainted by the $20,000 unearned emolument as to block
a dividend resultant on that unexpected corporate increment.

Thus Feldmann and Wilport have successfully leaped the only
two obstacles barring them from a welcome at the Newport window:
(1) *Personal culpability,* seemingly long since purged, and (2) *Sullied
shares,* now patently unsullied. All of which opens the lists for battle
between two equally eligible combatants for the ownership of the unsullied shares, since the battle was purposely deferred till now. He
who wins, Feldmann or Wilport, may legitimately claim the one

third of the $2.1 million. The ensuing analysis will confirm further the double eligibility—personal and shares—of Feldmann and Wilport.

(2) *The Severability of the Contracts*

The nub of the sole remaining question is the legitimacy of the simple sale of stock. Was the Feldmann/Wilport deal indivisible, involving a premium-bribe and the transfer of a controlling block of stock for a single sum of $8 million? Or did Feldmann and Wilport enter into two distinct contracts: (1) The sale of control by means of a $2.1-million premium-bribe and (2) The sale of a one-third stock block at the market price of $5.9 million?

The fate of any contract of premium-bribery is beyond question. As a crime in some jurisdictions and injury to corporation and shareholders everywhere, such an agreement would be void ab initio and unenforceable 'on account of public policy.' But when the contract of premium-bribery falls through invalidity, does it fall alone or carry down with it an inseparable sale of stock? If the stock sale can stand alone, Wilport keeps its shares, and a corresponding third of the $2.1 million. If not, the stock goes back to Feldmann and he gets the third.

The Intent of the Parties

Feldmann undoubtedly would argue—toward invalidation of the deal and return of the 37-percent block—that neither he nor Wilport ever envisaged anything but a single sale of a controlling block at a handsome price. In fact neither of them, so his story would go, would have ever entered into a simple stock sale without the surrender of the board. Wilport would counter with appropriate rebuttals—toward retention of the block—and the strong assertion that failing a control transfer the one-third block would nonetheless be more than a satisfactory beginning toward a legitimate 50-plus-percent majority. (Ironically the $2.1 million would have just made the difference, had Wilport purchased a minority 13 percent at market. That ridiculously assumes, of course, that Feldmann would also have sold his 37 percent at market.)

Feldmann undoubtedly would yield to the temptation to go all the way and allege his own crime of premium-bribery as the cause for invalidating the stock sale, with the resultant return of the shares to him. How a court would react to that, betimes.

But what the parties might have done had the invalidation been foreseen is gross conjecture. They contracted with other expectations. Since such conjectures on what might have been are otiose, the law must look at things as they actually were and conclude to the reasonable intent of the parties from all the circumstances surrounding the transaction.

In any attempt to penetrate to an unexpressed intent of such a collateral agreement the court has a task with a double aspect. Whenever faced with intertwining contracts—one patently void, the other not—the law as a rule, either rightly or wrongly, has correspondingly intertwined *public-policy considerations* with the *strictly private rights of the parties*. In facing such a complicated chore Levy and Law again should help somewhat. But the severability question requires more help than that. In the middle fifties two remarkably similar errants rode down an almost identical path. Their machinations and resultant Supreme Court litigation should elicit every needed principle toward the solution of this last remaining problem in the disposition of the $2.1 million.

Kelly v. Kosuga

As Levy and Law, Feldmann and Wilport before them, Jack H. Kelly and Vincent W. Kosuga had set themselves on a kindred criminal course, with only minor variations. Kelly and Kosuga, independent operators, "were both engaged in the marketing of onions,"[172] and unfortunately Mr. Kosuga had grossly overstocked his inventory. Towards unloading several carloads of this oversupply, Kosuga and his friend, Sam Siegel, concocted a doubly duplicitous plan whereby they would not only sell off the excess onions but 'stabilize' the market in the bargain.

By markedly overstating their supply—some "600 cars in the Chicago area and 400 more elsewhere throughout the country"— and boldly threatening poor Kelly and friends with a massive unloading "on the futures exchange for the purpose of depressing the futures price and the cash market price of onions," Kosuga and Siegel forced from hapless Kelly a contract of purchase for 50 carloads at $960 per car. Kelly's friends took 237 more, "fearful that this [dumping]

would cause them considerable loss." Finally, all parties contracted—Kelly and friends on one side and the Kosuga/Siegel group
on the other—that none would "deliver any onions on the futures
market for the remainder of the current trading season." Admittedly,
"this was 'for the purpose of creating a false and fictitious market condition,' and 'to fix the price of onions and limit the amount of onions
sold in the State of Illinois.'"[173]

In the event, Kelly actually accepted some of the contracted-for
onions, made a payment or two on account, but finally reneged on
37 of the 50 cars. The onions began to rot. And Kosuga "properly,
after repudiation of the purchase by [Kelly], withdrew the remaining
cars from storage and sold them for [Kelly's] account[,] . . . the market
price having declined in the interim."[174]

The facts were undisputed. Kelly admitted buying the onions.
He simply welshed on the deal, inspired possibly by the market drop.
To this Vincent Kosuga reacted by seeking court enforcement of the
onion sale. (Much as Wilport arguably should have done by similarly
seeking a declaratory judgment that the stock sale itself was likewise
valid—and carrying with it Wilport's right to share in the $2.1
million—even though the premium-bribe was illegal.) Jack Kelly
countered—much as Feldmann would have done had Wilport's
block been awarded a third of the $2.1 million and Feldmann been
unable to keep his third—"that the sale was made pursuant to and
as an indivisible part of an agreement which violated §1 of the Sherman Antitrust Act . . . ."[175] Thus Kelly argued that his onion contract
fell with the illegal price-fixing and that he was not bound to pay for
the onions. Just as Feldmann would have argued that his contract
of sale of stock fell with the premium-bribery and that he could recover his one-third block.

(Emphasize the anomaly in the relative Kelly/Kosuga and
Feldmann/Wilport adjudications. With Kelly/Kosuga the onion
contract would be totally invalid if tied inextricably to the price-
fixing. With Feldmann/Wilport the stock contract should likewise
be totally invalid if tied inextricably to the premium-bribery. The
analogy thus far would seem unassailable. But consider what the
Feldmann Court actually did: (1) The stock sale was treated in effect
as perfectly valid but (2) one isolated, but otherwise logical, concomitant of the sale was selectively blocked by a judicial denial of the
Wilport share of the then-disgorged-into-Newport $2.1 million. The
stock sale would stand. The effect of the sale—the right of Wilport's

37 percent to share in the $2.1 million—would fall. Thus the sale, the stock and all the attributes of the stock were fully valid, with one lone exception, the dividend flowing to the stock. This anomaly is implicit hereafter.)

"The District Court entered summary judgment [against Kelly] for the unpaid purchase price and storage charges, less the amounts obtained on the sale by"[176] Kosuga. The Court of Appeals for the Seventh Circuit affirmed. So also did the Supreme Court by Mr. Justice Brennan on "certiorari to consider the availability of [Kelly's] pleaded defense of illegality under the Sherman Act to this action to enforce the terms of a sale made under state law."[177]

To look at the final *Feldmann* problems through the eyes of *Kosuga* is eminently justified. The two cases are on all fours on the question of severability, with the marked difference that *Feldmann* never reached the problem, while *Kosuga* faced it with success.

Yet 'severability' is not an exact description of the question. As Justice Brennan said: "[A]nalysis in terms of 'divisibility' or some other verbal formula may well be circular . . . ."[178] Deeper down, both *Feldmann* and *Kosuga* faced a far more basic question: Was the contract of sale—stock or onions—a viable unit? May it, should it, stand alone on its own? Or must it fall with the concomitant criminal contract, the premium-bribery, the price-fixing?

The several principles underlying the problem of viability—some directly adduced by the *Kosuga* Court, some hinted at, others skirted—are an intriguing blend of the public and the private, the intrinsic and the extrinsic, the positive and the negative. Hand in hand with the *Kosuga* Court these principles must be dissected and evaluated.

The Presumption of Viability

In such a technical inquiry one might overlook inadvertently an elemental principle of law and human conduct. When two rational and reflective persons enter an important agreement, they generally have every intention of carrying through with it. An understandable presumption has developed over the history of contracting man that contracts are to be carried out, and that the law should enforce them without clear reason to the contrary. Hence cogent argument must be adduced to invalidate either the purchase of the onions or the sale—including, a fortiori, *all* effects of the sale—of Feldmann's stock. Why not presume that the parties meant what they said? The *Kosuga* Court was not far from this presumption: "[T]he federal courts should not be quick to create a policy of nonenforcement of contracts beyond that which is clearly the requirement of the Sherman Act."[179] As succeeding arguments are marshalled, therefore, bear in mind that the original, expressed intent should not be subverted for a slight reason.

But presumptions and extrinsic arguments aside, the overarching argument for the severability of the sale contracts from the premium-bribery and the price-fixing lies in the elementary analysis of the causal connection between the two. Levy and Law demonstrated the possibility of producing all the evils of premium-bribery without any stock sale at all. Kelly, Kosuga and Siegel could have cornered the market without ever an onion changing hands. A simple agreement to hold their onions from the market would have done the trick. And certainly Mr. Feldmann could have entrusted control of Newport to Wilport without any concomitant stock, as old man Alesch did when he installed Iowa Mutual as contrôleur of Le Mars Mutual (No stock existed to change hands). Clearly, then, in neither instance was there any *causal connection* between the criminal malefactions and any accompanying sales.

The sole question in *Kosuga* and *Feldmann* was the nature of the noncausal connection, tenuous as it was. Since not a cause, was the sale a condition, a sine qua non, to the price-fixing? Note again that the cornering operation admittedly could have succeeded without any purchase. Nor was the Feldmann/Wilport sale of stock any more intimately connected with the premium-bribery. Not only were the sales not causes of the crimes, they were not even conditions.

Undoubtedly, however, in both *Feldmann* and *Kosuga* there were some connections between contracts and malefactions. But the connections were only of time and place, mere accidentals in no way integral to the respective agreements. The stock block could have been sold many months before, or after, the premium-bribery, since control of Newport was referable to the proxy and the wide dispersal of shares. So too with the onions and the price-fixing. Mr. Justice Brennan could have been speaking for *Feldmann* as well as *Kosuga* when he described the true nature of the connection:

> [W]e do not think it inappropriate or violative of the intent of the parties to give [the sale] effect even though it fur-

nished *the occasion* for a restrictive agreement of the sort
here in question.
                    —*Kelly v. Kosuga,* 358 U.S. 516, 521 (1959)
                    (emphasis added).

In short here were two completely separate transactions. In
Kosuga it suited Kosuga's purpose to unload some onions. With
Feldmann some stock. As for Wilport, substantial stock support for
an anticipated mere-incumbency-control position, or a beginning
toward a majority, was not an undesirable thought. The sale alone
had advantages unrelated to premium-bribery. As for Kelly, he was
bludgeoned into the deal, but nonetheless as a marketer could use
the onions. Or so he thought. The price-fixing and the premium-
bribery were other matters indeed.

The *Kosuga* Court adduced another positive argument in support of viability. Taken in complete isolation, as separate deals in
their own right, the sales—onions and stock—both represented
completely integral agreements in themselves, with lawful terms,
commendable purpose, honest price. Nothing within the four cor-
ners could evoke attack, let alone invalidation. Hence, the Supreme
Court saw no reason not . . .

> . . . to give legal effect to a completed sale of onions at
> a fair price. And while analysis in terms of "divisibility"
> or some other verbal formula may well be circular, . . . in
> any event, where, as here, a lawful sale for a fair considera-
> tion constitutes an intelligible economic transaction in it-
> self, we do not think it inappropriate or violative of the
> intent of the parties to give it effect . . . .
>   —*Kelly v. Kosuga,* 358 U.S. 516, 521
>   (1959).

Public Protection

The public-policy arguments for invalidating such collateral
contracts are necessarily founded on one overriding purpose: The
protection of the public. In an excess of zeal one may forget that public protection is never needed without something to protect the public from. If a private contract offers no public threat, public policy
should scarce be invoked. The entire discussion of enforceability or

severability or divisibility, therefore, could have stopped logically with the intrinsic arguments. If a contract of sale of onions or stock is good in itself, no need for speculation on the harm such a contract could inflict on the public. If no intrinsic wrong, no need for extrinsic measures of protection. Of all the concepts supporting severability, the *Kosuga* Court relied most on this distinction between private contract and public protection, between intrinsic legitimacy and extrinsic factors, between positive and negative arguments. In his concluding statement Mr. Justice Brennan summarized this dichotomy:

> Accordingly, while the nondelivery agreement between the parties could not be enforced by a court, if its unlawful character under the Sherman Act be assumed, it can hardly be said to enforce a violation of the Act to give legal effect to a completed sale of onions at a fair price.
> —*Kelly v. Kosuga,* 358 U.S. 516, 521 (1959).

Which of course could be said equally of the premium-bribery agreement and "a completed sale of [stock] at a fair price."

The negative norm for a court in such circumstances is extremely limited. In *Continental Wall Paper* the allegedly legal purchases were integral to the price-fixing:

> The [*Continental Wall Paper*] Court was of opinion that to give judgment for the excessive purchase price so fixed in favor of such a vendor would be to make the courts a party to the carrying out of one of the very restraints forbidden by the Sherman Act. 212 U.S., at 261. Any thought that the Court might have been proceeding on broader grounds was shortly afterwards laid to rest by the unanimous opinion of the Court in the *Wilder* case. 236 U.S., at 177. The scope of the defense of illegality under the Sherman Act goes no further.
> —*Kelly v. Kosuga,* 358 U.S. 516, 520 (1959).

Scant danger of becoming a party to the crime faced the *Feldmann* Court in according Wilport full ownership of its stock and the inalienable right of that ownership, any just returns on that stock.

The civil court has no business in assuming the role of a public prosecutor. Mr. Justice Brennan carried this thesis to its logical conclusion:

> The Court [again in the *Wilder* case] observed that the Sherman Act's express remedies could not be added to judicially by including the avoidance of private contracts as a sanction.
>
> —*Kelly v. Kosuga,* 358 U.S. 516, 519 (1959).

How apropos of Mr. Levy, and correspondingly the Wilport Syndicate. If fine and imprisonment were efficacious, if tort damages for the perversion, successor unsuitability and illicit consideration were sufficient, if the $2.1-million premium-bribe was lost for good, if the sale itself is even admittedly valid, should the *Feldmann* Court 'add judicially' a further 'sanction' by the denial of a just share in the corporate increment, of a licit return on a licit investment?

> Supplying a sanction for the violation of the Act, not in terms provided and capricious in its operation, . . . is avoided by treating the defense [of illegality] as so confined [to cases where the courts would become a party to the crime].
>
> —*Kelly v. Kosuga,* 358 U.S. 516, 521 (1959).

If the *court's* role is so limited, a fortiori it ill behooves the *corporation* (should the matter not reach litigation) to assume the court's mantle by withholding a stockholder's proportionate share. Even were damages never mulcted or fines imposed elsewhere, the corporation arguably would have no right to rectify the omission in this collateral way. That rectification belongs to others at another time.

The *Kosuga* Court became understandably wroth—as the *Feldmann* Court should have been with Feldmann—when Kelly alleged his own crime in defense of his own breach of contract:

> "It has been often stated in similar cases that the defence is a very dishonest one, and it lies ill in the mouth of the defendant to allege it, and it is only allowed for public

considerations and in order the better to secure the public against dishonest transactions."

> —*Kelly v. Kosuga,* 358 U.S. 516, 519 (1959)
> (quoting *McMullen v. Hoffman*).

Once court and corporation have attributed to the proper parties the
crime, the damages and the restitution, what must be said of the malefactor himself who attempts to pervert his acknowledged crime to
his own advantage?

> If the defense of illegality is to be allowed as a collateral
> method of enforcement of the antitrust laws, as the
> breadth of [Kelly's] argument suggests, it must be said that
> his theory creates a very strange class of private attorneys
> general.
>
> > —*Kelly v. Kosuga,* 358 U.S. 516, 520
> > (1959).

The *Kosuga* Court touched briefly on the irrelevancy—to a collateral contract action—of any personal culpability of the
parties:

> While enforcement of a contract between wrongdoers
> may more frequently present such a situation . . ., the
> character of the parties is not in itself determinative.
>
> > —*Kelly v. Kosuga,* 358 U.S. 516, 520
> > (1959).

Thus the final anomaly of *Feldmann* emerges. In letting Wilport
keep its shares the Court correctly approved the contract of sale, but
in denying Wilport any returns on those shares, it reprobated it. If
the stock sale was legitimate, why emasculate the stock and leave
Wilport's $800,000 portion with Feldmann? (Premium-bribed
Feldmann, to boot.) If the stock sale partook so much of the invalidity
of the premium-bribery as to block a sharing in the $2.1 million, why
did not such invalidity invalidate the stock sale itself? The *Feldmann*
Court was doubly illogical.

The End of the Hypothetical

With this the matter seems concluded. The traditional law of *Sugden, McClure, Lionel, Rosenfeld, Le Mars,* would have awarded the $2.1 million directly to Newport Steel. Since premium-briber Wilport was personally purged, since the stock itself was untainted, and since the contract of sale was judicially severed from the collateral premium-bribery, shareholder Wilport would be welcomed at the Newport window for its portion of the $2.1 million, by then no doubt long since spent by Mr. Feldmann and his friends.

One parting adversion. As one wends his way through this thicket of premium-bribe-disposition ratiocination, the overgrowth could conceivably hide an overriding *fact* and a controlling *principle*. The fact? Feldmann had already accepted a premium-bribe. Feldmann had already committed the act of premium-bribery. This fact can never be undone. The principle? Premium-bribe dollars are necessarily—both according to law and according to intrinsic logic—disgorged. The corporation, Newport, should have already received the $2.1 million as a matter of right. Thus, if no premium-bribe had passed, if Wilport *had* justly paid a pro rata share of the $2.1 million to all, including Feldmann, then Feldmann would *not* be guilty of premium-bribery, would not therefore suffer the consequences of premium-bribery, and could properly keep his one third of the $2.1 million. But Feldmann has irretrievably and eternally committed premium-bribery. And all else follows ineluctably.

Perlman v. Feldmann, enhanced by its historic acclaim, has undoubtedly been the perfect incentive to a full analysis of the premium-bribe disposition. It laid out the basic truths so well, as an encouragement to begin, yet intriguingly left so much undone, as a challenge to carry on.

The elusive questions still out of the box leave further chores for this treatise.

Chapter 8

The Investment Value of Control Stock

[Jennings and Leech argue], for somewhat different reasons, that in general a corporate insider should not be allowed to sell his shares on terms unavailable to noncontrolling shareholders. It is the opinion of the present writer that such a blanket rule might well do more harm than good . . . .

> —Hill, *The Sale of Controlling Shares,* 70 HARV. L. REV. 986, 988 (1957).

[O]ne of the rights of the minority stockholders is to have an equal opportunity with all other stockholders to participate ratably in any sale of shares pursuant to a favorable offer for the purchase of controlling shares in their corporation.

> —Andrews, *The Stockholder's Right to Equal Opportunity in the Sale of Shares,* 78 HARV. L. REV. 505, 506 (1965).

In early 1968 when Cyrus Eaton, longtime contrôleur of Detroit Steel Corporation, exacted a $3.25-million 'premium' over market from Jakob Isbrandtsen and accordingly handed over control, he enunciated one of the most fundamental questions in this complex field of corporate control. Was this truly a premium-bribe that Isbrandtsen paid to Eaton? Or merely Isbrandtsen's investment evaluation of the control stock with Isbrandtsen in control? Was Eaton simply saying that a control block has an intrinsic and legitimate value considerably greater than a similar block without control? Were both maintaining that they alone, irrespective of the public owners, could determine in a private sale the 'considerably greater' value of that control block? The answers to these complex queries will form the last-but-one major segment in the Philosophy of Corporate Control.

Detroit Steel

From inauspicious beginnings in 1923, Detroit Steel Corporation had grown internally and through merger (Reliance Steel) and acquisitions (Craine-Schrage Steel, Portsmouth Steel, Tex-Tube) to $100-million annual sales in the midsixties. In its 45th year, 1967, DSC offered a wide range of steel products from pig iron and basic open-hearth steel, hot- and cold-rolled sheets to high-carbon spring wire and structural-steel tubing. With four producing mills and 18 sales offices Detroit Steel had become by 1967 a relatively substantial regional producer ranking just outside *Fortune's* select 500 top industrials. The 3.9-million shares outstanding in the hands of some 11,000 shareholders classified DSC as definitely a widely held corporation. No single shareholder, with the exception of the Eaton interests, owned over ten percent of the stock.

But that fiscal year ending just before Eaton's departure in March, 1968 had been a troubled one. Earnings before taxes showed a disturbing 32-percent drop from $7.9 to $5.3 million, registering the lowest per-share return in five years, $0.93. The common stock was trading on the NYSE in the midteens, with a two-million-share turnover in the seven months ending March, 1968. The volume for these months was undoubtedly increased appreciably by the frequent rumors of mergers and takeovers. The following is a rough capitulation:

September 1967	384,700
October 1967	179,300
November 1967	117,900
December 1967	455,200
January 1968	388,600
February 1968	312,300
March 1968	293,100
	2,131,100

The regular dividend of $0.60—down from a dollar in 1960—provided a below-average return.

Detroit Steel had "been the subject of takeover rumors for months. On Feb. 29 Georgia-Pacific Corp., Portland, Ore., producer of building materials and paper, called off merger talks with Detroit Steel."[180] But the rumors nonetheless persisted. A spring management shuffle saw the appointment of a new treasurer, the realignment of six vice-presidents and the replacement—after 44 years with the company—of the president, Max Zivian, with Charles A. Carter who came with the 1964 acquisition of Tex-Tube, Inc.

This was the gloomy panorama that Cyrus Eaton could so clearly discern from his Terminal Tower aerie. And he equally clearly saw that he wanted out. With astonishing speed—as late as March 8, 1968 the Annual Report still carried Mr. Carter's remark: "Currently we are exploring, with Georgia-Pacific Corp., the benefits . . . if the two companies are merged"—he got the out he wanted. A short 26 days after the Georgia-Pacific call-off came the startling announcement:

> NEW YORK—American Export Industries Inc. has purchased blocks of stock in Detroit Steel Corp. and Premium Iron Ores Ltd. from Cyrus S. Eaton, the Cleveland financier, and one of his associates for about $19,040,000.
>
> It marks a major withdrawal from the Midwest steel and iron ore industry of the 84-year-old Mr. Eaton, chairman of the Chesapeake & Ohio Railway. The other seller of the stocks was William R. Daley, long associated with Mr. Eaton in widespread business ventures.
>
> American Export paid them $25 a share for 525,000 shares, or about 13% of the outstanding shares of Detroit Steel Corp., a steel producer.
>
> —Wall St. J., Mar. 27, 1968, at 4, col. 2.

American Export Industries, Inc., Jakob Isbrandtsen contrôleur, was the parent of American Export Isbrandtsen Lines, a major steamship company, for years subsidized by the Federal government. "American Export has acquired at least three other companies within the past year."[181] (Control of Cleveland-Cliffs Iron Co. also passed with control of Detroit Steel.)

Since Detroit Steel shares had been struggling along for the month prior to the Eaton/Isbrandtsen deal in a range from 16¾ to 20¾, Isbrandtsen's $25 was $4.25 to $8.25 over market—a 20- to

49-percent markup—for a total premium ranging from $2.2 to $4.3 million, averaging out at $3.25 million. The spread for calendar 1967 was 11¼ to 22⅛. For 1966, 11¼ to 20.

The following conspectus tells a story in itself. The dates are for trading, not reporting, and run Monday through Friday.

Date	Volume	Closing
February 26, 1968	4700	20¾
February 27, 1968	4000	20¾
February 28, 1968	8000	20⅝
February 29, 1968	6500	20⅛

[On Feb. 29, a Thursday, Georgia-Pacific Corp. called off merger talks.]

March 1, 1968	26600	18⅛
March 4, 1968	17700	17¼
March 5, 1968	8900	16¾
March 6, 1968	16700	18¾
March 7, 1968	5300	18⅞
March 8, 1968	5900	18⅛
March 11, 1968	7600	18½
March 12, 1968	18200	19⅜
March 13, 1968	22900	20⅛
March 14, 1968	15600	19¾
March 15, 1968	9800	19¼
March 18, 1968	6000	19½
March 19, 1968	8300	18⅞
March 20, 1968	3100	19⅜
March 21, 1968	17400	19¾
March 22, 1968	9300	19⅞
March 25, 1968	20600	20½
March 26, 1968	73200	20¾

[American Export purchases stock from Cyrus Eaton]

March 27, 1968	18400	20¼
March 28, 1968	7900	19½
March 29, 1968	5600	19½

The 1967 earnings figure would have netted Mr. Isbrandtsen a 3.7-percent return on his investment.

The immediate upshot was predictable: "Jakob Isbrandtsen, president of American Export, and [his brother-in-law] Albert E. Rising Jr., vice president of American Export, replace Mr. Eaton and Mr. Daley as directors . . . ."[182] This left the seven-man board with two remaining Eaton nominees, Robert L. Kaiser, an attorney and 'Vice-President—Assistant to President' of the company, and Arnold D. Freydl, an outside director, in addition to Mr. Carter, Mr. Zivian and Roger A. Yoder, 'Vice-President—Finance.'

The premium figure of $3.25 million is arbitrary. Later analysis will establish guidelines for the determination of the amount of such a premium. This $3.25 million, moreover, does not include a second premium paid by Isbrandtsen to Max Zivian, the former DSC president, for his 219,000 shares.

The plan moved forward at the 1969 annual meeting: A third Isbrandtsen man, William H. Coleman, Chairman of Isbrandtsen-dominated Wheelabrator Corporation—later to become Wheelabrator-Frye, then Signal Cos., then Allied-Signal—replaced Roger Yoder. George E. Cullen, Jr. from the Carter Tex-Tube days succeeded Max Zivian who did not stand for reelection.

But Cullen's days were numbered. He did not fit into the final scheme of things which jelled in early 1970 with the addition of the fourth Isbrandtsen director on the seven-man board. With Cullen's demise came a presage of Mr. Carter's future and further bleak news of DSC profits and dividends:

> DETROIT—Ailing Detroit Steel Corp. elected Robert L. Cantor, former chairman, president and chief executive officer of National Equipment Rental Ltd. [an Isbrandtsen company], to the new position of chairman of the executive committee. He was also named a director. . . .
>
> Mr. Cantor will replace on the board George E. Cullen Jr., who will remain vice president of Detroit Steel. Mr. Cullen may possibly rejoin an expanded board in April.
>
> Charles A. Carter remains president and chief executive officer of the steel company.
>
> Detroit Steel's earnings plunged 88.4% to $405,000, or 10 cents a share, in the first nine months of 1969 from $3.5 million, or 88 cents a share, a year ear-

lier. Sales fell 10.7% to $83.8 million from $93.9 million. The company also omitted its third quarter dividend after paying 15 cents quarterly since 1962.

—Wall St. J., Jan. 26, 1970, at 21, col. 3.

Short days later the *Journal* reported that Detroit Steel suffered a $176,000 net loss in the fourth quarter, worse than a $131,000 loss in the like 1968 period.[183] And the last blow:

> [Earnings per year dropped sharply to] $229,000, or six cents a share, . . . from $3.4 million, or 85 cents a share, in 1968. . . .
>
> . . . Mr. Carter said the company's poor showing was primarily "the result of unsatisfactory operations at the Portsmouth (Ohio) Plant, including two major equipment failures and a fire."
>
> —Wall St. J., Mar. 23, 1970, at 28, col. 2.

Thus did the 1968 transfer of control of Detroit Steel see its implementation in measured steps over a two-year period.

The Issue Drawn

With this the scene is set for the answer to Cyrus Eaton's two questions. As the New York Court in *Gerdes v. Reynolds* in 1941 paraphrased Mr. Eaton:

> Is the price paid in reality a price paid for the stock, or is it, in part at least, a price paid for the resignations of the existing officers and directors and the election of the buyer's nominees?
>
> —*Gerdes v. Reynolds,* 28 N.Y.S.2d 622, 653 (Sup. Ct. 1941).

And, second, if it is "a price paid for the stock," does the right rest in Eaton and Isbrandtsen to set such price without regard to the market or the 87-percent minority?

The answers will be presented in a *Prelude* and four parts: *I. Contrôleur Increment and True Investment Value. II. The Disqualification of the Contrôleurs. III. The Solution: The Tender Offer. IV. The Legal Consequences of a Sale.*

The Prelude

> All shareholders are supposed to be treated about
> the same. It's not unusual to buy the control bloc
> before going after the rest of the company. But al-
> most invariably, the sellers of the control bloc in a
> public company insist that the acquirers agree to
> offer an equivalent deal to the other shareholders
> promptly, because of fairness and fiduciary
> obligations.
>
> —Sloan, *Everybody's Equal, Only Some
> People Are More So,* FORBES, May 26,
> 1980, at 61.

The sedulous reasoning of the many pages of this treatise has
carried the argumentation over some formidable obstacles. And by
now, after all this effort, if anything is clear—and it clearly is not the
legitimate-investment-value rationale—it should be the sale-of-
control premium-bribe. Segregate and understand this concept and
success in understanding the investment value of control stock is
largely assured. In this *Prelude,* therefore, recap the fundamentals
of the premium-bribe.

The early sale-of-control cases, *McClure, Porter v. Healy, Gerdes
v. Reynolds*—the progenitors of *Feldmann, Lionel, Ferraioli v. Cantor,
Rosenfeld v. Black, Le Mars*—offered utter simplicity of facts, and resultant clarity of law. Outstanding of these is *Gerdes v. Reynolds.*

Recall that only two cases in the centuries of sale-of-control history have treated both (1) the sale-of-control premium-bribe and (2)
the damages suffered by the corporation subsequent to the illegal
sale. *Bosworth v. Allen* by New York's highest court in 1901 was one.
Reynolds was the other.

Moreover, *Reynolds* in 1941—true, a product of New York's lowest court, but Justice Walter was outstandingly competent—was particularly apt in providing a superb matrix on which to superimpose
a more technical elucidation—Justice Walter did make an excellent
beginning—of the elusive concept of the investment value of control
stock. *Reynolds,* then, will supply the background for this major new
segment of the Philosophy of Corporate Control.

Reynolds

Single-handed the Reynolds (Metals) family have been prolific of voluminous control litigation. Their first assay into the barter of control came in late 1937 with the sale down the river of their own Reynolds Investing Company, Inc. (In a similar ploy some 20 years later Delaware let them get away with it—recollect *Manacher v. Reynolds*—but in New York in *Reynolds* they got caught.)

Three Reynoldses—and a factotum by the name of Woodward—were the sole officers and directors of this small investment trust.

> They were also stockholders, and, with members of their families, owned a majority of its common stock, which was the only stock having voting power and was junior to debentures and preferred stock outstanding in the hands of the public.
>
> —*Gerdes v. Reynolds,* 28 N.Y.S.2d 622, 629 (Sup. Ct. 1941).

A rather nondescript syndicate of ill-defined numbers headed by Sartell Prentice of the brokerage firm of Prentice & Brady cast covetous eyes on the liquid portfolio of Reynolds Investing. After complicated, even confusing, negotiations over many weeks the Reynolds family unloaded their entire interest in the firm, some 1,055,000 shares, for the stunning—as will be seen—price of $2 per share.

As the event would have it, John Gerdes, trustee in bankruptcy, instituted an action "to hold accountable therefor both those who sold and those who bought."[184] Justice Walter of the Supreme Court, New York, in a lengthy opinion concluded:

> In this case, however, it indisputably was a condition of the sale that all the officers and directors then in office should forthwith resign and that under their power to fill vacancies they should forthwith elect an entirely new directorate chosen wholly by the purchaser of the stock . . . .
>
> —*Gerdes v. Reynolds,* 28 N.Y.S.2d 622, 651 (Sup. Ct. 1941).

Moreover, "[n]either can they accept pay in any form or guise, direct or devious, for their own resignation or for the election of others in their place. *McClure v. Law* . . . ; *Bosworth v. Allen* . . . ."[185]

At this point the New York Court faced up to the question of segregating the premium-bribe from the investment value of the block:

> Is the price paid in reality a price paid for the stock, or is it, in part at least, a price paid for the resignations of the existing officers and directors and the election of the buyer's nominees?
>
> —*Gerdes v. Reynolds,* 28 N.Y.S.2d 622, 653 (Sup. Ct. 1941).

In his answer Justice Walter weighed the relevant factors in stock evaluation and summarized his position:

> Viewing all the elements which the fiduciary obligations of the officers and directors of Reynolds Investing Company required them to view I am convinced that $2,110,000 was so grossly in excess of the value of the stock that it carried upon its face a plain indication that it was not for the stock alone but partly for immediate . . . election of the purchasers' nominees as successors. The transaction was not one in which there was merely a sale of stock, with the right to elect directors passing to the purchasers as a legal incident of the sale . . . .
>
> —*Gerdes v. Reynolds,* 28 N.Y.S.2d 622, 658 (Sup. Ct. 1941).

The Court personally was convinced that six cents per share—not $2—should be the "maximum asset value of the shares."[186] But for slightly specious reasons an "additional something" was allowed "because of permissible hopes and expectations and other considerations already mentioned."[187] With that Justice Walter disposed of the matter:

> It nevertheless is a matter of fact which the trier of facts must find, and with due allowance for all elements I think that 75 cents per share is as liberal a finding as the evidence warrants. That gives $791,250 as the price paid for 1,055,000 shares of stock, and $1,318,750 as the price

paid for the resignations of the officers and directors and
their election of the buyer's nominees as their successors,
or, in other words, for what is termed the turning over of
control.

The conclusion ordinarily to be drawn from the foregoing is that, having violated their fiduciary duty, these
officers and directors must account to the corporation . . .
for the sum of $1,318,750 . . . .

> —*Gerdes v. Reynolds,* 28 N.Y.S.2d 622,
> 658-59 (Sup. Ct. 1941).

And that was the very conclusion the Court reached. As will be seen,
Justice Walter failed to carry the reasoning far enough, but his total
effort was commendable, especially for his times.

New York and the Premium-Bribe

Arguably and in practical effect the Court, with *McClure,*
"treated this transaction as a bribe paid to the directors."[188] Step by
step through page after page the New York Court deftly reasoned to
all the essential elements of that *McClure* sale-of-control premium-
bribe. The congeries of these essential elements leaves only one
conclusion, that the $1.3 million—$1.25 per share over
market—was . . .

> (1) Some form of consideration, monetary or otherwise,
> (2) Flowing to the incumbent contrôleur, (3) From or on
> behalf of the prospective contrôleur, (4) To induce the ap-
> pointment to the office of control, (5) Paid knowingly,
> scienter.
>
> > —Chapter 5: The Sale of Control and the
> > Premium-Bribe, *supra* at 171.

Which, of course, is the technical definition of the sale-of-control
premium-bribe so laboriously elaborated thus far.

What the New York Court did not spell out—understandably
so in the early year of 1941—was the underlying rationale for the
illegality of this premium-bribe. Undeniably, the Court did found its
decision on the correct philosophical base: "Officers and directors
always and necessarily stand in a fiduciary relation to the corporation
and to its stockholders . . . ."[189] However, a long line of arduous and

involved reasoning lies between this broad fiduciary duty and the
$1.3-million award to the corporation. But this arduous line none-
theless can be clearly traced, albeit with some effort, throughout the
Court's analysis. Necessarily, all three essentials—perversion of
judgment, illicit compensation, unsuitable successor—were
there.

Perversion of Judgment

First and foremost, throughout the opinion the Court continually adverted to the Reynoldses' specific fiducial obligation to scrutinize closely the personal suitability of their appointees, to guarantee
honest and competent successors. The Court further knew that any
money under the table was illicit, that such emolument belonged to
the corporation, not to the Reynoldses.

> Neither can they accept pay in any form or guise, direct
> or devious, for their own resignation or for the election
> of others in their place.
> —*Gerdes v. Reynolds,* 28 N.Y.S.2d 622, 651
> (Sup. Ct. 1941).

The violation of these two principles spelled only one thing: Perversion of judgment. Once determined to leave the firm, the fiduciary
duty of the Reynoldses bound them to only one norm in making their
appointment, the suitability of the successor. At that charged moment in the beginning when they undertook the custody of Reynolds
Investing they also dedicated themselves unreservedly to the *bonum
commune* of the company, especially in that most important official
act of all, the appointment of a new contrôleur.

Full in the face of this sole norm of contrôleur conduct they
turned their back on the corporation—and any thought of successor
suitability—and founded their judgment of selection on considerations of dollars. In a word, here was a $1.3-million perversion of judg-
ment in the appointment of Prentice to the control of Reynolds
Investing.

> Syllogistically: (1) The suitability of the successor is the
> sole final cause that may flow legitimately into the selec-
> tion of the new contrôleur. (2) The consideration of the
> premium-bribe is totally irrelevant, foreign, antagonistic,

to suitability. (3) Yet the premium-bribe consideration does flow as a final cause into the selection of a successor. Here is the quintessence of the perversion.

—Chapter 6: The Sale-of-Control Premium: The Intrinsic Illigitimacy, *supra* at 207.

Illicit Consideration

But, of course, the illegitimacy of the premium-bribe does not stop with the perversion of the contrôleur's judgment. Beyond this, the Reynolds family accepted, even demanded, $1.3 million for a corporate act, the most important of their corporate career, performed "in fulfillment of a corporate duty, in the course of official business, during the regular workweek, for which [they were] already amply remunerated."[190] The acceptance and the attempted retention of this $1.3 million was in and of itself the second element of the total turpitude of the premium-bribe. Here was illicit emolument that rightly belonged to the corporation. Here, moreover, was the direct rationale for the Court's award of the $1.3 million to the corporation.

Successor Unsuitability

Third and most subtle, and a point which seemed to flicker in the back of the Court's head, was the last coconstituent of the overall illegitimacy of the premium-bribe. The Reynolds family knew full well that the Prentice group were bribers, men (1) prepared to pervert the Reynolds judgment to the tune of $1.3 million, (2) prepared to pay this illicit cash not to the corporation but to faithless servants. Knowing all this the Reynoldses were nevertheless determined to foist such unsuitable men on the hapless firm. Thus, the premium-bribe-induced unsuitability was also a factor in the Court's illegality.

Thus the Court's amalgam of these three elements formed the essential turpitude of the premium-bribe:

> This tripartite illegitimacy could be defined as: (1) The perversion of the judgment of the incumbent contrôleur, engendered by an appointment of a successor induced by a cause other than suitability, (2) That is, for consideration illicit in itself, (3) Resulting in the appointment of a

candidate unsuitable by reason of his own active role in
the inducement.

> —Chapter 6: The Sale-of-Control Premium:
> The Intrinsic Illegitimacy, *supra* at
> 204-05.

Gerdes v. Reynolds, therefore, can serve throughout as the archetype
of the illegitimate sale: Illicit dollars improperly paid to the
contrôleur to premium-bribe an unsuitable successor into the office.

I. Contrôleur Increment
and True Investment Value

> I do not believe it would be desirable to shape
> a policy which might impede transfers of control,
> and consequently federal law should not view a pre-
> mium for control as the property of the corpora-
> tion, nor should controlling persons be required in
> all cases to obtain an equal opportunity for all
> shareholders to sell. This conclusion does not stem
> from a belief that there are no risks in control sale
> transactions; it grows out of a balancing of that risk
> against the opportunities which might be lost if
> control sales were impeded.
>
> —Schwartz, *Sale of Control,* 15
> N.Y.L.F. 674, 705 (1969).

With this *Reynolds* prototype so stark and clear, recur to the au-
thoritative Judge Swan forcefully dissenting in *Feldmann* and consider thoughtfully his viewpoint: "Concededly a controlling block of
stock has greater sale value than a small lot."[191] In response to the
majority's remand "for a determination of . . . the value of defendants' stock without the appurtenant control,"[192] Judge Swan
elaborated his position:

> The controlling block could not by any possibility be
> shorn of its appurtenant power to elect directors. . . . It
> is this "appurtenant power" which gives a controlling
> block its value as such block. What evidence could be

adduced to show the value of the block "if shorn" of
such appurtenant power, I cannot conceive, for it cannot be shorn of it.
—*Perlman v. Feldmann,* 219 F.2d 173, 180
(2d Cir. 1955) (Swan, J., dissenting).

What must be said of this elusive and unidentified tertium quid of
Judge Swan? Judge Swan—and Cyrus Eaton?—had something else
in mind beyond the simple, and legitimate, transfer of control without bonus or markup, and surely something other than the bald
premium-bribe of *Reynolds.* What is this third, legitimate something
of Judge Swan? Prescinding from the pro or con, what are the basic
factors—and what are not—that contribute to the presence of a legitimate investment value in a 'control block' of stock? Before arguing to its legitimacy, first define it precisely, then view the definition
from every reasonable angle.

One additional admonition is in order. For the present, prescind further from the second, and completely crucial, question of
who—the negotiating contrôleurs, the market, the minority
shareholders—has the ultimate right to establish 'the investment
value' of the 'control stock.' For now, simply define what it is. For
later: Who is to evaluate, how, and under what rules?

Beg the question for the moment and begin with this technical
definition:

> *The Legitimate Investment Value of Control Stock is the total
> current worth of that stock, (1) Resultant on the superadded
> contribution of the estimable abilities of a new contrôleur
> (2) To the existent corporate entity.*

Toward understanding this complex concept, one surpassing
truth can summarily brush away a long series of misconceived premises. A new man—the newly appointed contrôleur—with fresh and
different talents has just succeeded to the top spot in the corporate
hierarchy. This appointment is nothing other than a transfer of control, and this transfer has brought a new set of assets to the firm. The
increment referable to the qualities of this new contrôleur—the new
value a new contrôleur adds to the otherwise unchanged
corporation—is the all-important element in the investment value
of control stock. Here is the preeminent fact in the concept.

Thus certainly this new value is not related to *a sale of control,
the barter of the office,* which entails a premium-bribe and is intrinsi-

cally illegitimate. The value does not lie in control as such, but rather in the totality of the abilities the new man brings to the firm. The possession of control merely facilitates the exercise of the talents. The totality of his suitability is the differential between the value of the corporation before and after arrival, under former control vis-à-vis new control. 'Control' was always present. New talents made the difference. A direct ratio persists between these abilities and the investment value of the control stock.

'Control Stock'?

A second source of distortion has been the use of the term 'control stock.' The implication would seem to be that the investment value is limited *exclusively* to the control block. To the contrary, the accession of the new contrôleur benefits the entire entity and correspondingly enhances equally the value of all the stock outstanding, including, but only incidentally, the 'control block.'

The explanation of this usage of 'control block' is not difficult to discern. Although the increment to the entity attributable to the special talents of the new contrôleur is not peculiarly related to the 'control block,' nonetheless an accidental connection often exists between the new contrôleur—the party responsible for the increment—and the stock. It often happens—and outstandingly so in control litigation—that the successor contrôleur purchases a stock block from the incumbent at the time of appointment. The price set for this 'control stock' reflects for the first time the increment to the entity resultant on the new man's worth.

Correctly expressed, therefore, the investment value, enhanced by the appointment of the new man, is prorated equally to all stock of the entity, including, of course, but not exclusively, the 'control block' as well. Merely because the owner of the 'control block' happens also to be the new contrôleur does not mean that that stock is any more valuable per share than the stock owned by anyone else, whether he be the outgoing contrôleur or a minority public holder. In short, the investment value is unrelated to who the owner is, and hence unrelated to the 'control block' as such. In fact, ownership as a relevant factor would be ignored completely were not some owner, any owner, necessary.

Thus Judge Swan in his *Feldmann* dissent—"Concededly a controlling block of stock has greater sale value than a small lot"—was not only misleading, but probably never meant what he said. Judge

Swan certainly would never condone a premium-bribe. Elsewhere in his dissent:

> A director is privileged to resign, but so long as he remains a director he must be faithful to his fiduciary duties and must not make a personal gain from performing them. Consequently, if the price paid for Feldmann's stock included a payment for voting to elect the new directors, he must account to the corporation for such payment, even though he honestly believed that the men he voted to elect were well qualified to serve as directors. He can not take pay for performing his fiduciary duty.
>
> —*Perlman v. Feldmann,* 219 F.2d 173, 179
> (2d Cir. 1955) (Swan, J., dissenting).

Yet Judge Swan equally definitely recognized a "greater sale value" in "a controlling block of stock." How maneuver the Judge between this Scylla and Charybdis? The maneuver is a statement of what the Judge really meant, and an enunciation as well of the perspective proper to understanding the true nature of the investment value of '*control* stock':

> A '*controlling block of stock*' (or any other block) sold (or not sold) by the outgoing contrôleur (or by anyone) to his appointee (or to anyone) has '*greater sale value*' than '*a small lot*' (or any lot, including the '*controlling block*') had before the accession of the talented new contrôleur.

Furthermore, this proposition stated in question form would be the exact and technical question—the first of the two—that Mr. Eaton asked when Mr. Isbrandtsen handed him $3.25 million over market: Does the 'control block' have an intrinsic and legitimate value considerably greater than a similar block without control?

The answer to Mr. Eaton's question and to Judge Swan's quandary should supply a new set of legal principles fundamental to the Philosophy of Corporate Control.

The Elements of the Share Value

Toward the explication of Judge Swan's statement—as rewritten—recur to the Eaton/Isbrandtsen scenario. First adapt it slightly to present purposes, and later use it as it was.

The time as before is early 1968. The scene is the same. Mr. Eaton atop the Terminal Tower discerns the same gloomy panorama stretching back over Detroit Steel's fiscal 1967. The presage is there. As a "Detroit source said . . . 'Mr. Eaton became 84 last December. He has expressed on numerous occasions the desire to liquidate much, if not all, of his holdings and take it easy.'"[193] And again, being a sensible man, Mr. Eaton shortly determined to do just that.

Again, being also a conscientious man, Mr. Eaton undertook a thorough search for a suitable successor as contrôleur of Detroit Steel. His first selection did not measure up, or at any event aborted. Unfortunately, "[o]n Feb. 29 Georgia Pacific . . . called off merger talks with Detroit Steel."[194] But in his second effort Mr. Eaton found his 'suitable successor' in Jakob Isbrandtsen. In him, one could conjecture, were all the "personal qualities required for the corporate contrôleur . . . (1) Moral integrity, (2) Intellectual competence, (3) Managerial and organizational proficiency, (4) Social suitability and (5) Satisfactory age and health."[195] With this selection Mr. Eaton had satisfied his trust obligation to Detroit Steel.

But at this point the new script varies. Conceive rather that Messrs. Eaton and Daley had over recent years slowly sold off their 13-percent block of stock. *Ex hypothesi,* therefore, DSC shares were completely dispersed. No single shareholder owned more than ten percent *and Mr. Eaton himself had none.* His was the merest of mere-incumbency control, but with all the stability of IBM, thanks to the wide dispersal and his firm grasp on the proxy-solicitation mechanism.

As for Jakob Isbrandtsen, he was an empire builder much in the mold of a Cornfeld, a Vesco or a Posner. He wanted no stock, only the opportunity to put his unparalleled abilities to work for Detroit Steel. With the meeting of the minds the deal was sealed and the appointment made, with nary a share changing hands. As *Insuranshares* would put it:

> [E]verything they did [was] done without their owning more than directors' qualifying shares.
>
> —*Insuranshares Corp. v. Northern Fiscal Corp.,* 35 F. Supp. 22, 24 (E.D. Pa. 1940).

The seriatim replacements were perfunctory.

The obvious upshot? The consensus of informed buyers and sellers, established by the reasoned judgment of the Street, would shortly respond to Mr. Isbrandtsen's appointment by sending the market in Detroit Steel, for example, to 25.

The Person Is the Value

This variation on the original Detroit Steel facts should illustrate one principal point. The arrival of a supercontrôleur can enhance overnight the value of all stock equally, without any stock sale whatsoever, whoever the owner. The only requisite: The transfer of control, the appointment of a new contrôleur.

From the particular aspect of the share value, the crux of the problem lies with the personal qualifications of the successor contrôleur. The differential between a corporation before and after is the sole distinguishing element. At Detroit Steel this overnight differential lay between Cyrus Eaton and Jakob Isbrandtsen, between $18 and $25 per share.

At this point a new technical term could well be introduced into the argot of corporate control:

> *Contrôleur Increment is the increase in value to all stock of a corporation referable exclusively to the proven abilities of a new contrôleur, that is, the differential between the contributions to corporate value of the outgoing and incoming contrôleur.*

Note well the obvious: This *contrôleur increment* is totally legitimate and alone distinguishes the investment value of 'control stock' from the same block prior to the advent of the new contrôleur. Bearing forcefully in mind all the precautions of *The Prelude,* one should undertake the fascinating task of reading Judge Hincks's mind between the lines of *his* analysis of the contrôleur increment in the lower-court *Feldmann:*

> For instance, to the usual minority stockholder in a corporation the value of his stock necessarily depends on earnings which in turn depend on the abilities of its management. But one considering the purchase of a control block in a corporation may give less weight to past earnings since, if a change in management might be beneficial, the power to make such a change is in his hands. Thus, where the purchaser feels that the corporation's past record does not adequately reflect its realizable possibilities, he may well feel justified in paying more than

the quoted market price for a control block of its stock, on the theory that the present price probably has been determined in large measure by the corporate earnings under the old management. Surely this power through stock control to improve the corporate performance may be a factor of value attaching to a control block of stock.

> —*Perlman v. Feldmann,* 129 F. Supp. 162, 184 (D. Conn. 1952).

Whether the new contrôleur is to be a J. Peter Grace, a Roger Smith, a Lee Iacocca, or rather a John De Lorean, a Victor Posner, a Robert Vesco, will be the sole intrinsic determinant of the contrôleur increment and correspondingly of the investment value of the 'control block.'

How does the market discern these personal capabilities of an Iacocca or a Vesco? What are the guidelines for the evaluation of this sole essential of contrôleur increment?

The discernment of the contrôleur increment—and more important its isolation for evaluation—is not overly difficult. After all, the corporation itself necessarily remains unchanged during the accession of the new contrôleur, since the appointment obviously can occur only at a single instant in time. Any differential must be referable to the new contrôleur's talents. In such clear isolation the contrôleur increment is readily estimated, and the norms for estimation are simple and obvious.

The Nature of the Firm

As competent an empire builder as an Isbrandtsen may be, his abilities—and hence the resultant contrôleur increment—must be related to the circumstances he faces. Thus in the 1956 New York case of *Benson v. Braun:*

> It is trite but true to say that each corporation whose stock is evaluated must be viewed in relation to the facts peculiar to that particular enterprise. In this case factors were present which could well have been taken into account and have led to establishing a selling price well above the market quotations on the corporation's one listed stock.
>
> —*Benson v. Braun,* 155 N.Y.S.2d 622, 627 (Sup. Ct. 1956).

Even a Lee Iacocca would not be invaluable to a Reynolds Investing in the dismal months of late 1937. Who over the decades would have dared pretend to add any contrôleur increment to General Motors? To IBM? The current state of the nation, the economic bent of the government, the prospects for the industry, the health or infirmity of the firm itself, all form the milieu in which the new contrôleur exercises his talents. The scope for corporate improvement deeply affects contrôleur potential. Again *Benson v. Braun:*

> Far from the least of the factors to be considered in assessing possibilities for growth value is that of management. Moreover, the type of business in which this corporation was engaged is a matter of importance. In the search for reasons to explain the apparently high price paid for controlling stock, it is proper to inquire whether there were distinctive features of the corporation which might influence a purchaser to pay such a price.
>
> —*Benson v. Braun,* 155 N.Y.S.2d 622, 628 (Sup. Ct. 1956).

Past successes, proven ability, vast experience, can all be brought to naught—or enhanced—by these influences. Contrôleur increment, therefore, will fluctuate with the adaptability of the material at hand and the climate of the environment.

An Informed Market

A key cause for confusion in the evaluation of contrôleur increment has been the failure to distinguish the value of DSC shares under Eaton, for example, and the wholly new DSC plus Isbrandtsen. The market of DSC during the entire period prior to the public announcement of Isbrandtsen's accession could be lower, or higher, than the market afterwards. More to the point, sufficient time must elapse— witness the Court's treatment of the same problem in *Texas Gulf Sulphur*—for the informed public to assimilate the various effects the Isbrandtsen control will have on Detroit Steel. *Until all factors necessary for a reasoned judgment have sifted down,* the new market for DSC + Isbrandtsen is not a true norm of the contrôleur increment. Remember above all that the market for DSC + Eaton may have little relation to the DSC + Isbrandtsen market. In fact they could be far apart: By mid-1969 the Eaton 18 had fallen to an Isbrandtsen 11.

In the end, the free competitive market—able buyers with their own money on the line—is usually the best available norm. The market price of a listed stock reflects the full impact of Wall Street—securities analysts, investment advisers, industry specialists, market experts—as well as the 'willing seller, willing buyer' criterion. In fact the considered judgment of the money-in-hand investor would be the reliable distillate of all other value indices. These are admittedly simplistic assessments of a complex chore, but suffice for present purposes.[196]

This detailed disquisition on the existence and nature of 'contrôleur increment'—even to the canonization of a new term—was eminently necessary. Granted, the concept has a relatively limited use and would appear rarely outside the specific context of a sale of control. Such circumscribed utility would scarce warrant such attention had not a long line of Swans, Lumbards and Pollacks—and a conjecturally longer line of Feldmanns and Wilports, of Eatons and Isbrandtsens—taken refuge in the blind of 'true investment value' of a 'control block' of stock. 'True investment value' has long been a ready rebuttal—in fact, the last such possible rejoinder—to a charge of premium-bribery. And 'contrôleur increment' is the heart of 'true investment value.'

As long as the Swans, therefore, continue to see a "greater sale value" in "a controlling block of stock" and the Eatons persist in thus justifying questionable private sales, one must thoroughly define their position, if only to reject it out of hand.

The first of Mr. Eaton's questions has thus been answered, although not perhaps in the expected full affirmative. A 'control block'—or any block—may have an enhanced value resultant on the accession of a new contrôleur, the contrôleur increment. It should be clear, however, that the term 'control stock' is in truth a misnomer.

Contrôleur Decrement

But stop momentarily. This entire scrutiny of 'true investment value' saw only the rosy half. 'Contrôleur *decrement*' is a far more realistic factor, especially when a Posner or a Vesco 'buys' control. An incumbent contrôleur may be desperate to retire—through financial pressure, incompetence, age, ennui—and equally desperate in his selection of a successor. Thus, perhaps, the overnight value of DSC under Isbrandtsen was really 11 instead of 25. Maybe the market at 18 for DSC + Eaton was far too high for the new DSC + Isbrandtsen.

In all the foregoing pages, therefore, also read 'contrôleur decrement' and paint the picture black. In every future scrutiny always ask as well if 'contrôleur *increment*' is not in truth *'decrement,'* and the investment value that much less. 'Contrôleur decrement' is undoubtedly an equally important contribution to the control lexicon.

———————————

And now, what of the more crucial, second Eaton/Isbrandtsen question: Who has the right—the two contrôleurs, incoming and outgoing, the minority 87 percent, the market—to determine the amount of the contrôleur increment—*or decrement*—and hence the true investment value of the 'control block'? Or more to the point, who may act on such an evaluation in a good hard dollars-and-cents sale of that block? The answers to this multipronged question will form the second part of this inquiry into the investment value of control stock.

II. The Disqualification of the Contrôleurs

"Whether it be a director dealing with the board of which he is a member, or a trustee dealing with his co-trustees and himself, the real party in interest, the principal, is absent—the watchful and effective self interest of the director or trustee seeking a bargain, is not counteracted by the equally watchful and effective self interest of the other party, who is there only by his representatives, and the wise policy of the law treats all such cases as that of a trustee dealing with himself."

—*Cumberland Coal & Iron Co. v. Sherman,* 30 Barb. 553, 573 (N.Y. Sup. Ct. 1859) (quoting Plaintiff).

Admitting the unlawfulness of the sale [of the office] to its fullest extent, and that it is directly against public policy to sustain it, we can perceive no reason why the buyer is not to be regarded as guilty as the seller. He participated equally in the unlawful transaction.

—*Groton v. Waldoborough,* 11 Me. 306, 307 (1834).

Return now to the original Detroit Steel facts. Retrace each step from the first moment when Cyrus Eaton determined to resign as contrôleur. But pause for a moment at the events immediately after Mr. Eaton's selection of Mr. Isbrandtsen as his successor. Segregate conceptually the various stages of the negotiations between the two.

At the conclusion of Mr. Eaton's search, and his decision that Mr. Isbrandtsen embodied every requisite of contrôleur suitability, the question naturally arose: What of the Eaton 13-percent block? Should he sell it? After all, with Isbrandtsen in control the shares could be worth $25, and that was an appreciable increment over the recent market of $18. But if sell it, to whom? Perhaps the public? Or Max Zivian? Or possibly even Mr. Isbrandtsen himself? Further, reasoned Mr. Eaton, a complete severance from Detroit Steel, stock and all, might be the gentlemanly approach. Even further, the best interests of Detroit Steel might dictate a sizable stock ownership in the new contrôleur himself.

As for Mr. Isbrandtsen he shared these thoughts thoroughly, adding a secret surmise that his control position—founded, it is true, on the proxy and the dispersal—would certainly not be less secure with that 13-percent block in hand, rather than the oral, albeit unquestionable, assurances of Mr. Eaton, or even an unassailable Eaton-issued voting-trust certificate in his pocket.

With such unanimity of attitude, agreement was readily reached. Mr. Isbrandtsen was to have his 13-percent block. But now what? Could Eaton sell Isbrandtsen his own 13 percent forthwith? If so, at what price? The market had hovered around 18, but both Eaton and Isbrandtsen were convinced—or so it would seem—that the contrôleur increment resultant on Isbrandtsen in office actually lifted the value to 25. The two contrôleurs faced the most vexing of questions: Who is to name the price? Could they personally set it at 25—as they actually did—and close the sale accordingly?

If ever everything could not be said at once, it is at this moment when the simultaneous conjunction of several seemingly disparate factors crowds the mind and defies all orderly progress. But each of these factors can be put in place. And as each is so arranged, the result becomes an arresting revelation, especially to Messrs. Eaton and Isbrandtsen, and any other sale-negotiating contrôleurs. The orderly conjunction of these factors spells out forcefully the essential illegality of any private evaluation of the contrôleur increment or decrement by the two contrôleurs, outgoing and incoming. As a guide for ready reference, a formal statement of this illegality would perhaps help toward tracing the line of argumentation:

> *At the time of the transfer of control and the sale of the 'control stock' inter se, a personal evaluation of that stock—whether actually correct or not—by the two contrôleurs, incumbent and appointee, is intrinsically reprobate under the Benefit-to-Beneficiary and No Inquiry Rules, since both contrôleurs are acting throughout as strict trustees of the entity.*

This technical enunciation of the major thesis set for proof should meet head-on the second of the Eaton/Isbrandtsen questions.

Strict Trustees

At this point little doubt should remain about the *potential* existence and reality of a marked, dollar differential—a truly legitimate differential—in value between a Detroit Steel under Eaton and the same corporation moments later under an Isbrandtsen. In the Detroit Steel scenario Eaton and Isbrandtsen set this overnight contrôleur increment at $25 million, a $3.25-million premium for the 13-percent 'control block.' Less sanguine investors might have seen, to the contrary, a $25-million contrôleur decrement, with a true market at 11. No naysayers can gainsay either potential. The question, therefore, is not the possibility of some contrôleur increment or decrement, but the right and conditions in determining it.

In this direct attack on the personal evaluation by Eaton and Isbrandtsen, the pervasive philosophical premise, the ultimate rationale—sufficient with little more—is the Custodial Concept of Corporate Control. In assuming the stewardship of Detroit Steel, Cyrus Eaton promised unqualifiedly all his "time, energy, imagination, judgment and skill"[197] to the well-being and benefit of the corporate entity. As a strict trustee he was bound firmly by the Benefit-to-Beneficiary Rule. Beyond his agreed compensation, no recompense whatsoever could pass to Mr. Eaton for his transfer of the corporation to Mr. Isbrandtsen. He was "bound to forgo any emolument of any kind connected with the trust corpus. The very hypothesis of a trust relationship is the Benefit-to-Beneficiary Rule."[198] As for Mr. Isbrandtsen he, too, had undertaken the duties of a strict trustee. Thus, "at that charged instant when control passes from contrôleur to appointee, the complete custody of the corporation hangs precariously in the grasp of each, the one relinquishing, the other assuming."[199] Both had identical obligations.

The Appointment to Control and the Sale of Stock

The first of two highly operable facts along the line of argumentation is the consummated appointment of a new contrôleur. No public announcement has yet been made, but Eaton has irrevocably selected Isbrandtsen as the new steward of Detroit Steel. For all practical purposes complete custody of the corporation has already passed into Isbrandtsen's hands. Into these hands has been entrusted the corporate *bonum commune,* the future well-being of the entire entity. The first operable fact: Isbrandtsen's appointment is final.

The second operable fact has absolutely no *intrinsic* connection with the first. Whether Cyrus Eaton is to resign as contrôleur of Detroit Steel, no matter. Merely because Eaton has appointed Isbrandtsen his successor, also no matter. In any case and irrespective of the transfer of control, for reasons peculiar to each, Eaton has decided to sell and Isbrandtsen to buy the 13-percent block of 'control stock.' Either the control transfer or the stock sale could have been effected separately, the one without the other.

This essential dichotomy between *control transfer* and *stock sale* is the key to understanding the entire transaction. If Eaton were to have forced Isbrandtsen to buy his 13 percent *as a condition precedent to the appointment,* any attempt to relate the $3.25 million to the stock would be laughable, since the appointment to control would have thus been inextricably dependent on the dollars: No dollars, no appointment. Both Eaton and Isbrandtsen must staunchly live or die with one assumption: The appointment of Isbrandtsen was made on merit alone, was a fait accompli, had absolutely nothing to do with any stock, or especially nothing to do with the payment to Eaton of a premium over market *in the guise of* $3.25 million in contrôleur increment. With any other assumption Eaton and Isbrandtsen would be skewered on one prong or the other of a very painful dilemma. Either Eaton appoints Isbrandtsen for merit alone, and nothing more, especially nothing more connected with control-stock dollars, or Eaton wants something more for Isbrandtsen's appointment than Isbrandtsen suitability. Which by definition is premium-bribery. The appointment goes with the merit, the dollars go with the stock. Eaton and Isbrandtsen, therefore, must treat the valuation and sale of the stock in utter, albeit conceptual, isolation from the conceptually prior appointment. Both must stoutly maintain that the entire amount passing from Isbrandtsen to Eaton, $13 million, was referable to the stock price and not a cent—for example, $3.25 million—was paid for control. Any other treatment is disastrous.

The 50-plus-Percent Block

This essential severability may be readily understandable when the control stock is a minority interest, but the mind shudders a bit at the prospect of a majority-block sale. When the incumbent contrôleur owns 50-plus percent of the stock, would not a transfer of control *necessarily* entail the simultaneous sale of the control block? Are not the appointment of the successor and the stock sale inseparable when the control is actually attached to the stock? To the contrary, the presence of a majority-stock block alters none of the basics. The same fundamental principles govern the selection of the successor, his appointment and the transfer of control. One accidental difference, however, is the understandable cause for hesitation.

In most of the hypotheticals thus far adduced, the control position of the contrôleur was founded on nondemocratic mere incumbency, the wide dispersal of shares and the domination of the proxy-solicitation mechanism. The shift to a majority-stock-ownership control base only changes one thing, the manner—but not the essentials—of the control transfer. Even with a 50-plus-percent block, the stock sale itself is unrelated—or related only accidentally—to the transfer of control. The transfer is the appointment. The stock sale is collateral at most. Any of the standard control devices—pooling agreement, proxy coupled with an interest, voting trust—can achieve the same objective. Or, of course, the sale of the control block. The sale of stock is merely one of many means of effecting the appointment, but in no wise the necessary one.

Although the transactions are essentially unrelated and independent—as the two contrôleurs must steadfastly aver—nevertheless Eaton and Isbrandtsen have decided to join the two (which is the invariable case in any but the most bold-faced sales of control). The simultaneous appointment of a new contrôleur and the sale of a substantial stock block to the appointee by the very person appointing melds these two *intrinsically disparate acts* into a *functionally indivisible unit*. Any realistic view of the circumstances makes it impossible to consider one facet without the other. The two deals are extrinsically inextricable. Future argument assumes this inseparability.

Another valid assumption would eliminate, and correctly so, from the Detroit Steel facts any other collateral transactions that might divert attention from the control-transfer/stock-sale exchange just now conjoined. Were a substantial lump sum to have passed—admittedly unconnected with the stock sale—from Isbrandtsen to Eaton, a rebuttable presumption of premium-bribe presence would become immediately operative and put the parties on the defensive. Many explanations for such a premium are possible, but few are convincing. Isbrandtsen could have taken the occasion of his appointment to pay off a long-overdue $3.25-million Eaton debt. Or perhaps express the depth of his respect and regard for Mr. Eaton in a gracious gift in a similar amount. Either of these— debt payment, gracious gift—could for some valid reason, or pure fortuity, accompany the transfer of control, and thus rebut the presumption. But fortunately for the instant investigation, no such distracting collateral extra has intruded into the DSC facts. For the present, therefore, the single unencumbered control-transfer/stock-sale stands alone for scrutiny. No dollars other than the price for the stock need disturb the concentration.

Overvaluation: A Premium-Bribe

With the control transfer and the stock sale all alone in the spotlight, the looming importance of the evaluation takes its proper perspective. Absolutely the only money involved is the $13 million Isbrandtsen paid Eaton for the stock. No spurious collaterals—debt, gift or whatever—cloud the issue. Any chicanery that might be afoot, therefore, must lurk in those stock-sale dollars, or it is nowhere. If a premium-bribe is to be laid at the Eaton/Isbrandtsen doorstep, it can be found in only one place, the amount fixed as the investment value—was there contrôleur increment or rather even decrement? —of the 'control block.'

With this comes the crux. Any *overvaluation* of the stock, however little or much, becomes necessarily an unqualified premium-bribe paid by Isbrandtsen to Eaton for his appointment to the office of control. 'Overvaluation' by definition denotes the deliberate appraisal of a salable object at a figure *over* its true value. Such an appraisal entails perforce the purposeful attribution of dollars in excess of honest worth. Any such dollars, therefore, beyond the value of the stock by inexorable logic have no connection with the stock. They represent money passing from appointee to incumbent with no justifiable relation to the stock sale.

Since the Eaton/Isbrandtsen deal is extrinsically indivisible—but intrinsically separate—any excess dollars not referable to the stock value are willy-nilly referable to the control transfer. No other explanation is possible. Unless, of course, one wishes to indulge in the overdue-debt, gracious-gift gambit (But then why secrete the debt or gift in the stock value?). The same inexorable logic would then describe, equally necessarily, such excess dollars in only one way: The price to be paid for control, the primitive premium-bribe.

With this the circle is complete. Even the slightest, deliberate overvaluation satisfies by that very act the five requisites of the illicit premium-bribe. Here unmistakably would be (1) palpable consideration (2) destined to flow from would-be contrôleur Isbrandtsen to (3) incumbent Eaton (4) to induce the appointment—since no other explanation was proffered—to the office of control of DSC. As astute businessmen both Eaton and Isbrandtsen (5) knew full well, scienter, what they were doing.

Special note: True, any *over*valuation is necessarily premium-bribe. But that does not rule out some legitimate contrôleur increment. Thus the dollars over the then market may contain (1) honest contrôleur increment *and* (2) dishonest overvaluation. Bear this in mind passim.

Traffic in the Trust

Concede for the moment that two such putative contrôleurs did deliberately overvalue the 'control block' in order thus to camouflage a $3.25-million sale of control. (Recall, however, that this $3.25 million figure is tentative. Should later analysis conclude to contrôleur *decrement*, $3.25 million would be correspondingly too little.) Carry out this assumption, strictly arguendo, to its logical limits. Would such a control sale, particularly the overvaluation deeply embedded in the deal, be the official act of two corporate agents performed pursuant to their contrôleur duties, or a completely independent transaction between two private parties acting in their own personal capacities? Would that control-transfer/stock-sale exchange, and the overpricing essential to it, be a proper—here improper— function of the trust office, or merely a collateral business deal between two individual entrepreneurs?

The sale of control can be disguised behind many masks. In *Laurenzano v. Einbender* the premium-bribe was tucked away in the sale of a subsidiary at "an excessive price."[200] In *Lionel* appointee Sonnabend was prepared to approve a $75,000 outlay in the form of consultation fees to the former contrôleur, the Muscat group. In *Le Mars* the premium-bribe was 'hidden' in the 'collateral' sale of an insurance agency. In *Porter v. Healy,* to the contrary, all duplicity was eschewed with a naive lump-sum payment.

Merely because the sale of control hides behind the stock-investment-value subterfuge in no way alters its essentials. The very heart of the act remains the conscious transfer of the custody of the entire trust corpus from incumbent to appointee. Concomitant, but nonetheless integral, to this transfer is the payment of a price for the appointment, in this case a price established by the overestimation of the value of the corporation as allegedly enhanced by the advent of an Isbrandtsen and the departure of an Eaton. This overvalued contrôleur increment, or overlooked decrement, correspondingly inflates falsely the price for the 'control stock,' thereby passing the premium-bribe. This bipartite act involves simultaneously and inextricably the transfer of custody and the personal overvaluation of the entity.

Once adopt the stock-investment-value ploy as a sale-of-control device, and the overvaluation thereby becomes a necessary constituent of the premium-bribe. And the premium-bribe of course is the essence of the sale of control. Cyrus Eaton, continuing arguendo, would never have considered the Isbrandtsen appointment without the prior assurance of the premium-bribe, and consequently without the overvaluation as the vehicle to carry the cash. And Jakob Isbrandtsen would never have joined in the overvaluation—and thereby parted with otherwise unnecessary and unrelated dollars— were not excess dollars a precondition to an appointment untrammeled by the uncomfortable strictures of appointee suitability binding a legitimate transfer of control.

A congeries of related functions, therefore, combines to produce one indivisible act, the transfer of custody for a price. As such, this multifaceted act—the mock valuation of the stock, the payment of the premium-bribe, the sale of control—is the most important of all official corporate transactions. Here are two strict trustees performing a complex but single corporate act, in their official capacities, on corporate time, for the avowed good of all, pursuant to the mandates of their office, and involving directly the entire trust corpus, the corporate entity. This sale of control is not a strictly private matter between two independent businessmen, and therefore regulated by the loose rules of the marketplace. Rather such transfer of custody is subject in all its details to the utmost stringencies of trust law, particularly the Benefit-to-Beneficiary and No Inquiry Rules. The sale of control, through overvalued stock, is truly trafficking in trust 'assets'—namely the entire corporate entity and all its possessions—and is governed accordingly. Were one, therefore, to indulge in the supposition of a purposeful overvaluation to effect a premium-bribe, the result would necessarily be traffic in the trust, and the consequent imposition of strict-trust rules.

Note well, moreover, that all this is not airy persiflage. These Benefit-to-Beneficiary and No Inquiry Rules bind in grim and specific application to the ad hoc situation at hand. Such cocontrôleurs, incipient and incumbent, are not strict trustees in a vague academic sense, bound by ivory-tower generalities. They are face to face with exact rules geared to a highly particular trust context: A sham overvaluation in order to buy custody of a corporation.

Conflict of Interest

In its broadest statement the Custodial Concept of Corporate Control stipulates that a corporate steward guide, guard and nurture the beneficiaries' assets without benefit to self. In his month-to-month, year-to-year administration the contrôleur must strive for the best possible corporation in terms of management, corporate structure, personnel. If possible, a contrôleur's duties heighten at that critical second when he entrusts the entity to a new steward. If ever, then does the Benefit-to-Beneficiary Rule come into play. But more to the point, when a *licit* control transfer is transformed into an *illegitimate* sale for a price measured in overvalued stock, the Benefit-to-Beneficiary Rule correspondingly adapts to the occasion.

Faced with the twin *possibility* of (1) diversion of illicit dollars away from the corporate till and (2) the appointment of an unsuitable contrôleur, the corporate custodian finds his obligation triply specified: (1) He must be a vigilant *representative* of the corporate interest, (2) His representation must extend through the entity-beneficiary to *all* subbeneficiaries without exception and (3) The utmost *impartiality* must be his rule. The contrôleur has been entrusted with 'other people's money.' Although he may hold 13 percent of the entity himself, as did Eaton, he nonetheless must represent the 'other' 87 percent with the same evenhandedness as his own. This 87 percent, or 100 percent, or 0.01 percent—even the mite is much to the widow—is entitled to equally impartial treatment.

Yet at this trust-charged instant the two custodians are locked in an excoriating conflict of interest. Behind closed doors is the bargaining table. At one end sit an Eaton and Isbrandtsen, two strict trustees, avowedly dedicated only to the stockholders' interest. At the far other end sit two level-eyed entrepreneurs, the same Eaton and Isbrandtsen (If Pooh-Bah could do it, why not they?) impelled by only one personal desire: To extract the best possible deal from themselves as trustees. With an eye to the dollar these two gentlemen as astute businessmen wish only to outmaneuver themselves as custodians. The interests are antipolar. But wherein lies the substance of the conflict? What, for example, would an Eaton and Isbrandtsen want that would be so inimical to the 87-percent public?

The Public Interests

Were the DSC minority represented at the bargaining table their desires would have been simple indeed, reducibly twofold: (1) The elimination of a premium-bribe (say $3.25 million?) by means of an honest stock evaluation and (2) The appointment of a suitable contrôleur (say an Isbrandtsen?).

Since any overpricing of the stock becomes *eo ipso* a premium-bribe, and since the premium-bribe money goes invariably into the pocket of the incumbent contrôleur (when it rightly belongs to all equally), the minority 87 percent want above all a very vigilant eye at the valuation. Every extra dollar is simply larceny from the corporate safe. To the contrary, if the stock valuation is exactly correct, no premium-bribe will pass and the shareholders are cheated of nothing. Here is the Benefit-to-Beneficiary Rule in elementary application: No premium-bribe dollars may pass to a trustee at the expense of the beneficiaries. Such illicit cash is one of the coconstituents of the triple turpitude of the premium-bribe. Were the public minority, therefore, assured of impartial scrutiny of the dollar assessment of the stock, half their wishes would be met.

But more than half the battle is won for the minority once impartial evaluators succeed in eliminating the premium-bribe. Without the inducement of premium-bribe dollars the deliberate appointment of an unsuitable contrôleur is understandably unlikely. Remove the pressure of possible overpricing, say to the extent of $3.25 million, and Cyrus Eaton would assay the suitability of his appointee with an eye single to personal qualifications. Obviously and necessarily the premium-briber would thereby be eliminated from contention for the office. The readiness—perhaps indicative of a propensity—to premium-bribe his way into control is a principal element of the unsuitability of any prospective contrôleur. (It is again submitted that a premium-briber generally recoups his outlay at the expense of the corporation.) This very act of premium-bribery would certainly disqualify any candidate for the custody of others' assets. (Unless perhaps a small premium-bribe could be conceived to be insufficiently culpable to warrant disqualification?)

The addition, moreover, of premium-bribe-induced unsuitability to the illicit cash would supply a second constituent of the triple turpitude of the premium-bribe. The third requisite, the perversion, would be effected by the appointment itself. Thus use of overvalued stock to conceal the cash does not create any new species of premium-bribe. The result is the same tripartite illegitimacy which has been "defined as: (1) The perversion of the judgment of the incumbent contrôleur, engendered by an appointment of a successor induced by a cause other than suitability, (2) That is, for consideration illicit in itself, (3) Resulting in the appointment of a candidate unsuitable by reason of his own active role in the inducement."[201]

Once, however, the impartial scrutiny of a third party forestalls a premium-bribe, the assumption is justified that the incumbent contrôleur is trustworthy enough to adhere closely to the fivefold norm of successor suitability: "(1) Moral integrity, (2) Intellectual competence, (3) Managerial and organizational proficiency, (4) Social suitability and (5) Satisfactory age and health."[202]

The Conflicting Interests

Set off against these legitimate shareholder expectations are the deeply antagonistic goals of the trustees-turned-entrepreneurs. When two such competing entrepreneurs join battle over the amount of the premium-bribe to be lodged in the stock valuation, neither battler is worrying about the public minority.

Of the two, perhaps the conflict of interest is more glaring in the incumbent contrôleur. After an Eaton has decided to sell the office for overpriced stock, he obviously will fight tenaciously—else why enter the arena in the beginning?—for the highest possible overpricing. With the market at 16 to 20, why should an Eaton settle for 22 if he can force the bid to 25 (or 26.5 as Max Zivian did)? For the premium-bribed, the top dollar is the only sensible course.

With this approach, one might think the seller is the primary, even the sole, villain in the script. After all, he not only selected the successor but he sold the office. Perhaps even pushed the matter, since he exacted the premium-bribe. Most of all, he has actually pocketed the putative premium-bribe, possibly even more than the $3.25 million.

To the contrary, in an arm's-length negotiation between two hardheaded entrepreneurs the prevailing assumption would cast both in the identical roles of equals, one as able to take care of himself as the other. The success of such a deal postulates mutual agreement. It takes two consenting parties to make a bilateral contract. Even more, the would-be contrôleur is the active party. He wanted the office. He would do the premium-bribing, and might well have been the instigator. American Export Industries wanted steel (DSC), iron ore and ships (Cleveland-Cliffs), to fill out the pattern, as its Annual Report put it, for "the development of a total system for the domestic and international transportation and distribution of freight." This was, after all, "transition year plus one" for American Export. Thus an Isbrandtsen will pay an Eaton or a Zivian whatever it takes to buy control, especially since premium-bribe dollars obviate any inquiry into suitability. Not that unsuitability is the objective, but at least suitability is not the sole norm. This is the prevailing point for Isbrandtsen. Dollars not merit are now the issue. If merit alone were involved, Eaton would never demand overvalued dollars, or would Isbrandtsen think of paying them. On merit alone Isbrandtsen never would have gotten the job. Else why the overpayment? Eaton obviously wanted more than Isbrandtsen, or his talents. And Isbrandtsen wanted less than the shareholder scrutiny of his suitability. Reflection reveals that both parties are equally guilty, since both are equally responsible. Both are strict trustees. One received the money, but the other passed it. If an Eaton was premium-bribed, an Isbrandtsen was the premium-briber. Eaton and Isbrandtsen, therefore, formed a united front in their antagonism to the interest and welfare of the 87 percent. One sought premium-bribe dollars. The other, other than suitability. Toward the minority they were a single unit of opposition.

To this would come strong Eaton/Isbrandtsen rebuttal in the Swan tradition:

> Concededly a majority or dominant shareholder is ordinarily privileged to sell his stock at the best price obtainable from the purchaser.
> —*Perlman v. Feldmann*, 219 F.2d 173, 179
> (2d Cir. 1955) (Swan, J., dissenting).

If Eaton is determined to get the "best price obtainable" and Isbrandtsen the lowest, who is to say that such an arm's-length struggle is not as objective as any other competitive market? Isbrandtsen's suitability is beyond question. Concededly his appointment on merit alone has been consummated. Why must the two delay to seek the bids of others? Especially since no one knows the product better than Eaton and Isbrandtsen.

The pitched battle over the investment value is not difficult to imagine. Eaton might demand more, but probably would soon settle firmly and finally at 25. In support of his price he would simply detail Isbrandtsen's proven success in building American Export into an "international transportation" colossus, with acquisitions and subsidiaries stumbling one over the other: Eastern Express, National Carloading, DSC, Cleveland-Cliffs Iron, Premium Ore, The Equity Corp., etc., etc. (In a surge of modesty Eaton might even cite his own team's recent failures.) Isbrandtsen would be loath to gainsay the contrôleur increment he would bring to Detroit Steel.

But the dollar sign would restore sanity and Isbrandtsen would counter with the undeniable and pervading presence of the ready market on the NYSE—some two-million-share turnover in seven months—at the arresting reality of 18. To pay Eaton 25, or Zivian

26.5, would be abject folly when he could lift the telephone and pay only 18. Further, would not such a purchase at 25 be self-damning? An admitted premium-bribe? Assuredly Mr. Isbrandtsen, or any incoming contrôleur, could have no special predilection for Mr. Eaton's particular shares of stock, especially when they carried a $7 markup. Why not pay 18 at market?

But before the phone is lifted Eaton presses some equally arresting facts. Should DSC + Isbrandtsen be really worth 25, or even 30, as both in their heart know, what of a forceful suit under Section 10(b) of the Securities Exchange Act by the minority deceived into selling to Isbrandtsen at 18, alleging, and justly so, failure to disclose the material fact of the public shares' true value, 25, enhanced by the Isbrandtsen contrôleur increment? The litigation expense alone would eat up the saving, and recovery besides would not be unthinkable. In the same vein, Eaton evidences a tendency to jump the gun with an early announcement of the appointment, and watch the market go to 30 before Isbrandtsen can buy Eaton's shares. Isbrandtsen reconsiders. With these possibilities, Eaton's shares at 25 look persuasive—as does Section 10(b)—or at a possible 30, or more.

Of course, argues Isbrandtsen, the Isbrandtsen advent might mean contrôleur *decrement,* and therefore 15, or even 11. But the absurdity of this is apparent to both and the figure is firmed at 25.

This brief interlude, so the argument would go, is exactly reflective of any arm's-length negotiation between any two bargaining shareholders possessed of inside information of *Texas Gulf Sulphur* magnitude. Contrôleur increment may be the subject of an arm's-length deal. Or contrôleur decrement.

But all this is fantasy. One tends to wander off in a dreamworld of stock-sale negotiations and forget the surrounding reality. These two are *not* Tom and Dick shareholders dickering over the price of the stock. If they were, the fantasy would be reality. At this moment these two are contrôleurs, strict trustees, passing control of millions in assets. They are negotiating in the real world of a gross conflict of interest. Both are far more interested in the sale of control than the sale of the stock. The latter is incidental. Eaton and Isbrandtsen, and Swan and Lumbard and Pollack, fail to emphasize that the stock sale—at an overvalued, premium-bribe price?—can never be fully divorced from the transfer of custody. At that moment an Eaton can see premium-bribe dollars and an Isbrandtsen a merit-free, voteless appointment to control. As long as a control transfer accompanies a stock sale, the stock sale is necessarily involved in traffic in the trust. That stock sale is necessarily suspect.

True, when Eaton and Isbrandtsen sat down together, a knock-down-and-drag-out battle did ensue. But it was not an open, arm's-length negotiation between one dogged and impartial investor and another. To the contrary, one must assume that it was two tough-minded businessmen hammering out in private the amount of premium-bribe necessary to buy control of Detroit Steel. To Eaton and Isbrandtsen the overnight contrôleur increment, with Isbrandtsen in and Eaton out, adding instantaneously $25 million to the overall worth of the Detroit Steel Corporation and correspondingly netting Eaton $3.25 million for his 'control block,' was an artful ruse. Doubly artful if the increment was actually decrement. (If the true value of DSC + Isbrandtsen was 11, the premium was correspondingly greater.) Such rather was the Eaton/Isbrandtsen consensus of the sale value of control to a ready and willing premium-briber. Stock valuation was in fact premium-bribe negotiation. Otherwise, why not a competitive price on a free market?

The *Insuranshares* Court knew what happened:

> The buyers were primarily interested in getting control of the corporation together with such stock ownership as would make that control secure and untrammelled, and the sellers were primarily interested in getting as much money as possible for what they had to sell—both the control and their interest in the assets.
>
> —*Insuranshares Corp. v. Northern Fiscal Corp.*, 35 F. Supp. 22, 24 (E.D. Pa. 1940).

The No Inquiry Rule

Note well: The sole subject of this back-room 'valuation' was a totally unknown entity. Not a soul had any clear idea of the value of Detroit Steel under an Isbrandtsen. No one even suspected the combination was in the offing. True, the cold eye of the market had calculated Detroit Steel under Eaton at an average 18. But Detroit Steel plus Isbrandtsen was presumably another thing. The contrôleur increment, or decrement, the differential before and after, was the lone subject of 'valuation,' and not one person beyond Eaton and Isbrandtsen had even heard of it.

Next, the 'valuation' itself was strictly ex parte. Behind closed doors and alone, Eaton and Isbrandtsen upped Detroit Steel's value $25 million, by simply subtracting Eaton and adding Isbrandtsen. No impartial person—a ready buyer with dollars in hand—was called in to put a price on the stock without control. No public announcement asked an objectively competitive market to evaluate Detroit Steel plus Isbrandtsen. Obviously, such an evaluation—whether by ready buyer, general market, or even the 87-percent minority—would eliminate any conflict of interest. No longer would the 'valuation' be that of Eaton and Isbrandtsen. The competitive evaluation would become their evaluation. In effect this impartial third party would supplant Eaton and Isbrandtsen, acquisitive entrepreneurs, at the bargaining table. Then Eaton and Isbrandtsen, strict trustees, would be out of the conflict.

But the doors were never thus opened, and the 'valuation' of this questionable increment was strictly a private matter. No outside scrutiny, no current corroboration, no possible double check. To this add the dedicated devotion to their own interests, a palpable conflict of interest, and Eaton and Isbrandtsen have set the scene for the unswerving application of the No Inquiry Rule.

Over the decades the Anglo-Saxon law of trusts has gained some remarkably reliable insights into man's nature and conduct. Paramount among these has been the categorical conviction that a fallible human person on both sides of a bargain with a personal stake in the outcome is essentially incapable of impartiality. Centuries of legal wisdom have long since placed such detached objectivity far beyond the rational powers of *homo rationalis*. This ultimate principle of human conduct is founded simply on the consistent fragility of human nature and the basic loyalty incumbent on both trustees and founded on the Custodial Concept of Corporate Control.

Age-old recognition of this basic handicap of acquisitive man led inevitably to the formal enunciation of the so-called No Inquiry Rule:

> *The law of trusts has been unrelentingly adamant in the automatic disqualification from any attempt to represent both sides in an adversary negotiation of any single person with a personal interest in one side. So unremitting is the prohibition that the courts will not even initiate an inquiry into the result.*

The absolute inflexibility of the No Inquiry Rule is amply fortified by the fusion of two separate factors: (1) The private evaluation
of a wholly unknown subject with no independent corroboration,
(2) By a single person with interests deeply in conflict with those of
the absent party. Understandably the result is automatic
disqualification.

Further reflection can penetrate more deeply into the rationale
of the No Inquiry Rule. When an Eaton and Isbrandtsen, trustees-
turned-entrepreneurs and hence a unitary 'person,' personally
priced a new entity—DSC+Isbrandtsen—without the check of a
free market, the result could be high of the mark, or low, or exactly
reflect true value. From the strictly factual standpoint Eaton and
Isbrandtsen could stoutly stand by $25 million in contrôleur *incre-
ment,* whereas detractors among the public minority could argue ob-
streperously that the transition from Eaton to Isbrandtsen was rather
a contrôleur *decrement* of $25 million (witness a year later), that
Isbrandtsen was far from a Roger Smith, J. Peter Grace or Lee Iacocca.
But both claims are equally irrelevant. The nub is the intrinsic incom-
petency of an Isbrandtsen to set a value on Isbrandtsen, especially
with help from an Eaton who wants the highest dollar. Whether high,
low or exactly correct, therefore, is not the point. The real crux is
twofold: (1) *The ever present possibility of overvaluation* and (2) *The
utter impossibility of knowing what the correct value might have been.*
The complete absence of a free-market countercheck plus the
proven conflict-of-interest compulsion renders the chance of
overvaluation invariable. In the light of the cupidity of humankind
such possibility is rather likelihood.

With such inescapable possibility—even likelihood—and the
inability ever to know, the law is forced to regard such overvaluation
as a certainty. Since the law can never depend on the absence of
overvaluation, it must always presume its presence. A necessarily
possible overvaluation must be viewed legally as an actuality. The
conclusion: All private conflict-of-interest valuations are *legal*
overvaluations, and must be treated as such in their legal consequences.

Such personal price-setting, then, is necessarily reprobate, not
extrinsically because the figure could be correct (Some contrôleur
increment could well be present), but intrinsically because of the innate, conflict-of-interest disability and the postulated rejection of a

competitive countercheck. The right itself is impugned, not the possible correctness of an evaluation. Any unsupervised valuation by partial parties necessarily becomes at law an overvaluation. (Recall John L. Counsellor, Sr., and his malefactions.)

All this explains the assumption throughout that Eaton and Isbrandtsen overvalued. Now at long last the validity, and necessity, of that irritating and long-prolonged 'assumption strictly arguendo' of an Eaton/Isbrandtsen mock 'valuation' should be apparent. Such assumption is unavoidable, albeit regrettable, as long as partial parties insist on ignoring the independent market. What began as an assumption must end as a fact. Only thus can the law of trusts protect the helpless beneficiaries.

The view from the textbooks always left the No Inquiry Rule looking harsh and unnecessarily unremitting. In the abstract, some concession seemed in order. But its applicability becomes vivid when an Eaton and Isbrandtsen sit all alone 'pricing Detroit Steel plus Isbrandtsen' at a figure personally congenial to both, and smacking of a sale of control.

Thus the last of the several factors has been proven. As proven it joins with the others to prove the proposition originally set for proof:

> At the time of the transfer of control and the sale of the 'control stock' inter se, a personal evaluation of that stock—whether actually correct or not—by the two contrôleurs, incumbent and appointee, is intrinsically reprobate under the Benefit-to-Beneficiary and No Inquiry Rules, since both contrôleurs are acting throughout as strict trustees of the entity.
>
> —Chapter 8: The Investment Value of Control Stock, *supra* at 312.

Here then is the essential ineligibility, the necessary disqualification, of the trustees-turned-entrepreneurs. The No Inquiry Rule interdicts absolutely any independent evaluation and sale.

But if Eaton and Isbrandtsen are forever precluded from a private estimate, what to do? Will such a rigid rule stifle all control transfers? Is any sale possible? If so, how best?

III. The Solution: The Tender Offer

> The thoughtful and scholarly writings of the
> academic commentators on sale of control have
> had surprisingly little influence on the way courts
> decide cases. With only infrequent and relatively
> minor exceptions, the courts still adhere to the tra-
> ditional view that a shareholder, irrespective of
> whether he is also a director, officer, or both, may
> sell his shares, just as he may sell other kinds of per-
> sonal property, for whatever price he can obtain,
> even if his shares constitute a controlling block and
> the price per share is enhanced by that fact.
>
> —O'Neal, *Introduction* to *Symposium:*
> *Sale of Control,* 4 J. CORP. L. 239
> (1979).

Cyrus Eaton was determined to resign. Painstaking research
had produced a successor eminently suitable for the stewardship of
Detroit Steel. Jakob Isbrandtsen had acceded to the selection and
was prepared to dedicate himself absolutely to the *bonum commune*
of the corporation. The board changeover was settled. Mr. Eaton also
felt that the best interests of all, including Detroit Steel, suggested
that he unload his entire interest and quit the field completely. Besides, he was tired. And he wanted cash for his stock. So too did Max
Zivian.

Jakob Isbrandtsen on his part—better than any conscious of his
own capabilities—had estimated the value of his own personal contribution to the firm at $7 per share. He was convinced that the
contrôleur increment with Isbrandtsen in and Eaton out was approximately $25 million in all. More to the point Mr. Isbrandtsen felt that
a substantial stake in Detroit Steel would give him greater incentive
toward diligence and productivity. His current financial state indi-
cated a 13-percent interest as feasible. He was determined to buy.

Both Mr. Eaton and Mr. Isbrandtsen had only one all-pervasive
consideration: The selection of a most suitable successor to the office
of control. Certainly, no thought of a sale of control or a premium-
bribe ever entered their heads. If, incidentally, Mr. Isbrandtsen could
also purchase a 13-percent block at $25, all the better.

With both determined, one to sell, the other buy, several powerful impulses tortured them. How to rein in these forces, and still effect the sale and purchase to the satisfaction of both?

In the first place, Cyrus Eaton was frank to admit that he was not about to sell at a market 18. And certainly he would never admit 'contrôleur *decrement*' to 11 or more. He knew DSC+Isbrandtsen was worth 25. Isbrandtsen had to agree, especially since he saw the real dangers of a Section 10(b) action if he bought up 525,000 public shares at 18 without disclosing his appointment and a consequent true value of 25. And a premature announcement *might* send the market to 30. Which confirmed Isbrandtsen in his agreement to the 25.

Next, as unlofty as the motive was, neither dared risk even the accusation of a premium-bribe. In their more moral moments they knew a private partial 'valuation' included just that. The sale/purchase had to avoid that stigma. Straight common sense, or even gross dollar-and-cents motivation, would send both incumbent and successor headlong to protect their names. They would recall:

> [O]f all the acts of his corporate career the most important is probably the contrôleur's appointment of a successor, an act fraught with deep trust implications, determinative of the long-term future well-being of the corporation. How completely unthinkable and unlikely for men of prudence to pass unrelated consideration at this time. Even schoolboy discretion would caution a contrary course. . . . [O]nly a rare trustee would not heed such elemental warnings . . . .
>
> —Chapter 5: The Sale of Control and the Premium-Bribe. *supra* at 186-87.

The attitude of both Eaton and Isbrandtsen would be colored deeply by strong desires to remove even the tincture of suspicion.

Finally, both Eaton and Isbrandtsen translated their trust obligations into a firm desire to give the 87-percent minority an equal opportunity to share in any sale which would reflect the legitimate contrôleur increment or decrement actually effected by the advent of Isbrandtsen.

Impelled by these desires, some altruistic, some selfish, but all legitimate, Eaton and Isbrandtsen could well have thought of a way, a reconciliation of all the apparent ambivalence. The solution lay in a flanking operation. Oscar Wilde notwithstanding, the best way to overcome temptation is to flee it. Had Eaton and Isbrandtsen wished to avoid the stigma of suspicion and the cries for an explanation, a simple side step would have achieved both. The risk of premium-bribe or Section 10(b), the loss of a just sale or a fair purchase, the inequity of leaving the 87 percent outside, could all be obviated in the simplicity of an uncluttered tender offer.

A straightforward letter to all the shareholders over the signatures of Messrs. Eaton and Isbrandtsen could squarely present all the facts and factors. The letter could begin with Mr. Eaton's decision to retire, his selection of Mr. Isbrandtsen, a full but objective list of those Isbrandtsen capabilities so impressive to Mr. Eaton, and move on to Mr. Isbrandtsen's desire to buy into the firm. The letter could conclude with a firm Isbrandtsen offer to purchase at $25 per share—$7 over current market—13 percent of all outstanding stock prorated equally for all, including of course Mr. Eaton.

Subsequent to the success of the offer and as part of the plan, Mr. Eaton on his part could take immediate advantage of the $25 market and sell—in paced sales over the NYSE—the remaining 87 percent of his original 13-percent block (but only after he had made up from his own shares any deficiency in the tenders, thereby assuring Mr. Isbrandtsen of his full 13 percent). Thus in one simple flanking operation, Eaton and Isbrandtsen would achieve their every objective, without even a smidgen of suspicion.

The Outgoing Contrôleur

Such a stratagem puts everyone on his mettle, Mr. Eaton particularly as incumbent contrôleur. His judgment of successor selection would be subjected to the collective scrutiny of an informed market. If the public shareholders of DSC concurred in Eaton's judgment of Isbrandtsen's rosy promise, *none of the public 87 percent would sell*. Who would run away from a good thing? Better keep the stock and ride high with Isbrandtsen. Thus would Eaton's judgment be vindicated and his original intentions implemented. He would then sell his entire 13-percent block to Isbrandtsen and reap his full $7 of contrôleur increment. And he could retire gracefully from the scene exactly according to plan.

To the contrary if his vision had been blinded by an unfounded glamor in Mr. Isbrandtsen, an astute evaluation of Detroit Steel under Isbrandtsen would send sell offers pouring in. And Mr. Eaton, able to sell only 13 percent of 13 percent, would be forced to live—or die—with 87 percent of his investment in the stewardship of Isbrandtsen. (Isbrandtsen might well wish to stipulate that such an event would prompt Eaton to disburse his shares on the market over an agreed period, and thus remove any discomfiture Isbrandtsen might feel in having his predecessor too close at hand.)

If Eaton's estimate was egregiously wrong in the eyes of the Street, if *decrement* rather than increment was the correct word, Detroit Steel would invariably slip back down to the realistic 18 (or to the 11 it actually hit about a year after). With such sobering alternatives before him an incumbent contrôleur would not be hasty in either his selection of a successor or his estimation of contrôleur increment.

The Incoming Contrôleur

Except for the shared expense of the shareholder letter, such a tender offer should have considerable appeal to Mr. Isbrandtsen. Even the relatively slight expense would be amply offset by the several advantages. First, he has achieved his prime objective, the opportunity to devote his talents toward the development of Detroit Steel. As a result, his 13-percent block not only carries the present enhanced value of the contrôleur increment but the incentive of future appreciation under his aggressive leadership. Next, Mr. Isbrandtsen certainly cared not a whit who sold him what particular shares (assuming the stipulation that Eaton later leave, if and when). With no intent of cheating anyone, he was perfectly ready to pay the fair price of 25—reflecting the legitimate contrôleur increment—to any seller ready to sell. But most of all, as an incipient trustee, Mr. Isbrandtsen wanted to shun all taint of premium-bribery—and danger of Section 10(b)—so easily done with a tender offer.

The Public Shareholders

The scattered minority have everything to gain. Granted, if the stewardship of Isbrandtsen should go sour—assuming they held their shares—they would deeply regret Eaton's appointment. But even this contingency was freely chosen. They could have opted out, at least partially, at 25. This option to stay in or sell is far better than the forced acceptance of a new contrôleur. Further, the NYSE might momentarily follow the tender-offer price and the minority might sell all their 87 percent at 25.

The tender offer gives the public holders the chance to realize their $7 contrôleur increment on a pro rata basis equal to the outgoing contrôleur. Such a contrôleur-trustee should not enjoy a favored opportunity to reap an early reward merely because of his position. This is one of the handicaps of being a custodian. Even then this handicap only holds the contrôleur to a fair price. The result is not a penalty, merely a bar to cheating. The offer was made to Eaton as incumbent contrôleur-trustee by Isbrandtsen as incipient contrôleur-trustee. Thus does the tender offer anticipate the rudimentary demands of equity without the need of postdelictum litigation. As the California Court of Appeal puts it in the 1969 *Brown v. Halbert*:

> The rule we have adopted here simply is that it is the duty of the majority stockholder-director, when contemplating the sale of the majority stock at a price not available to other stockholders and which sale may prejudice the minority stockholders, is to act affirmatively and openly with full disclosure so that every opportunity is given to obtain substantially the same advantages that such fiduciary secured and for the full protection of the minority.
>
> —*Brown v. Halbert*, 76 Cal. Rptr. 781, 793-94 (Cal. App. 1969).

The chief advantage to the public, however, lies in the knowledge that the steward of their assets will exercise every vigilance in selecting a suitable successor. The built-in safeguards will add realistic muscle to the contrôleur's fiducial obligation to represent the corporate beneficiary and all the shareholders—and incidentally himself—in his successor selection and during an arm's-length negotiation of the investment price, including the contrôleur increment or decrement. And it would be truly arm's length with the free market setting the price. Since the minority are at the mercy of the contrôleur at any event, far better to face the dangers of a control transfer with an option to bail out than to sit by and watch control pass to a looter or incompetent. With a suitable appointee, moreover, the minority will not feel the necessity of selling their remaining shares.

This suggested solution is redolent of that Solomonic parental device for sharing the apple. With such an arrangement—and so too with the tender offer—the only unhappy party is the avaricious one.

Many possible variants could perhaps improve this tender-offer plan. The prospective contrôleur could be required to purchase a minimum of ten- or 15-percent of the corporation. Or perhaps the outgoing contrôleur should not share in any sale to his successor until the public have tendered all they wish, up to the agreed limit.

But whatever the variant, obviously none of the proposals need be mandatory, even the tender offer itself. After the public announcement of the Isbrandtsen appointment, several paths lay open. Eaton and Isbrandtsen could have each bought and sold separately over the NYSE. Or they could have forgone a sale altogether.

But if Eaton and Isbrandtsen insist on a sale inter se, only one narrow route is open: The price for the stock must be established by a freely competitive market—either general public or minority tender—with full knowledge of any potential contrôleur increment or, more to the point, decrement that Isbrandtsen might bring to DSC. The crux? The market for DSC + Eaton is strictly irrelevant to a new market for DSC + Isbrandtsen. It may stay at 18, or go to 25, or 26.5, or 30—or drop to the 11 it did.

The ever present possibility, therefore, of this ready and waiting freely competitive market in the persons of the public minority pushes the issue to the ultimate: Do the trustee contrôleurs intend the appointment of a suitable successor, accompanied incidentally by a legitimate sale and purchase of stock, or would they prefer a gross sale of control for a handsome premium-bribe?

But if that straight and narrow path of a tender offer is eschewed, what then?

IV. The Legal Consequences of a Sale

First, the equal opportunity rule has been rather soundly rejected. *McDaniel v. Painter* [10th Cir. 1968]. Second, the rule, if applied, would likely result in the stifling of many financial transactions due either to a purchaser's inability to purchase the additional shares, or from a lack of inclination to purchase those shares.

> —*Clagett v. Hutchison,* 583 F.2d 1259, 1264 (4th Cir. 1978).

[The claim] baldly asserts that a purchaser of control has a duty to purchase all the stock at the same price. Such an "all or nothing" principle has been embraced by no case or commentary of which we are aware.

> —*Doleman v. Meiji Mut. Life Ins. Co.,* 727 F.2d 1480, 1484 (9th Cir. 1984).

Were a court faced with a consummated sale along the lines of the Detroit Steel sale of control, the devious path of reasoning so painfully elaborated thus far should point the way to a plausible adjudication.

The first step would strip away the camouflage that hid the traditional old-line premium-bribe. Underneath lay the blunt £75 slipped under the table in *Sugden v. Crossland,* the almost gauche $15,000 Levy handed Law, the naive sale of control from Muscat to Sonnabend for $135,000 in straight cash in *Lionel,* the undisguised $300,000 Iowa Mutual passed to John Alesch in *Le Mars.* The only difference? The dollars wore a different garb, and could barely be recognized in the 'true investment value' of the stock.

To begin, the court would juxtapose (1) The transfer of custody of DSC from Eaton to Isbrandtsen against (2) The private sale at 25 by partial parties of an unknown entity, DSC+Isbrandtsen, untested, and never to be tested, by a free market, with not a thought of the 87-percent minority or any competitive bid. How remarkable that Eaton and Isbrandtsen should choose the occasion of this most delicate act of their tenure for the sale of such a block at a price unconfirmed and unconfirmable.

In the face of such conflict of interest the No Inquiry Rule would become immediately operative. How much of the $13-million sale figure was pure premium-bribe? Was there contrôleur increment? Or decrement? No one would or could ever know. At the time of the actual sale no disinterested dollars were asked to bid against the partial price of 25. With that moment gone forever, steel shortages or steel glut, Vietnam, Iran, Afghan hopes or scares, franc devaluations or mark advaluations, the baneful effects of inflation, the inflationary potential of SDRs—and, of course, the actual impact of Isbrandtsen on Detroit Steel—could send the market skyrocketing to 40, or plummeting to the later 11. All the paid appraisers in the world, with their own dollars inside their pockets, can never adequately reconstruct the true investment value of DSC shares as of March 26, 1968. *The Wall Street Journal* put it well in praising the German move to a free-floating mark:

> The problem is: What is the mark worth? Instead of closeting some financial wizards to dream up the answer in a vacuum, the Bonn government chose to let the market decide. Specifically, it will permit the dollar-mark exchange rate to find its own level . . . .
>
> —Editorial, Wall St. J., Oct. 1, 1969, at 18, col. 1.

In the end, then, a court would have no other choice: Secret traffic in the trust rendered the then true value of the shares unknown and unknowable.

The Amount of the Premium-Bribe

At this juncture, therefore, the court would face the necessary chore: How determine the dollar amount of those shares? Isbrandtsen chose to pay, and Eaton accept, 25, Zivian 26.5, in secret deals. After the open market absorbed the news of the Isbrandtsen takeover, what was the available price? The dollar differential between the price Eaton actually received and the correct price later available on the market determines the amount of the premium-bribe.

And to say 'dollar differential' only begins the chore. Dollar differential for whom? And when? Were Eaton to have hunted an impartial buyer for his 525,000 shares, he would have cautiously sold on the Big Board over several months. He might have gotten as high as 27. Isbrandtsen, however, would have been just as cautious and might have bought at 11. Whose efforts, Eaton's or Isbrandtsen's, are to set the market price against the 25 actually paid? Eaton exacted the premium-bribe, but Isbrandtsen was the premium-briber. Regardless of who is to be the protagonist, what conjectural price is to govern? The highest for Eaton? The lowest for Isbrandtsen? In between? And when?

Since two strict trustees saw fit to place themselves in a clear conflict with beneficiary interests, since both rejected the ready opportunity to get the best deal at competitive prices in a free market, since both refused at the proper time to establish the true dollar value of the stock, they cannot now complain when the court is forced to set the figure for them. Only thus can the law protect the neglected beneficiary. In such an after-the-fact situation the court is willy-nilly hamstrung. It alone must find the price. More to the point, as between active malefactors and injured victims the court has little choice. The law must select that stock-price figure most favorable to the impotent minority and least so to the contrôleurs who concocted the deal and spurned an impartial price at the time. Learned Hand faced a similar problem in *Gratz v. Claughton* in 1951: How to determine the profits in short-swing dealings when many sales and many purchases could not be matched with certainty?

> The situation falls within the doctrine which has been law since the days of the "Chimney Sweeper's Jewel Case," [*Armory v. Delamirie,* 1722] that when damages are at some unascertainable amount below an upper limit and when the uncertainty arises from the defendant's wrong, the upper limit will be taken as the proper amount.
>
> —*Gratz v. Claughton,* 187 F.2d 46, 51-52 (2d Cir. 1951).

Learned Hand—and any court, it is submitted—would decide the instant question the same way. The only legal assumption available: The premium-bribe base—to set off against the actually paid 25— would be the lowest market price possible, within a reasonable time after the announcement of the appointment. Further, an Eaton/ Isbrandtsen court would in fact have an 'ascertainable amount': The best buy an energetic and dollar-minded Isbrandtsen could find, to wit, the lowest figure available for a 13-percent block.

Not only must the court select the lower "limit . . . as the proper amount," but the time span for the purchase must extend as long as a reasonable buyer would wait. Nothing compelled Isbrandtsen to buy privately on March 26. Had he or Eaton wanted immediate action a public deal or a tender offer was available. Isbrandtsen could have spread his purchases over six months to a year, or longer, watching the market for the most favorable, lowest moment. Next to the tender offer itself the surest earnest of honesty would have been just such a calculated delay until the objective market evaluated DSC + Isbrandtsen. In short, any "uncertainty [arose] from the defendant's wrong."

Thus the handicap the two contrôleurs assumed in refusing a free competitive offer would send the court to the lowest feasible figure within a reasonable time of the transaction. Such search would not be difficult. Roughly a year after the March 26 sale the market hovered for some time in the 13s, even hitting the 11s. On this basis the tentative premium-bribe figure of $7 would undoubtedly be supplanted by a more realistic $12. For Max Zivian, $13.5. Consequently the Eaton premium-bribe would be $6.3 million. For Zivian, $3 million. Total: $9.3 million.

In fine, Isbrandtsen—or the court on his behalf—simply needed time and deftness. The 3.9-million DSC shares outstanding, plus a two-million-share volume in the seven-month period ending March 26, 1968, should settle the matter.

The Illegality of the Premium

The determination of the free-market figure for Isbrandtsen's purchase should not unduly occupy a court, and from that point forward precedents governing premium-bribe illegality abound. Given the fact of a premium-bribe, the applicable law should long since be clear. True, even faced with a proven premium-bribe—its existence established and amount determined—the courts are still widely split. But guidelines are emerging, and the answers have been attempted in considerable detail. Respectable authority—*Sugden, McClure, Bosworth v. Allen, Porter v. Healy, Reynolds, Perlman v. Feldmann, Lionel, Ferraioli v. Cantor,* the 1969 *Brown v. Halbert,* the outstanding Second Circuit *Rosenfeld v. Black,* the Iowa *Le Mars* and the 1985 Missouri *Forinash*—has ordered over the premium-bribe to the corporation. The question should be closed. The 'premium' for the sale of control is illegal, and belongs to the corporation.

The Disposition

But once awarded to the corporation, how would the total $9.3 million be distributed? May 19.3-percent-stockholder Isbrandtsen share in the 'windfall'? Must Eaton and Zivian disgorge the total $9.3 million, or only the 87-percent public's share? Over the decades these extremely subtle questions have received almost total neglect at the hands of both court and commentator. Recall that *Perlman v. Feldmann* has been the only court to advert directly to the problem posed by the disposition of the premium-bribe. *Feldmann* righteously refused—albeit without support of precedent or reason—to let premium-briber Wilport, now with a third of Newport Steel, share in the $2.1 million ostensibly destined for the corporate treasury, even though its *stock purchase* (sans premium) from Feldmann was perfectly legitimate. On the other hand the Court, mirabile dictu, allowed *premium-bribed* Feldmann to keep a third of the premium-bribe. To the contrary, the *Lionel* court never mentioned the problem, and permitted Sonnabend's three percent to share in the $135,000 he originally paid to premium-bribe Muscat.

The Eaton/Isbrandtsen facts are of course on all fours with *Feldmann* and *Lionel*. The small share of Sonnabend may have escaped the court, but the Isbrandtsen 13 percent—19.3 percent, with Max Zivian's sale—would loom almost as large as the Feldmann/Wilport third. Recall *Feldmann* and compare it to Eaton/Isbrandtsen. As between premium-bribed Feldmann and premium-briber Wilport why *Feldmann* favored Feldmann one will never know. The Court's error is probably referable to its earlier error: No attempt was made to mulct civil damages from Wilport for its breach of trust in buying control of Newport Steel. Recall further that no criminal prosecutions were pressed against Wilport for commercial bribery. Civil damages and criminal fines, if not imprisonment—to say nothing of its 'loss' of the $2.1 million—would have completely cleansed Wilport of culpability. With its triple debt paid, no court would further bar Wilport personally from its just share in the corporation. As to the stock itself, it was scarcely tainted, since the sale of a valuable commodity at an honest price was fully severable from the turpitude of the premium-bribe. Such reasoning should permit Wilport—and an analogous Isbrandtsen—to enjoy the benefits of the entire award to the corporation. As for an Eaton, he too would be mulcted in civil damages, fined, even imprisoned, for 'commercial-bribe receiving,' and possibly for larceny by embezzlement. Thus both would seemingly be equally purged. The upshot would find Eaton and Zivian with their $9.3 million disgorged, Isbrandtsen without his original $9.3 million but still holding the purchased 19.3 percent.

The Office of Contrôleur

But what of control of Detroit Steel? Eaton, guilty of premium-bribery and breach of trust, convicted of assorted crimes, would certainly never be restored to his original control position. Correspondingly, Isbrandtsen equally proved his unsuitability by covering himself with the triple turpitude of premium-bribery. The civil damages, criminal sanctions, loss of the $9.3 million, all are resultant on his active role in effecting the tripartite illegitimacy of the premium-bribe:

> (1) The perversion of the judgment of the incumbent contrôleur, engendered by an appointment of a successor induced by a cause other than suitability, (2) That is, for consideration illicit in itself, (3) Resulting in the appointment of a candidate unsuitable by reason of his own active role in the inducement.
>
> —Chapter 6: The Sale-of-Control Premium: The Intrinsic Illegitimacy, supra at 204-05.

Isbrandtsen consciously set about (1) to pervert Eaton's judgment, (2) with illicit cash and (3) thereby foist a premium-briber on DSC. His removal—at least under these egregious circumstances—is foregone and simple. With him, of course, would go his entire team, all those directors who executed the takeover.

> The stock sales had the full approval of the companies in which Mr. Eaton and Mr. Daley had their interests . . . and these companies welcome the chance of tying up with a major steamship enterprise.
>
> —Wall St. J., Mar. 27, 1968, at 4, col. 1.

But the implementation of that removal carries real problems: (1) How elect his successor? (2) And keep him elected? What of the 19.3-percent Isbrandtsen block? The astute *Lionel* Court in 1964 faced its Isbrandtsen—and the identical problems—in the senior Sonnabend. A. N. Sonnabend not only bought control of Lionel for $135,000, but was prepared to sweeten the premium-bribe with $75,000 in postresignation salaries and consultation fees for the selling contrôleur Muscat. More than that, Sonnabend was about to unleash several 'dogs' on Lionel, notably *Mad,* from his Premier Corporation. With Sonnabend incumbent a new election would find the sheepish proxies putting Sonnabend right back into office.

> Therefore, some restrictions of the present board are required, so that the Sonnabend group may not take advantage of the position they hold.
>
> —*Matter of Lionel Corp.,* N.Y.L.J., Feb. 4, 1964, at 14 (Sup. Ct., N.Y. County).

The New York Court handled the matter in a most enlightened way. (Subsurface of course was an unexpressed impugning of the outmoded 'democratic' processes of the widely held annual meeting.)

> They shall be restricted to current management problems and other matters necessary for the proper functioning of the corporation and they shall not be permitted to use their present offices as the means to secure stockholder approval for their designated directorial slate, or dealing in matters involving self interest, such as proposed acquisitions from Premier Corporation of America.
>
> —*Matter of Lionel Corp.,* N.Y.L.J., Feb. 4, 1964, at 14 (Sup. Ct., N.Y. County).

The 87-percent public minority shareholders of Detroit Steel are in exactly the same fix as the 97 percent of Lionel:

> It would appear the interests of all the corporate body politic require that some method be evolved so that the holders of the other 97 per cent. of the corporate stock be given an opportunity to express and disseminate their views and suggestions and take whatever appropriate action they wish to with respect to both, the future management of the corporation and the acquisition proposals which are about to be submitted to them. In other words, what is called for is some neutralizing element which will

see to it that no undue advantage is arrogated to it by the current group and that other groups, which may form, will have an opportunity to take such action in the premises as they deem advisable.

> —*Matter of Lionel Corp.*, N.Y.L.J., Feb. 4,
> 1964, at 14 (Sup. Ct., N.Y. County).

The 'neutralization' of the Sonnabend/Isbrandtsen power 'position' could be approached on two fronts: (1) The share dispersal and (2) Domination of the proxy-solicitation mechanism. The former seemed beyond change, so the *Lionel* court 'neutralized' the latter:

> In some jurisdictions, the device of a Master in Chancery to supervise the election has been utilized for such purpose [citations]. In this and other states there have been instances of the appointment of a referee to perform like functions [citations]. Even within the confining limits of former section 25 of the General Corporation Law, a New York court recently designated such a supervisor under similar circumstances [citations].
>
> —*Matter of Lionel Corp.*, N.Y.L.J., Feb. 4,
> 1964, at 14 (Sup. Ct., N.Y. County).

Of course, the New York Court was not truly circumscribed by "the confining limits of former section 25" and did not need to rely on the successor Section 619 which "empowers the court to 'take such other action as justice may require' in the premises."[203] Since these are merely statutory enunciations of the broad equitable power possessed by every chancellor since the early 1300s, an equity court therefore could readily emulate New York:

> The court, in order to take such action as "justice may require" must assure the use of the corporate proxy machinery for the best interests of all the stockholders of the corporation. To this end the court will designate a referee on the order to be entered herein. The said referee will perform such acts as may be necessary to effectuate the decision of the court.
>
> —*Matter of Lionel Corp.*, N.Y.L.J., Feb. 4,
> 1964, at 14 (Sup. Ct., N.Y. County).

In the late seventies the Iowa court in *Le Mars* reached the same result. *Le Mars* ordered a Special Master and a court-supervised election:

> "Wherever a situation exists which is contrary to the principles of equity and which can be redressed within the scope of judicial action, a court of equity will devise a remedy to meet the situation, though no similar relief has been given before."
>
> —*Rowen v. Le Mars Mutual Ins. Co.,* 282 N.W.2d 639, 656 (Iowa 1979) (quoting H. MCCLINTOCK, HANDBOOK OF THE PRINCIPLES OF EQUITY).

With this the matter would seem to be closed. But what of the foreboding presence of the Isbrandtsen 19.3-percent block brooding over the new DSC contrôleur—assuming, of course, a *new* man—at every succeeding meeting over the coming years? Here an equity court could perhaps take a page from the Government's book in its unraveling of the knotty Du Pont/General Motors antitrust problem in the fifties. A forced sale can be decently done. Du Pont was able to disburse 63-million shares of General Motors without apparent damage. After all, two-million shares of Detroit Steel changed hands in a short seven months in 1967-68. Thus a negotiated plan of disbursal spread over several years and subject to the scrutiny of a court-appointed referee could adequately remove the Isbrandtsen threat for the future, and do Isbrandtsen no more harm than he deserves.

The Detroit Steel sale of control offered a very appropriate vehicle toward the elucidation of the most complex of the sale-of-control problems. No longer should 'true investment value' successfully disguise a raw premium-bribe. With this, only one major study remains.

Chapter 9

The Noninvestment Value of Control Stock

> In the view of many, there is something morally wrong in taking a premium price for controlling shares. As already indicated, this judgment is quite unfounded. The premium bid for control is merely a measure of the value of the shares to a bidder confident of his ability to increase the corporate profits. This is a value inherent in a controlling block.
>
> —Katz, *Responsibility and the Modern Corporation,* 3 J.L. & ECON. 75, 83 (1960).

In the 1968 Federal case of *Christophides v. Porco* Charles Bluhdorn and his expansionist Gulf and Western were accused of passing a premium to Fasco, the incumbent contrôleur, for the control of the Brown Company, a diversified paper manufacturer. The Court dismissed this accusation summarily:

> [A] purchaser is free to offer a premium for a block of control stock. This is so, even though control stock is purchased pursuant to a plan to acquire the remainder of the shares at a lower price . . . .
>
> —*Christophides v. Porco,* 289 F. Supp. 403, 405 (S.D.N.Y. 1968).

(*Porco* received unqualified support, but without elaboration, from the Tenth Circuit in the 1969 *McDaniel v. Painter.*) As for Fasco the recipient, such a sale-of-control premium was equally blameless:

343

"Even assuming that Fasco realized a premium for its controlling block, that alone would not entitle plaintiffs to relief."[204] Judge Pollack saw no reason for looking more deeply into the matter, since a . . .

> . . . controlling stockholder is under no duty to other stockholders to refrain from receiving a premium upon the sale of his stock which reflects *merely the control potential* of that stock. There is no obligation under such circumstances, to 'share and share alike'.
>
> —*Christophides v. Porco,* 289 F. Supp. 403, 405 (S.D.N.Y. 1968) (emphasis added).

What legitimate values did the New York Federal District Court—and arguably Charles Bluhdorn and Gulf and Western—envisage in "merely the control potential" of the 23-percent block of Brown stock? Is it possible to break down this "control potential" into its constituent—and salable—elements? Once broken down, moreover, why do these control elements belong exclusively to the "controlling stockholder"? Why is there "no obligation under such circumstances to 'share and share alike'" with the 77-percent public shareholders?

These questions surrounding the various values of control stock have haunted both courts and commentators for decades. The answers come fittingly at the end of the Philosophy of Corporate Control and will be attempted in a *Prelude* and five parts: *I. Total Contrôleur Contribution. II. Total Corporate Compensation. III. The Ownership of the Control Assets. IV. The Sale-of-Control Premium-Bribe. V. The Analysis in Summary.*

The Prelude

> The control potential of a large block of shares has a value, and equalizing per-share prices is simply interfering with the market forces determining the value of control. As the price of control blocks is raised in this artificial fashion, fewer "purchases" of control will occur. Many shareholders will simply receive no premium at all for their shares—a high price to pay for shareholder equality.
>
> —Henry G. Manne, Letter to the Editor, Wall St. J., Nov. 5, 1969, at 22, col. 6.

Over the decades of this confusion, court and commentator have been mizzled by a plethora of 'control values,' some attached to the control itself, some integral to the concomitant stock, some legitimate, some illegitimate. This variegated mix of underlying control advantages has been difficult to sort out, as if one had three or four jigsaw puzzles in a single box, and did not know it. The first chore, therefore: To separate the puzzles, and work on them one at a time.

Illegitimate Desires

The readiest exclusion from this present study is that large class of 'values' resultant on control which are simply and callously outright marauding. In the long-famous looting cases of the early forties, *Reynolds* and *Insuranshares,* the prize of control was the liquid portfolio. In *Lionel* the prospect of unloading the several corporate 'dogs'— held by his Premier Corporation, but destined for Lionel—motivated Sonnabend to buy control from Muscat. In *Feldmann* Wilport sought a captive steel supply at favoring rates. In *Le Mars* Iowa Mutual wanted a pliant customer for 'management services' and its computer.

Understandably Charles Bluhdorn and his G+W—and certainly Judge Pollack in *Porco*—had none of these 'values' in mind in seeking "the control potential" of the Brown Company. Nor should such illicit aspects of corporate control be relevant to the noninvestment value of control stock. Infinite are the varieties of larceny, from the crass to the subtle, and none are peculiar to corporate control. Such a study would be barren. Recall throughout, therefore, that the present concern must only be the benefits legally flowing from control. Any illicit returns not only break the rules of the corporate game but render futile any reasoned dissection of the noninvestment value of control stock. Looting is thus excluded.

Investment Value

The sorting out of the second alien puzzle in the jigsaw box is far more difficult. Unwittingly the *investment* value of the *stock* itself has been indiscriminately grouped—and with baneful results—with the congeries of *noninvestment* values inhering in the *control* alone. Yet the one puzzle has absolutely nothing to do with the other, except for the happenstance of being in the same 'control-stock' box. The investment value of 'control' stock has essentially nothing to do with the control, and everything to do with the stock. The noninvestment value of control 'stock,' correspondingly, has nothing to do with the stock, and everything to do with the control.

At this point a brief review of the '*investment* value of control stock' will facilitate this segregation of the '*noninvestment* value.' Begin with a paraphrase of the technically exact definition constructed with such particularity over so many pages:

> *The Investment Value of 'Control Stock' is the total worth of a given block of stock, composed of two elements: (1) The base value of the stock antedating the advent to the corporation of a new contrôleur and (2) The increment to the block attributable to the superadded talents of the new contrôleur.*

One does not find difficulty with the generic concept of 'investment value'—the worth inherent in the stock itself, dependent on the dollars-and-cents return in dividends and capital gain—but the specific limitation to 'control stock' mystifies, and rightly so, because it is a misnomer. Recall that the accession of a new contrôleur with his estimable contribution to the firm enhances the value of *all* stock equally, whether 'control' or otherwise, whoever the owner, however held. True, a 'control block' may happen to be the accidental concomitant of a transfer of control, may pass at the time of the appointment of a new contrôleur to head the firm. Yet the sale of such stock is *intrinsically* unconnected with the change of control. A new contrôleur at IBM would hardly refer his tenure to stock holdings—since he would have relatively none—but rather to the domination of the proxy and the share dispersal.

The crux of the concept of the *investment* value of 'control stock' was found to consist in the personal qualifications of the successor contrôleur, the difference between the corporation before and after. Technically, the totality of these new-contrôleur talents is the contrôleur increment:

> [T]he increase in value to all stock of a corporation referable exclusively to the proven abilities of a new contrôleur, that is, the differential between the contributions to corporate value of the outgoing and incoming contrôleur.
>
> —Chapter 8: The Investment Value of Control Stock, *supra* at 306.

This understood, the investment value, enhanced by the advent of a new contrôleur, is scarcely limited to any particular block of stock. The efforts—and predictable successes—of the new contrôleur are directed to the entire corporate entity and correspondingly increase the value of every single share, willy-nilly. Yet in the past this value has been erroneously attributed to the 'control stock' exclusively.

But the Court in *Porco*—and correspondingly Bluhdorn and his G+W—made no mention of the *investment* value of 'control stock.' 'Contrôleur increment' was not advanced as their rationale for the "premium for a block of control stock." They, and this present investigation, therefore, have no concern with the investment value.

Noninvestment Value

Arguably the subject of Judge Pollack's discussion, and of the instant study, is rather a set of control advantages "which reflects *merely the control potential* of that stock," those values which would flow from the later exercise of control, completely irrespective of any stock.

If one were to assume, arguendo but justifiably, a complete separation and segregation of control from stock (hence the impossibility of *investment,* and the necessity of *noninvestment,* value) what advantages attach—with control isolated and alone—to control itself? Begin with a tentative, even loose, working definition, with the objective of continual technical refinement over succeeding pages:

> The 'Noninvestment' Value of 'Control Stock' is the totality of those legitimate values which inhere in the power of control, "merely the control potential," (irrespective of, and in contradistinction to, the investment value, including particularly the contrôleur increment, of the concomitant stock) and flow from the right and duty to direct the corporation through the domination of the board of directors.

With the noninvestment-value puzzle alone left in the box, how put the pieces together in an intelligible pattern?

Judge Hincks on the trial level in *Feldmann* was deeply confused in his overall philosophy of corporate control—witness his reversal by the Second Circuit—but he nonetheless correctly knew that "the control potential" was in itself a value much to be desired. He sets the general scene, moreover, toward an item-for-item enumeration of the many species and subspecies of the genus "control potential."

> When the distribution of a corporate stock is such that as a practical matter under the corporate charter and by-laws a given block—whether a majority block or one somewhat less—can control the election of the directors, the power is one that may be utilized to control the corporate management. . . . It is obvious, I think, that some at least of the *specific applications of the power* have inherent value . . . .
>
> > —*Perlman v. Feldmann,* 129 F. Supp. 162, 184 (D. Conn. 1952) (emphasis added).

At another point Hincks expresses the same idea when he refers to "the incidents of the electoral power . . . which contributes value to the entire bundle of rights and powers."[205]

In the illustrious *Green Giant* in 1962 Judge Nordbye showed himself much of a mind with Hincks in his control philosophy. But he also fully appreciated—perhaps more realistically than Judge Hincks—the very real cash-money value of corporate control.

> No . . . shareholder could be expected to forego the power of control of a company of this size without receiving in return a consideration commensurate with the value of the control which he foregoes.
>
> > —*Honigman v. Green Giant Co.,* 208 F. Supp. 754, 758 (D. Minn. 1961).

Underlying this sweeping reference to "the power of control" Judge Nordbye had before his mind's eye, and also in the *Green Giant* briefs, a methodical—some might even call it a Machiavellian— itemization of those "specific applications of the power" to which Hincks referred.

The Glore, Forgan Report

When the Cosgrove family finally realized that their Green Giant could grow no taller without a healthy infusion of the green of public dollars, they consulted Glore, Forgan & Co., the Chicago brokerage house, (impellingly redolent of Ko-Ko's consultation with

Pooh-Bah, as private secretary, or perhaps more apropos as his solicitor, anent his nuptials) toward an estimate of the dollar value of their control over Green Giant. In the event, Glore, Forgan and Judge Nordbye both concluded to the premium of roughly $2 million ("Although there are broad limits to the control power . . . , and hence to its value, there is no question that this value is real and substantial"[206]) even though the Cosgroves never actually parted with control, merely relinquished absolute-majority for equally effective mere-incumbency control. For nearly two decades thereafter they remained very much the contrôleur of Green Giant.

But arrestingly pertinent to the present purposes, the result of the Glore, Forgan counsel was the detailed 27-page report to the Green Giant board, that is, the Cosgrove family, detailing a "Plan of Recapitalization for the Green Giant Company," with unblushing emphasis on the *"Advantages . . . of Control."* These several pages were aimed at, and arguably were successful in, establishing, as Judge Nordbye put it, the "consideration commensurate with the value of the control" of Green Giant. Reducibly, therefore, the question was simple: What control advantages were worth $2.1 million to the Cosgroves? Even though the Cosgroves never handed them over.

It was as if the Glore, Forgan Report had set itself especially to search out and analyze Hincks's "specific applications of the power" of control. The opening paragraph, even its subheading, is certainly apposite to introduce a systematic breakdown of those "advantages of control" which constitute "merely the control potential," to wit, the noninvestment value of control.

> *Specific Areas of Advantage*
> In considering the advantages of control . . . we are not primarily concerned with advantages from the possible illegal actions [sic]. However, there are many possible actions which . . . are either legal or on the borderline. Specific plans of such action are as follows.
> —Glore, Forgan Report, Record on Appeal at 338, *Honigman v. Green Giant Co.,* 309 F.2d 667 (8th Cir. 1962).

The Control Advantages Specified

The Glore, Forgan Report will serve as a matrix, but no more, for the development of a comprehensive pattern of those values flowing from "merely the control potential." Remember, especially when the Report strays too near "the borderline," that all illegitimate objectives have by postulate been excluded from present consideration. Moreover, this capitulation is neither all-inclusive nor hierarchical as to importance.

"Adverse Contracts"[207]

Glore, Forgan was "not *primarily* concerned with advantages from the possible illegal actions."[208] But if such contracts are truly "adverse," the Report has already stepped well over "the borderline." In fact, the border line becomes more like a tightrope as the Report describes these contracts.

> Entering into contracts with suppliers or agents owned by the [controlling] stockholders could be advantageous. However, opportunities to do this are probably limited and the advantages small. Contracts not made on an arms-length bargaining basis would certainly be open to attack.
>
> —Glore, Forgan Report, Record on Appeal at 339, *Honigman v. Green Giant Co.,* 309 F.2d 667 (8th Cir. 1962).

Assuredly the law would attack any contract that did not insist on a legitimate quid for the corporate quo. The power, however, to allocate many kinds of corporate contracts, even on stringently legitimate terms, can be highly beneficial to an incumbent contrôleur.

As with suppliers so too with consumers. Judge Hincks ranked such contract allocation high on his list of desiderata.

> Turning to another specific application of the power of corporate control . . . , it is obvious, I think, that the power to control the selection of the customers is a factor adding materially to the value of the block of stock to which the power is appurtenant. It is another one of the incidents of the electoral power of stock which contributes value to the entire bundle of rights and powers which is wrapped in a control block of stock.
>
> —*Perlman v. Feldmann,* 129 F. Supp. 162, 184 (D. Conn. 1952).

If one were to concede—probably unjustifiably—the legitimacy of the Feldmann plan of interest-free prepayments by end-users of Newport's steel during the Korean gray market, these "corporate opportunities"[209] might be classed as a licit control advantage.

"Liquidation"

"The not unusual practice of obtaining control in order to secure a capital gain by liquidating the Company"[210] *could be* a perfectly legal maneuver if two prerequisites were satisfied: (1) Statutory compliance with liquidation provisions and (2) The fairness of any plan. Liquidation was the objective in the 1910 Pennsylvania *Commonwealth Title v. Seltzer,* in which the Continental Hotel Company possessed as its sole asset a valuable piece of real estate. (The sale of control in *Seltzer* was struck down for reasons other than the projected liquidation itself.)

"Elimination of Dividends"

"The cutting or elimination of dividends to avoid personal income taxes"[211] would seem to be clearly over the border line. As Glore, Forgan admits:

> Furthermore, if the case were extreme the Company might well develop problems with the Department of Internal Revenue.
>
> —Glore, Forgan Report, Record on Appeal at 339, *Honigman v. Green Giant Co.,* 309 F.2d 667 (8th Cir. 1962).

Perquisites

The use of the company jet, executive limousine or yacht, membership in city, country and boat clubs, "plus other perquisites of the office including such things as stock options, pensions, insurance coverage, et cetera,"[212] all are legitimate and highly desirable habiliments of the office of control. This is true even though the Report felt that:

> The areas in which control stock can exercise direction [discretion?] in the matter of granting of stock options

are not regarded as very important in view of existing law and generally accepted corporate practice.

> —Glore, Forgan Report, Record on Appeal at 339, *Honigman v. Green Giant Co.,* 309 F.2d 667 (8th Cir. 1962).

"Mergers and Consolidations"

"The practice of arranging mergers and consolidations advantageous to the controlling persons' outside interests might prove difficult to carry out. Minnesota law requires that all shareholders be notified of such proposed action."[213] Here again the Report seems properly skittish about its footwork.

> Although a certain amount of alertness would be needed, the [public] stockholders undoubtedly could block such actions by dissenting and demanding the fair cash value for their shares.
>
> —Glore, Forgan Report, Record on Appeal at 339, *Honigman v. Green Giant Co.,* 309 F.2d 667 (8th Cir. 1962).

A merger was the very legitimate objective in the Delaware *Manacher v. Reynolds* in 1960. In *Lionel,* to the contrary, Sonnabend had several illegitimate mergers in mind. In *Porter v. Healy* in Pennsylvania in 1914 the American Gas Company sought control of Pottstown Light toward its eventual absorption.

The Intangibles

At a certain point, purely financial considerations invariably give way to more subtle human urgings. Such natural drives are difficult of monetary evaluation, but nonetheless are powerful propellants toward corporate control. The triple incalculables: (1) Prestige, (2) Power, (3) Inner satisfaction of accomplishment, are foremost among control values. A dollar sign can be set opposite them only during ad hoc negotiations between corporation and incipient contrôleur.

"Management and Salaries"[214]

Glore, Forgan's brazen treatment of this most palpable of all legitimate control advantages has a certain collateral fascination that would seem to warrant full presentation:

The major advantage to the [controlling] stockholders which might be adverse to the interests of the [public] stockholders is the right to select the management and to establish salary levels. Even here there are certain practical limits to the extent of this advantage.

1. Obviously there are outside limits to the salaries which might be paid without becoming subject to court attack on the basis of violation of fiduciary responsibilities.

2. The action of replacing a large proportion of the officers of the Company with incompetent friends or relatives in the long run would be acting against the controlling party's own interest.

3. If such employees were capable, the action might not be adverse to the [public] stock unless the salaries were exhorbitant [sic]; that might be attacked in the courts.

From a practical standpoint, it would seem that the chief advantage of control is the right to elect the principal officer of the corporation and thereby to obtain the largest salary that could not be attacked in the courts plus other perquisites of the office including such things as stock options, pensions, insurance coverage, et cetera.

—Glore, Forgan Report, Record on Appeal at 340, *Honigman v. Green Giant Co.,* 309 F.2d 667 (8th Cir. 1962).

As with supplier and consumer contracts, salary awards both to self and friends or relatives can carry distinct and calculable benefits even though the corporation's right to a generous quid pro quo is scrupulously observed.

Corporate Improvement

One of the most subtle—and hence worthy of some later discussion—of all the values attaching to corporate control was mentioned by Judge Hincks in his attempt to present some "specific applications of the power."

For instance, to the usual minority stockholder in a corporation the value of his stock necessarily depends on earnings which in turn depend on the abilities of its management. But one considering the purchase of a control

block in a corporation may give less weight to past earnings since, if a change in management might be beneficial, the power to make such a change is in his hands. . . .
Surely this power through stock control *to improve the corporate performance* may be a factor of value attaching to
a control block of stock.

> —*Perlman v. Feldmann*, 129 F. Supp. 162,
> 184 (D. Conn. 1952) (emphasis
> added).

This opportunity to "improve the corporate performance" can be
viewed from many aspects, and so it will betimes. For the present,
classify it as one more legitimate reward of corporate control.

This conspectus of the legitimate—and one must be vigilant to
keep them so—advantages of control will constitute the wherewithal
in facing the question posed by Pollack in *Porco* and allegedly by
Bluhdorn, G + W and Fasco. These various specifications of "merely
the control potential" of the block of Brown stock can serve for ready
reference throughout. The first question, therefore, was indeed
answerable:

> [It is] possible to break down this "control potential" into
> its constituent—and salable—elements.
>
> > —Chapter 9: The Noninvestment Value of
> > Control Stock, *supra* at 344.

But what of the other questions?

> Once broken down, moreover, why do these control ele-
> ments belong exclusively to the "controlling stock-
> holder"? Why is there "no obligation under such
> circumstances to 'share and share alike'" with the 77-
> percent public shareholders?
>
> > —Chapter 9: The Noninvestment Value of
> > Control Stock, *supra* at 344.

I. Total Contrôleur Contribution

> [T]heir interest may lie less in the profit-making
> possibilities of the corporation in respect of which
> they have or seek control, and more in their ability

to direct the purchases or sales of the corporation
in the direction of some other interest . . . .

—Berle, *"Control" in Corporate Law,* 58
COLUM. L. REV. 1212, 1214
(1958).

Synthetic Stockman Nut and Rivet, Inc., had been the only child
of the three Stockman brothers. Based in Syracuse, Synthetic Stockman had a net worth of $150 million, ranked 482 in *Fortune's* select
500 industrials, and generally enjoyed the highest respect in the
community. But, retired and now in their midseventies, the three
brothers faced a delicate control problem with their firm.

Some ten years earlier the three had decided, after some 40
years at the grindstone, that their startling successes with Synthetic
Stockman warranted the sun and leisure of Lauderdale. Their solution to their dilemma—and also to their problem of preserving and
increasing SS's assets for the benefit of their joint charity—had been
a voting trust holding the third interests of each. The voting trustee
had been a 'hard charger,' much in the Stockman mold, who had
prosecuted the corporate *bonum commune* with the same successes
of the halcyon days. But the idyll was now threatened with the reluctant resignation—the ten-year term of the trust was expiring—of
their 'hard charger' contrôleur. Who to succeed to the office?

The headhunters were put on the spoor and the field for a successor contrôleur was narrowed to two, a Stockman relative and a
brash interloper by the name of J. Peter Cocca. The Stockmans had
determined to reinstate the voting trust, but with the added provision
in a joint will that the new contrôleur would carry on after the brothers' death under a new strict trust and appoint his successor, and thus
ad infinitum.

Successor Suitability

The years of experience had given the Stockmans a very crystallized concept of the manifold qualifications required of a competent
contrôleur of Synthetic Stockman, or for that matter of any corporation. As sole owners they were not bedeviled by any moral or legal
fiduciary duty to strive to select the most competent personnel, especially the successor contrôleur—not that they were blind to the interests of their charity—but the brothers were, nevertheless,

determined that their appointee meet the elemental, fivefold norm of successor suitability: (1) Moral integrity, (2) Intellectual competence, (3) Managerial and organizational proficiency, (4) Social suitability and (5) Satisfactory age and health.

The Stockmans were astute observers of human nature. In both young Cocca and the aspirant Stockman, the brothers saw highly capable competitors. Both were honest to a fault. There would be no walking "the borderline," let alone any concern, even secondarily, "with advantages from the possible illegal actions." As to talents it was a toss-up. Both moreover could be expected to work long devoted hours. Finally, since neither would-be contrôleur owned any stock, neither would be tempted to minority-shareholder-serving maneuvers.

In a word, each would bring to the corporate bargaining table substantial assets in the form of contrôleur talents. Although each had different personal qualifications, the total contrôleur contribution of each to the corporation would indeed constitute valuable consideration in the negotiation of the employment contract.

A resolution of the quandary of equal suitability was found in interviews and negotiations with the prospective contrôleurs.

II. Total Corporate Compensation

> The interest of prospective purchasers of controlling shares typically springs from a belief that increased profits may be made from innovations in product or in production or merchandising policies; and under competition society gains when such beliefs may freely be put to the test. From this viewpoint one may question the desirability of a legal rule which would restrict such transfers of control.
>
> —Comment, *Sale of Corporate Control,*
> 19 U. CHI. L. REV. 869, 871
> (1952).

Over against the respective talents offered by the candidates— the totality of services *to* the corporation—the Stockmans decided to lay out the corresponding corporation consideration—the totality of compensation *by* the corporation—notably the "specific areas of advantage" surrounding the office of control of Synthetic Stockman Nut and Rivet, Inc.

Since each prospect presented comparable credentials—and the Stockmans had estimated the contrôleur contribution of each *to* the corporation to be worth $130,000—and since the demands of the office were both stable and estimable, the Stockmans offered an identical package of *tangible* inducements to both. The predecessor's salary of $100,000 was to be augmented by a sliding scale of profit-based bonuses. Since SS's $100 million in annual sales would predictably increase at the recent 10-percent rate, this could net at least $10,000 in the early years. Beyond the usual perquisites—the firm's boat, the company Cadillac, an executive assistant—SS had usually underwritten the initiation fee and 75 percent of the annual dues at both the Century Club and the Onondaga Country Club. The outgoing contrôleur had placed these collateral benefits at $3,000 a year. Group health and life policies, the pension plan and stock options exercisable for the life of the trust totaled another $7,000. As the Stockman brothers saw it, in *tangibles* alone the corporation's offer would total roughly $120,000 per year in compensation. The corporation, then, would offer each aspirant an identical amount in total *tangible* compensation for an identical personal contribution in total services and talents.

The Intangible Negotiations

Here lay the resolution of the quandary of the equality of aspirant talents. Begin with young Stockman. In a highly communicative meeting with the Stockman scion, the three old brothers realized that their cousin, even without a single share of Synthetic Stockman, was driven by a deeply sincere—and to the brothers a highly creditable—desire to build the firm that bore his name to a position of preeminence in the nut-and-rivet world. ("At least, it is worth $5,000 a year if they let me see this outfit succeed.") With thoughts of loco parentis the three old Stockmans were not unhappy. To them here was the pure altruist with only one thought, to build for the benefit of others.

Apart from this Robin Hood, man-on-the-white-horse approach young Stockman anticipated a certain personal, almost Germanic, satisfaction in the hard work, the palpable progress, the orderly organization of his very own creature. ("Their offer goes up another $5,000 just for the privilege of doing things in my own precise way.") Young Stockman agreed with Judge Hincks:

> Surely this power through . . . control to improve the corporate performance may be a factor of value attaching to . . . control . . . .
>
> —*Perlman v. Feldmann,* 129 F. Supp. 162, 184 (D. Conn. 1952).

Thus the *intangible* compensation flowing to Stockman reached $10,000.

The upshot of the interview: All four Stockmans agreed that the total, tangible and intangible, corporate remuneration of $130,000 should adequately compensate young Stockman for his total contrôleur contribution—services and talents, worth $130,000 —to the future of Synthetic Stockman Nut and Rivet, Inc.

As a study in human energy and ambition, Cocca was even more interesting. He had had no connection whatsoever with Synthetic Stockman. Not only was he shareless, but he would come from an archcompetitor, and had been acquainted with the company only on a business basis. Further, apart from equal qualifications, Cocca was the antipolar extreme to Stockman. While Stockman could put a $5,000 price tag on the opportunity to enhance the family name, Cocca saw the same value in the chance to build a personal empire. Cocca was a lineal descendant of Samuel Insull, the Van Sweringens and the Rockefellers. His modern counterparts headed up Genesco, IT&T, City Investing, Textron. Synthetic Stockman Nut and Rivet, Inc., would soon become SSNR Industries, Inc., and each new acquisition would be one more diadem for the Cocca royal head.

Beyond this sense of power, this absolute authority, Cocca was ready to admit that the prestige of the position—contrôleur, chairman of the board, chief executive officer of 'SSNR Industries, Inc.'— was as good as another $5,000 in the bank. Synthetic Stockman was a prestigious name in Syracuse. Its top executives had long been civic notables. All this added dollars to the corporate offer.

But Cocca parted company with young Stockman on another important item of control value. Cocca saw a very attractive program of self-advancement and self-benefit in the day-in-and-day-out allocation of the many corporate contracts with suppliers, consumers, top-level executives. Not that Cocca was dishonest. To the contrary. He had no thought of even approaching the Glore, Forgan border line. He reasoned this way: It would be worth $10,000 a year personally to appoint a hitherto unknown, albeit impressively competent, 'comer' to the presidency of the firm, to help out a struggling but honest die manufacturer, to assure a certain construction company of a fair deal and a steady source of rivets. In every instance the deal would be a rigid quid pro quo with absolutely no conflict of interest, but the legitimate advantage would be nonetheless appreciable, even if unconscionably long-range.

The Premium for Control

With the cards thus on the table, the three Stockmans, and young Cocca, sensed that the *intangibles* in the corporate offer were far more valuable—$10,000 more—to Cocca than to young Stockman. Whereas SS offered each exactly $120,000 in tangible remuneration, the corporation could pay Cocca a full $10,000 more in intangibles. Taking stock within himself, J. Peter Cocca had realized this difference when he compared in dollars and cents the total emolument he would personally receive from SS—a figure of $140,000 per annum in corporate compensation, tangible and intangible— with SS's comparable offer to Stockman, which totaled only $130,000. The $10,000 annual differential in the corporation's offer impressed Cocca with his superior bargaining position. After much calculation he concluded that $50,000—the annual differential accumulated over a five-year period—would be a sensible investment toward "the control potential" that would predictably extend well beyond such a short tenure.

Armed with this conviction, and an almost oppressive desire to control 'SSNR Industries, Inc.,' Cocca approached the three Stockmans with a proposition: He would accept the contrôleurship of Synthetic Stockman on the terms discussed *and,* to cinch the deal, therewith agree to pay the three brothers a $50,000 premium for the control of the company. Cocca was almost childlike in his forthright enumeration of the many control values he sought. Knowing that SS regarded its offers to each as identical—at least the tangible offers— Cocca was convinced that the premium would win the day. The three brothers were not unimpressed.

Confident of young Cocca's honesty, ability and above all his driving ambition for the firm, the founders and owners of Synthetic Stockman Nut and Rivet, Inc., had already determined that young Cocca embodied all five requisites of contrôleur suitability, and was definitely the man for the job. But what of his premium for control?

The Fatuity of the Premium

They could not, however, restrain a wry smile at the proffer of the premium for control. Cocca was almost callow in his inability to correlate the proffered premium with the collateral contract of contrôleur employment. As they pointed out to Cocca, they were, after all, the sole owners of SS, and all the corporate assets were effectively theirs. Moreover, SS had just formulated a deal whereby the corporation would pay him some $140,000 consideration in exchange for his labor and industry. Every item of this consideration—whether salary, perquisites, options or pensions, whether the intangibles of power, prestige or contract allocation—was a corporate asset flowing under the contract from SS to Cocca. How fatuous, therefore, for the three brothers to receive $50,000 from Cocca with one hand while paying him twice that amount in salary with the other.

The simple solution: Set off the 'premium' against the tangible dollars of the salary, and thereby maintain the original stipulation of $130,000 in corporate remuneration. Thus reduced, the total corporate compensation would equal Cocca's total contrôleur contribution to the company. Merely prorate the $50,000 'premium' over the five-year period, and cut the salary accordingly to $90,000 per annum.

True, salary, perquisites, prestige, power, are all estimable and legitimate control values. As valuable, they are salable. Cocca could do well to 'buy' every one of them by 'paying' a substantial 'price' for their 'purchase.' But since the corporation is the owner of each, since only the owner sells, and since the corporation disburses these very assets to Cocca for his work for the firm—they form the congeries of emolument at the disposal of the corporation for the remuneration of the incumbent contrôleur—Cocca should 'pay' the 'premium for control' to the owner, by lowering his salary in the agreed amount. Any 'premium' should be recognized as simply such a deduction, an acknowledgment that the corporate remuneration had been too great.

After this circuitous return to reality, the Stockmans and young Cocca closed the deal at $90,000 in salary, plus $40,000 per annum in fringe benefits, tangible and intangible. Which was the same total amount—$100,000 in salary, plus $30,000—SS would have paid young Stockman, had he won the day.

The Stock-Enhancement Factor

Vary the suppositions of the mythical Synthetic Stockman in one particular, but otherwise leave all the facts intact. Assume, in the fairy-book Stockmans/Stockman formula, that the brothers Stockman, then dreaming of the day now arrived, had each bestowed at the young Stockman's birth a third of a share of SS on their newborn cousin and heir apparent. Thus, now some three decades later, the Stockman scion approaches the same bargaining table armed with his same high ideals, family aspirations, overall contrôleur suitability, but holding in his hand a further factor of moving importance, his one share—one percent, $1.5-million worth—of Synthetic Stockman Nut and Rivet, Inc.

Granted, the total ownership of SS had scarce been altered. Each brother still owned a third, and the one percent against the 99 would change the bargaining impact not a whit. But to young Stockman—apart from any clout at the table—that one share gave rise to an appreciable dollars-and-cents consideration as he totted up the several "advantages of control" and estimated his total corporate compensation from SS.

This stock-enhancement thought was not lost on Stockman. Quick arithmetic showed him the full situation. If his own considerable contrôleur talents could up SS's annual five-percent after-tax return to seven—as he was ready to gamble they would—his personal extra annual increment would be $30,000 on his $1.5-million holding. Were he to forgo an annual $10,000 of that $30,000 to guarantee his appointment—and hence his stock increment—the net would still be a yearly $20,000 beyond his return at the firm's present pace. Moving further in his calculations, Stockman decided on a five-year gamble (of the annual $10,000) for an accumulated $50,000 toward the projected $150,000 extra increment, especially since his youth gave every prospect of many years longer than five.

From this point forward the drama took on all the aspects of a replay of the Cocca negotiations. Cumulating the annual $10,000 in stock-enhancement compensation, Stockman, as had Cocca, proffered a $50,000 premium for the control of SS.

Once again came the same wry smile, the same restrained wonder at the callowness of youth, the same patient explanation of the realities of the relation between Stockman's contrôleur contribution, labor, industry, honesty, and SS's corporate compensation, salary, perquisites, power, prestige, and now the opportunity to enhance the value of his one-percent 'block.' The upshot was the same. Young Stockman realized that this extra control advantage should be 'paid for' not with a $50,000 premium, but rather by a simple reduction of the stipulated $100,000 in salary. With that deal sealed, family considerations prevailed and Stockman became contrôleur with compensation at $130,000, tangible and intangible, which was the same amount SS would have paid Cocca, had he won the day. The further absurdity occurred to them all: To the extent of his ownership of SS, Stockman would in effect be paying a premium to himself.

Thus this 'opportunity' "to improve the corporate performance" is merely another asset in the corporate treasury, available on proper occasion for disbursement as contrôleur compensation. Note, however, that this particular 'opportunity to improve the firm'—the stock-enhancement factor—is not the same 'control value' as either the Robin Hood's pleasure in helping the firm or the Germanic satisfaction in building, both of which are 'control values' and could also both be properly called the 'opportunity' "to improve the corporate performance."

This addition of the stock-enhancement factor should complete the list of those "advantages" flowing from "merely the control potential" of the office.

III. The Ownership of the Control Assets

Contrary to the position evidenced by most state courts, that sale of control at a premium is permissible provided the transaction does not fall

> within any of the recognized exceptions, several
> commentators have suggested that the general rule
> permitting sale of control at a premium is
> wrong.
>
> —Schiff, *Sale of Control,* 32 BUS. LAW.
> 507, 509 (1977) (citing Berle, Jen-
> nings, Andrews and Bayne).

Implicit in these SS fantasies has been a realization—too arcane for the past—that could well dispel much of the confusion clouding the concept of control value. Both parties to the Synthetic Stockman contract fully sensed, albeit subliminally, the governing truth that all these control advantages belonged without exception to the corporation, that the contrôleur personally did not produce any of these assets for himself, that all were for the firm. But this is only half the matter. The other half of the Stockman perception was a series of subtle distinctions far at the base of the various corporate-control values. An exact analysis of these distinctions should give deeper understanding to the Stockman negotiations, and the noninvestment value of control stock.

Corporate Administration

In the theoretical, but very real, beginning of every corporation the shareholder owners in a deliberate appropriation entrust the corporate assets to the untrammeled dominion of that necessary top-level authority, the contrôleur. In acquiescing to this appropriation the contrôleur thereby assumes custody of the entity, with all its duties and rights. Technically, therefore, corporate control is a relation of total custody subsisting between the subjective term, the office of control, and the objective term, the corporate entity itself. In this office of control inhere all the corporate rights and duties. In accepting this stewardship the contrôleur dedicates himself unremittingly to the overall corporate welfare. He acknowledges himself a strict trustee and accepts the stringencies of the Benefit-to-Beneficiary and No Inquiry Rules. His sole undertaking: To administer the corporation and utilize its assets to the exclusive advantage of the shareholder owners.

In this administration of the corporation *ad bonum commune* the contrôleur, as the chief corporate agent, has been burdened with the complexus of corporate duties originally imposed by the state, at the instance of the incorporators, and enumerated in the corporate purposes and powers of the charter. These corporate duties have become necessarily the contrôleur's duties. Thus, for example, Sears has formally undertaken a broad public service. The duties incurred by this undertaking are legion, from the vast retailing empire and the insurance services of Allstate to the real-estate network of Coldwell Banker and the supermarket service of the Dean Witter investment and brokerage organization.

Set off against these manifold duties is a perfectly correlative set of corporate rights, ranging from the appointment of top executives—including incidentally, if need be, a successor contrôleur—to the allocation of major contracts with suppliers and consumers, the negotiation of complex financial deals, on down to the employment of clerks, insurance and real-estate salesmen and stockbrokers.

All these rights and duties inhere essentially in the corporate entity. Incumbent on the entity is the performance, through its agents, of this broad corporate obligation of public service, and all the subobligations implicit in it. Correspondingly, to the corporate entity attach all the rights necessary for the performance, through its agents, of all the corporate duties. Sitting as he is at the top of the corporate hierarchy, the contrôleur, therefore, must see to the performance of these duties, the exercise of these rights, all to the entity's benefit and the consequent benefit of the shareholder beneficiaries.

The office of control—in the person of the contrôleur and as representative of the entity—possesses the totality of these corporate rights and duties. In fact the ambit of the contrôleur's official authority and responsibility—the limits of his job—is coterminous with the rights and duties of the corporation as spelled out, or implicit, in its charter. The contrôleur is hired to prosecute the corporate goals by performing the corporate rights and duties. Thus all the rights of the contrôleur qua contrôleur are control rights. And all the duties, control duties. Because of the virtual identification of the contrôleur with his office, and the corresponding relation of the office to the entity, this is a justifiable viewpoint for the study of the noninvestment control values.

The Direct Returns of Corporate Control

In going about his day-to-day duties the contrôleur is presumably visited with some success. The enlightened managerial policy of Sears's contrôleur produces an upswing in the earnings record, and healthy profits for dividends or expansion. A sound corporate structure encourages investment and hence capital increment. The selection of aggressive personnel increases further the profit potential and ultimately augments the assets. All these advantages flowing from contrôleur endeavors in the corporate behalf are by no means limited to high-level administration but include the most menial, from the productivity of the Sears Tower personnel in Chicago to the devoted labors of the thousands of employees the world over. But all these returns—profits and capital increment—from the energy of the contrôleur are very real control values and are directly and primarily referable to the performance of the corporation's duties and the exercise of its rights under the contrôleur's general guidance.

The Indirect Advantages

But the corporate rewards of the contrôleur's industry are not all primary and direct. The competent contrôleur creates a corporate climate that encompasses a broad list of assets of extreme value to the company. Thanks to the same enlightened managerial policy, all the employees—from the lowliest salesman on up even to the contrôleur himself—enjoy their work, feel the exhilaration of accomplishment, the satisfaction of good working conditions, the prestige of their positions with Sears, or possibly reap the legitimate by-products of contract allocation, managerial appointments, customer selection, or even the enhancement of their Sears stock. A solid corporate structure plus superb personnel gradually effect a substantial going-concern value and notable corporate goodwill. All these collateral benefits are corporate assets adding to the overall worth of the firm.

The utilization by the contrôleur of the control rights and the performance of the control duties, therefore, result in a broad spectrum of benefits, products, profits, the sum of corporate assets produced through the corporate administration entrusted to the office of control. The totality of these benefits, *direct* and *indirect*, represents the totality of control advantages, the collective fruit of the custodial administration of the corporation, the exercise of control. Quite clearly this totality is by no means limited to those "control advantages" laid out in the Stockman—or Glore, Forgan—list. Some of these values flow from the labor expended toward the direct and primary objectives of the corporate business, some are secondary and collateral gains. But *all* are the result of official corporate effort. All are produced by corporate agents on corporate time toward the corporate well-being pursuant to the charter purposes, and ultimately under the direction of the corporate contrôleur. All consequently are corporate assets. Here, then, is the totality of control values.

The Rights of the Human Person

But how dovetail these corporate duties and rights into the personal rights and duties of the humans—especially the human contrôleur—who man the entity? Generally speaking, all the employees, from janitor, telephone operator, salesman on up to the chief executive officer and finally the contrôleur, come to their jobs at Sears with the same class of personal duties and rights. Their duty is fivefold: To be honest, adequately intelligent, industrious and proficient, socially adaptable, physically fit. In a word, to do their best for the firm. Their rights are corresponding: To receive sufficient salary, health-and-retirement benefits, the respect and dignity of the position, the satisfaction and exhilaration of the job, the opportunity to improve the firm.

Thus the duty and right to sell the clothes, the insurance, the home, the securities, belong to Sears. The duty and right to represent Sears in the performance of its duty and right belong to the employee. For the performance of his personal duty—labor, honesty, industry—Sears recognizes the employee's personal right to salary, perquisites, prestige and power. In fulfilling, as agent, the corporate duties and exercising the corporate rights, the employee, including the contrôleur, earns his appropriate compensation disbursed from the corporate assets, whether from the store of direct control assets, e.g., salary, options, perquisites, or the indirect, e.g., prestige, power, satisfaction.

The Corporate vis-à-vis the Personal

At this point the sharp control-value dichotomy, the direct and the indirect, plus the setoff of personal from corporate rights and duties, prompt the introduction into the control lexicon of two new technical terms embodying these various distinctions:

> *Personal Control Advantages* are corporate-control values flowing either primarily and directly or secondarily and collaterally from the performance of official corporate duties and rights, and *passed on by the corporation to the human occupant of the office of control* as his total corporate compensation for the performance of his personal duties and rights.

Over against these strictly personal rewards of control are other concomitant corporate benefits:

> *Corporate Control Returns* are corporate-control values flowing either primarily and directly or secondarily and collaterally from the performance of official corporate duties and rights, and *necessarily retained in the corporate net worth.*

In both cases, *Personal Control Advantages* and *Corporate Control Returns,* these control values are corporate assets accruing to the corporation as a result of corporate effort expended toward the corporate welfare. In the former, the corporation simply sees fit to disburse these corporate assets, direct or indirect, to the person holding the position of control, as recompense for a job well done. In the latter, the corporation retains necessarily the benefits, direct or indirect, as the sought-for fruits of the corporate program toward profit making. The key concepts are *disbursal* and *retention.* Nothing else distinguishes them. Both are species of the genus *Corporate-Control Values,* corporate assets broadly referable to the overall corporate administration of the contrôleur. Ultimately, of course, and here is the catch in the whole piece, all these 'control values' are simply subproducts of the total corporate product viewed, by force of the multiform problems raised by the sale of control, from the slightly forced aspect of the person who happens to hold the office of control, or the one who wants to 'buy' it.

But in the view of any other observer, these values are no more 'control values' than they are directorial values or chief-executive-officer values or presidential values. They are simply corporate assets. Nothing more. But over the decades contrôleurs have tried to sell them off as if they were really their own personal possessions, as if 'control value' meant an asset belonging to the human in control rather than an asset produced under the corporate administration of the office of control. Hence a spate of misnomers and a botch of fallacies. Which leads to the last major point.

IV. The Sale-of-Control Premium-Bribe

> There's nothing illegal about giving control-block stockholders a better deal than ordinary stockholders. That's life.
>
> —Sloan, *Waiting for the Dough,* FORBES, Apr. 27, 1981, at 33.

For the last time, recur to Synthetic Stockman Nut and Rivet, Inc., and make two last, but major, alterations in that hardy hypothetical. As before, the brothers Stockman—founders of the firm, joint holders of every voting-trust certificate, long ready to retire—face the imminent expiration of the voting trust and the vexing necessity of selecting a successor contrôleur to guide the firm's future. Both the Stockman scion and the aggressive young Cocca are again in the wings, ready to serve.

But beyond all this, everything is not the same. The ten years of the trust had not been kind to the three Stockmans. Pressed by parlous times, each succeeding year had seen their personal finances fail. The regretful solution: A sizable stock split, 10,000 for one, and a successful public offering of their entire 99 percent. Since each sale was extremely small and, more to the point, the purchasers were widely scattered, none of the new owners held more than two percent of the company. Thus the three brothers, although completely shareless, nonetheless held unassailable mere-incumbency control through the proxy mechanism and the wide dispersal. But to their dismay they also held the awesome and onerous obligation of entrusting $150 million in other people's money into the unfettered hands of a new contrôleur.

Onto this deeply altered scene walked Bernie Veswolf, *entrepreneur extraordinaire,* who knew a good thing when he saw one. Fully apprised of the many control values in SS's offer to Stockman and Cocca—and of possibilities as well that never occurred to these conscientious young men—Veswolf joined his name to the list of prospective contrôleurs, but with a difference. Whereas Stockman and Cocca had both seen the fatuity of their $50,000 premiums for control, Veswolf was not so perspicacious, or perhaps more so. Veswolf not only saw the 'control advantages' in the tangibles—salary, options, perquisites—and the intangibles—power, prestige, the opportunity to improve the firm—but he looked even beyond this $140,000. After all, the Stockman brothers would be gone on the morrow, and his mere-incumbency control would be absolute. He further knew as no one else the true worth of his talents, and saw no reason against a substantial salary increase at an early date. Glore, Forgan's words kept running through his mind:

> From a practical standpoint, . . . the chief advantage of control is . . . to obtain the largest salary that could not be attacked in the courts plus other perquisites of the office . . . .
>
> —Glore, Forgan Report, Record on Appeal at 340, *Honigman v. Green Giant Co.*, 309 F.2d 667 (8th Cir. 1962).

Veswolf tolled off a long litany of control values—especially contract allocations to cronies, large salaries for "incompetent friends or relatives," maybe even eventual liquidation—that were foreign to the thoughts of Stockman and Cocca. In a word, perhaps Veswolf was "not *primarily* concerned with advantages from the possible illegal actions," but his secondary concern was compelling. Nor did he fear stepping over the border line.

To give proper expression to these sentiments Bernie Veswolf concluded to an offer of a $100,000 sale-of-control premium, which he promptly presented to the brothers Stockman.

The Premium-Bribe

For the three Stockmans no astute argumentation was necessary to penetrate to the heart of Veswolf's deal. No need now to restrain a wry smile. No longer was it a case of three owners receiving

$100,000 with one hand while paying out the same amount in salary with the other. True, the owners would still be paying the salary—and the perquisites, power, prestige, whatever—but the owners would not be receiving the $100,000 premium. As with Stockman and Cocca, how fatuous not to set off the premium directly against the salary. But more pertinently, how dishonest to pay the premium to the nonowners Stockman when it belonged to the owner shareholders scattered across the country.

Here was nothing other than the primitive sale-of-control premium-bribe:

> (1) Some form of consideration, monetary or otherwise, (2) Flowing to the incumbent contrôleur, (3) From or on behalf of the prospective contrôleur, (4) To induce the appointment to the office of control, (5) Paid knowingly, scienter.
>
> —Chapter 5: The Sale of Control and the Premium-Bribe, *supra* at 171.

Armed with this realization, and all the implications of the unsuitability of a premium-briber—particularly his predictable propensity to recoup his premium-bribe at the expense of a hapless ownership—the three Stockmans threw the charlatan out and betook themselves to their old problem of choosing between their cousin and his competitor.

Fatuity Becomes Fraud

The innocent and callow 'sale-of-control premium' of the SS aspirants ceases to be merely fatuous and becomes downright dishonest when the payment goes not to the owner but to a noncorporate third party. It becomes singularly shocking when that third party is a trusted agent who has dedicated himself to the very owners he is cheating. The *factual* nub of the premium-bribe, therefore, is the payment of a 'rebate'—otherwise merely foolishly circuitous—to the wrong person.

One may admit to certain personal advantages flowing from the office of control. As valuable, they may be 'sold.' But if 'sold,' the 'sellers' must invariably be the owners. When they in truth were the owners, the Stockmans could have entered into the ridiculous circuity of a 'sale of control.' No matter. If the new public owners of Synthetic Stockman want to indulge in a similar absurdity, also no matter. But if the nonowners Stockman attempt to 'sell' the control they no longer 'own'—or Veswolf attempts to 'buy' it—the result is aggravated larceny in the subtle and oft undetected guise of premium-bribery. Imbedded in this larceny is the triple turpitude, the intrinsic illegitimacy of the premium-bribe:

> (1) The perversion of the judgment of the incumbent contrôleur, engendered by an appointment of a successor induced by a cause other than suitability, (2) That is, for consideration illicit in itself, (3) Resulting in the appointment of a candidate unsuitable by reason of his own active role in the inducement.
>
> —Chapter 6: The Sale-of-Control Premium: The Intrinsic Illegitimacy, *supra* at 204-05.

V. The Analysis in Summary

> It is to be hoped that either now or eventually the courts will give legal recognition to the widespread belief in the business community that a sale of control shares should be accompanied by a general offer, and thus reject the philosophy that, in this situation, the right to a special profit is simply a perquisite of control.
>
> —Jennings, *Trading in Corporate Control*, 44 Calif. L. Rev. 1, 39 (1956).

With all the distinctions and subdivisions, the correlatives and the antitheticals in the background, what can be said overall of *'The Noninvestment Value of Control Stock,'* and the many concepts and subconcepts surrounding it? Concisely, what is the exact import of the subject? The answer lies in an orderly process of exclusion and refinement, a step-by-step narrowing from general to specific, down to the point of an intelligible, and practical, delineation of a major burden of this study. Conclude with a recap.

Control Value

Here probably is the chief devil in the piece. 'Control value' is so hopelessly generic a term as to be practically useless. It includes everything, legitimate/illegitimate, stock/nonstock, investment/noninvestment, direct/indirect, anything in any way pertaining to any benefits, advantages, values, inuring to corporation or contrôleur or anyone, through the impact of corporate control. Further, it is indeterminate about the ownership of these values. Are they 'owned'? And if owned, may they be sold? And if salable, who may sell them? Or buy them? The use, or misuse, of the term has left court and commentator in an ill-defined state of chaos. Witness *Feldmann* and *Porco.* In short, 'control value' should be condemned to oblivion, except as an introductory phrase demanding immediate technical qualification.

Illegitimate Control Values

The first such technical qualification must be the elimination from consideration of all illegitimate returns milked from and through the office. Strictly, such returns are not properly referable to control at all, but are simple larceny effected in a control context. Any gain even secondary from "the possible illegal actions" or activity along "the borderline" should be and is outside the definition of 'control value.'

The Investment Value of Control Stock

The next narrowing saw the exclusion from the concept of 'control value' of that possible increment to the stock itself—*stock about to be purchased*—attributable to the advent of a talented new contrôleur. Here, the adjective 'control' is a transposed epithet which properly modifies neither 'stock' nor 'value' but applies exclusively to the changed quality of the corporate administration. The *'control change'* heightens the investment value of all stock. Control administration benefits the entire entity. Since the entity is merely the conduit for every shareholder interest, any such gains flow perforce to all equally. This 'investment value' applies to every share, not just those about to be sold, whether 'control' or no, by whomever. As only remotely related to 'control,' 'investment value' is scarcely a 'control value,' or at best only in some metonymic sense. Such use without immediate qualification, therefore, is also anathema.

The Noninvestment Value of Control Stock

Whereas 'investment value' referred solely to the purchased stock and not at all to the distant 'control,' the 'noninvestment value of control stock' refers only to control and not a bit to the 'stock.' To a great extent their connection is an historical anachronism. In earlier days a controlling block generally accompanied a control transfer. Even today control is often passed by a 50-plus-percent stock block. Strictly, however, control itself is not connected necessarily with the stock. 'Control' is exercisable without relation to the base on which its tenure is founded, whether voting trust, proxy, mere incumbency, however. Control can be total without any stock at all, e.g., of IBM.

With the 'stock' thus removed, the subject now becomes "The Noninvestment Value of Control." But is not 'noninvestment' also superfluous? After all, it was used only to negate the concept of 'investment' and eliminate any connection with the stock. With 'stock' gone, why talk of 'noninvestment' at all? Investment is only in stock, perforce. Absent the need to eradicate the historical anachronism, both words are unnecessary. The elimination of both 'noninvestment' and 'stock' leaves a better title: The Value of Control.

Corporate-Control Assets

Thus circumscribed, the proper perspective begins to appear. The only 'values' correctly denominated 'control' are those corporate benefits, products, profits, produced through the control administration. As such, every last one of them is a corporate asset. But when the average layman—if ever he were to blunder onto the term—refers to 'the noninvestment value of control stock'—or better, 'the value of control'—he would never mean *all* the corporate-control assets. The concept is still too inclusive.

Corporate Control Returns

Even though they are in every sense 'control assets,' those corporate returns from the contrôleur's administration retained in the corporate net worth—annual profits, capital increment, going-concern value—are never referred to as 'control values.' Why? Although ultimately *produced* by the work of the contrôleur—and to this extent 'control values'—they are not *paid out* to him personally, thus never become doubly the contrôleur's own. The discussion of corporate control returns was necessary only to distinguish them from the last remaining class of 'control values.'

Personal Control Advantages

Here then is the end of the line. Some corporate assets, once in the corporate treasury through the contrôleur's efforts—hence 'control values'—are then *disbursed* to the contrôleur himself in payment for his work for the firm. These are the 'control values,' doubly so in a sense, of which the layman—and the lawyer, judge, writer—should speak. The technically correct title should then read: The Personal Control Advantages Accorded the Contrôleur as Corporate Compensation.

Two Parting Adversions

With the title thus changed and the concepts clarified, no further questions should arise about the ownership of these corporate assets, or their salability, or their purchase for a premium. As corporate assets originally and as contrôleur remuneration eventually, the thought of 'selling' or 'buying' them is fully as callow as the Stockman/Cocca $50,000 'premium' for the 'sale of control.'

Finally, equally otiose should be any discussion of the intrinsically illegitimate Veswolf premium-bribe. Granted the fatuity of the Stockman/Cocca 'premium,' at least the $50,000 was destined for the true owners. Veswolf on the contrary was prepared to pay an illicit $100,000 to nonowners Stockman, an act of premium-bribery.

All the misnomers strewn through this chapter—notably the title itself—and the fallacies behind them had their genesis, as with Hincks in *Feldmann*, Pollack in *Porco,* in one pervasive misconception: That *somewhere* amid all those control values—salary, perquisites, prestige, power, particularly the opportunity to improve the corporate performance—*something* must be the personal possession of the contrôleur himself. That somehow corporate control could legitimately be sold.

Which, of course, set the purpose of this chapter: To lay these misnomers and fallacies to rest once and for all. To show simply that the values resultant on control can never be sold, except by the owners. To establish above all that the contrôleur is not an owner, merely an employee. To prove that the contrôleur, as an employee, produced these assets for the corporation, not for himself personally. To convince, finally, that any ostensible 'sale' of these unowned assets—at the time of a transfer of control—is simply a not so subtle subterfuge for premium-bribery.

Epilogue

> As yet, the conception of control has not been up-dated to conform to existing conditions.
>
> —Berle, *"Control" in Corporate Law,* 58 COLUM. L. REV. 1212, 1214 (1958).

> The courts and legislatures have apparently accepted some of the theoretical underpinnings of the theories of Professors Berle and Bayne, although rejecting their ultimate solutions.
>
> —Hazen, *Transfers of Corporate Control,* 125 U. PA. L. REV. 1023, 1061 (1977).

The first hope for *The Philosophy of Corporate Control* has been to erect a substantial, complete, tenable, corpus of principles—to define at last the elusive 'fiduciary duty'—for the governance of the contrôleur in his most important role as the top-level officer of the corporation. Perhaps, now, in Mr. Berle's words, "the conception of control has . . . been up-dated to conform to existing conditions."

It has been the glory of both moral theology and the Anglo-American common law—understandably because both are the products of the same ethicolegal rational mind—that each succeeding thinking generation has refurbished, refined, expanded, the scholarly work of each earlier generation. The second hope, therefore, has been that *The Philosophy of Corporate Control* would be sufficiently cohesive and credible as to warrant the further study of scholars, thoughtful commentary, development, elaboration. Or at the worst, so the hope has gone, the Custodial Concept of Corporate

Control might elicit volumes of critical scrutiny toward the improvement of the law of corporate control and the fiduciary duty of the contrôleur.

As to the bench and bar, *The Philosophy of Corporate Control* will have to stand or fall on its merits.

Footnotes

The conventions of legal citation observed in the text are continued in the footnotes (*see* Prenote: The Mechanics). Readers requiring a complete entry should turn to the following Tables, where all cases and other literature noted here are repeated in full citation.

Chapter 1

1. Perlman v. Feldmann, 219 F.2d 173, 174 (2d Cir. 1955).

2. 129 F. Supp. 162, 186 (D. Conn. 1952).

3. 219 F.2d at 175.

4. *Id.* at 176 (quoting Cardozo, C.J., Meinhard v. Salmon).

5. *Id.* (quoting Schemmel v. Hill).

6. Honigman v. Green Giant Co., 208 F. Supp. 754, 762 (D. Minn. 1961).

7. Perlman v. Feldmann, 219 F.2d at 175.

8. *Id.* at 176.

9. *Id.* at 175.

10. *Id.*

11. *Id.* at 176 (quoting Schemmel v. Hill).

12. *Id.* (quoting Schemmel v. Hill).

13. *Id.*

14. *Id.* at 178.

15. Honigman v. Green Giant Co., 309 F.2d 667, 671 (8th Cir. 1962) (quoting the trial court).

16. 208 F. Supp. at 759.

17. *Id.* at 758.

18. 309 F.2d at 670.

Chapter 2

19. Bazelon, *Clients Against Lawyers,* Harper's, Sept. 1967, at 104, 112.

20. Sugden v. Crossland, 65 Eng. Rep. 620 (V.C. 1856).

21. *Id.* at 621.

22. *Id.*

23. Sept. 1964, at 139.

24. In re Caplan's Petition, 246 N.Y.S.2d 913, 915 (App. Div. 1964).

25. Gabriel Indus. v. Defiance Indus., N.Y.L.J., June 17, 1964, at 13, col. 8 (Sup. Ct., N.Y. County).

26. 65 Eng. Rep. at 621.

27. Lepaulle, *An Outsider's Viewpoint of the Nature of Trusts,* 14 Cornell L.Q. 52, 57 (1928).

28. T. Lewin, The Law of Trusts and Trustees 15 (London 1837).

29. Hoover, *Basic Principles Underlying Duty of Loyalty,* 5 Clev.- Mar. L. Rev. 7, 33 (1956).

30. 1 A. Scott, The Law of Trusts §2.6 (3d ed. 1967).

31. *Id.*

32. Lepaulle, *An Outsider's Viewpoint of the Nature of Trusts,* 14 Cornell L.Q. 52, 55 (1928).

33. Roman Catholic Bishop of Jaro v. De La Pena, 26 Phillipine 144, 146 (1913).

34. 1 A. Scott, The Law of Trusts §1, at 4 (3d ed. 1967).

35. Johnson, *Corporate Directors as Trustees in Illinois,* 23 Ill. L. Rev. 653, 670 (1929).

36. A. Berle, Studies in the Law of Corporation Finance 51 (1928).

37. 44 Harv. L. Rev. 1049 (1931).

38. N. Lattin & R. Jennings, Cases & Materials on Corporations 717 (3d ed. 1959).

39. Dodd, *For Whom Are Corporate Managers Trustees?*, 45 HARV. L. REV. 1145, 1157 (1932).

40. Scott, *The Fiduciary Principle*, 37 CALIF. L. REV. 539, 541 (1949).

41. Clapp, *A Fiduciary's Duty of Loyalty*, 3 MD. L. REV. 221 (1939).

42. *Id.* at 236.

43. *Id.* at 221-22.

44. RESTATEMENT (SECOND) OF TRUSTS §170(1), at 364 (1959).

45. 49 HARV. L. REV. 521 (1936).

46. Scott, *The Fiduciary Principle*, 37 CALIF. L. REV. 539, 540 (1949).

47. J. ROYCE, THE PHILOSOPHY OF LOYALTY 16 (1930) (emphasis omitted).

48. *Id.* at 15 (emphasis omitted).

49. Scott, *The Fiduciary Principle*, 37 CALIF. L. REV. 539, 555 (1949).

50. Roman Catholic Bishop of Jaro v. De La Pena, 26 Phillipine 144, 146 (1913).

51. Turner v. Bouchell's Ex'rs, 3 H. & J. 99, 106 (Md. 1810).

52. Willis, *Duties and Responsibilities of Trustees*, L. LIBR. 79 (1835).

53. *Id.* at 59.

54. *Id.*

55. *Id.* at 79.

56. Lepaulle, *An Outsider's Viewpoint of the Nature of Trusts*, 14 CORNELL L.Q. 52, 55 (1928).

57. Kilpatrick v. Penrose Ferry Bridge Co., 49 Pa. 118, 122 (1865).

58. Record on Appeal at 299, Honigman v. Green Giant Co., 309 F.2d 667 (8th Cir. 1962).

59. *Id.* at 300.

60. *Id.*

61. *Id.*

62. *Id.*

63. T. LEWIN, THE LAW OF TRUSTS AND TRUSTEES 376-77 (London 1837).

64. G. BOGERT, TRUSTS AND TRUSTEES §543, at 200 (rev. 2d ed. 1978) (quoting CAL. CIV. CODE §2233).

65. J. ROYCE, THE PHILOSOPHY OF LOYALTY 15 (1930).

66. *Luke* 16:8.

67. Metropolitan Elevated Ry. v. Manhattan Ry., 14 Abb. N. Cas. 103, 272 (N.Y. Sup. Ct. 1884).

68. Meinhard v. Salmon, 164 N.E. 545, 546 (N.Y. 1928) (Cardozo, C.J.).

69. J. MESSNER, SOCIAL ETHICS 218 (1949).

70. *Id.* at 219.

71. Clapp, *A Fiduciary's Duty of Loyalty,* 3 MD. L. REV. 221, 232 (1939).

72. 149 Rev. Rep. 32, 40 (H.L. 1854).

73. T. LEWIN, THE LAW OF TRUSTS AND TRUSTEES 15, 377 (London 1837).

74. Barnes v. Brown, 80 N.Y. 527, 535 (1880).

75. 478 F.2d 817, 824 n.9 (citing Diamond v. Oreamuno).

Chapter 3

76. Essex Universal Corp. v. Yates, 305 F.2d 572, 580 (2d Cir. 1962).

77. 65 Eng. Rep. at 621.

78. A. BERLE & G. MEANS, THE MODERN CORPORATION AND PRIVATE PROPERTY 70 (1932).

79. *Id.* at 376.

80. 219 F.2d at 176.

81. *Id.* at 175.

82. *See* Bayne, *A Legitimate Transfer of Control: The Weyenberg Shoe-Florsheim Case Study,* 18 STAN. L. REV. 438 (1966).

83. N.Y. Times, Feb. 3, 1965, at 43, col. 6.

84. United States v. E.I. Du Pont De Nemours & Co., 366 U.S. 316 (1961).

85. *See* Wise, *The Curious Pursuit of Pure Oil,* FORTUNE, July 1965, at 112.

86. 305 F.2d at 580.

87. 219 F.2d at 175.

88. Honigman v. Green Giant Co., 208 F. Supp. at 759.

89. 305 F.2d at 576.

90. Manne, *Some Theoretical Aspects of Share Voting,* 64 COLUM. L. REV. 1427, 1433 (1964).

91. Berle, *"Control" in Corporate Law,* 58 COLUM. L. REV. 1212, 1215 (1958).

92. Sheehan, *Coal Man at Chrysler,* FORTUNE, Sept. 1962, at 102.

93. Perlman v. Feldmann, 219 F.2d at 174.

94. 208 F. Supp. at 759.

95. Bayne, *A Legitimate Transfer of Control: The Weyenberg Shoe-Florsheim Case Study,* 18 STAN. L. REV. 438, 439 (1966).

96. 219 F.2d at 175.

Chapter 4

97. Record on Appeal at 75 (testimony of W.F. Dietrich), Honigman v. Green Giant Co., 309 F.2d 667 (8th Cir. 1962); *see also id.* at 100 (testimony of L.E. Felton).

98. Manacher v. Reynolds, 165 A.2d 741, 748 (Del. Ch. 1960).

99. *Id.* at 755.

100. 219 F.2d at 175.

101. Record on Appeal at 338, Honigman v. Green Giant Co., 309 F.2d 667 (8th Cir. 1962).

102. Porter v. Healy, 91 A. 428, 432 (Pa. 1914).

103. Record on Appeal at 86, Honigman v. Green Giant Co., 309 F.2d 667 (8th Cir. 1962).

104. 219 F.2d at 178.

105. Record on Appeal at 87, Honigman v. Green Giant Co., 309 F.2d 667 (8th Cir. 1962).

106. Commonwealth Title Ins. & Trust Co. v. Seltzer, 76 A. 77, 78 (Pa. 1910).

107. *Id.* at 79.

108. Glore, Forgan Report, Record on Appeal at 338, Honigman v. Green Giant Co., 309 F.2d 667 (8th Cir. 1962).

109. Record on Appeal at 63, Honigman v. Green Giant Co., 309 F.2d 667 (8th Cir. 1962).

Chapter 5

110. Wall St. J., May 16, 1968, at 1, col. 6. *See also,* Wall St. J., Aug. 28, 1968, at 1, col. 6; Feb. 21, 1968, at 11, cols. 2 & 3; Dec. 19, 1967, at 6, col. 1.

111. Wall St. J., Nov. 2, 1967, at 4, col. 4.

112. Wall St. J., Mar. 26, 1968, at 6, cols. 2, 3.

113. Wall St. J., Mar. 27, 1968, at 4, col. 2.

114. McClure v. Law, 55 N.E. 388 (N.Y. 1899).

115. Porter v. Healy, 91 A. at 430 (quoting C.P., Montgomery County, Pa., below).

116. 141 N.W.2d 36, 45 (1966).

117. Matter of Lionel Corp., N.Y.L.J., Feb. 4, 1964, at 14, col. 5 (Sup. Ct., N.Y. County).

118. Matter of Carter, N.Y.L.J., May 26, 1964, at 17, col. 3 (Sup. Ct., N.Y. County).

119. 165 A.2d 741, 754 (1960).

120. 305 F.2d at 576.

121. 91 A. at 430 (quoting the court below).

122. McClure v. Law, 47 N.Y.S. 84, 85 (App. Div. 1897).

123. McClure v. Law, 55 N.E. at 388.

124. United States v. E.I. Du Pont De Nemours & Co., 366 U.S. 316 (1961).

125. Jennings, *Trading in Corporate Control,* 44 CALIF. L. REV. 1, 5 (1956).

126. Essex Universal Corp. v. Yates, 305 F.2d at 575.

127. Berle, *"Control" in Corporate Law,* 58 COLUM. L. REV. 1212, 1220-22 (1958).

128. Wall St. J., Dec. 3, 1962, at 16, col. 3.

129. Laurenzano v. Einbender, 264 F. Supp. 356, 358 (E.D.N.Y. 1966).

130. *Id.* at 359 (emphasis added).

131. Wall St. J., Mar. 26, 1968, at 6, col. 2; Kahan v. Rosenstiel, 424 F.2d 161, 164-65 (3d Cir. 1970).

132. Wall St. J., Mar. 27, 1968, at 4, col. 2.

133. *Id.* As president of an Eaton interest, Otis & Co., Mr. William R. Daley found himself in the midst of a Street-shaking securities litigation. *Kaiser-Frazer Corp. v. Otis & Co.,* 195 F.2d 838 (2d Cir.), *cert. denied,* 344 U.S. 856 (1952). For a detailed study of this case, *see* Bayne, *Kaiser-Frazer v. Otis: A Legal and Moral Analysis,* 2 DE PAUL L. REV. 131 (1953).

134. 305 F.2d at 576.

135. 219 F.2d at 180.

Chapter 6

136. Wall St. J., Nov. 2, 1967, at 4, col. 4.

137. Chapter 4: The Fiduciary Duty of Corporate Control, *supra* at 157.

138. *Id.* at 165.

139. 305 F.2d at 576.

140. N.Y.L.J., Feb. 4, 1964, at 14, col. 5 (Sup. Ct., N.Y. County).

141. Meinhard v. Salmon, 164 N.E. at 546.

Chapter 7

142. Berle, *"Control" in Corporate Law,* 58 COLUM. L. REV. 1212, 1214 (1958).

143. Andrews, *The Stockholder's Right to Equal Opportunity in the Sale of Shares,* 78 HARV. L. REV. 505, 506 (1965).

144. Jennings, *Trading in Corporate Control,* 44 CALIF. L. REV. 1 (1956).

145. Perlman v. Feldmann, 219 F.2d at 174.

146. *Id.* at 175.

147. *Id.* at 178. *See* Perlman v. Feldmann, 154 F. Supp. 436, 446 (D. Conn. 1957).

148. 219 F.2d at 176.

149. *Id.* at 175.

150. *Id.*

151. *Id.* at 176.

152. *Id.* at 177.

153. *Id.* at 176.

154. *Id.* at 178.

155. *Id.*

156. 154 F. Supp. at 446.

157. N.Y.L.J., Feb. 4, 1964, at 14, col. 4 (Sup. Ct., N.Y. County).

158. Insuranshares Corp. v. Northern Fiscal Corp., 35 F. Supp. 22, 24 (E.D. Pa. 1940).

159. 55 N.E. at 389.

160. Chapter 6: The Sale-of-Control Premium: The Intrinsic Illegitimacy, *supra* at 207.

161. 289 F. Supp. at 405.

162. Matter of Lionel Corp., N.Y.L.J., Feb. 4, 1964, at 14, col. 5 (Sup. Ct., N.Y. County).

163. Meinhard v. Salmon, 164 N.E. 545, 546 (N.Y. 1928).

164. Chapter 6: The Sale-of-Control Premium: The Intrinsic Illegitimacy, *supra* at 220.

165. 47 N.Y.S. at 85.

166. *Id.*

167. *See* N.Y. PENAL LAW §§ 180.00, 180.05 (McKinney 1967).

168. *See id.* §70.15-2.

169. *See id.* §80.05-2.

170. *See id.* §80.05-5.

171. 129 F. Supp. at 188.

172. Kelly v. Kosuga, 358 U.S. 516, 516-17 (1959).

173. *Id.* at 517.

174. *Id.* at 518.

175. *Id.* at 516.

176. *Id.* at 518.

177. *Id.*

178. *Id.* at 521.

179. *Id.* at 519.

Chapter 8

180. Wall St. J., Mar. 27, 1968, at 4, col. 2.

181. *Id.*

182. *Id.*

183. Wall St. J., Feb. 16, 1970, at 16, col. 2.

184. 28 N.Y.S.2d at 630.

185. *Id.* at 651.

186. *Id.* at 658.

187. *Id.*

188. 55 N.E. at 389.

189. Gerdes v. Reynolds, 28 N.Y.S.2d 622, 651 (Sup. Ct. 1941).

190. Chapter 6: The Sale-of-Control Premium: The Intrinsic Illegitimacy, *supra* at 220.

191. 219 F.2d at 180.

192. *Id.* at 178.

193. Wall St. J., Mar. 27, 1968, at 4, col. 2.

194. *Id.*

195. Chapter 4: The Fiduciary Duty of Corporate Control, *supra* at 148.

196. *See* Metz, *Deciding How Much a Company Is Worth,* Wall St. J., Mar. 19, 1981, at 29, col. 4.

197. Chapter 2: The Custodial Concept of Corporate Control, *supra* at 62.

198. Chapter 5: The Sale of Control and the Premium-Bribe, *supra* at 186.

199. *Id.*

200. 264 F. Supp. 356, 359 (E.D.N.Y. 1966).

201. Chapter 6: The Sale-of-Control Premium: The Intrinsic Illegitimacy, *supra* at 204-05.

202. Chapter 4: The Fiduciary Duty of Corporate Control, *supra* at 148.

203. *Matter of Lionel Corp.*, N.Y.L.J., Feb. 4, 1964, at 14 (Sup. Ct., N.Y. County).

Chapter 9

204. 289 F. Supp. at 405.

205. 129 F. Supp. at 184.

206. Glore, Forgan Report, Record on Appeal at 345, Honigman v. Green Giant Co., 309 F.2d 667 (8th Cir. 1962).

207. *Id.* at 339.

208. *Id.* at 338 (emphasis added).

209. Perlman v. Feldmann, 219 F.2d 173, 176 (2d Cir. 1955).

210. Glore, Forgan Report, Record on Appeal at 339, Honigman v. Green Giant Co., 309 F.2d 667 (8th Cir. 1962).

211. *Id.*

212. *Id.* at 340.

213. *Id.* at 339.

214. *Id.* at 340.

Table of Cases Cited

Note: This Table carries the full citation for every case mentioned in the text for whatever reason. Moreover, all major sale-of-control opinions of interest to scholar and practitioners are highlighted by an asterisk.

Literature

Articles

Andrews, *The Stockholder's Right to Equal Opportunity in the Sale of Shares,* 78 HARV. L. REV. 505 (1965).

Bayne, Book Review, 35 FORDHAM L. REV. 393 (1966) (reviewing D. BAUM N. STILES, THE SILENT PARTNERS: INSTITUTIONAL INVESTORS AND CORPORATE CONTROL (1965).

_____, *Corporate Control as a Strict Trustee,* 53 GEO. L.J. 543 (1965).

_____, *The Curse of Corporate Control: A Mutual Insurance Company: A Brief on Behalf of Society,* 1979 B.Y.U. L. REV. 227.

_____, *The Definition of Corporate Control,* 9 ST. LOUIS U.L.J. 445 (1965).

_____, *The Investment Value of Control Stock,* 54 MINN. L. REV. 1265 (1970).

_____, *Kaiser-Frazer v. Otis: A Legal and Moral Analysis,* 2 DE PAUL L. REV. 131 (1953).

_____, *A Legitimate Transfer of Control: The Weyenberg Shoe-Florsheim Case Study,* 18 STAN. L. REV. 438 (1966).

_____, *The Noninvestment Value of Control Stock,* 45 IND. L.J. 317 (1970).

_____, *A Philosophy of Corporate Control,* 112 U. PA. L. REV. 22 (1963).

_____, *The Sale-of-Control Premium: The Definition,* 53 MINN. L. REV. 485 (1969).

_____, *The Sale-of-Control Premium: The Disposition,* 57 CALIF. L. REV. 615 (1969).

_____, *The Sale-of-Control Premium: The Intrinsic Illegitimacy,* 47 TEX. L. REV. 215 (1969).

_____, *The Sale-of-Control Quandary,* 51 CORNELL L.Q. 49 (1965).

_____, *The Sale of Corporate Control,* 33 FORDHAM L. REV. 583 (1965).

Berle, *"Control" in Corporate Law,* 58 COLUM. L. REV. 1212 (1958).

Berle, *Corporate Powers as Powers in Trust,* 44 Harv. L. Rev. 1049 (1931).

———, *The Price of Power: Sale of Corporate Control,* 50 Cornell L.Q. 628 (1965).

Boyle, *The Sale of Controlling Shares: American Law and the Jenkins Committee,* 13 Int'l & Comp. L.Q. 185 (1964).

Bromberg, *Bootstrapping-II,* 5 Rev. Sec. Reg. 885 (Aug. 16, 1972).

Brudney, *Fiduciary Ideology in Transactions Affecting Corporate Control,* 65 Mich. L. Rev. 259 (1966).

——— & Chirelstein, *Fair Shares in Corporate Mergers and Takeovers,* 88 Harv. L. Rev. 297 (1974).

Clapp, *A Fiduciary's Duty of Loyalty,* 3 Md. L. Rev. 221 (1939).

Cohn, *Tender Offers and the Sale of Control: An Analogue to Determine the Validity of Target Management Defensive Measures,* 66 Iowa L. Rev. 475 (1981).

Connolly, *Perlman v. Feldmann and the Sale of Control–A Brief Reconsideration,* 26 Bus. Law. 1259 (1971).

Dodd, *For Whom Are Corporate Managers Trustees?,* 45 Harv. L. Rev. 1145 (1932).

Easterbrook & Fischel, *Corporate Control Transactions,* 91 Yale L.J. 698 (1982).

Enstam & Kamen, *Control and the Institutional Investor,* 23 Bus. Law. 289 (1968).

Fellows & Painter, *Valuing Close Corporations for Federal Wealth Transfer Taxes: A Statutory Solution to the Disappearing Wealth Syndrome,* 30 Stan. L. Rev. 895 (1978).

Gibson, *The Sale of Control in Canadian Company Law,* 10 U. Brit. Colum. L. Rev. 1 (1975).

Grass, *The Sale of Corporate Control,* 19 Corp. Prac. Ser. (BNA) (1980).

Hayes, *Sale of Control of a Corporation: Who Gets the Premium?,* 4 J. Corp. L. 243 (1979).

Hazen, *Premium in the Sale of Corporate Control—Common Law Fiduciary Duties and the Role of the Federal Securities Laws* (outline), in Institute of Securities Regulation, Eleventh Annual Institute on Securities Regulation 651 (1979).

———, *The Sale of Corporate Control: Towards a Three-Tiered Approach,* 4 J. Corp. L. 263 (1979).

Hazen, *Transfers of Corporate Control and Duties of Controlling Shareholders—Common Law, Tender Offers, Investment Companies—And a Proposal for Reform*, 125 U. PA. L. REV. 1023 (1977).

Hill, *The Sale of Controlling Shares*, 70 HARV. L. REV. 986 (1957).

Hoover, *Basic Principles Underlying Duty of Loyalty*, 5 CLEV.-MAR. L. REV. 7 (1956).

Hornstein, *Corporate Control and Private Property Rules*, 92 U. PA. L. REV. 1 (1943).

Javaras, *Equal Opportunity in the Sale of Controlling Shares: A Reply to Professor Andrews*, 32 U. CHI. L. REV. 420 (1965).

Jennings, *Trading in Corporate Control*, 44 CALIF. L. REV. 1 (1956).

Johnson, *Corporate Directors as Trustees in Illinois*, 23 ILL. L. REV. 653 (1929).

Kaplan, *Fiduciary Responsibility in the Management of the Corporation*, 31 BUS. LAW. 883 (1976).

Katz, *Responsibility and the Modern Corporation*, 3 J. L. & ECON. 75 (1960).

———, *The Sale of Corporate Control*, 38 CHI. B. REC. 376 (1957).

Keeton, *The Director as Trustee*, 5 CURRENT LEGAL PROBS. 11 (1952).

Leech, *Transactions in Corporate Control*, 104 U. PA. L. REV. 725 (1956).

Lepaulle, *An Outsider's Viewpoint of the Nature of Trusts*, 14 CORNELL L.Q. 52 (1928).

Letts, *Sales of Control Stock and the Rights of Minority Shareholders*, 26 BUS. LAW. 631 (1971).

Lewis, *The Legitimate Transfer of Corporate Control: A Paradigmatic Study of the Custodial Concept*, 13 CREIGHTON L. REV. 463 (1979).

Long, *The Definition of a Trust*, 8 VA. L. REV. 426 (1922).

Lorne, *A Reappraisal of Fair Shares in Controlled Mergers*, 126 U. PA. L. REV. 955 (1978).

Manne, *Mergers and the Market for Corporate Control*, 73 J. POL. ECON. 110 (1965).

———, *Some Theoretical Aspects of Share Voting*, 64 COLUM. L. REV. 1427 (1964).

Newman & Pickering, *A Premium for Control*, 28 Tex. B.J. 735 (1965).

O'Neal, *Sale of a Controlling Corporate Interest: Bases of Possible Seller Liability*, 38 U. Pitt. L. Rev. 9 (1976).

———, *Symposium: Sale of Control, Introduction*, 4 J. Corp. L. 239 (1979).

Pam, *Interlocking Directorates, The Problem and Its Solution*, 26 Harv. L. Rev. 467 (1913).

Ratner, *The Government of Business Corporations: Critical Reflections on the Rule of "One Share, One Vote"*, 56 Cornell L. Rev. 1 (1970).

———, *Section 14(f): A New Approach to Transfers of Corporate Control*, 54 Cornell L.Q. 65 (1968).

Santoni, *The Developing Duties of Controlling Shareholders and Appropriate Restraints on the Sale of Corporate Control*, 4 J. Corp. L. 285 (1979).

Schiff, *Sale of Control: The Equal Opportunity and Foreseeable Harm Theories Under Rule 10b-5*, 32 Bus. Law. 507 (1977).

Schwartz, *The Sale of Control and the 1934 Act: New Directions for Federal Corporation Law*, 15 N.Y.L.F. 674 (1969).

Scott, *The Fiduciary Principle*, 37 Calif. L. Rev. 539 (1949).

———, *The Trustee's Duty of Loyalty*, 49 Harv. L. Rev. 521 (1936).

Sealy, *The Director as Trustee*, 1967 Cambridge L.J. 83.

Sommer, Jr., *Who's "In Control"?—SEC*, 21 Bus. Law. 559 (1966).

Sterrett, *Reward for Mutual Fund Sponsor Entrepreneurial Risk*, 58 Cornell L. Rev. 195 (1973).

Stickells, *Stockholder's Duty in Sale of Stock*, 31 B.U.L. Rev. 191 (1951).

Tarver, *The Arrogance of Corporate Power: A Study of the Evolution of the Fiduciary Duty Owed by Management to the Corporation or Its Shareholders*, 42 Tul. L. Rev. 155 (1967).

Weisbrod, *Trading in Business Ownership*, 1954 U. Ill. L.F. 465.

Willis, *Duties and Responsibilities of Trustees*, L. Libr. (1835).

Notes and Comments

Duties of Controlling Shareholders in Transferring Their Shares, 54 HARV. L. REV. 648 (1941).

An Examination of the Neglected Role of Sale-of-Control Law and Theory in the Valuation of a Control Block of Stock for Federal Estate-Tax Purposes, 2 J. CORP. L. 91 (1976).

Fiduciary Duties of Majority or Controlling Stockholders, 44 IOWA L. REV. 734 (1959).

Mutual Fund Control-Transfer Profits: Congress, the SEC, and Rosenfeld v. Black, 58 VA. L. REV. 371 (1972).

Opportunity Lost: More of the Same in Sale of Corporate Control Cases, 58 NEB. L. REV. 891 (1979).

Restrictions on the Transfer of Controlling Stock, 40 VA. L. REV. 195 (1954).

Rule 10b-5 and the Control Premium: Duties of Disclosure and Invitation, 10 B.C. IND. & COM. L. REV. 743 (1969).

The Sale of Control of the Widely-Held Corporation and the Strict Trust Doctrine, 59 IOWA L. REV. 1286 (1974).

Sale of Corporate Control, 19 U. CHI. L. REV. 869 (1952).

The Sale of Corporate Control: The Berle Theory and the Law, 25 U. PITT. L. REV. 59 (1963).

Sales of Corporate Control and the Theory of Overkill, 31 U. CHI. L. REV. 725 (1964).

Sales of Corporate Control at a Premium: An Analysis and Suggested Approach, 1961 DUKE L.J. 554.

Shareholder's Liability for Sale of Controlling Interest, 22 U. CHI. L. REV. 895 (1955).

Recent Cases [*Manacher v. Reynolds*], 109 U. PA. L. REV. 887 (1961).

Case Note [*Rowen v. Le Mars Mutual Ins. Co.*], 29 DRAKE L. REV. 673 (1980).

Other Sources Cited

Books:

A. Berle, Studies in the Law of Corporation Finance (1928).

_____ & G. Means, The Modern Corporation and Private Property (1932).

G. Bogert, Trusts and Trustees (rev. 2d ed. 1978).

Z. Cavitch, Business Organizations (1963).

W. Cook, A Treatise on the Law of Corporations (4th ed. 1898).

L. Gower, The Principles of Modern Company Law (2d ed. 1957).

N. Lattin & R. Jennings, Cases and Materials on Corporations (3d ed. 1959).

T. Lewin, The Law of Trusts and Trustees (London 1837).

F. Maitland, _The Unincorporate Body,_ in 3 Collected Papers of Frederic William Maitland 272 (H. Fisher ed. 1911).

H. McClintock, Handbook of the Principles of Equity (2d ed. 1948).

F. Mechem, Outlines of the Law of Agency (4th ed. 1952).

J. Messner, Social Ethics (1949).

V. Morawetz, A Treatise on the Law of Private Corporations (2d ed. 1886).

J. Noonan, Bribes (1984).

J. Perry, A Treatise on the Law of Trusts (5th ed. 1899).

J. Royce, The Philosophy of Loyalty (1930).

A. Scott, The Law of Trusts (3d ed. 1967).

J. Strahan & G. Kendrick, Digest of Equity (1909).

H. Taylor, Law of Private Corporations (3d ed. 1894).

Articles:

Bazelon, _Clients Against Lawyers,_ Harper's, Sept. 1967, at 104.

Brown, _What's in It for Eddie, Bob, and Vic?,_ Fortune, Sept. 1, 1964, at 139.

Metz, _Deciding How Much a Company Is Worth,_ Wall St. J., Mar. 19, 1981, at 29, col. 4.

Sheehan, _Coal Man at Chrysler,_ Fortune, Sept. 1962, at 102.

Sloan, _Everybody's Equal, Only Some People Are More So,_ Forbes, May 26, 1981, at 61.

_____, *Waiting for the Dough,* FORBES, Apr. 27, 1981, at 33.

Stone, *The Public Influence of the Bar,* 48 HARV. L. REV. 1 (1934).

Vanderpoel, Chi. Sun-Times. Oct. 10, 1951, (Finance Sec.), at 47, col. 1.

Wise, *The Curious Pursuit of Pure Oil,* FORTUNE, July 1965, at 112.

Statutes and Research Materials:

An Acte againste Buyinge and Sellinge of Offices, 1551, 5 & 6 Edw. 6, c. 16.

CAL. CIV. CODE §2233 (1955).

Glore, Forgan & Co., *Plan of Recapitalization for Green Giant Co.,* Record on Appeal at 338, *Honigman v. Green Giant Co.,* 309 F.2d 667 (8th Cir. 1962).

ILL. REV. STAT. ch. 32, §8.70 (Supp. 1984).

MISS. CODE ANN. §97-11-11 (1972).

12 N.Y. JUR. *Corporations* §§ 717, 724 (rev. ed. 1971).

N.Y. PENAL LAW §§ 70.15-2, 80.05-2, 80.05-5, 180.00, 180.05 (McKinney 1967).

RESTATEMENT OF RESTITUTION §§ 128, 138, 197 (1937).

RESTATEMENT (SECOND) OF TORTS § 8A (1965).

RESTATEMENT (SECOND) OF TRUSTS §§ 2, 170(1), 203, 206 (1959).

Rev. Rul. 59-60, 1959-1 C.B. 242.

Index